A Northern Cheyenne Album

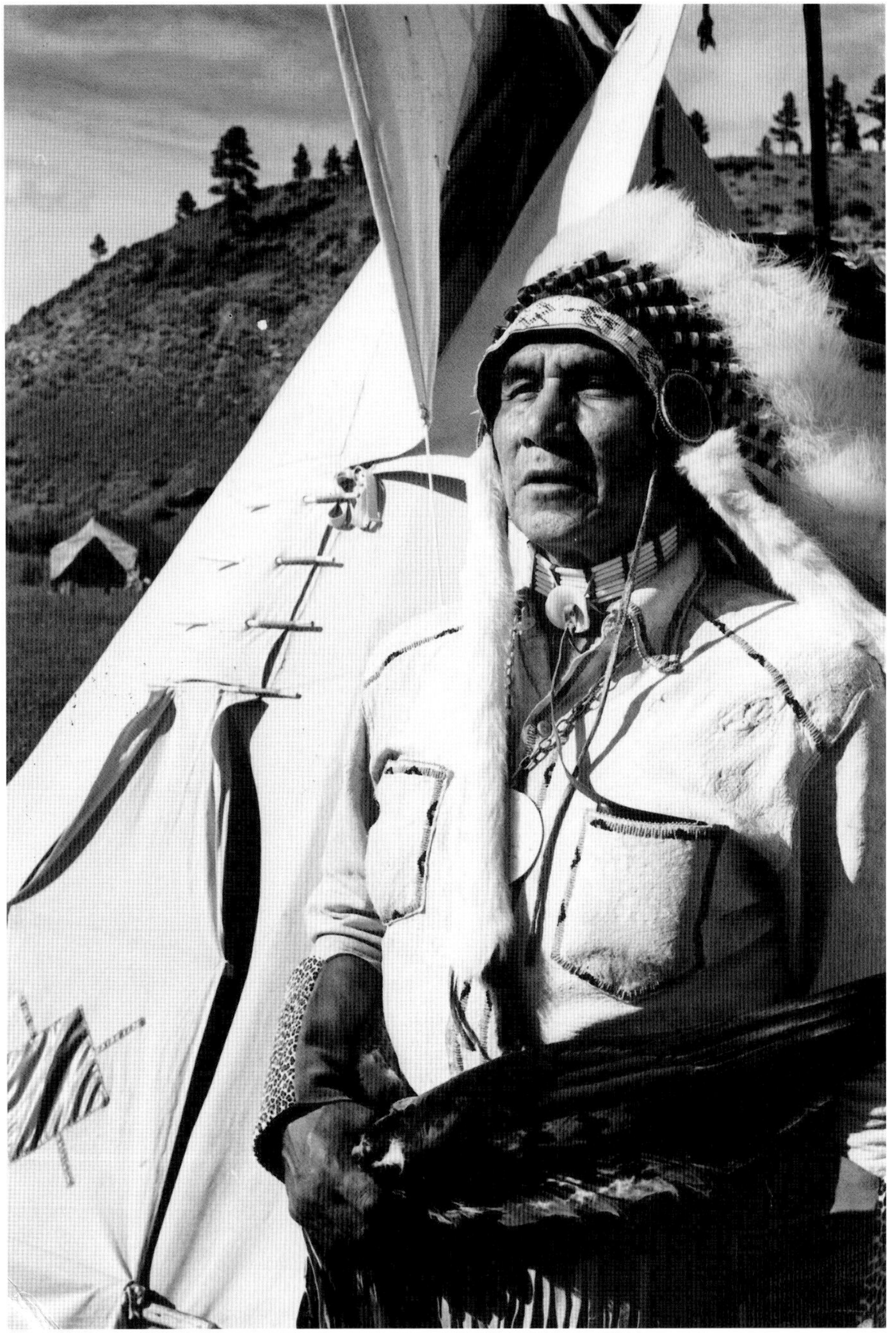

John Woodenlegs, Northern Cheyenne Tribal Chairman and leader of the reservation research team, circa 1960. Photographer unknown.

A Northern Cheyenne Album

Photographs by Thomas B. Marquis

Margot Liberty, Editor

Commentary by John Woodenlegs

University of Oklahoma Press : Norman

Publication of this book is funded in part by a grant from the Montana Committee for the Humanities, an affiliate of the National Endowment for the Humanities.

Also by Margot Liberty

Cheyenne Memories (New Haven, 1967, 1998)

(ed.) *American Indian Intellectuals of the Nineteenth and Early Twentieth Centuries* (St. Paul, 1978; Norman, 2002)

(e.d., with W. Raymond Wood) *Anthropology of the Great Plains* (Lincoln, 1980)

(with Barry Head) *Working Cowboy: Recollections of Ray Holmes* (Norman, 1995)

Library of Congress Cataloging-in-Publication Data

Liberty, Margot
A Northern Cheyenne album / Margot Liberty editor ; photographs by Thomas B. Marquis ; commentary by John Woodenlegs.
p. cm.
Includes index.
ISBN 978-0-8061-3749-0 (cloth)
ISBN 978-0-8061-3893-0 (paper)
1. Cheyenne Indians—History—Pictorial works. 2. Cheyenne Indians—Social life and customs—Pictorial works. 3. Montana—History. I. Marquis, Thomas Bailey. II. Woodenlegs, John, d. 1981. III. Title.
E99.C53M365 2006
978.6004'973500222—dc22
2005052956

The paper in this book meets the guidelines for permanence and durability of the Committee on Production Guidelines for Book Longevity of the Council on Library Resources, Inc. ∞

2 3 4 5 6 7 8 9 10

To the memory of my father, Henry F. Pringle

Contents

Photographs

Preface

THIS BOOK IS the result of a collaboration that spans several decades and involves numerous contributors, editors, and Cheyenne informants. Basic to it are photographs by Thomas B. Marquis, taken in the 1920s when he first came to the Northern Cheyenne Indian Reservation in Lame Deer, Montana, to serve as agency physician. Having been defeated by the U.S. Army and turned from a nomadic nation into subsistence farmers, the Cheyennes were experiencing ongoing and rapid social change. These photographs offer a unique view of their early reservation life.

Marquis lasted for less than a year as a doctor, but he remained in the area until his death in 1935 and took the photographs that appear in this book. He became an astute student of Cheyenne culture and tradition, authoring *Wooden Leg: A Warrior Who Fought Custer* (1957, first published in 1931), the best Indian account of the Custer fight. He also wrote much other material that can be found in *The Cheyennes of Montana* (Marquis 1978) as well as a controversial account of the Custer fight, *Keep the Last Bullet for Yourself* (Marquis 1976).

When he arrived in Lame Deer, Marquis owned three Kodak cameras: a Brownie No. 2, a pre–World War I Premoette, and a 4-by-5 view camera. He carried the Brownie in his medical bag but later abandoned it for the Premoette, which had a faster lens and produced a larger 2\F1/2 by 4\F1/2 negative. His pictures were used in his small Custer Battle Museum at Hardin, Montana, as well as in scattered publications, including a series of pamphlets on the Custer fight (for example, Marquis 1933a).

Marquis enjoyed remarkable rapport with his subjects. The pictures presented here are completely devoid of studio settings and props. All were made in and around the Lame Deer agency or in neighboring communities. He recorded many events, including fairs and rodeos. The photographs have not been published, except for a few in the Marquis pamphlet series. Among the most important historically are the pictures of about twenty Custer battle veterans in their old age, taken at or near the time of the fiftieth anniversary of the battle in 1926.

Marquis died in 1935. His daughters, Minnie Ellen Hastings and Anna Rose Heil, eventually gave his negatives to John Woodenlegs, a distinguished political and religious leader of the Northern Cheyenne tribe.

Woodenlegs was tribal president in the 1950s. He was also a major proponent of the reservation cattle industry and a national leader of the Native American Church. This Native church came to the Cheyennes about

1900, a decade or so later than the Catholic and Mennonite missions. It augmented continuing Cheyenne belief in the traditional Sun Dance, the Sacred Medicine Hat, and the Sacred Medicine Arrows (kept by the Southern Cheyennes). The fourth big traditional ceremony, the Massaum or Animal Dance, did not survive—its last performance is shown in figure 92.

After 1960 Woodenlegs joined in an educational effort that identified about 150 of the best Marquis pictures for use in a manuscript intended for reservation schools. Hap Gilliland of the Council for Indian Education (a publisher of classroom materials for use in Indian education) in Billings, Montana, was instrumental in this project, as was Missoula journalist Tom Weist. Also fundamental to its completion was Billings resident Betty Clark Wilson. Negatives of the Marquis collection (about 500 images, from which this book has been compiled) were bought from Gilliland by the Buffalo Bill Historical Center museum in Cody, Wyoming, several years ago. Some other Marquis negatives are held by the National Anthropological Archives at the Smithsonian Institution in Washington, D.C., and at Little Bighorn Battlefield National Monument in Crow Agency, Montana.

Jerry Mader, a photographer from Missoula, made prints from the selected Marquis negatives by means of Johnson O'Malley grants to Lame Deer School District No. 6. A reservation research team including John Woodenlegs, Tom Weist, and Betty Clark then gathered caption material in tape-recorded interviews, which appear here as caption series A. Some additional interviews were recorded as late as 1981. Pictures and caption materials were assembled into a large manuscript, which failed to find a publisher. After a telephone call from Clark to Margot Liberty of Sheridan, Wyoming, the material was sent to her in 1998. Liberty then forwarded it to the University of Oklahoma Press, recommending further editing and publication.

University of Oklahoma Press editors agreed that much of the value of the manuscript lay in the narrative "feel" of the initial series of captions. The reservation research team had used the actual words of elders to describe each photograph, especially in the narratives of John Woodenlegs, who had taken the leading information-gathering role. These original captions vary a good deal in length and focus, but they have a distinctive Indian character and outlook and give a sense of the voice of Woodenlegs. The editors therefore decided to retain these original narratives "as is." Their content is somewhat uneven and the tone informal, however, so the Press asked Liberty to augment the original captions with a second series of more scholarly captions, here presented as caption series B. Each photograph is therefore accompanied by two captions.

Material in caption series B relies primarily on four major sources in addition to Liberty's own experience with the Northern Cheyennes (she was a teacher in the Birney school, 1954–58). First is *Cheyenne Memories* (Stands in Timber and Liberty 1997), a book of tribal history including material on many of the subjects of the Marquis pictures.

Second is *The Cheyennes of Montana* (Marquis 1978), particularly the introduction and the Marquis biography by editor Tom Weist. Weist also wrote *A History of the Cheyenne People* (1977), which contains a few additional Marquis photographs (as does *The Cheyennes of Montana*).

Third is Robert Pringle's unpublished thesis: "The Northern Cheyenne Indians in the Reservation Period" (1958), which contains an excellent historic overview of the early reservation years.

A fourth important contemporary reservation account, which details the printing of the pictures by Jerry Mader, is *The Road to Lame Deer* (Mader 2002).

Acknowledgments

THIS MANUSCRIPT IS the result of a major cooperative effort spanning generations and cultures and could not have happened without the dedication and efforts of Thomas Marquis, John Woodenlegs, and the Cheyenne elders. Nor could it have come into being without the interest and assistance of the Marquis daughters, Minnie Ellen Hastings and Anna Rose Heil. Very important likewise were Hap Gilliland, Betty Clark, Tom Weist, Jerry Mader, and the editors of the University of Oklahoma Press. John Drayton at the Press deserves special thanks for ongoing encouragement and help. Alessandra Jacobi of the University of Oklahoma Press and Winifred Galloway of Sheridan, Wyoming, provided important assistance in the final manuscript preparation. Thanks also to Shmuel Ben-Dor and Scott Burgan.

A Northern Cheyenne Album

Introduction

When Thomas Marquis began service as a doctor at the Northern Cheyenne Agency in 1922, the reservation had been in existence for about forty years or roughly two generations. The Cheyennes were still in the process of adapting from a nomadic to a settled way of life. If the U.S. government had prevailed, the Northern Cheyennes might have been sent to join the Southern Cheyennes in Oklahoma in 1877, to remain there permanently. But the Northern Cheyennes ended up in Montana, their chosen homeland.

These were people who had won the admiration of their enemies—among them Capt. Frederick Benteen, who had ridden against them and who survived in June 1876 when Custer and his command were wiped out. Benteen said that they were "good shots, good riders and the best fighters the sun ever shone on" (Grinnell 1956: viii). A number of the elderly men and women who appear in these pages lived through the last bloody fights and treks of the Cheyennes.

First documentation of the Cheyennes appeared in the eighteenth century, when French traders began recording this people's migration from the Minnesota region at the headwaters of the Mississippi past the Black Hills into the high plains. Before that time they were neighbors of other Algonquian and Athabascan-speaking tribes in southern Canada. Their westward move accelerated in response to pressure from enemy tribes, who had been receiving guns and ammunition from invading whites farther east.

Never a large tribe, the Cheyennes split into Northern and Southern divisions after the Year the Stars Fell, 1833 (the year Bent's Fort was built on the Arkansas River). In response to better hunting and trading opportunities the newly equestrian Cheyennes spread out across nearly a thousand miles of plains.

The Cheyennes reckoned descent bilaterally, through both parents. No clans existed; instead, they lived in ten nomadic hunting bands that came together for summer ceremonies like the Sun Dance. They had a famous council of forty-four chiefs that met at this time; otherwise the people were dispersed into the component hunting bands for most of the year. There were also six soldier bands or military societies (divided among the ten bands), which also convened only during the summer, at the major tribal gathering.

The total number of Cheyennes came to about four thousand at the time of European contact (an average of four hundred people per band), although these numbers are not clearly known. The population during the buffalo years was increasing. Grass and game were generally more plentiful in the North, although the majority of bands followed the Southern division of the tribe. The Southern Cheyennes in general sought better trade and raiding opportunities south of the Platte River, while the Northern Cheyennes generally roamed north of the river.

When the Cheyennes reached the Black Hills and eastern plains of Wyoming, a period of fierce intertribal warfare ensued against the Crow, Shoshone, and Kiowa enemies over rich new game lands made irresistible by the recent acquisition of horses. Peace was made with the Kiowas in 1840, and the main thrust of Cheyenne warfare soon turned against invading whites.

The Cheyennes appear as major players in western U.S. military history for more than three decades, beginning with the 1854 "Mormon cow incident" (when the killing of a stray cow precipitated the first major engagement of the final struggle for the plains) near Fort Laramie and ending with the famous outbreak from Oklahoma in 1878–79. During this time more than fifty engagements with troops and civilians took place before the surrender of most of the Southern Cheyennes on March 6, 1875, and the piecemeal surrender of the Northern Cheyennes in several groups in 1877. The Southern Cheyennes had suffered severe defeats by Anglo-American forces in attacks on Black Kettle's villages at Sand Creek in 1864 and at the Washita in 1868.

Four major U.S. attacks took place against the Northern Cheyennes in 1876. The March 17 attack by Joseph Reynolds on Old Bear's village on the Little Powder River, Montana, ended in a draw. The Indians won the next two fights, first on June 17 against George Crook at Rosebud Creek and next on June 25–26 against George Custer at the Little Bighorn. But on November 25 federal troops led by Ranald Mackenzie overran the main Northern Cheyenne camp at Crazy Woman Creek, Wyoming, and broke the back of Northern Cheyenne resistance.

The surrender of the Northern Cheyennes soon followed, and various groups and subdivisions scattered widely. In April 1877 the Two Moons band surrendered at Fort Keogh, Montana, and the Little Wolf/Dull Knife band at Fort Robinson, Nebraska. The Fort Robinson group was transferred (May 28 to August 5) to the Cheyenne-Arapaho Agency in Oklahoma, but they broke out and fled north on September 8, 1878. A number of engagements with pursuing soldiers and with settlers ensued.

In October 1878 the fugitives divided. Little Wolf's band (126 people) surrendered in the spring of 1879 and was allowed to join the Two Moons band at Fort Keogh. Another 149 Cheyennes under Dull Knife were held at Fort Robinson and ordered to return south, however, leading to a second outbreak on January 9, 1879. During the escape and the follow-up pursuit, more than half of Dull Knife's followers were killed. The remnants of this band eventually reached Fort Keogh, as did a third band, the White River Cheyennes under Little Chief. That band had gone to Oklahoma in 1878 (passing the main body of Northern Cheyennes on their flight from the south) and then to Pine Ridge in 1881. By October 1891 all Northern Cheyennes were finally reunited at the Tongue River in Montana, which had become the eastern boundary of their reservation in 1884.

The reservation period thus began ca. 1875 in the south and ca. 1880 in the north. During this interim period, the Cheyennes moved frequently until 1884, when the Northern Cheyenne reservation was officially designated.

By the time Marquis arrived in 1922, he found an active religious and social climate on the reservation. Catholic and Mennonite missionaries had introduced the Northern Cheyennes to Christianity. They also had the Sun Dance, a spectacular annual summertime festival shared by most of the equestrian Great Plains tribes.

The Cheyennes had been influenced briefly by the Ghost Dance, a prophetic movement that appeared among the Plains tribes during the early reservation years in the 1880s. The Ghost Dance, which predicted the departure of whites and the return of the buffalo, was particularly prevalent among the Teton or Lakota Sioux. Fearing a renewed uprising among the Plains tribes, the government suppressed the Ghost Dance quickly and brutally—the massacre at Wounded Knee in 1890 being the most famous event.

More important to the Cheyennes was the widespread adoption by 1900 of the new pan-tribal Native American Church, which coexisted with the Sun Dance, Sacred Hat, and Sacred Arrows as well as with various traditional forms of "medicine" or Native healing.

Although the government and missionary groups opposed most of these Native American religious practices, they worked actively to suppress only the Sun Dance. Whites objected to it principally because of the spectacular self-torture voluntarily engaged in by the dancers. The Sun Dance continued despite repeated government and missionary attempts to suppress it between 1883 and 1933. It went underground during many of these years. There are numerous references to these religious developments in the following pages, as well as some detailed discussion of the Native American Church.

Religious and government schools had introduced Western-style education by the time Marquis arrived. Most tribes were expected to allow their children to attend off-reservation boarding schools. By 1900 a number of Northern Cheyenne children were thus sent away, but most children remained on or near the reservation at St. Labre's (a Catholic mission just off the reservation at Ashland) or at Busby (a government boarding school in one of the five reservation communities). The off-reservation schools were often strict in requiring conformity (for example, haircuts) and prohibiting the use of Native American languages. This was a harsh factor in the forced assimilation of Cheyenne children and contributed to their partial loss of culture and tradition. Children in boarding schools came into contact with members of many other tribes, however, with whom they could exchange ideas freely for the first time in newly acquired English. Previous communication had been possible only through interpreters or through the Plains Indian sign language.

Woodenlegs and the elders in this book talk freely about these events as well as about shared social functions, such as dancing and music, rodeos, visiting back and forth, various games (including "hand games," traditional team organized betting contests), and "giveaways." These elements have since evolved into the modern complex of powwows and other cultural events now widely shared by Indian groups throughout the plains.

The photographs and narratives here also give us glimpses into economic changes taking place on the reservation—from the issue of rations to cattle raising and dry farming—and sometimes leave a clear impression of the bureaucratic and cultural blindness behind some of the government's policies.

Still, the Northern Cheyennes were more fortunate than the Southern Cheyennes, because they retained possession of most of their land. Under the federal Dawes Allotment Act of 1887, land was allotted to individual

Southern Cheyennes, but nearly all of it was lost through sale to whites after 1892. The Northern Cheyennes did not receive individual allotments until 1925, and most of their land base of 445,000 acres has been retained in individual or tribal ownership.

The people revealed in these pages are far from being the pitiful concentration-camp inhabitants that some outsiders have imagined. Instead we see adaptable individuals who frequently exhibit a telling sense of humor. Marquis and Woodenlegs and the reservation research team have done a remarkable job of preserving a record of many aspects of their way of life, as seen through the eyes of Cheyenne elders of several generations ago.

A Note to Custer Scholars

SCHOLARLY AND POPULAR writing on the Battle of the Little Bighorn in southeastern Montana, June 25–26, 1876, continues to proliferate. This book contains several items that should be of interest to Custer scholars.

A number of Northern Cheyennes who participated in the Custer battle appear in this book in their late old age. Those whose pictures have not been published elsewhere include Sun Bear, Isaac Black Bird, Big Beaver, Porcupine, Hairy Hand, Laban Little Wolf, Issues, Stump Horn, Beaver Heart, Pine, Grasshopper, Bobtailed Horse, Iron Shirt, and Turkey Legs. Five women included here are identified as being in the Cheyenne camp at the time of the battle: Mrs. Limpy, Susan Iron Teeth, and Maud Arapaho Chief, Laura Arapaho Chief, and Lenora Arapaho Chief. Kate Bighead is the only woman known to have been on the field during the battle.

In some cases these individuals appear in group pictures where their faces are not distinct, but all were identified by Marquis at the time the pictures were taken.

The two most significant pictures herein are figure 22 (Limpy and his wife) and figure 118 (Maud Arapaho Chief and Lenora Arapaho Chief Two Birds).

In figure 22 Limpy is pointing to a bullet wound in Mrs. Limpy's breast. The reservation research team identified this photograph as showing the scar from a bullet wound that Mrs Limpy received in the Indian village on June 25, 1876.

Maud Arapaho Chief (figure 118) and her daughters Laura and Lenora were in the Cheyenne camp at the time of the fight. Laura and her sister were young girls. The source of this caption by the reservation research team was Sylvester Knows His Gun, who was Lenora's grandson. He stated that Laura saw a column of horsemen crossing the river and asked who they were. Her mother told her: "Those are the people who have come to kill us!" Laura was so frightened by this that she fainted. We do not have a picture of Laura, just her sister Lenora and her mother.

Sylvester Knows His Gun was told that when the soldiers began to cross the river, one of their number was hit and collapsed in his saddle. Two other soldiers supported him from either side as the column reversed its line of march and did not enter the village. Knows His Gun speculates that this wounded man, presumably an officer, might have been Custer. He heard the story from Maud, his great-grandmother.

According to this new evidence, the Custer command did indeed approach and enter the river for at least a short time. This matter has been keenly debated by Custer scholars, some of whom (including Marquis 1933b) have written that Custer and some of his command remained back near the ridge east of the river, called Custer Hill today, where his body was found.

George Bird Grinnell (1956: 357–58), however, wrote: "It seems that a part of Custer's command did come down nearly to the ford, and if the two companies that reached that point . . . had kept on and crossed the river, they no doubt would have been followed by the rest of the command, and a great victory might have followed."

These two pictures (figures 22 and 118) offer evidence that at least some of the Custer soldiers may have started to cross the river. At any rate they got close enough to wound a woman and badly frighten a little Cheyenne girl.

—Margot Liberty

Photographs

The pictures presented here were taken between 1922 and 1935 by Thomas Bailey Marquis, M.D. (d. 1935). They are accompanied by two sets of captions. Caption series A was recorded from numerous Northern Cheyenne informants by John Woodenlegs, Tom Weist, and Betty Clark Wilson, mostly in the 1970s and ending in 1981. Caption series B was written by Margot Liberty in 2003 and 2004.

The spellings of Cheyenne names are not consistent because they have never been standardized. Sometimes they are spelled as one word, sometimes as two or more words. The Cheyennes themselves use more than one spelling, as in the captions here. The spellings, phrasing, and punctuation of the captions have been preserved, in keeping with the editorial policy of retaining the original content and style.

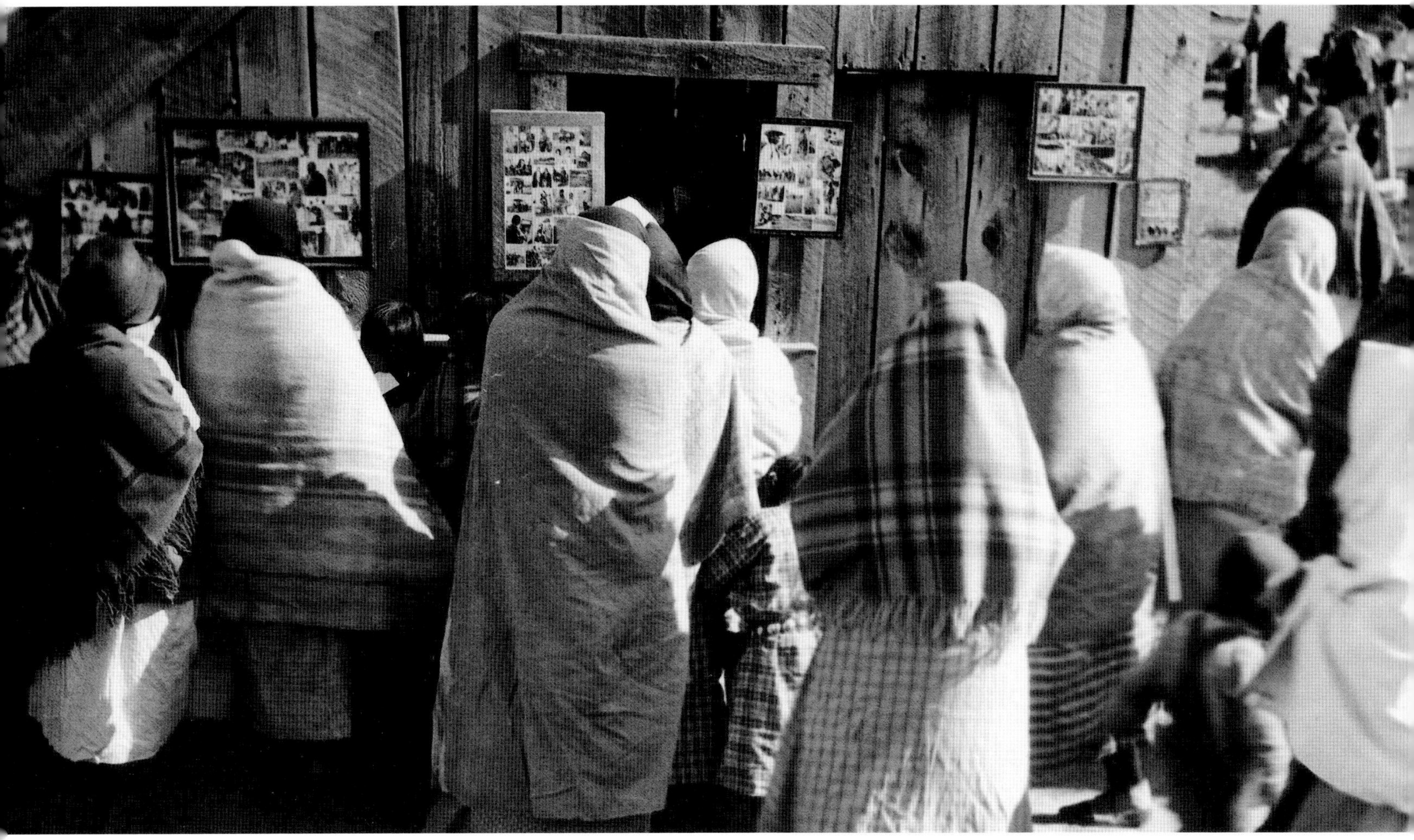

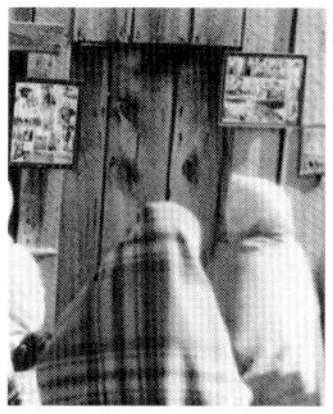

1. Ladies Looking at Pictures (1922)

INFORMANT: JOHN WOODENLEGS

1a. These are Cheyennes at the Busby fairgrounds. Now the photographer must have put up a lot of pictures alongside of that grandstand. So all these women are looking at these pictures. They've all got handkerchiefs around their heads and their shawls on and the photographer took the picture. Looks like one of them is wearing a hat. The children are kind of hiding behind their mothers. Dr. Marquis put the pictures up so the people could see them. This young girl has a leather belt with round conchos on it. One lady is wearing moccasins; part of it is leather and part of it is canvas. They are all good people.

1b. Busby is one of five Northern Cheyenne Reservation communities that still exist. The others are Ashland, Lame Deer, Birney, and Muddy. The Busby community is sometimes referred to as White River, because Cheyennes from the White River area at Pine Ridge, South Dakota, settled there in 1891.

Marquis posted his prints for his subjects to enjoy at the Busby fair and rodeo in 1922. Other celebrations at Busby, Ashland, and Lame Deer are illustrated in this volume.

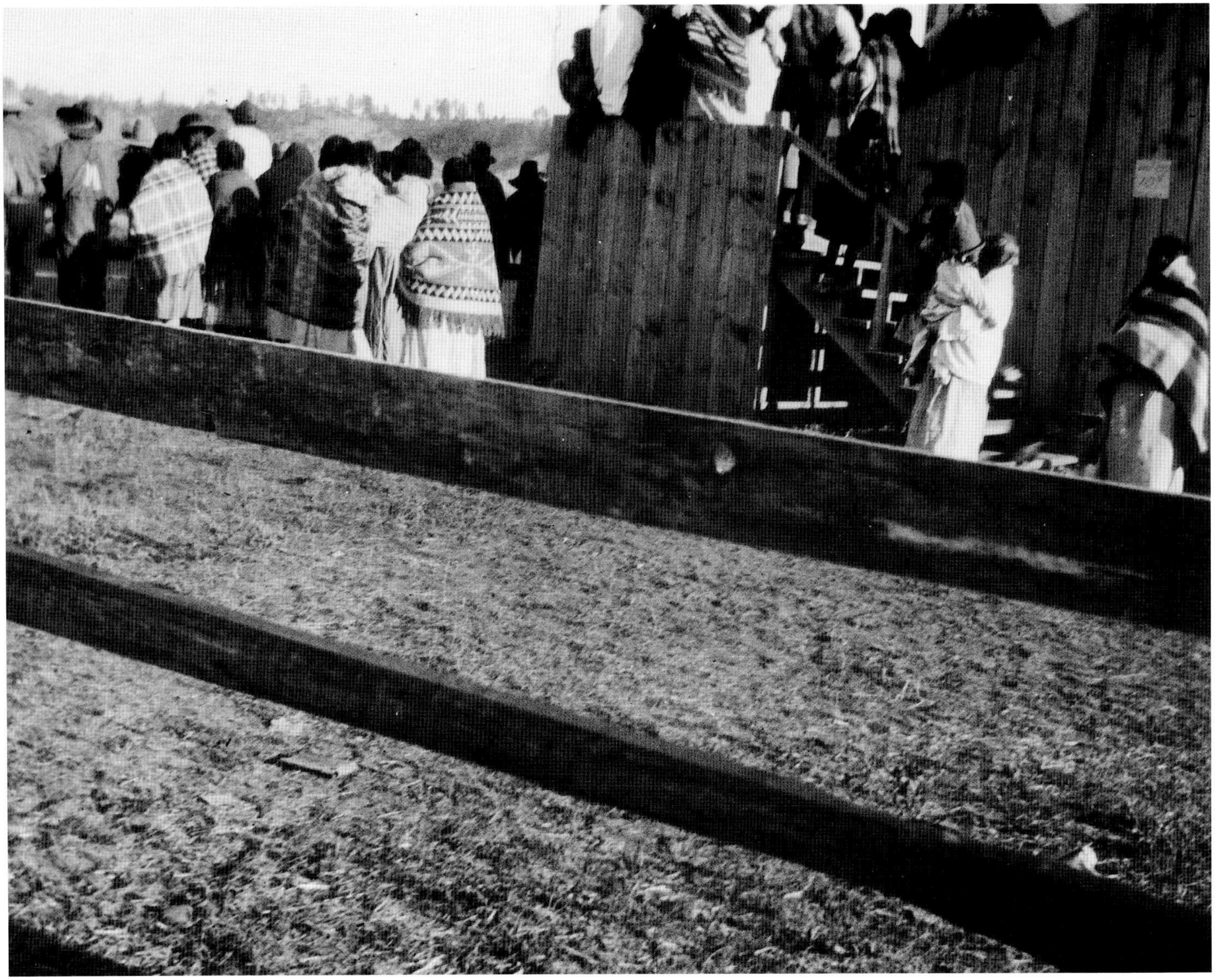

2. Watching the Rodeo

INFORMANT: JOHN WOODENLEGS

2a. This is at Busby at the rodeo and fair. It's all mostly women with their blankets and their children—striped blankets and long dresses. They were all looking at the races and the rodeo. The babies are on their backs. There's some men there too with their backs to the photographer. They have suspenders on and big hats. Nobody is posing. Two of the children on the backs of their mothers look like they are playing or shaking hands with each other.

2b. Reservation fairs, which often included rodeo events and horse races, were encouraged by government officials in the vain hope that they would replace Native American ceremonies. These people are dressed up in their "Sunday best," next to the judges' stand at the racetrack. Such fairs have been replaced today by powwows and school athletic events throughout the year.

Reservation clothing styles have changed with the times, especially the black cowboy hats or "reservation hats" formerly worn by men.

The comment by Woodenlegs that "nobody is posing" is an important feature of the Marquis photography, which is unusual in its depiction of Indian subjects in the reservation setting. Most photographers of Indians at this time used studio settings and props.

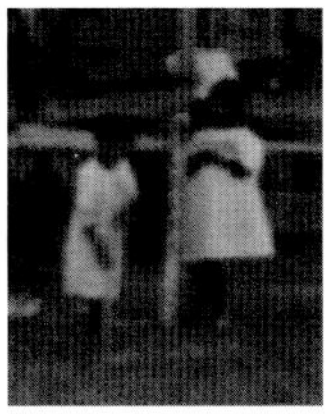

3. Grandstand at Busby

INFORMANT: JOHN WOODENLEGS

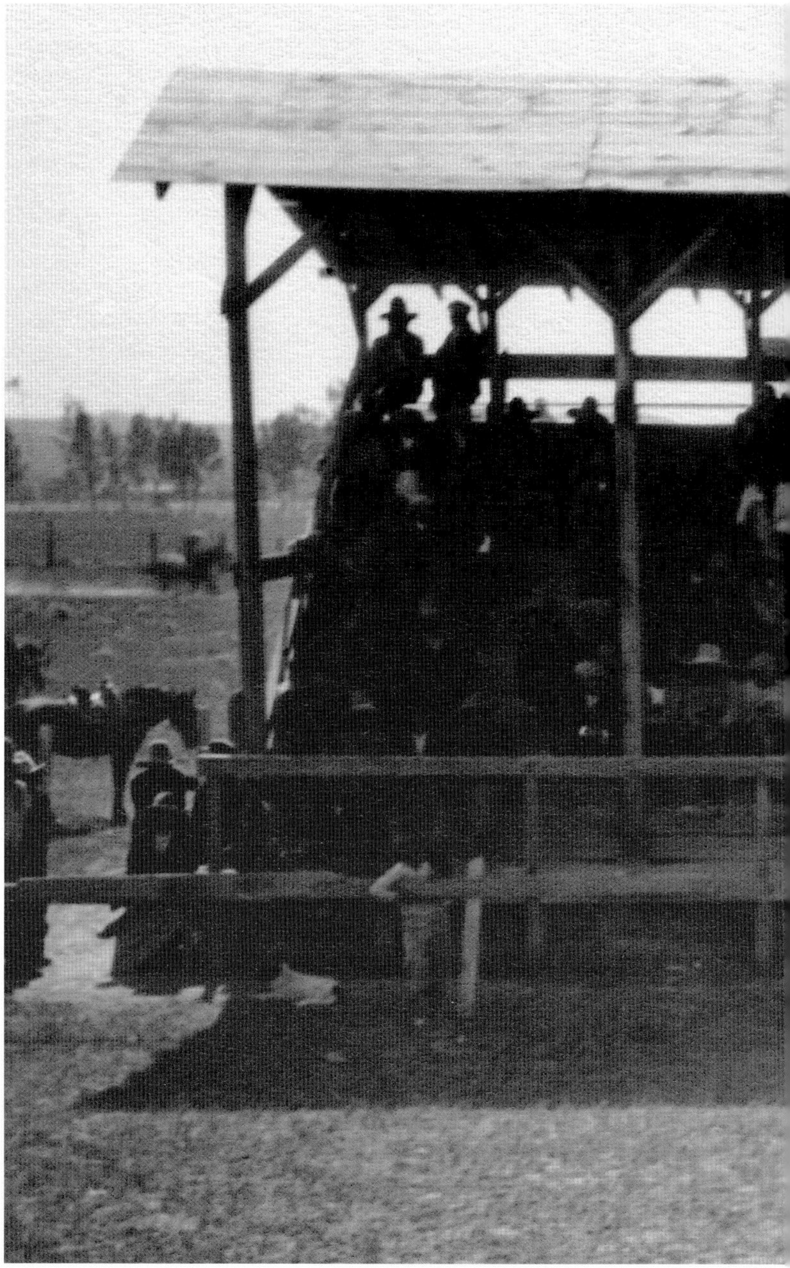

3a. This is the grandstand at Busby. There are a lot of people and a lot of children in the front. There's some saddle horses and a Model T Ford. Up in the top left, a fellow has a reservation hat. This is where they had their races, rodeos, and bucking horses.

3b. The adoption of ranch and cowboy culture, including rodeos, was widespread throughout Plains reservation communities. From about 1900 through the 1920s and 1930s, government policy sporadically encouraged and supported tribal and individually owned Indian cattle herds. Cheyenne and other tribal cowboys (such as the Sioux and Arapahos) wore the same clothing as neighboring non-Indian ranchers.

The Model T here probably belonged to Marquis, who owned such a car in his doctor days in 1922. He gave rides to some of his patients, including Porcupine, the famous leader of the Cheyenne Ghost Dance.

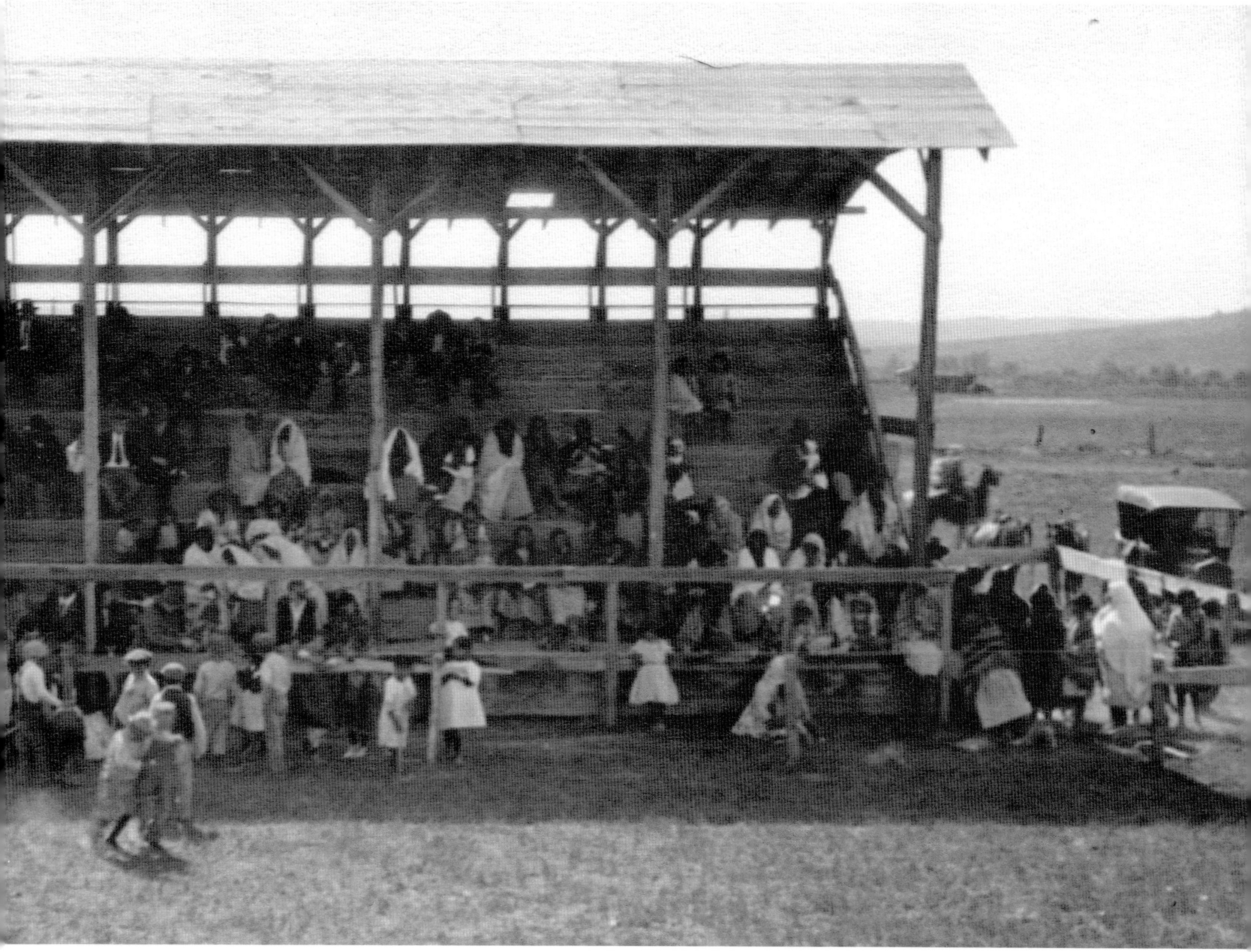

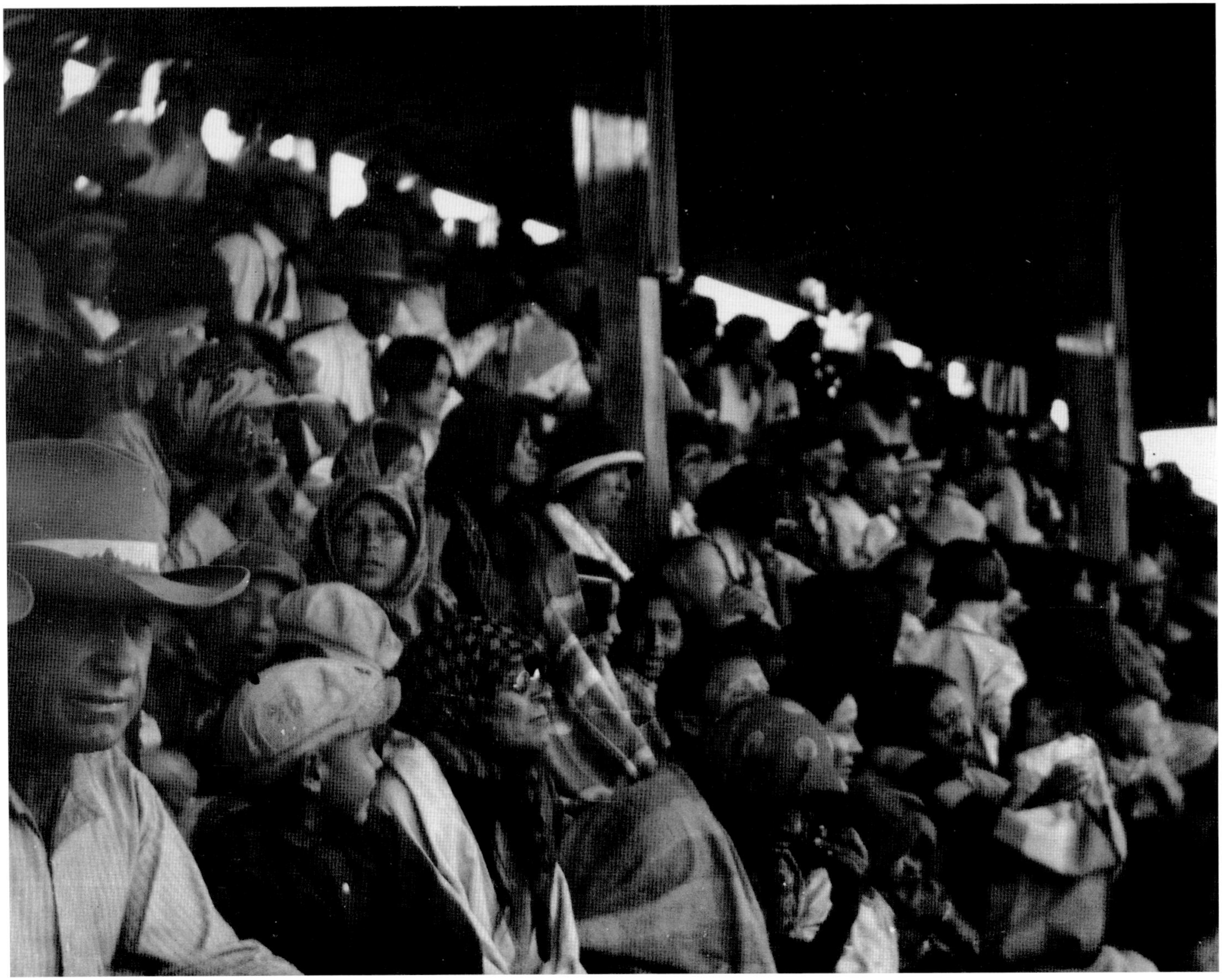

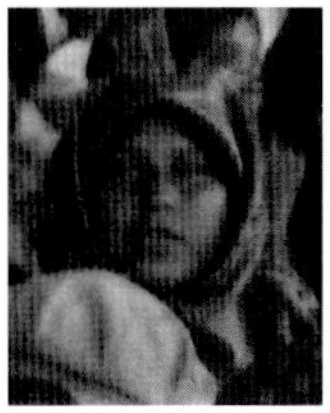

4. Faces at the Rodeo

INFORMANT: JOHN WOODENLEGS

4a. This is the Busby grandstand full of people, lots of faces. Holding their babies and old ladies with handkerchiefs around their heads. There's Crow women and men and Cheyennes and white people all sitting watching the rodeo. They all seemed to dress neat and they're all interested in the rodeo. It's a good picture.

4b. By the early 1900s frequent Crow and Northern Cheyenne social interaction was taking place, as shown here. Formerly the bitterest of enemies, the tribes retain a certain amount of rivalry. Their native languages were totally different, so that conversation took place in English or in the Plains sign language

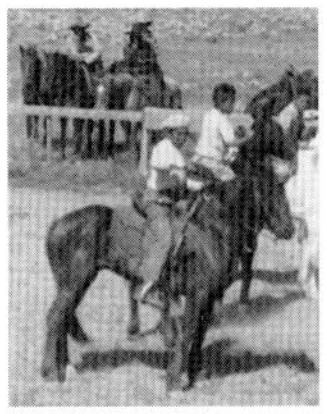

5. Lining up for the Race

INFORMANT: JOHN WOODENLEGS

5a. This picture is at Busby getting ready for the race. There's the judges' stand with about 15 judges up there. These are young boys riding, maybe riding as jockeys. The race track only has one rail. There's older men watching. Some are leading horses. Some may own horses that are in the race. There's seven horses there getting ready, and there's a man standing there with a big hat. Looks like Willis Deafy. There's two boys wearing hats and two without any hat and three wearing a cap. They turned the cap around so it won't blow off. Three are riding bareback and the others have saddles. They're getting ready to go! It's quite an excitement for these boys to go around the track.

5b. Horse races were very popular. The Cheyennes' love for their horses was very great. A calamity almost as bad as losing the buffalo happened in the 1920s when the government forced them to slaughter their horses for food or for the two-dollar bounty paid for a pair of ears. This was done to free reservation grazing resources for use by cattle. During this time the Cheyennes were encouraged to raise home gardens, and food rations were continued.

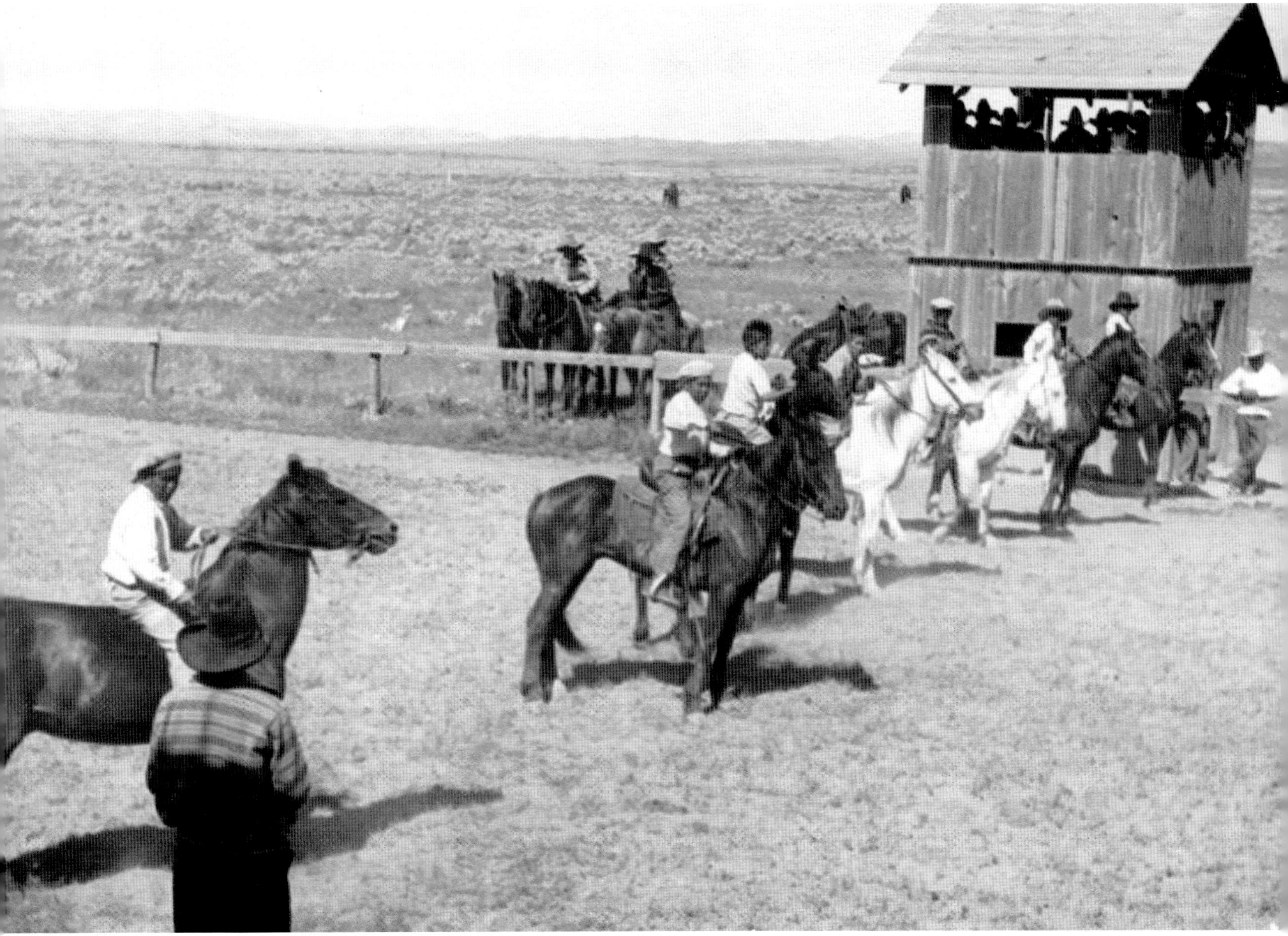

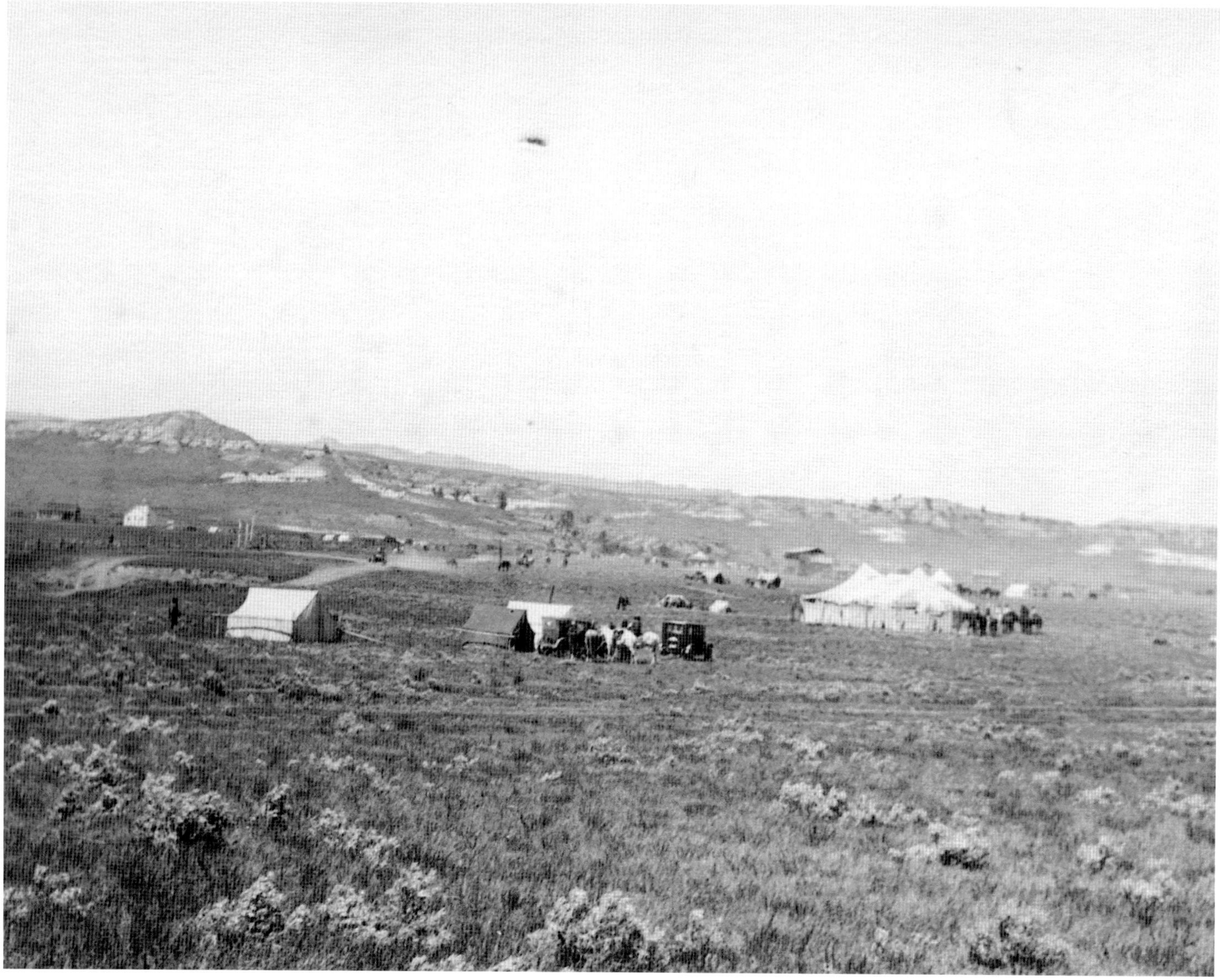

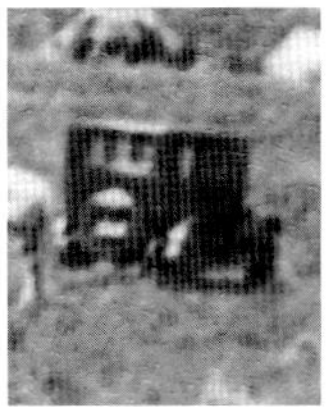

6. Busby Dance Hall Tent

Informant: John Woodenlegs

6a. This picture was taken at Busby right there where all the houses are now. The white building on the left is the Mennonite Church and the log house close to the church, these two buildings are still there. The Busby people had this big circus tent for a dance hall. They could take it down or put it up, and it belonged to the Busby district, the Busby people, the White River Cheyennes. In the back there is a grandstand and the race track. There's a few tents set up, and they had their dances there right in that big tent. Sometimes they took it further up toward Kirby and set it up there for Christmas doings and other celebrations. They had hand games and dances in this big tent. Now there are a lot of houses all over this area.

6b. The continuity of communities and social groups that were derived from earlier nomadic bands and families was one of the more positive features of reservation life. So too were freedom from pursuit by soldiers and a steadier supply of food and clothing than in the last years of bitter warfare.

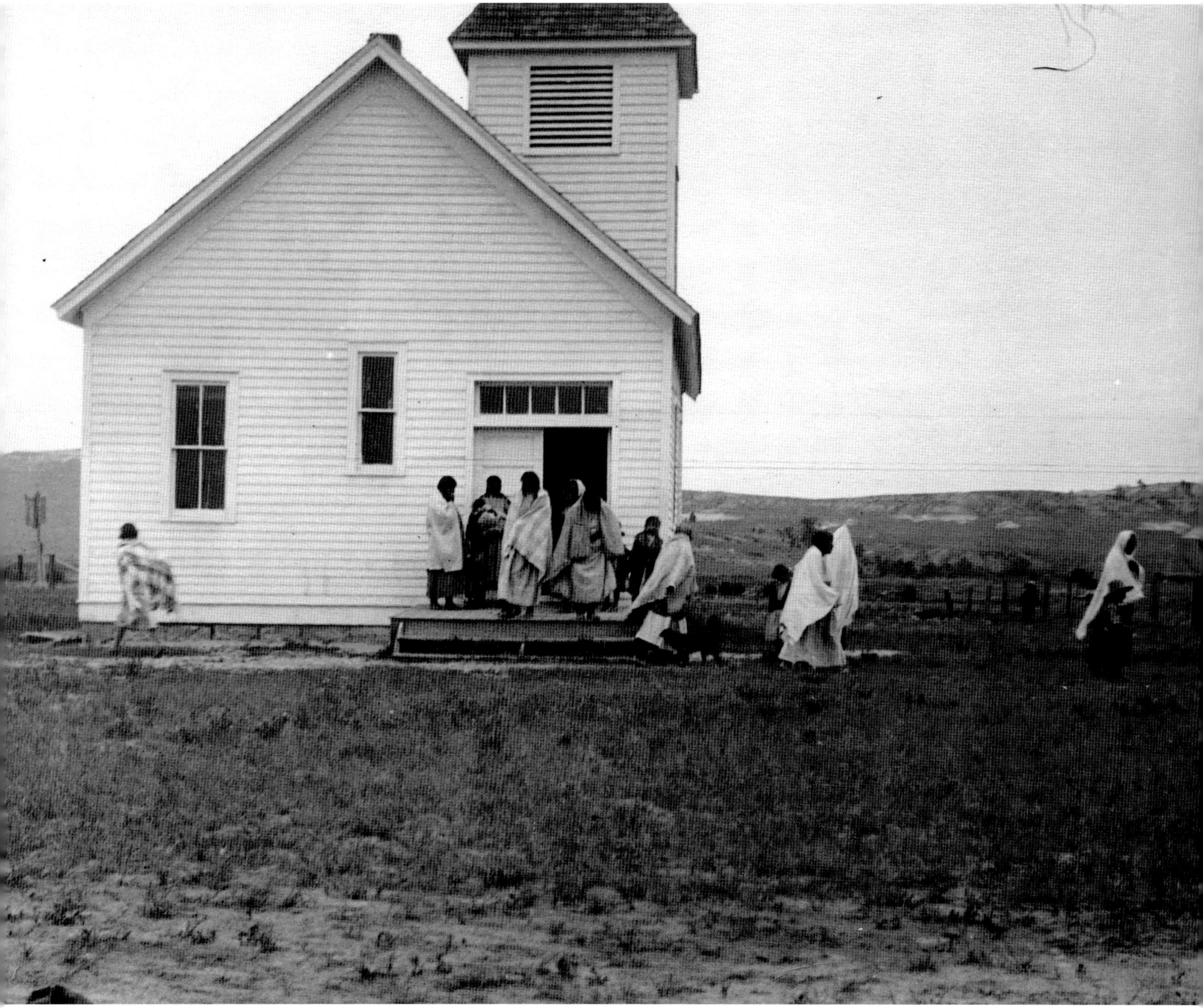

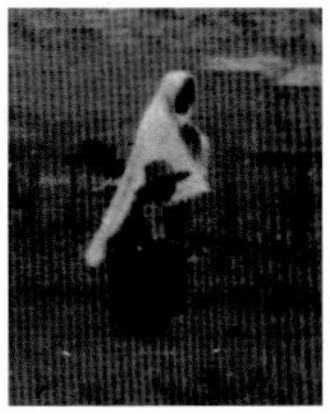

7. Busby Mennonite Church

INFORMANT: JOHN WOODENLEGS

7a. This is the Busby Mennonite Church. It looks real good. These are Cheyenne women and children coming out of the church, wearing white blankets and different colored blankets. This must be Sunday after the service. This church is still standing today.

7b. The Mennonite mission to the Cheyennes included the Swiss linguist Rodolphe Petter, who had formerly served as a missionary among the Southern Cheyennes in Oklahoma. When he arrived speaking their extremely difficult language, the Northern Cheyennes thought that he must be the Messiah, whose coming was predicted by the Ghost Dance. An earlier church was the Catholic mission St. Labre's at Ashland. Both missions still exist.

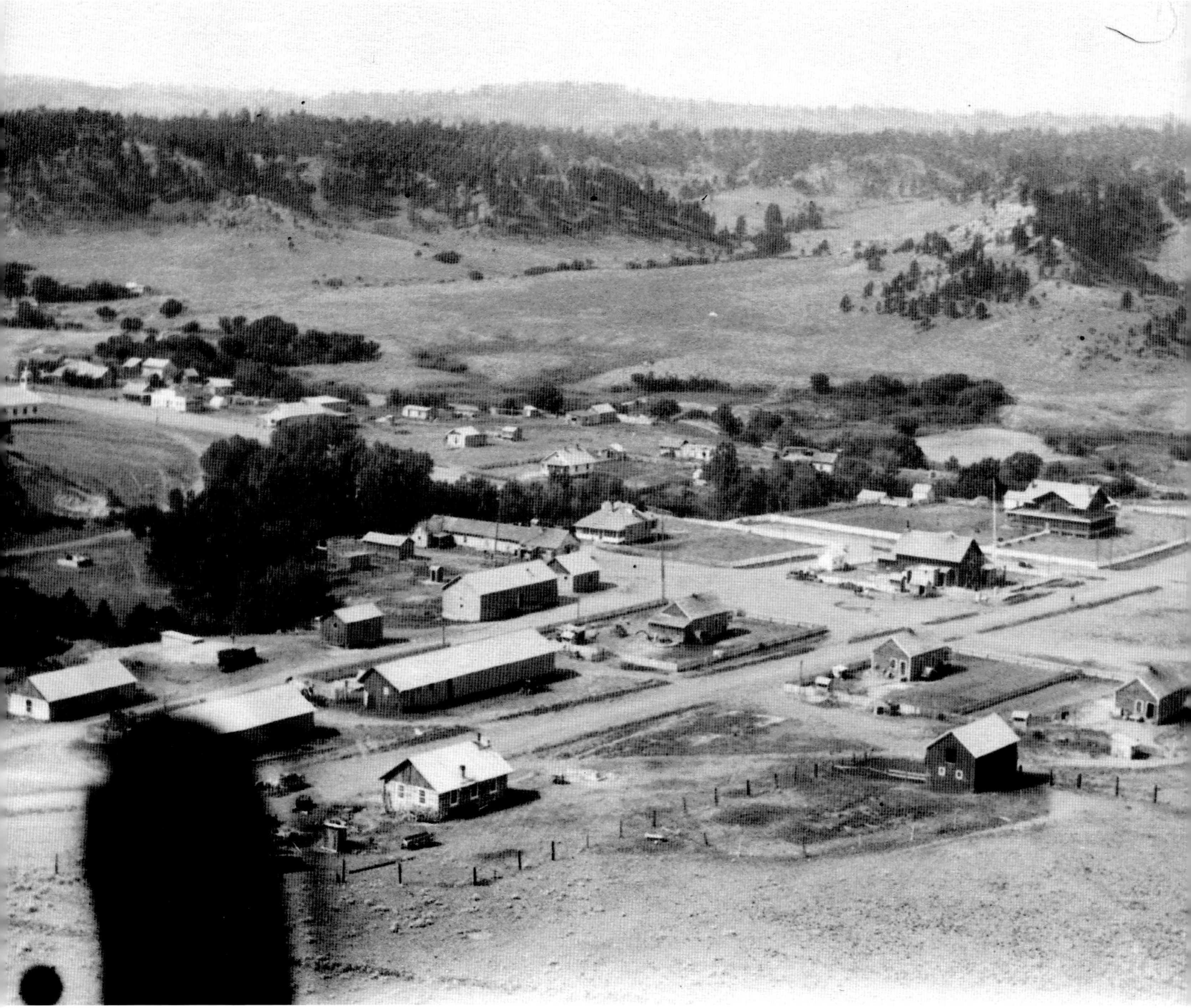

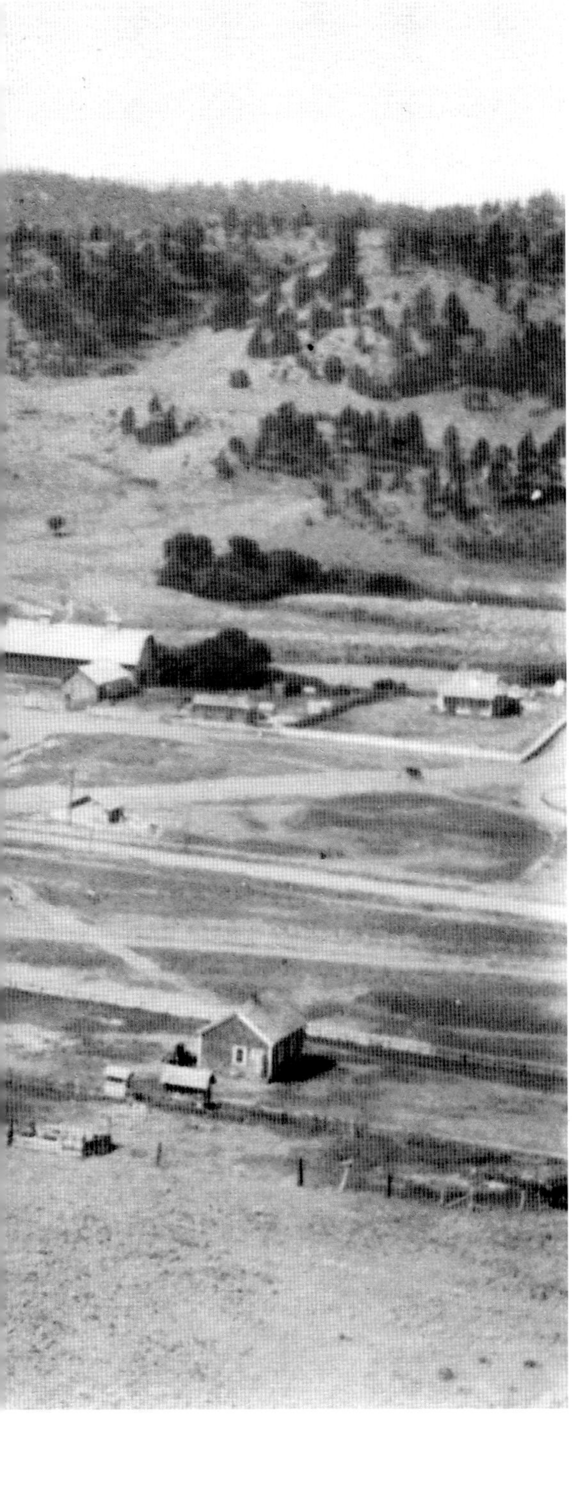

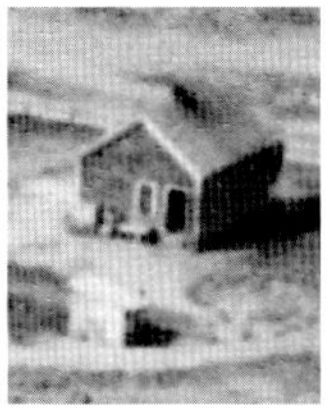

8. Lame Deer around 1927

INFORMANT: JOHN WOODENLEGS

8a. This is Lame Deer, around 1927. The Catholic Church (left center) is still there.

8b. Lame Deer, the agency headquarters town, was established in 1884 on the site of the original Walt Alderson place described in A Bride Goes West *(Alderson and Smith 1942). Their ranch was burned by angry Cheyennes in 1884 when one of the Alderson hands shot the hat from the head of a sleeping tribesman. The Cheyennes did not think it was a joke. The Aldersons were away at the time in Miles City for the birth of their first baby. They returned to find their new house in ashes and never had another home to equal it.*

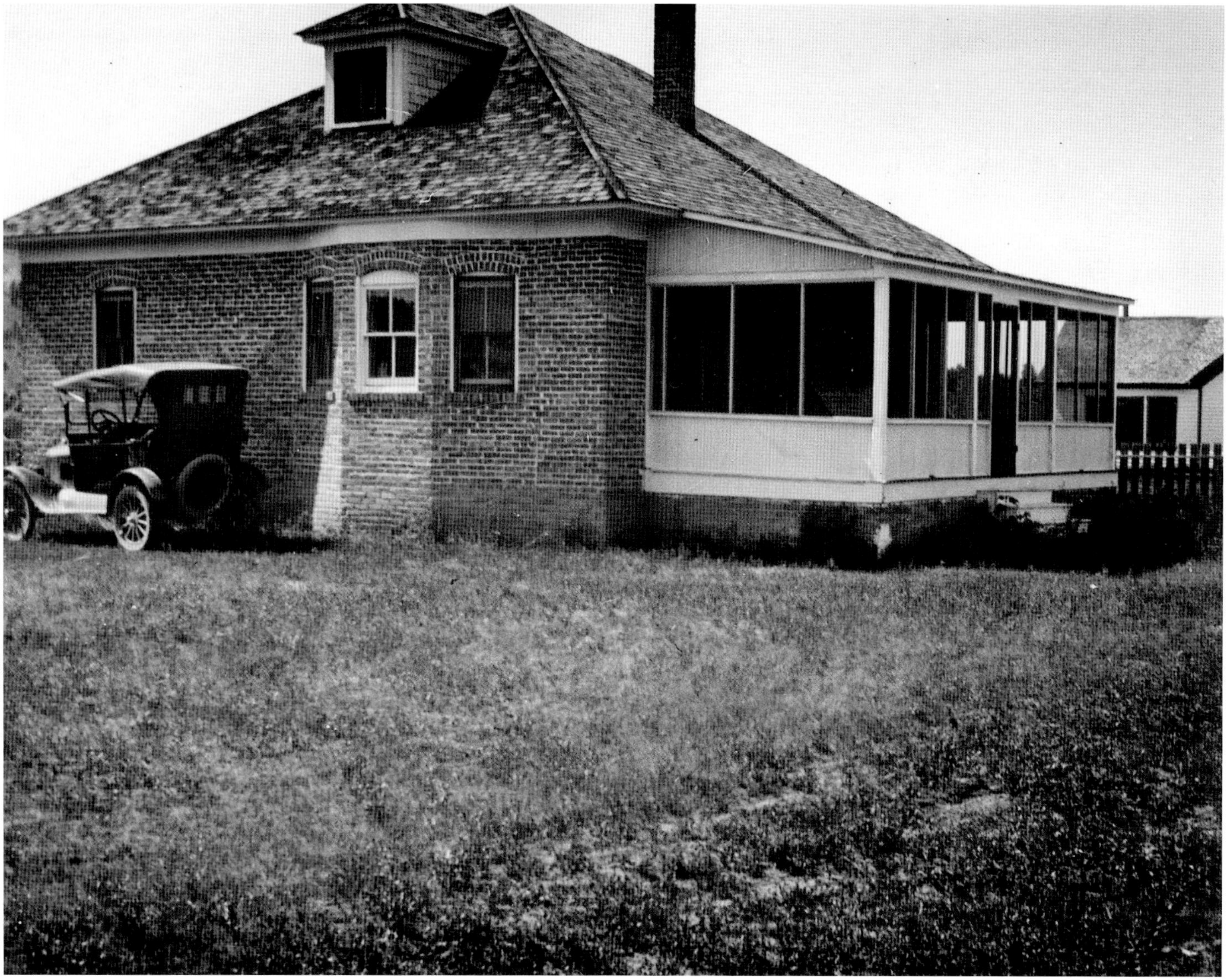

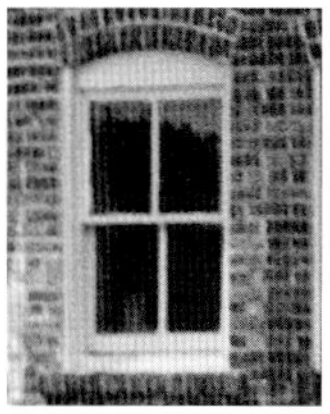

9. Physician's Residence, Lame Deer

Informant: Notes of Dr. Thomas Marquis

9a. This is the house where Dr. Marquis lived during his time as agency physician in Lame Deer. The picture was taken in July 1922. The teachers' residence is in the background.

9b. These Marquis notes have been missing for years.

Marquis did not last long as an agency doctor. He began service in 1922 but quit before the end of the year. Marquis remained in the vicinity of the Cheyenne and Crow reservations, however, until his death in 1935. During this time he not only took pictures but purchased numerous artifacts. Many of them are on exhibit today at Little Bighorn Battlefield National Monument (formerly Custer Battlefield National Monument). He also founded his own small museum in Hardin, Montana, and wrote numerous articles on local history for the Billings Gazette *plus a series of pamphlets and books that are treasured by historians (see the references).*

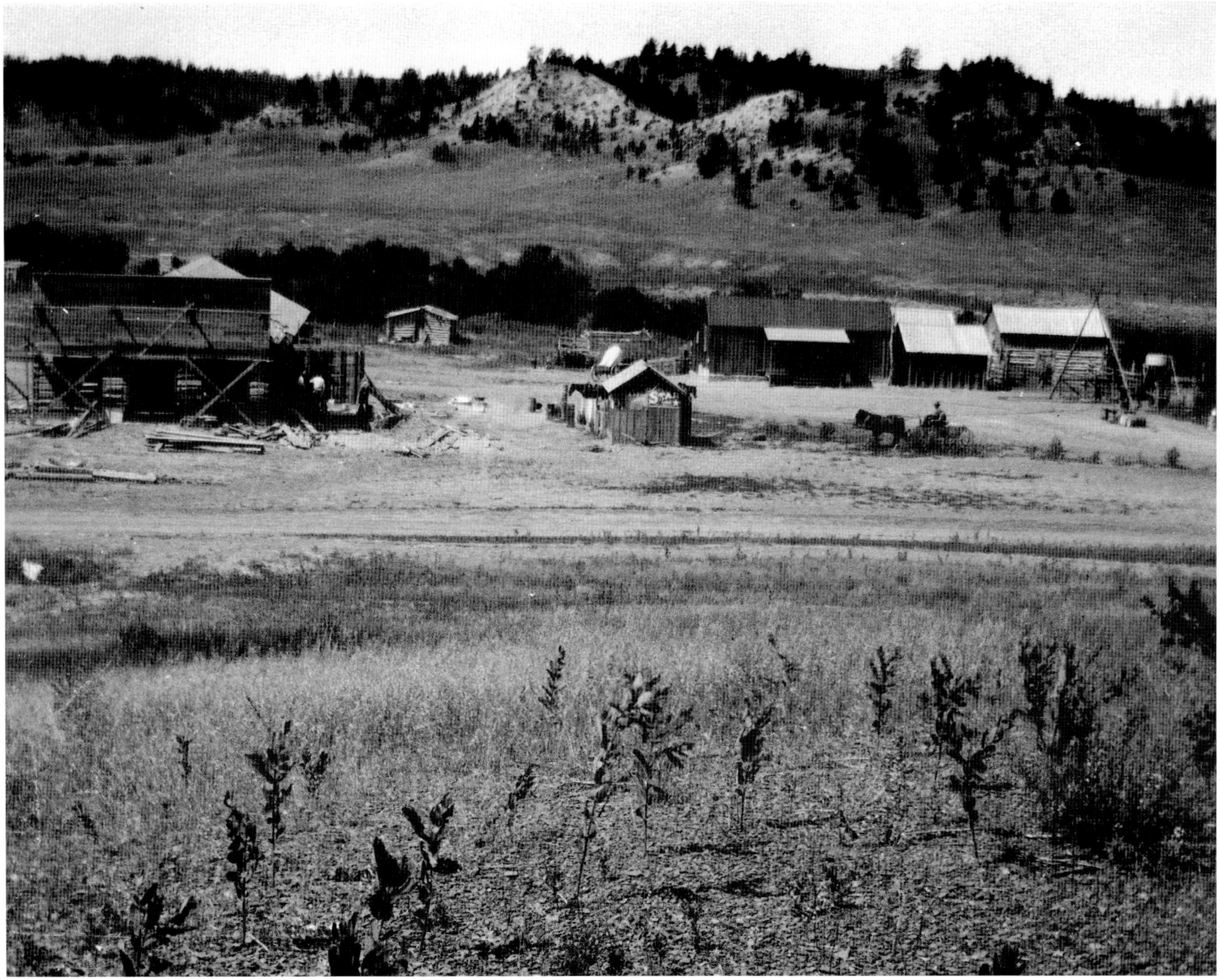

10. Lame Deer Store

Informant: John Woodenlegs

10a. This is the Lame Deer store. A white fellow ran this store and they called him "Big Nose." He married Jules Seminole's daughter. She was my aunt, my dad's half-sister. Her name was Jennie. She married this white fellow and had two or three children. They called him George Walters, Sr. In this picture they are rebuilding the front part of that store. It had burned down. There's shacks and a hitching post with saddle horses tied up and a covered wagon. They used the back granary as a store while they were rebuilding. They have a big sign here that says "Star Chewing Tobacco." Cheyennes bought a lot of this plug tobacco to mix with kinnick-kinnick [red willow bark or Indian tobacco] so they could put it in their pipes and smoke it. There's a man here with a team of horses and a buggy. These old shacks are still here today. There's another log house that a Spaniard had. He wanted to live close to the store. His wife and children died off and he was alone. He married into the tribe. He was a good gambler.

The road runs right in front of the store, north and south. Now the store has a big addition to it and it's called an IGA store, but the old store had the post office inside of it and hardware, groceries, clothing and saddles, harness, boots. It had everything in that store! When Mr. Walters got old and quit running that store, he sold it to Mr. Stohr. The Cheyennes named that white guy, Mr. Stohr, "Lop-sided Nose." First we had "Big Nose" and then "Lop-sided Nose" owned the store. After Stohr died, different people handled it until Jim Mullins took over. Inside this store there was a big, high counter so nobody could reach over. You had to ask for different things and the clerks would give it to you, and you had to pay for it. I never heard of anybody ever stealing out of that store. It seemed like some people thought Indian people were thieves, but they never stole out of there.

There's a picture of a hayrack on a wagon here, and also a covered wagon and some saddle horses. This store had a really good well for water. That log house near the store is still there, it's been remodeled. Some of the old buildings, log houses that were built around there are still there today. At the time Mr. Mullins came in to run the store, his dad was running one at Busby. Mullins wanted to open that store up to let the Indian people take stuff off of the shelves and put it in a cart and take it up to the clerk to have it checked out. A lot of white people told him, "You're going to lose your shirt—you're going to let Indians pick the stuff off the shelves? You're going to lose!" A lot of people didn't trust the Indians. Mr. Mullins said, "I trust them, I'm going to run it that way." At the time I was president of the Tribal Council. He asked me to come and help him to show the Indians to take the stuff off the shelves. They didn't want to do that, it would look like they were stealing or something. They didn't know how to do that, to put it in a cart and push it up to be checked out. We kind of had to show them what they should do. After a while they did go ahead. Mr. Mullins is still running that store today, and I always kind of thank him for trusting the Cheyennes. But the older storekeepers said that the older Cheyennes were really honest people. It would be good if that would rub onto the younger ones today. This is such a good picture of the old Lame Deer store, called Lame Deer Trading Post. We have a joke now—IGA means "Indians Grab Anything" store.

10b. The Big Store remains the most important grocery and general goods business on the reservation.

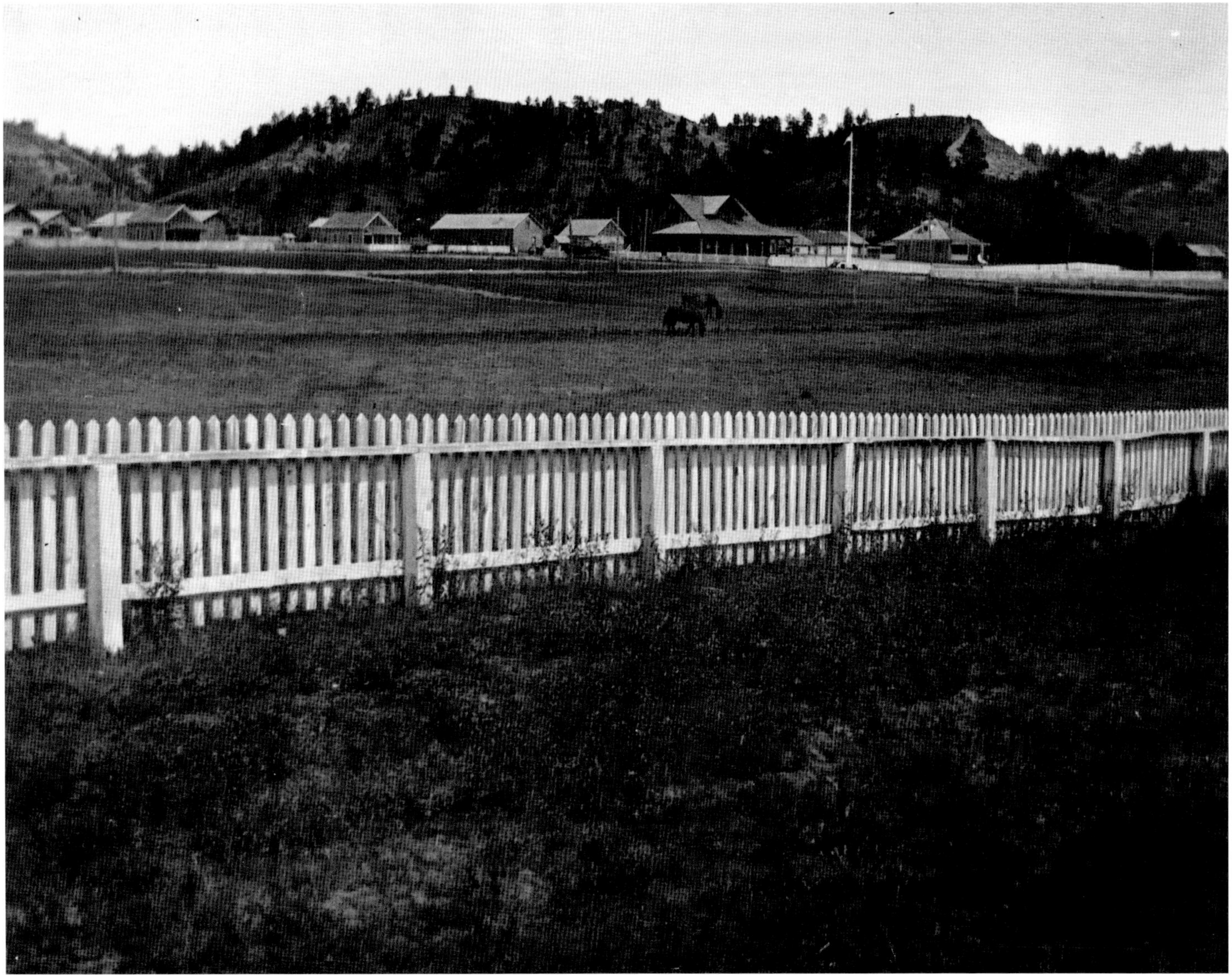

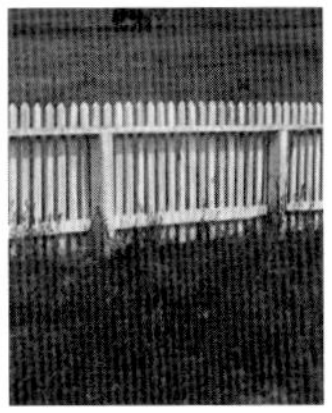

11. First Northern Cheyenne Agency

INFORMANT: JOHN WOODENLEGS

11a. This is the Northern Cheyenne Agency—the big building there with the flagpole close to it. It's the office of the Bureau of Indian Affairs, with the superintendent and all his staff. The house to the right is the chief clerk's house. The one made out of brick, behind the flagpole is the Lame Deer School, and right behind the office towards the east is the jail house. The next building is the Issue House, where they issued rations. Then they had four new buildings built for the policemen and the judge and the employees. Right behind those buildings is another storehouse or warehouse, and behind that is the blacksmith shop. The road runs right in front of the office and the buildings, goes on across to the Lame Deer town. It crosses Alderson Gulch or Alderson Creek. You can see the top of the Lame Deer Public School. I went to school at that day school when I first went to school, and later I went to the public school. The Agency building on the north (left) side of it, you can just barely see a hay rack and a wagon and a team of horses. They had a scale there and they weighed hay there, where they used to butcher cattle on ration day. They weighed the hay there and sold it to the government.

11b. The ration period extended from the Northern Cheyenne surrender in 1877 until about 1900, when cattle raising and later dry farming were promoted by the government in order to encourage Cheyenne self-sufficiency. Both efforts were hurt by periodic cycles of drought.

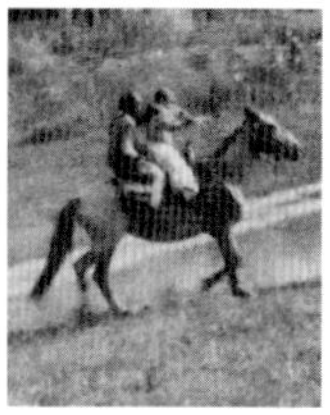

12. Lame Deer Flour Mill

INFORMANT: JOHN WOODENLEGS

12a. This is the flour mill in Lame Deer. The government at one time had the Cheyennes plant a lot of wheat. They plowed with horses, even farmed up on top of the divide, and they raised a lot of grain. So they had a flour mill right there in Lame Deer. There are two girls riding horseback, riding double and they're driving two other horses. The way the Cheyennes rode, they took a blanket and wrapped their legs—looks like they have chaps on. The flour mill did really well for the Cheyenne people, they ground up their own wheat and sold part of it and used some of it for flour. A white fellow named Mitchell ran the mill, and Indians were helping. They used coal to run a steam engine in the mill.

12b. Cheyenne women were skilled with horses from buffalo days. They handled them for packing and moving camp, and most were expert equestrians. A few, such as Buffalo Calf Road Woman, even participated in battles alongside the men (Stands in Timber and Liberty 1997: chapter 11).

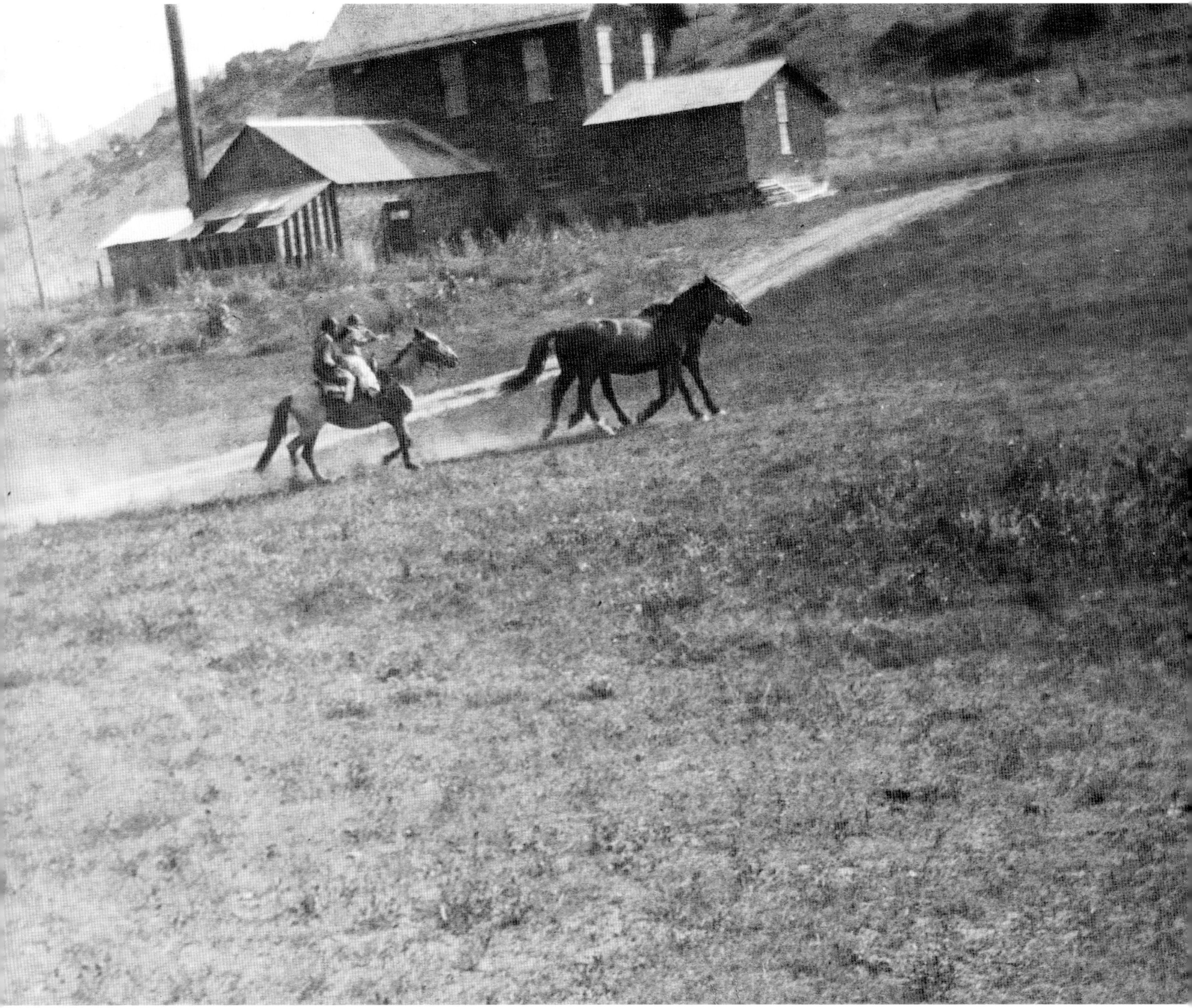

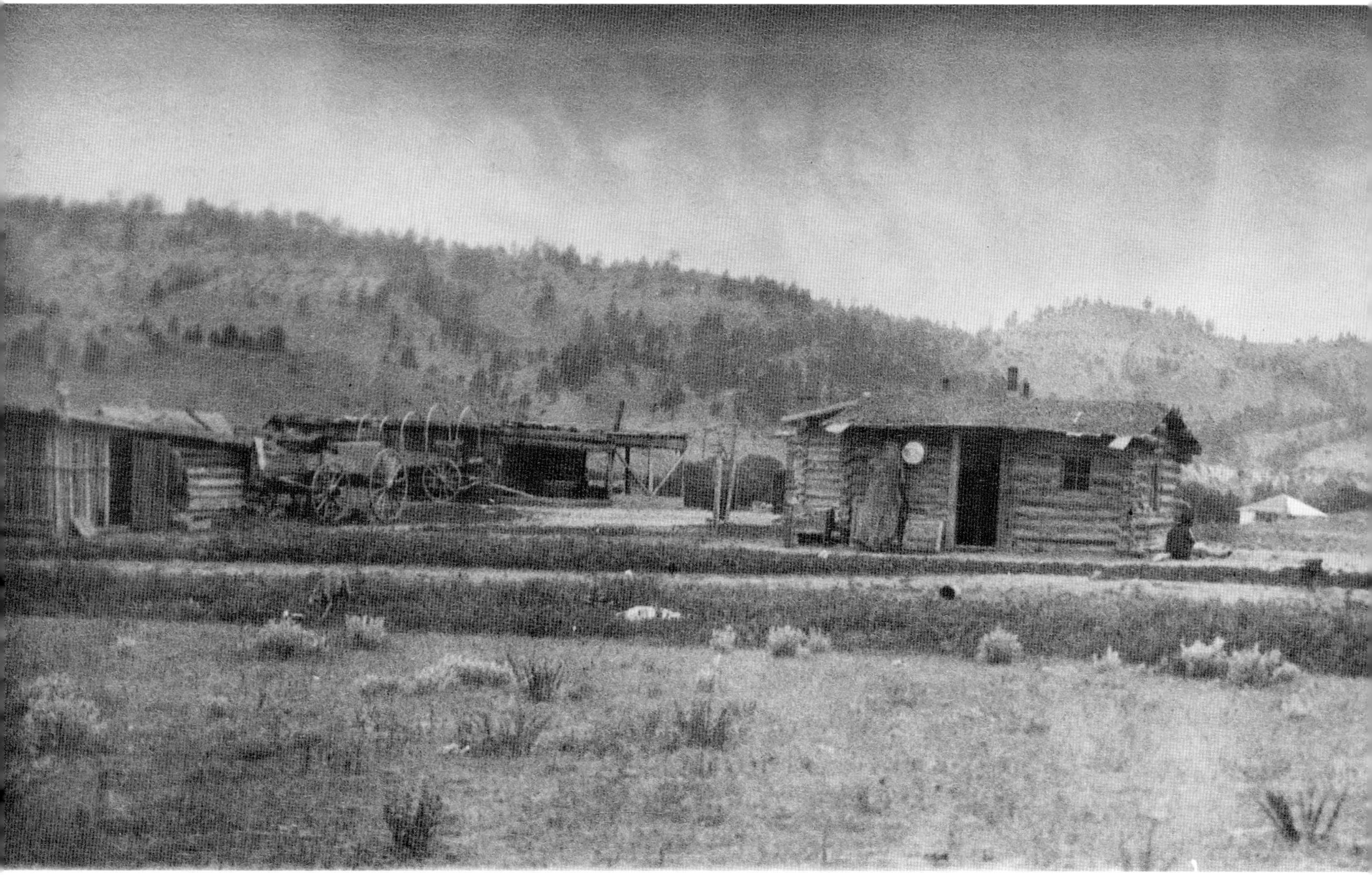

13. Log Houses in Lame Deer

INFORMANT: JOHN WOODENLEGS

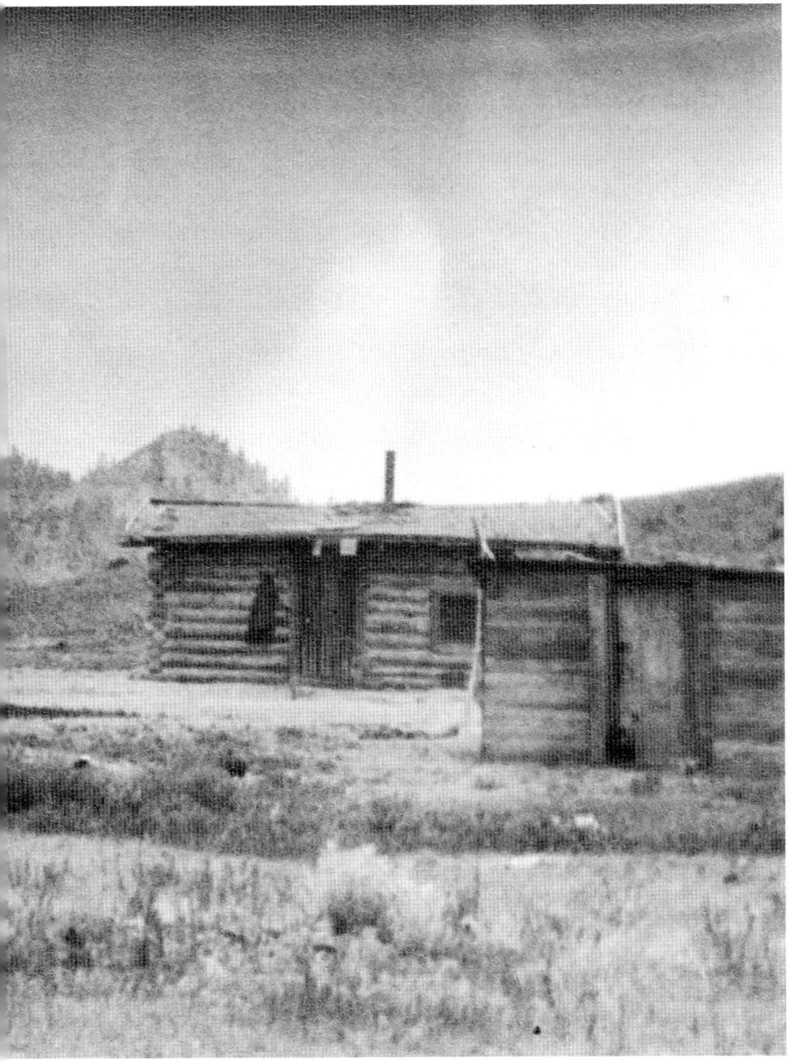

13a. This picture is also in Lame Deer, just above the Lame Deer store. These are log houses that people built themselves—cut the trees down. One of them was Jennie Issues and she lived there. She had two or three daughters, and then Black Horses built their house there because they were related. Louis Seminole built one house there. He was married into the Black Horse family. There were other houses and different kinds of board shacks they had. They had wagons with a bow on the wagon box. Now these houses had logs chinked with mud or clay, one window and dirt floors. They were not fixed very good for ventilation—it was just a place to live. The big cook stove for heat, and they all lived in there, and whatever disease anybody might have, everyone would be in contact. They all slept in there inside. They had to go after water to the creek or to a well, and they had outhouses. Nobody showed them about how to have a screen door or screen window for ventilation. They cut the logs themselves; they helped one another. You can still see some of those old houses along Rosebud Creek—they were really small houses.

13b. Early reservation log houses were patterned after the one-room homestead cabins of white pioneers. Sanitation problems became acute in fixed settlements for a people who had traditionally remained only a short time in one camping place.

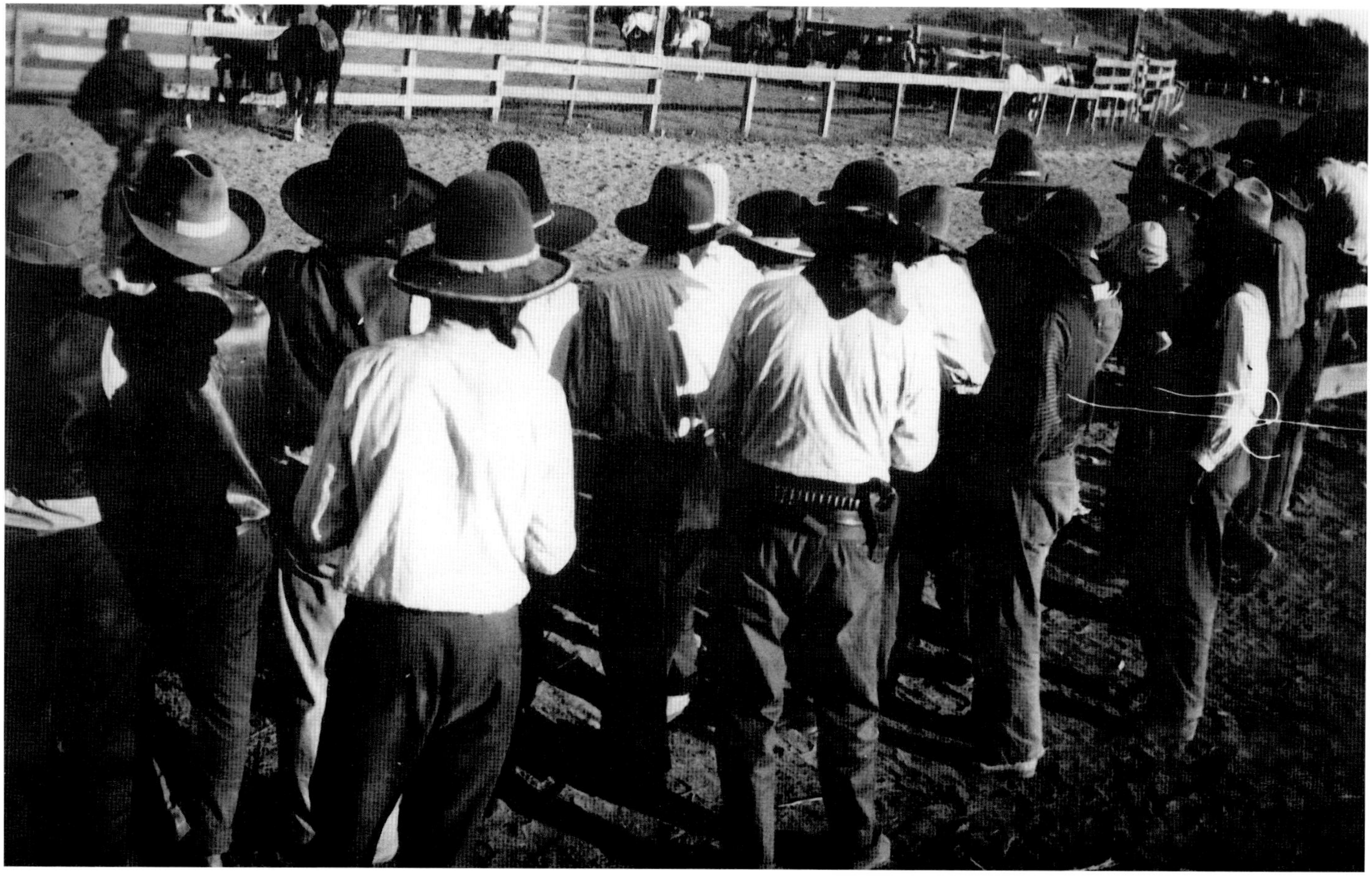

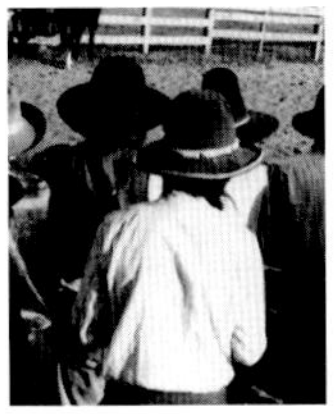

14. Waiting for the Races

INFORMANT: JOHN WOODENLEGS

14a. This is at the Lame Deer fairgrounds. They are getting ready for a race or a relay race. There's a lot of men standing, with their backs to the photographer. Some of these I know from their back. Some are Crows, some are white people. George American Horse is one of them and John Russell. The one with the reservation hat is Austin Texas. There's a policeman with his gun and shell belt, with his handkerchief on his head and his hat on top of it. Now they have horse races, a quarter mile, three-eighths, and half a mile. Some are mile horses, mile and a half, or two mile horses. They sure took good care of them. I don't know how they did it, but they did. Some of the races were relay races. They fixed a paddock where the horses were and that's where they would change horses and come out for the next stretch. It used to be a good fairgrounds, a good race track. They had prizes for these horses and then they had match races with their own horses, or the Crows or with white people. White people came to these fairs to ride and to race. They had young boys and young men foot races, also young girls and old lady races. They'd run even with their long dresses, kind of comical. They had pulling contests, a team of horses pulling a heavy load. Everybody had fun, everybody was sincere. They all had a good time. They had dances, the powwow. They danced in front of the grandstand, contest dances. They had a tug-of-war with a big rope. Seemed like the judges paid the money right away when you won. They had the cash. They must have been honest people.

14b. The events at fairs or celebrations were varied and highly popular. Whether "old lady races" (foot races for older women) existed on other reservations is not known, but they must have been wonderful events. The lives of reservation women and their predecessors had more advantages than suggested by the "downtrodden squaw" stereotype so widely circulated in mainstream culture to this day.

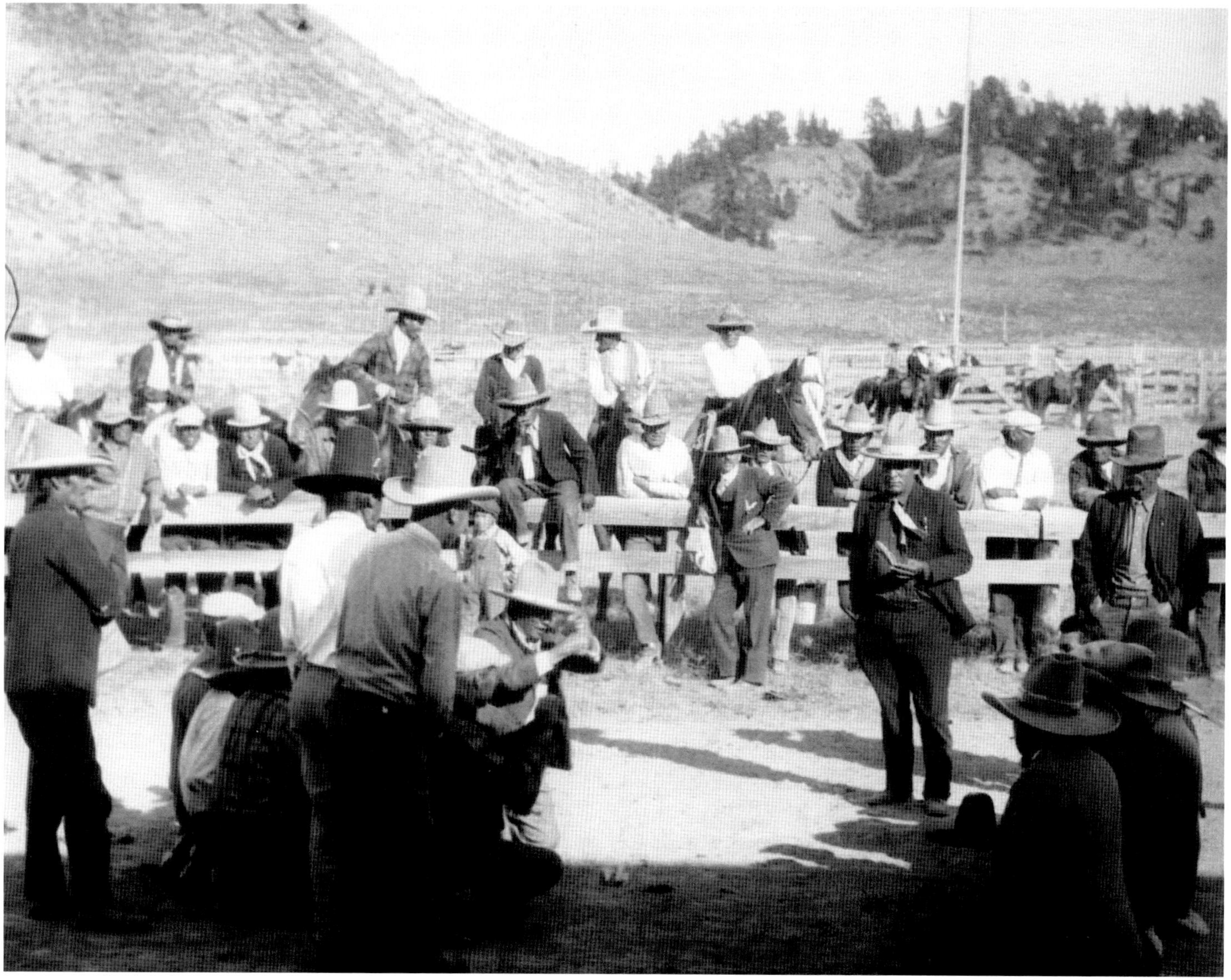

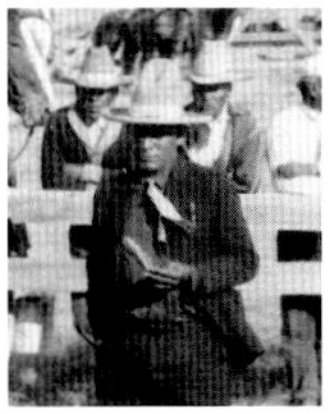

15. Playing a Stick Game

INFORMANT: JOHN WOODENLEGS

15a. This was taken in Lame Deer at the fairgrounds during the fair and rodeo. There's quite a few people on horseback and on foot, leaning against the fence and there's two sets of stick game players. During these fair celebrations, they had all kinds of events to take part in. One of them was these stick games. These are Crows playing against Cheyennes. The Cheyenne that has the bones and is playing them is Ghost Bull. Whoever wins will get paid—it's kind of a contest. These men are all good people. The old men that I know still look good: Wolf Tooth (front, left), American Horse, Wounded Eye, Ghost Bull, Stands in Timber, La Rance, and four or five Crows that are sitting. Then along the fence is (I don't know the first one) but then Monothy, Charles Sitting Man, Sr., Charles Kills Back, Strange Owl. The man sitting on the fence is Willie Two Moons, smoking a cigarette. He's got a ribbon tied; he must be one of the officials. There's a man standing there I don't know and then there's a white man. The next one is Martin Kills Night. That's just the way I know him. Floyd High Walking, Alex Brady, Jerome Bear Tusk, and there's an uncle of ours, Louis Seminole. There's some on horseback; they're all looking on. Ben Black Wolf and Frank Hart are there too. Frank is a bronc rider, then Fred Round Stone, one of the older calf ropers and rodeo men, riding a sorrel, bald-faced horse. I know him, he wore that hat, and he calf roped—then there's some more corrals and chutes. They used to have a pole in the middle of this fairgrounds where they put up the flag. Today there's houses all over this fairground. It's good to see some of these good old people, the way they looked, kind people.

15b. The stick game or hand game, a gambling contest between opposing teams accompanied by drumming and singing, is still highly popular in reservation communities. It is a guessing game in which the guessing team must locate the sticks or bones concealed in the hands of one of the members of the hiding team—a sort of musical "Who's Got the Button." A lot of money is often wagered at these events. Wolf Tooth, identified here, was the grandfather of John Stands in Timber (the Cheyenne tribal historian) and a prominent figure in many events in Cheyenne Memories *(Stands in Timber and Liberty 1997).*

Stands in Timber wears a dark suit and a tie and a white hat.

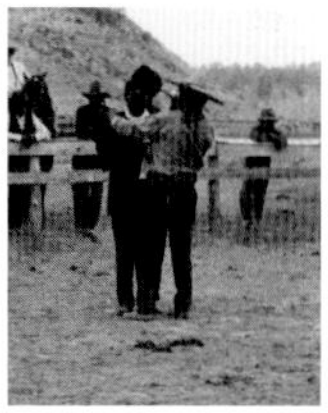

16. At the Fair

INFORMANT: JOHN WOODENLEGS

16a. This is at the Lame Deer fairgrounds, right in front of the grandstand, in front of the judges' stand. One of the contests was to walk a wire that was strung in the air. They walked the wire, these Cheyennes. The judge is explaining to this young man about this kind of contest, to walk this wire across. I don't know how high, maybe ten or twelve feet. Some of them practiced. There were some older men like Little Chief, Samson Medicine, and Pete Risingsun on horseback with his braids on. This man that's instructing the young man has a reservation hat and a black handkerchief, his gun scabbard, and his belt. Half of the judges' stand is showing and the hill in the background.

16b. The site of the old Lame Deer fairgrounds and racetrack is covered today by contemporary housing. Any child of an enrolled Cheyenne parent is eligible to become an enrolled member of the tribe. Like other supposedly "Vanishing Americans," the Cheyennes did not vanish. From a population of 900 in 1890, Northern Cheyenne numbers reached 1,450 in 1942 and have more than doubled since that time.

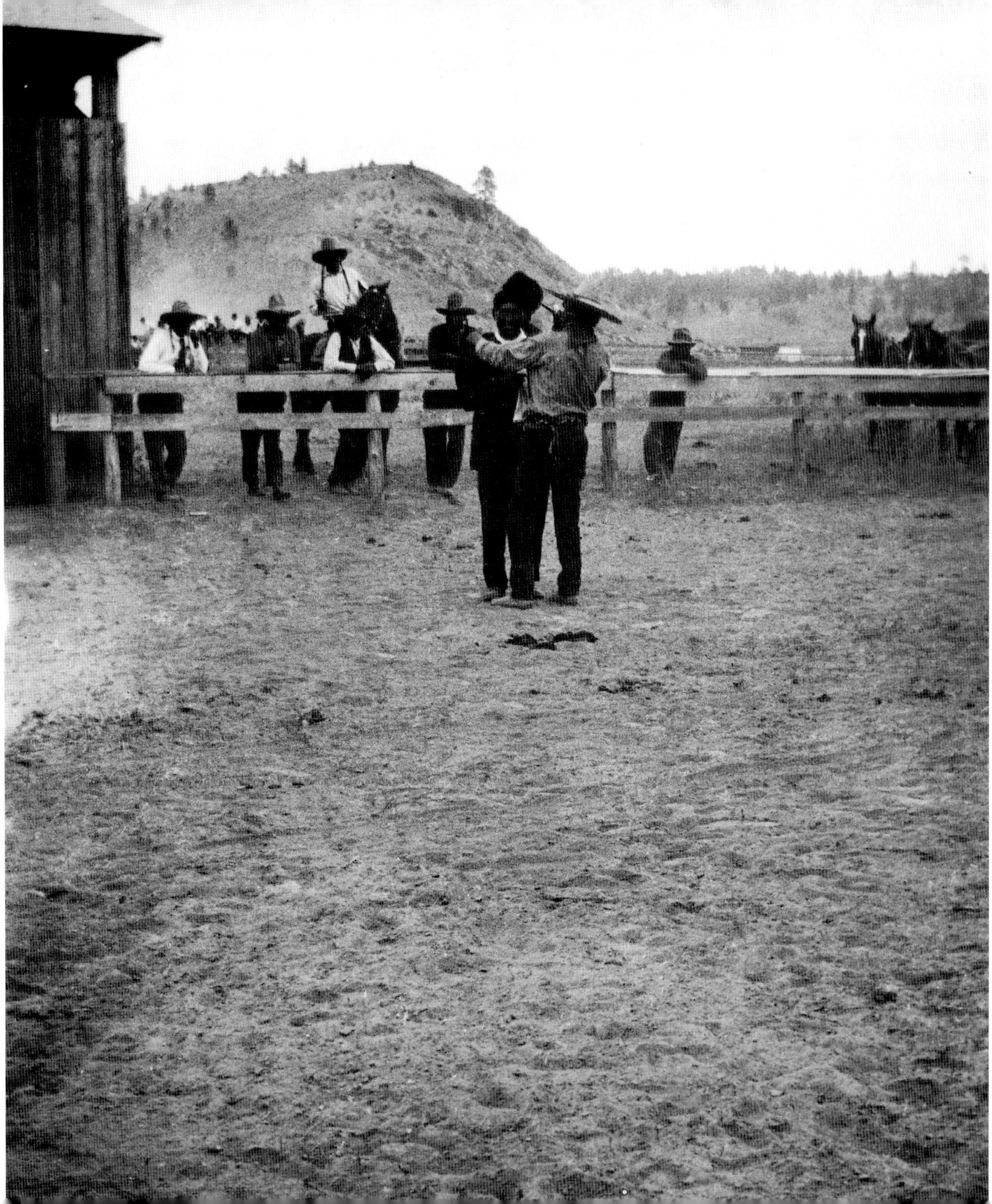

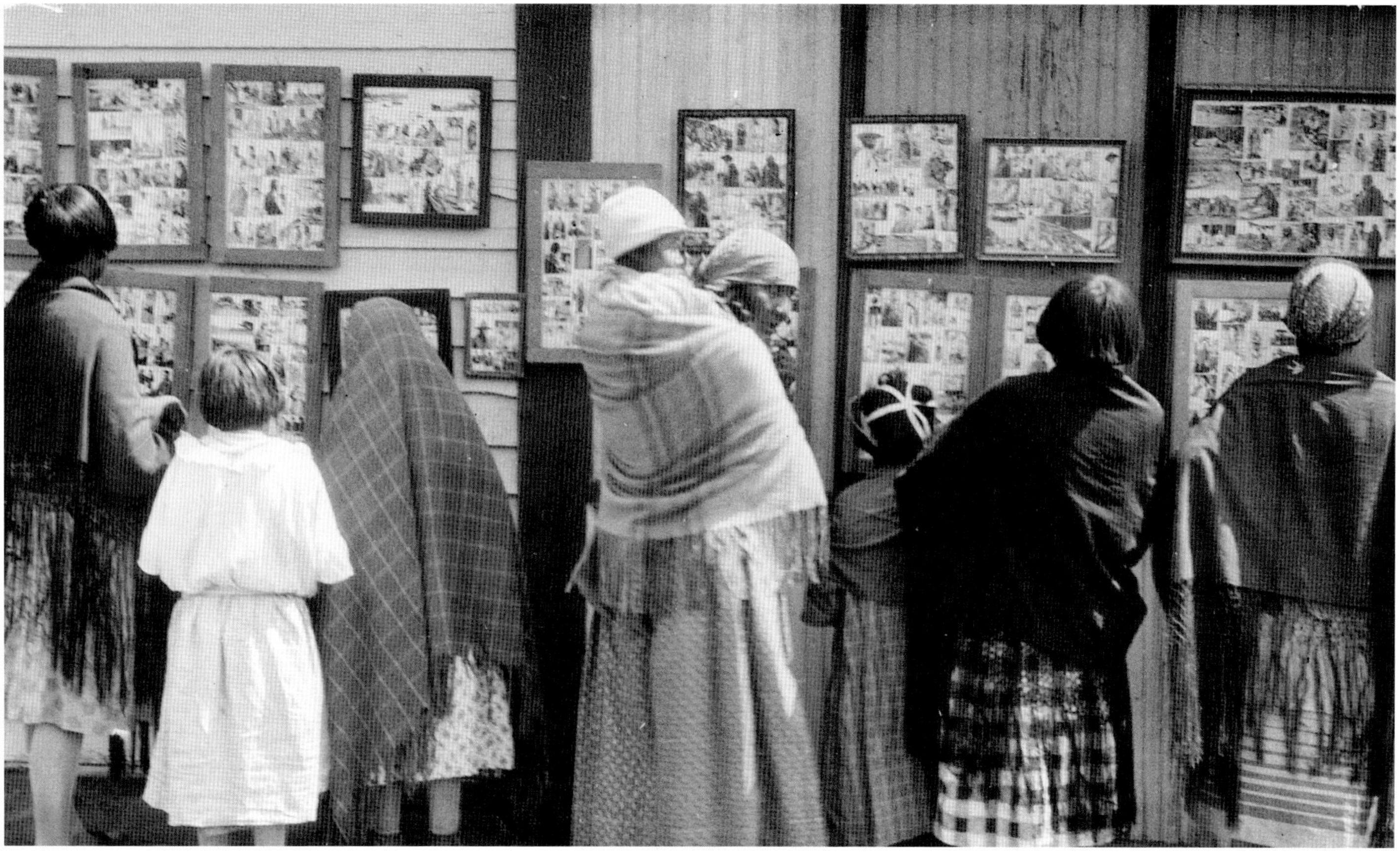

17. Marquis Photo Exhibit

Informant: John Woodenlegs

17a. Women and girls viewing Thomas Marquis photo exhibit at the Cheyenne fair in Lame Deer, September, 1926.

17b. Marquis took about 500 Northern Cheyenne photographs in all. For the story of their return to the tribe, see The Road to Lame Deer *(Mader 2002: 61–68).*

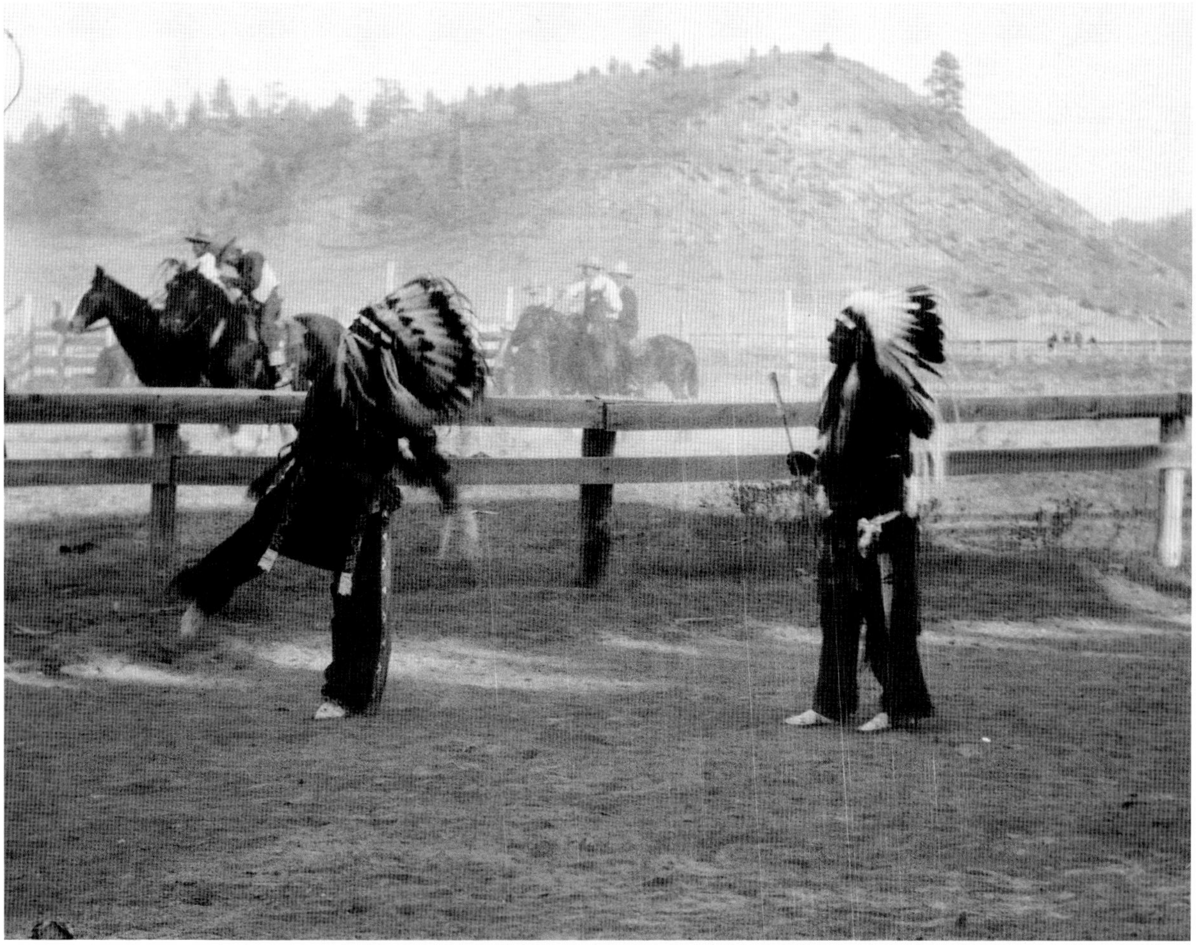

18. Arrow-Throwing Contest

INFORMANT: JOHN WOODENLEGS

18a. Men liked to take part in throwing arrows—a contest to see who could be most accurate. This was another event at the Cheyenne fair in Lame Deer. These men have good outfits on, including their moccasins. Indian people still enjoy arrow throwing contests today.

18b. The war bonnets used here in 1920s athletic contests were a rare and valuable possession, and the value has gone up—one appraised at $75,000 was recently returned to the tribe after rescue by a non-Indian from a thrift shop in California.

Today it is illegal for any non-Indian to possess eagle feathers or eagle-feather regalia.

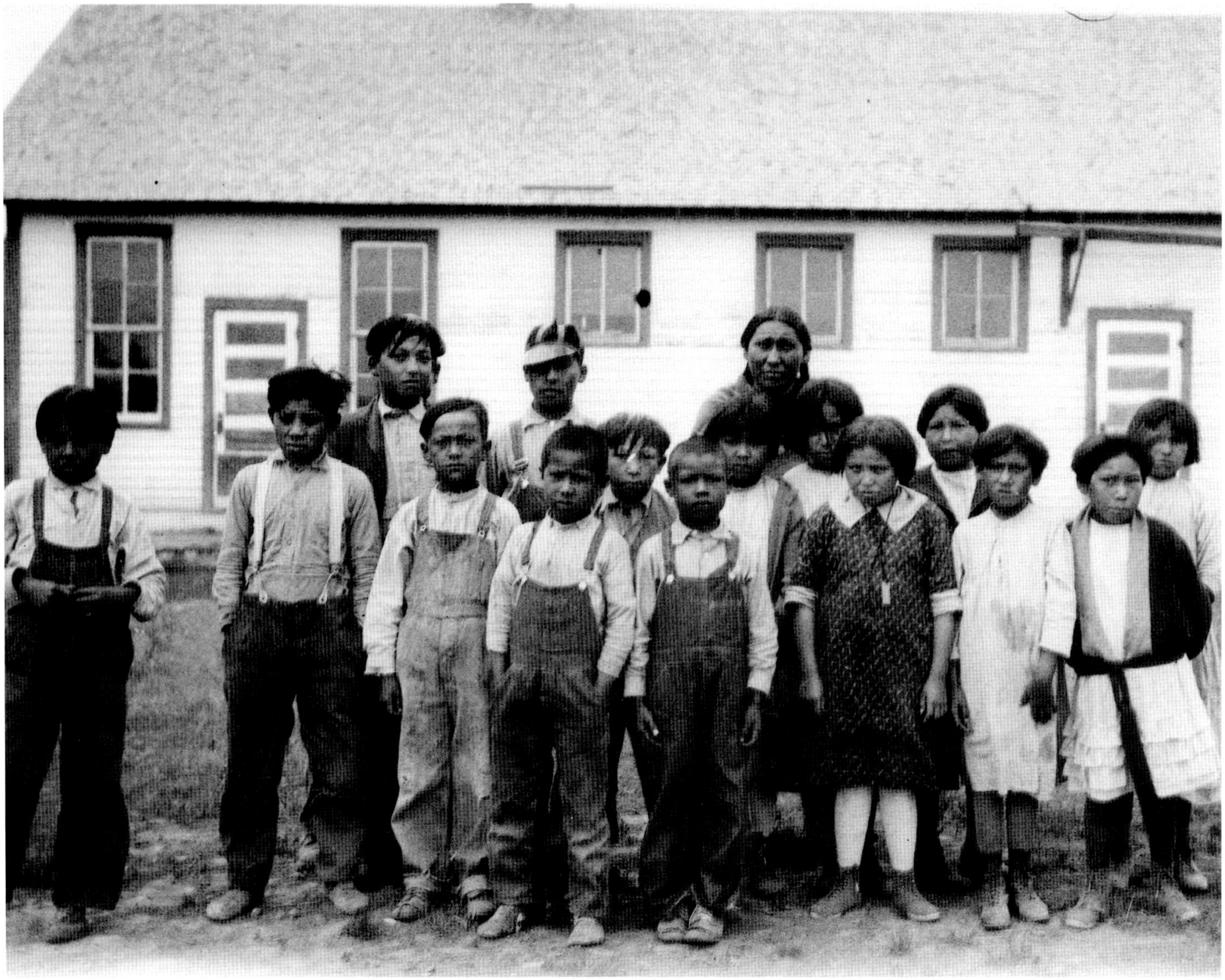

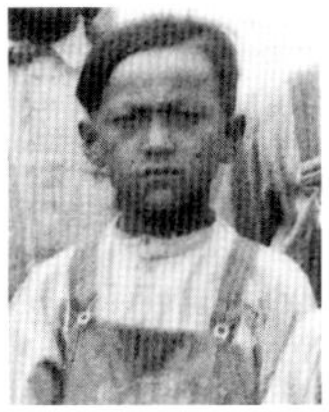

19. Lame Deer Schoolchildren about 1926

INFORMANT: JOHN WOODENLEGS

19a. These are children going to school at Lame Deer Day School. In the front row, left to right: John Stands in Timber, Jr., Max High Walking, unknown, Ira Issues, Henry Scalpcane, Grace Rowland, Harriet King, Rose King. In the back row: George Texas, James King (cap on), Sam Dives Backwards, Ramona Brady, Rose Red Cherries, Fannie Walks Along, Elsie Tall Whiteman. Emma King is the lady. James King is her son. Emma probably was a teacher's aide.

This was the second day school they had in Lame Deer. I went to the first one, and I went to this one too for six months. These buildings are all gone now, and these boys and girls are grown up. They are parents and grandparents. Some got a good education. There is just one boy here we don't know who he is. The first day school we went to was made out of logs, kind of a house, then they added onto it for a dining room and kitchen. We had dinner at noon. That was my first contact with white people. The teacher was a white man. I must have been a real good boy, I got a whipping the first day!

19b. Boarding schools existed at Ashland and at Busby, while there were day schools at Birney and at Lame Deer. Ashland was operated by St. Labre's Catholic Mission, Busby and Birney by the Bureau of Indian Affairs, and Lame Deer by the Montana public school system. The day schools were preferred by Indian families because children were not taken out of the home for long periods. The children who were sent away were often orphans who had no parents to resist.

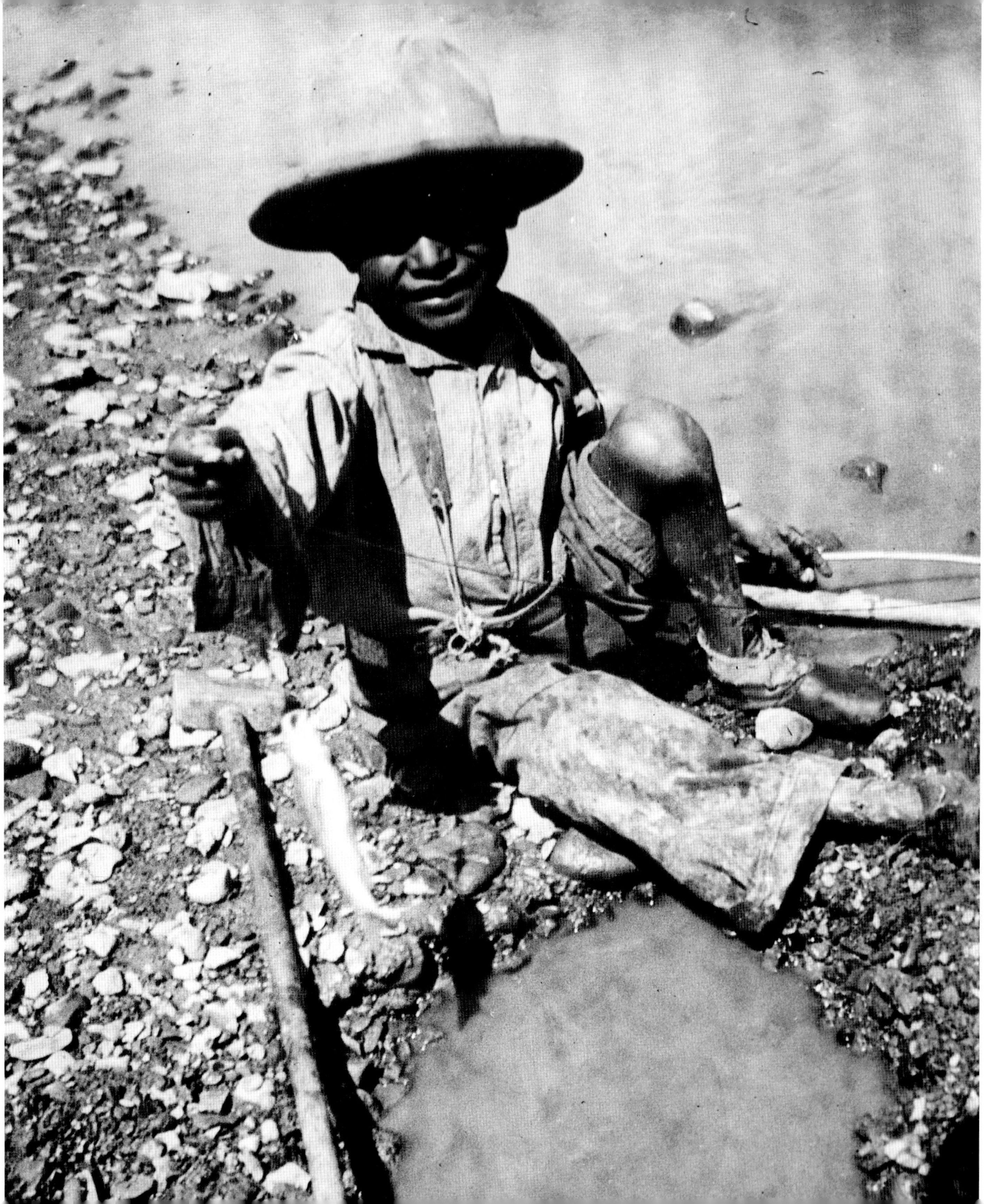

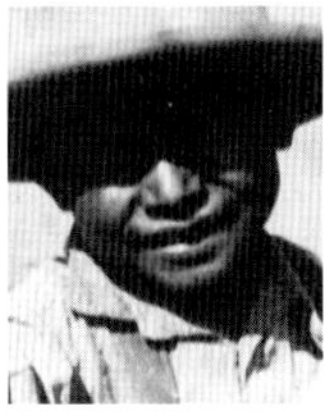

20. Boy Fisherman

INFORMANT: NOTES OF DR. MARQUIS

20a. Paul Big Foot, a crippled boy, is sitting by the river. He has caught a fish and holds it up to view. Marquis got two old broomsticks, and had the carpenter make him a pair of crutches.

20b. The caption information cited by Woodenlegs above was taken from the notes of Dr. Marquis on the photographs, now lost, along with other archival materials.

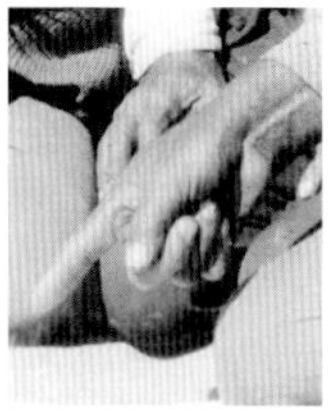

21. Discussing the Battle

INFORMANT: JOHN WOODENLEGS

21a. Four Cheyennes who fought at the Battle of the Little Bighorn, left to right: Little Sun, Wolf Chief, Big Beaver, and Wooden Leg, 1927. The map of the Custer Battlefield they are examining was drawn by Marquis.

21b. Locally reproduced as a postcard, this is one of the better-known pictures of the Custer fight Cheyennes by Marquis, who knew them so well. His book Wooden Leg: A Warrior Who Fought Custer *(Marquis 1957) is one of the very best Indian accounts of what took place on the Little Bighorn on June 25–26, 1876. About twenty such participants appear in this book.*

Major commemorative events took place on the fiftieth anniversary of the Custer battle in 1926, when many survivors came together at the battlefield to share their stories. The Hunkpapa Sioux leader Gall, a member of Sitting Bull's following, "buried the hatchet" that day with Gen. E. S. Godfrey, an officer who served under Custer. A memorial exhibit can be seen near the battlefield at the Montana post office of Garryowen.

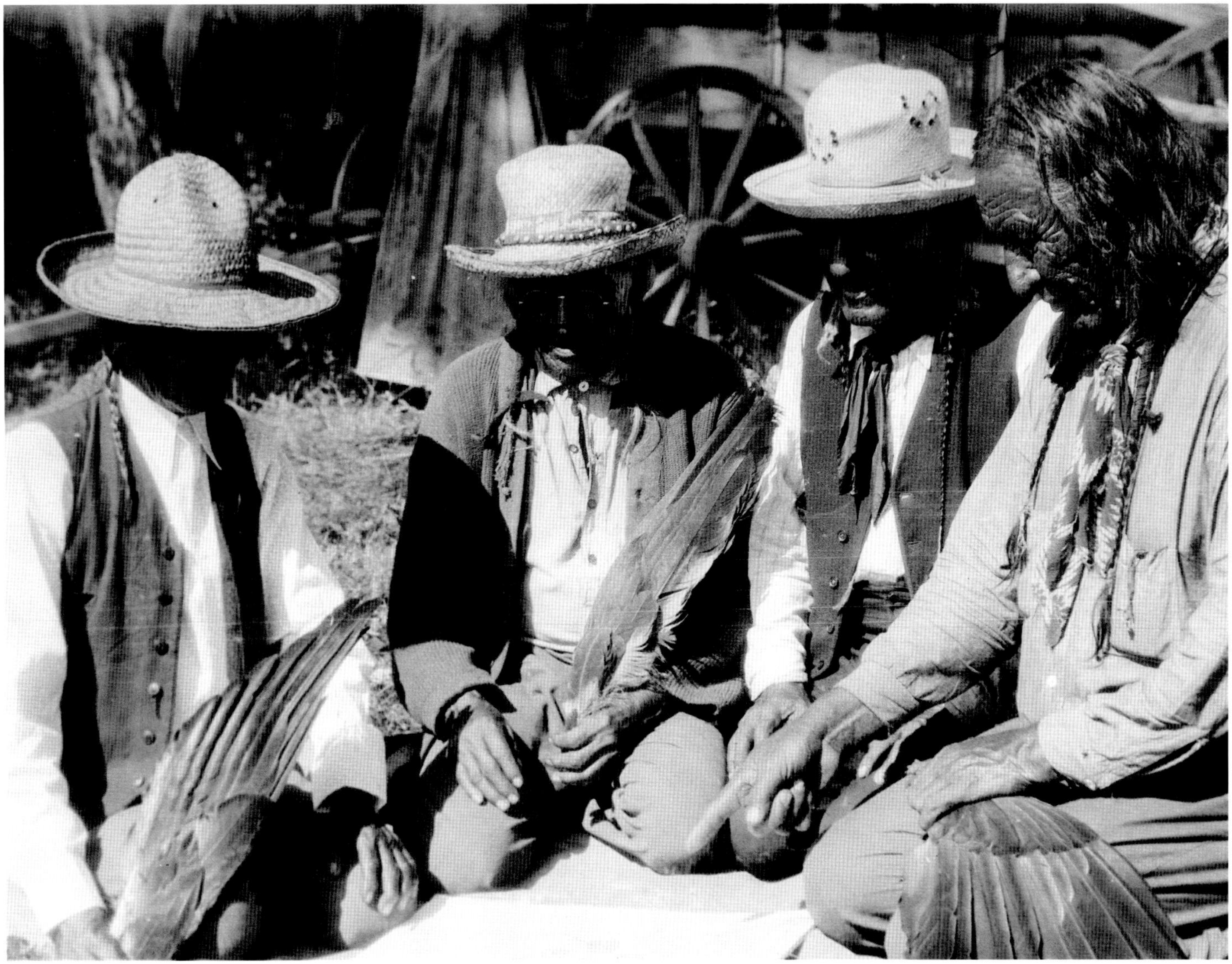

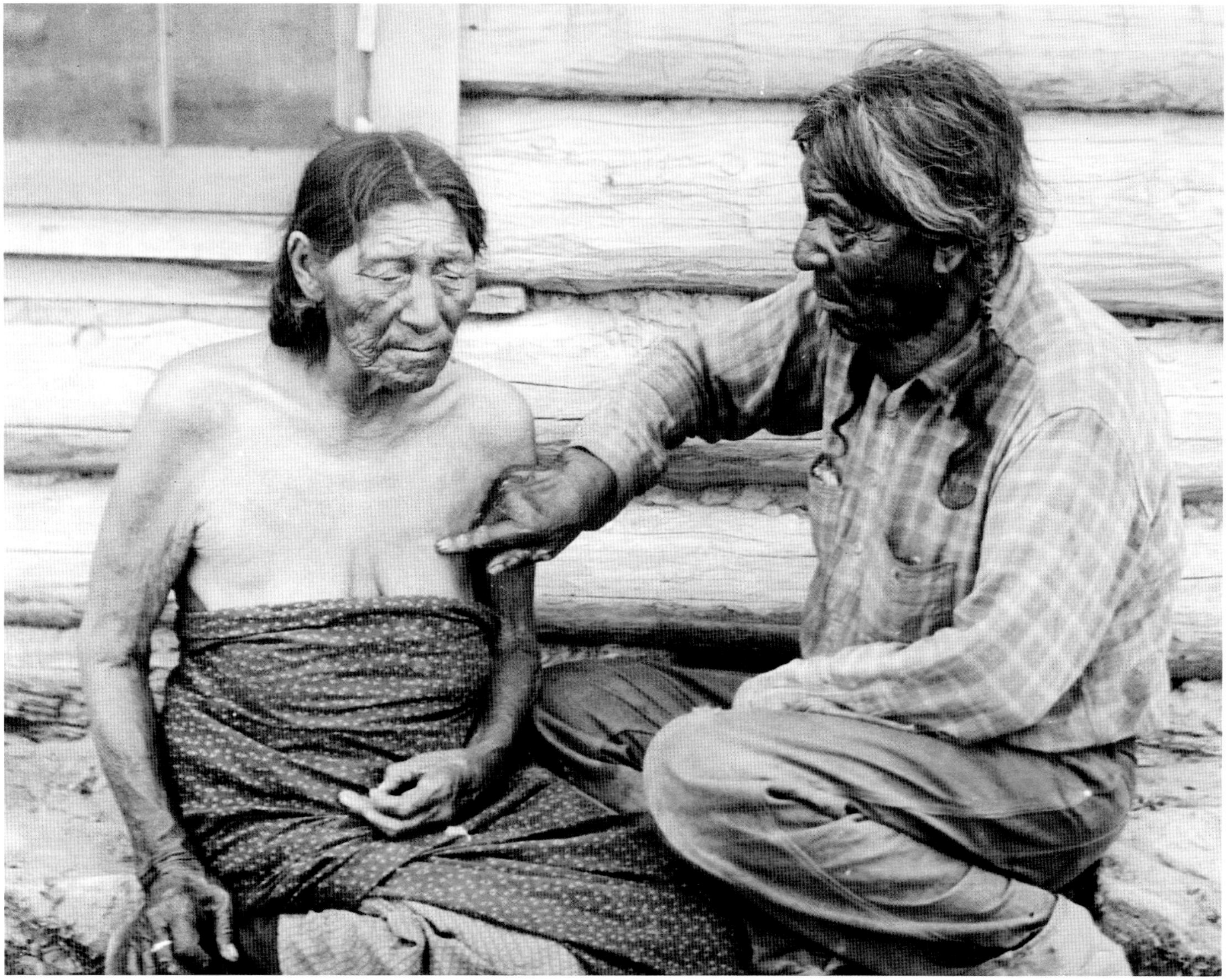

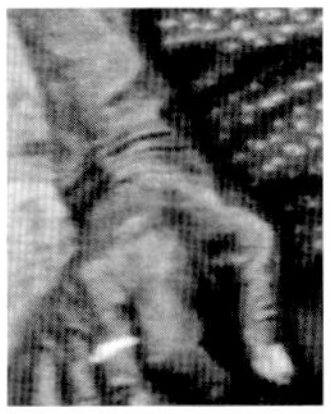

22. Limpy and Wife

INFORMANT: NOTES OF DR. MARQUIS AND JOHN WOODENLEGS

22a. This is Limpy with his wife. He is pointing to a bullet scar on his wife's breast. She was shot in 1876, during the Battle of the Little Bighorn. This picture was taken in August 1930. Limpy was crippled all his life, that's why they called him "Limpy." These folks lived in Busby.

22b. This is a very important picture historically, because it documents the near approach of the Custer forces to the Cheyenne village. Limpy was better known to white historians for his action in the Rosebud Battle of June 17, 1876. A marker exists at "Limpy's Rocks" on that field.

Women and children were often casualties of engagements with U.S. troops, especially the Cheyennes, who suffered more disastrous attacks on their villages than all other tribes combined. Horrendous destruction of Cheyenne villages took place at Sand Creek in 1864 and at the Washita in 1868, where Custer was also in command prior to his adventure on the Little Bighorn. Dull Knife's village on the Powder River was destroyed by troops under George Crook in November 1876.

According to Marquis, the other tribes believed that there was a particular army vendetta against the Cheyennes and that they—not the Sioux—were the primary Indian combatants in 1876.

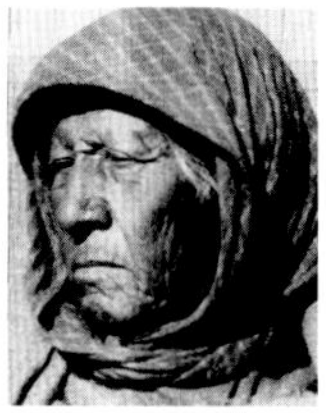

23. Kate Big Head in 1926

INFORMANT: JOHN WOODENLEGS

23a. This is Kate Big Head, who was the narrator of *She Watched Custer's Last Battle,* by Thomas Marquis. The young girl is Mary White Horse, Kate's grandchild.

23b. Kate Big Head's account (which is reprinted in the Marquis book Custer on the Little Bighorn*) has been important for Custer battle scholars. At the time of Custer's attack she rode onto the battlefield to aid her nephew Noisy Walking, a Cheyenne suicide warrior who was mortally wounded near the death site of the Cheyenne leader Lame White Man. Red stone markers have been placed at these locations near the main battlefield road.*

Big Head also gives an account of Custer's alleged mistress Maotzi or Monaseta. Despite its wide circulation in the Marquis pamphlet (Marquis 1933a), the story that Custer had a half-Cheyenne son by Monaseta is generally discounted by historians.

The Marquis pamphlets, today collectors' items, were sold at the battlefield for many years. The cover designs bore the red and blue heart symbol of Marquis, meaning "My Heart Is Half Indian."

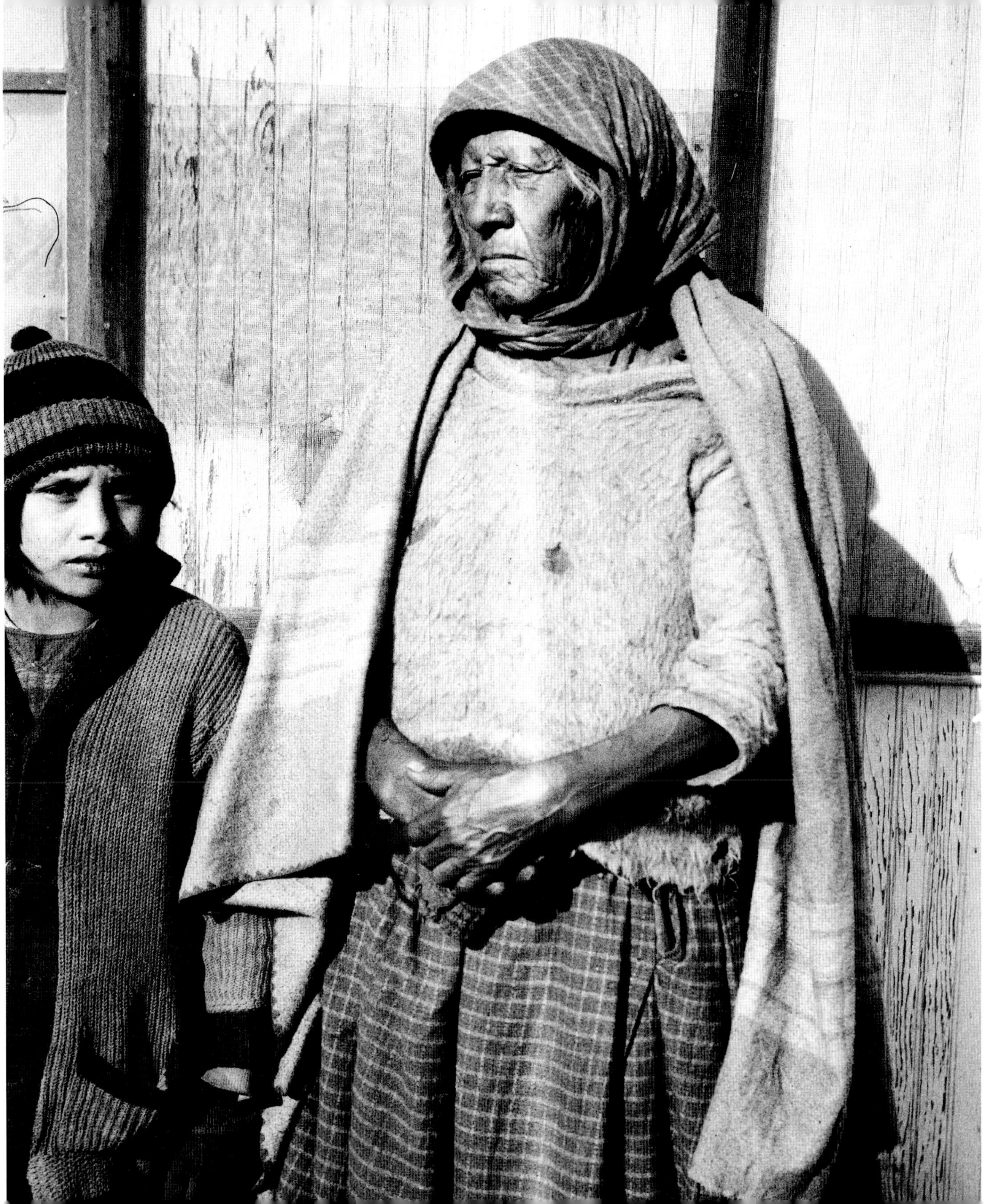

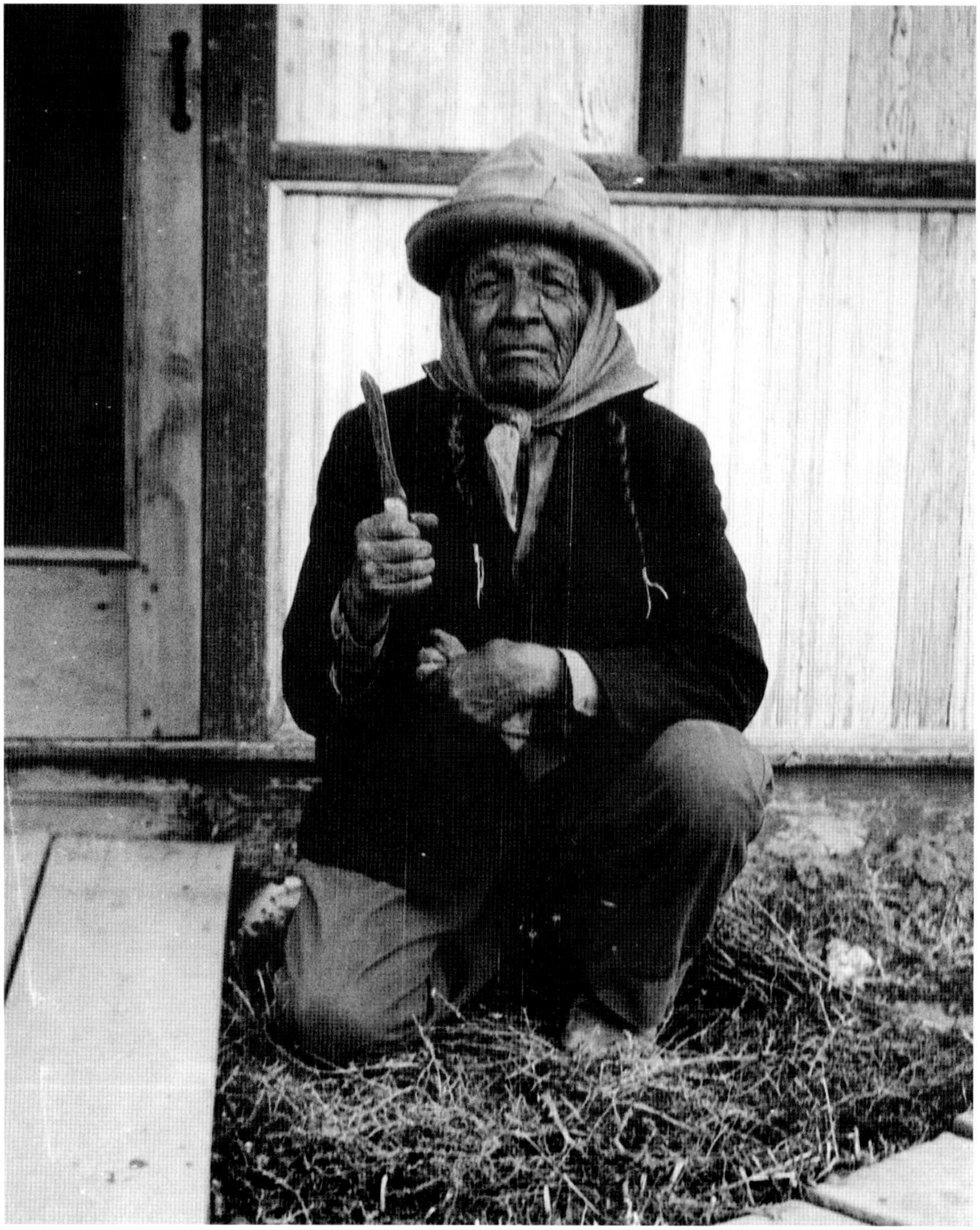

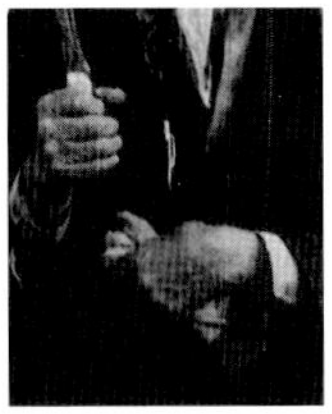

24. Sun Bear

INFORMANT: TOM WEIST

24a. This is Sun Bear, age 83, 1926. He was the narrator of "A Cheyenne Old Man," told in *The Cheyennes of Montana* (Marquis 1978). He fought at both the Fetterman Fight, December 1866, and the Battle of the Little Bighorn a decade later.

24b. Sun Bear is probably holding the knife in this fashion for the photographer because it was used in battle during Cheyenne fights with the soldiers. Marquis began buying such artifacts in 1927, first displaying them in his own little museum in Hardin, Montana. They later became an important component of National Park Service exhibits at Little Bighorn Battlefield National Monument in Montana.

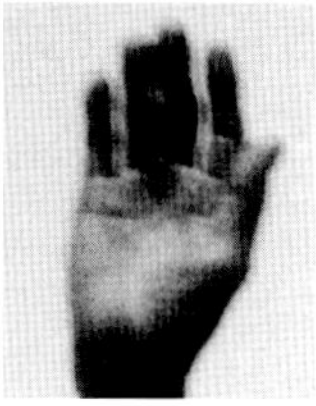

25. Praying at Custer Battlefield

INFORMANT: JOHN WOODENLEGS

25a. Isaac Black Bird was Keeper of the Sacred Hat. This picture was taken in 1928 at the Custer Battlefield by his friend, Dr. Marquis. When Isaac was eleven years old, he had watched this battle and he probably told what he knew. At this time, he has his eagle wing fan and he is praying to God. He has his shirt and his braids and he has a black handkerchief around his head. He has it knotted in front. He has Bull Durham in his shirt pocket. He was such a good old man, kind, and prayed for everybody. He lived there at Busby. The Sacred Hat tepee was at his place. He had children and grand children and great-grandchildren. He really talked good to people. People really respected him.

25b. The Sacred Medicine Hat and the Sacred Arrows are the two primary sacred relics of the Cheyenne tribe. The Medicine Hat was brought to the Northern Cheyennes by their Suhtai division. It is maintained at tribal expense to this day in a special tepee by a specially appointed keeper, such as Isaac Black Bird, pictured here. Believed to protect the welfare of women, it stood in the Cheyenne village at the Custer fight and has remained in custody of a succession of Northern Cheyenne priests on the reservation for over a century. The Sacred Arrows are still maintained with similar care and respect by the Southern Cheyennes in Oklahoma.

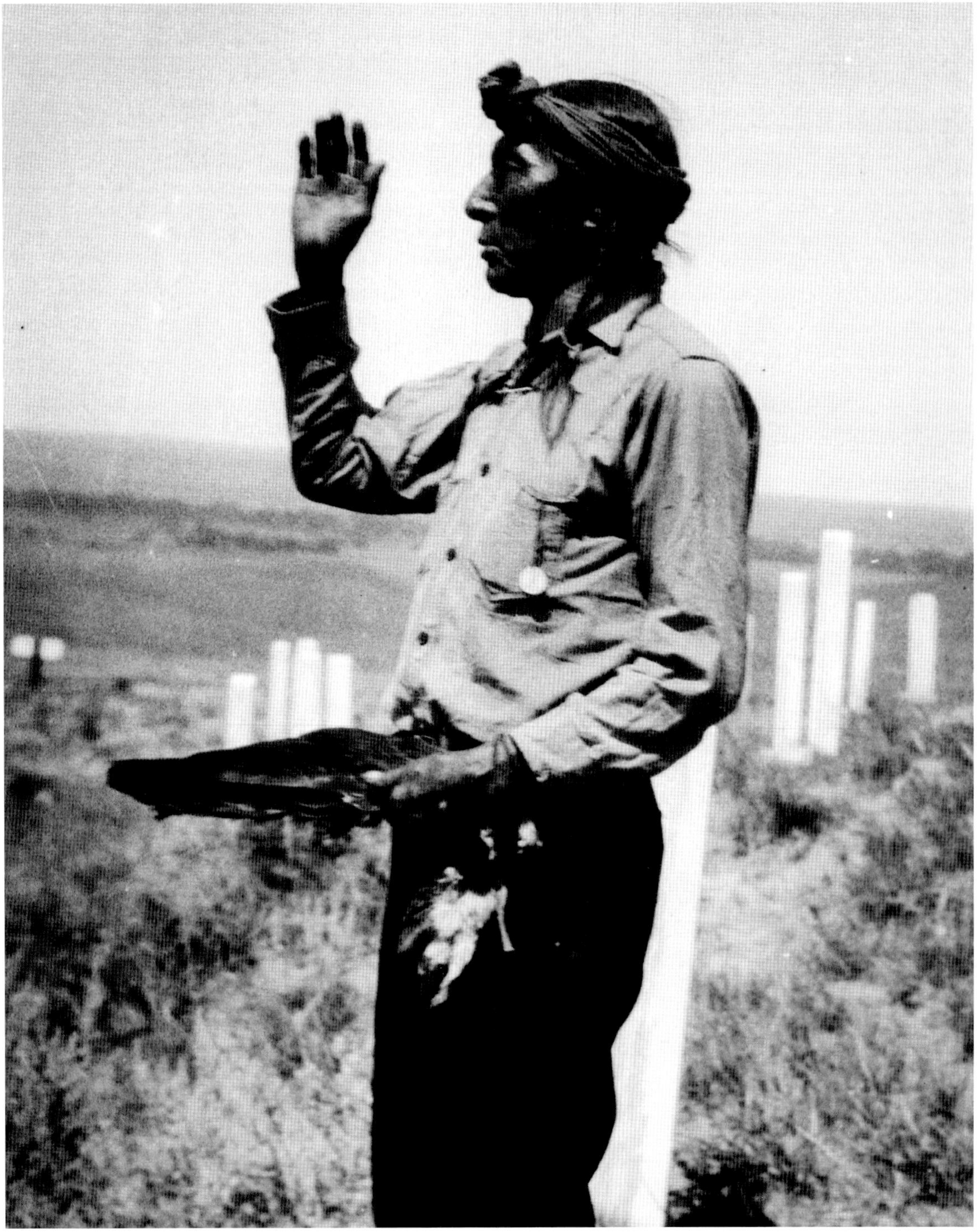

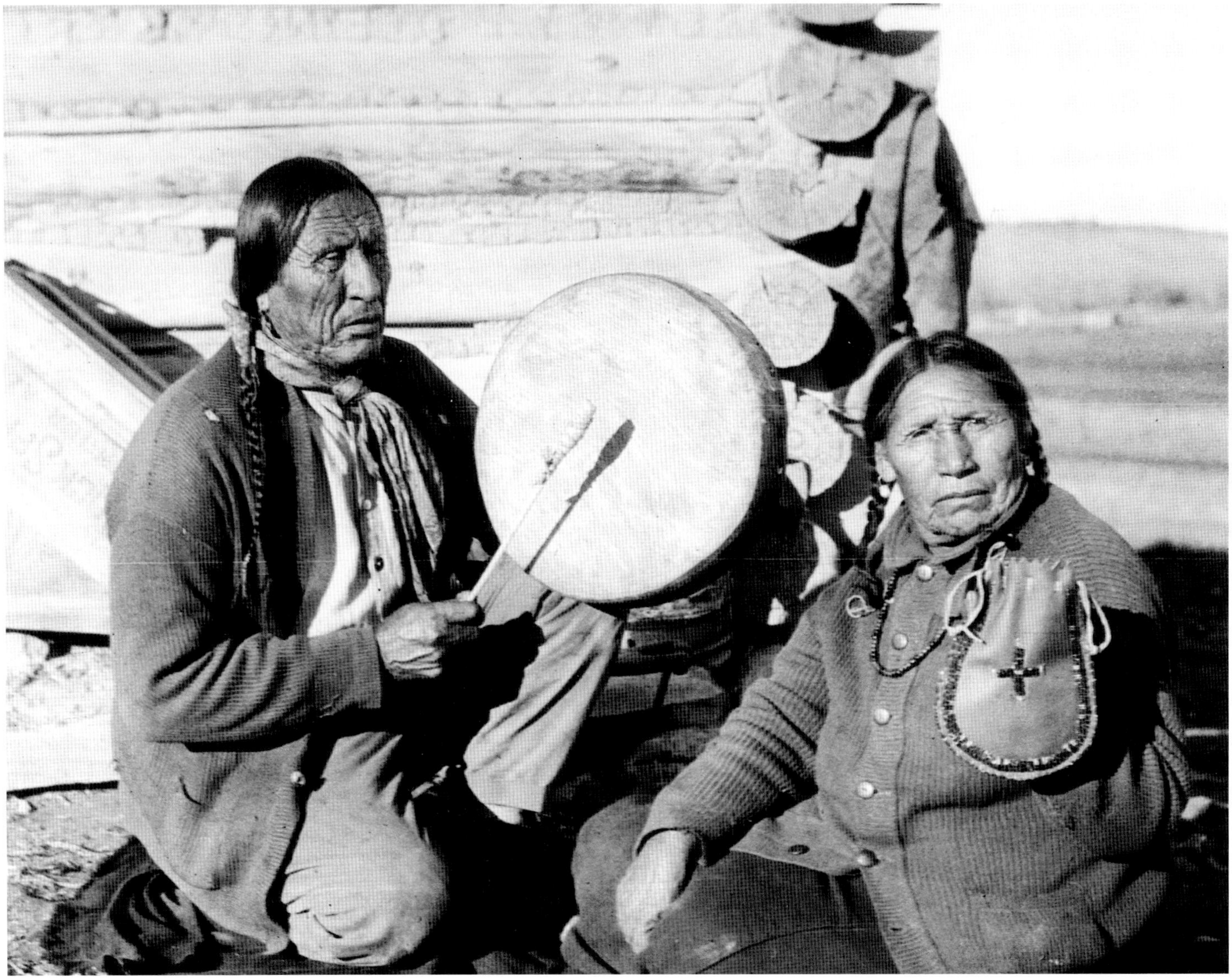

26. Woodenlegs and Wife

Informant: John Woodenlegs

26a. My grandfather Richard Woodenlegs and his wife, Sophie, are close to their house. Dr. Marquis was his friend and he took pictures when they were fixing a book, *A Warrior Who Fought Custer* (Marquis 1931). My grandfather, Woodenlegs, is the subject of that book. He was contented at the time living with this wife. He did have two wives before, but being a judge, he had to set an example to have only one wife and be legally married. This picture shows one of the drums he made. He was quite an old man at the time this picture was taken. His wife has a beaded bag that she fixed and beaded. These old people could do things. He fixed these drums and he could sing. He had some real good songs and he fixed flutes and he played flutes. He was a scout for the U.S. Army in Miles City and he also fought in the Custer battle. Quite a few times I would go to him and try to take care of things around the home there. They lived close to Ashland where their daughter had gone to school. He had cattle and he lived out on a ranch about six miles west of Ashland. He built his house there, and in winter he would move down near Ashland so his children could go to school at the Mission. He had a herd of cattle, horses and he traveled in a big wagon with big horses. His wife traveled in a buggy with a buggy team. He would tie his saddle horse on the side. He had quite a few head of cattle, and haying equipment. He planted a garden. His brother lived up there with him. People would come and help him and camp on his place.

The old man was self-supporting. His name was Flying Buffalo, Tall Man, Goat Whiskers, and Woodenlegs. One of his uncles was named Woodenlegs. He was a good runner and walker. Richard was like that too, so he was called Woodenlegs also. His brother's name was "Twin." My dad was named after his uncle Twin. I have taken care of Woodenlegs when he was a little sick. I took him to the hospital. Another time he had pneumonia. This time he didn't want to go to the hospital. He said, "I think I'm through." His wife had passed on and a lot of his friends. He said, "I seem to be lonely here. I better go where everybody went, my friends. Thank you for trying to help me to take me to the hospital. But I think it's my time and I want to go." On the Cheyenne Road of Life, you have four directions: east is a new baby, new child is to grow up in a good way; south is a teenager; west is an adult; and north is a grandfather. He said, "I've lived around the circle, and thank the Spirit, and I want to go back to the Spirit." The old people, like my grandfather, were not afraid of death. When it was time to go, to do this or that, they went ahead and did it. Whenever it was time, they were ready. He said, "It's time now."

He was always kind of a self-supporting man. He really knew how to butcher and to make jerky. Different things he did. The old lady, Sophie, was such a good old lady, kind to everybody, good to everybody. This is a good picture of them and the work they did making drums and beaded bags. He was a tall man, over six feet, very strong and healthy. For being a scout, he got a pension, so much a month after he got to be 60 years old. He had a lot of good friends, and he danced and he sang for the dances. He doctored sick people. He had a brand for his cattle, number 259. The cattle that he owned stayed around the place there. He had a fence there, he even put in alfalfa. I guess the Army trains people good and that's where he got his training. He was a judge for the Indian Court. He had to go from his ranch in a wagon to Lame Deer and stay overnight, maybe a couple nights. He got $10 a month. That's what the government paid him. Later they raised his wages.

He was a hard worker and a good grandfather. I helped care for them when I had time, gather wood for them and some hay for his horses. He would go to Miles City in a wagon, travel down there. Some of the people went down there for celebrations, also to Broadus. He had draft horses, smaller horses for the buggy. He had machinery and a lot of tools that they got from the government. They had ID on them: hammers, shovels, and axes. He took good care of his tools and the things he needed. I guess he was trained that way from his folks. They were such good people. He belonged to the Elk Society. He never was a Chief. My grandfolks lived on their allotment. Now my daughter

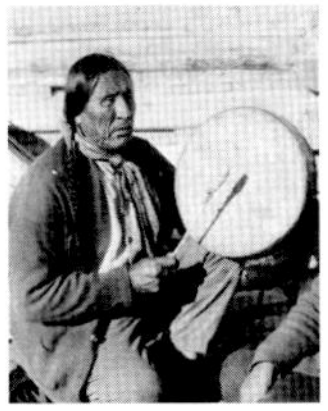

lives there and we all go there to that home place. We pray there and have Prayer Meetings and thank God that we can still go to that place, because my daughter is the fourth generation from Richard, my dad, myself, and her. She has four children, two boys and two girls. They seem to be really happy there. They have a house and a fence, electricity and water. The ranch has good water going through, called Stebbins Creek. A few people are beginning to live around there between Ashland and Lame Deer.

26b. Marquis researched the book cited as A Warrior Who Fought Custer *(first published in 1931 and published in paperback by the University of Nebraska Press in 1957 and 1961) in part through his skilled use of the Plains sign language.*

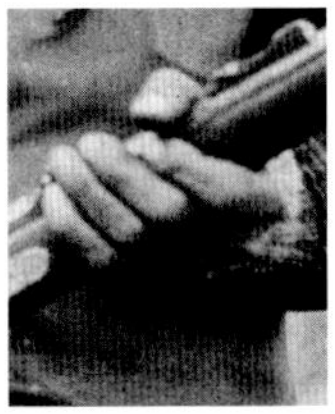

27. Richard Woodenlegs with Rifle

INFORMANT: JOHN WOODENLEGS

27a. Richard Woodenlegs was one of the scouts for the U.S. Army at Fort Keogh. He has his mackinaw on and his handkerchief around his neck, his braids, and his gun. He had a gun called 7MM. I think it was a German gun. He's holding it in his hand. He got one of these guns at the Custer Battle. He still had some of his Indian clothes when he worked down there at Fort Keogh. As a scout they built roads with a shovel and pick with their Indian dress on–stove-pipe leggings and moccasins. That's what they first did there. Later on they got their Army suits. The families camped around there at Miles City. Sometimes they had dances and celebrations and stick games.

This picture was taken in 1927.

27b. The Northern Cheyennes who surrendered at Fort Keogh, Montana, in 1877 provided scouts for service with U.S. troops in continuing campaigns of the Indian wars, including pursuit of the Nez Perces.

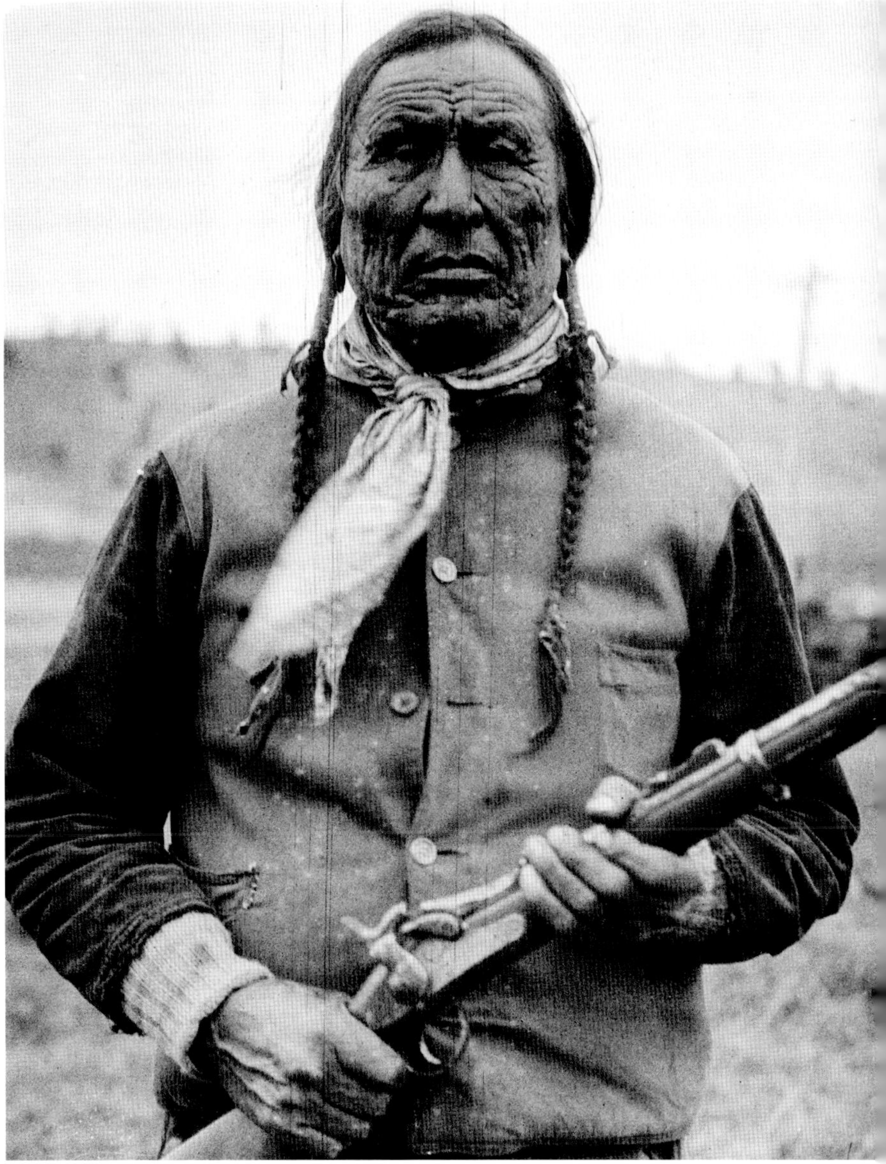

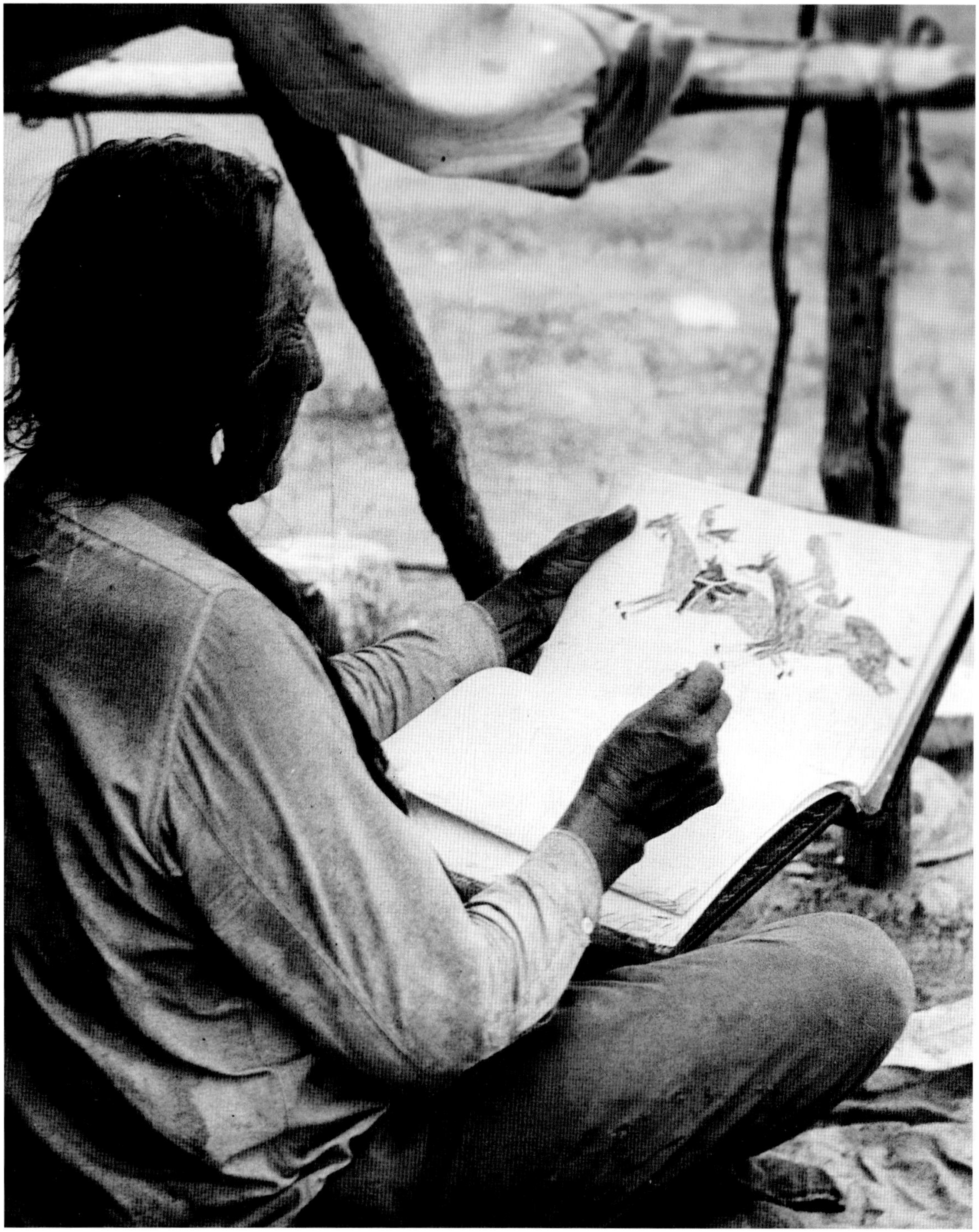

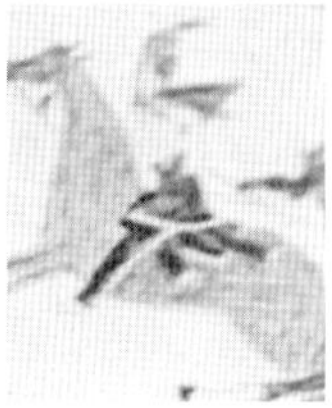

28. Woodenlegs Sketching

INFORMANT: JOHN WOODENLEGS

28a. Woodenlegs made a number of sketches showing different things he saw during the Custer battle. Some of these sketches are now at the museum at the Custer Battlefield.

28b. Ledger books of art by Plains warrior artists are hot items in the Western art market today, bringing as much as several thousand dollars per page.

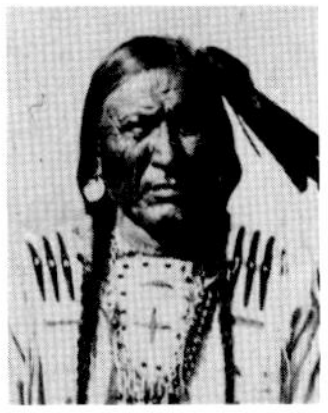

29. Woodenlegs with Wife and Daughter

INFORMANT: JOHN WOODENLEGS

29a. After the Custer Battle, Woodenlegs, who was about age 19, went to Oklahoma with all the Cheyennes who were sent there. It was while he was there that he married Sophie, who was a Southern Cheyenne. They were both age 20. Woodenlegs did not come north with the Cheyennes led by Little Wolf and Morning Star, but came north about 1883. He became a scout at Fort Keogh in 1889 under Lt. Ned Casey.

After he returned from the south, he took a second wife named Daisy. At that time, having more than one wife was alright. Daisy was my father's mother. My father's name was Thomas Woodenlegs. Richard had to give up one wife after he became a judge, so the families decided which wife he should let go, and that was Daisy.

29b. The circumstances surrounding this formal portrait of the Woodenlegs family are not known.

The Court of Indian Offenses, for which Woodenlegs served as the first judge, began at Lame Deer before 1900. Such Custer battle veterans made an amazing adaptation to early reservation life (Hagan 1966).

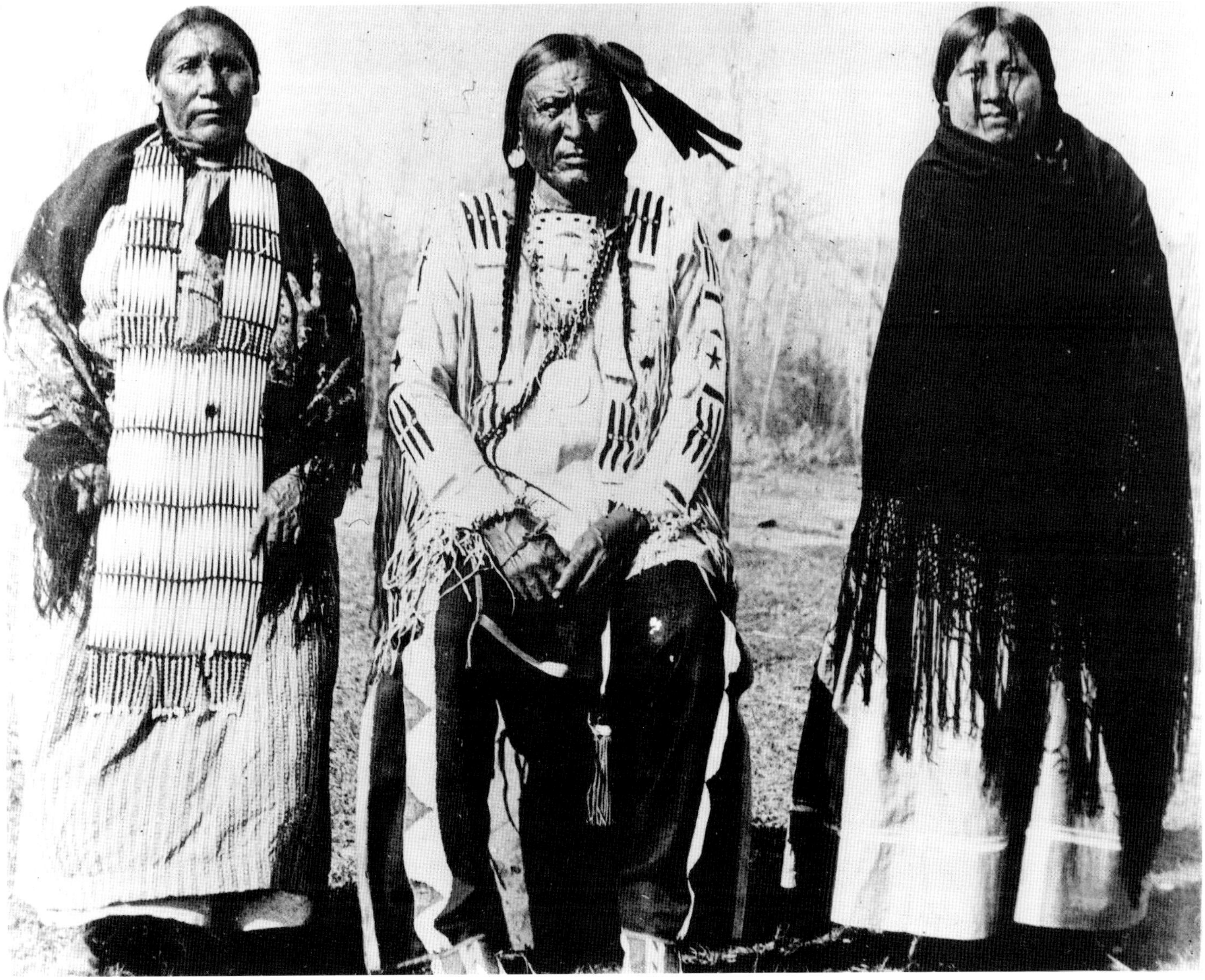

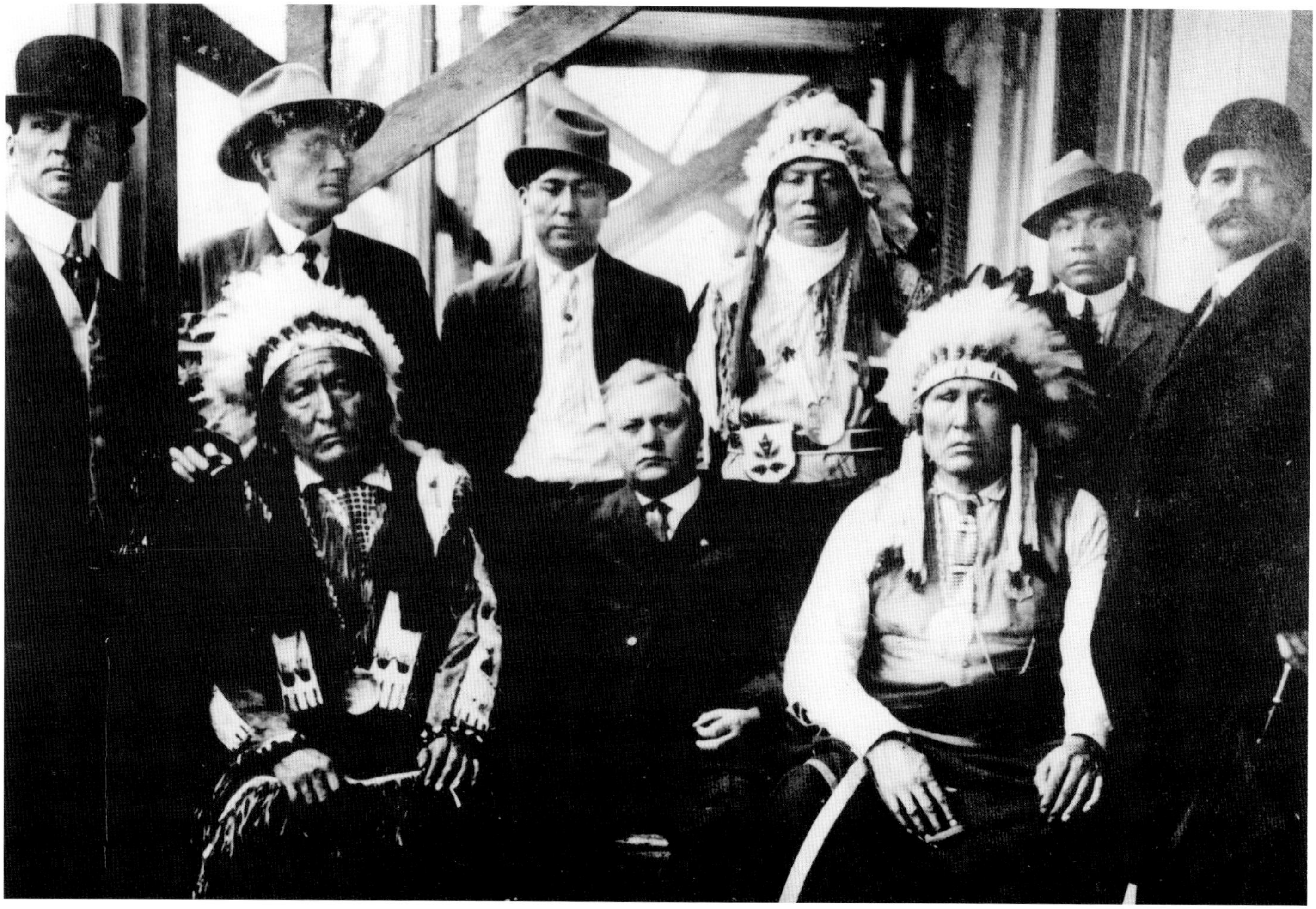

30. Cheyenne Delegation

INFORMANT: JOHN WOODENLEGS

30a. This picture shows a group of Cheyennes and some white people. It must have been a delegation of some sort.

In the back row, left to right: a white man, Willis Rowland, Milton Whiteman, John Black Wolf, Ben Shoulderblade, a white man. Front row: Laban Little Wolf, a white man, and Richard Woodenlegs.

30b. This is the only picture in this volume not taken by Marquis. Identified by Woodenlegs as the Northern Cheyenne delegation of 1913, it was included here by the research team because of its portrayal of Richard Woodenlegs with five other Cheyennes.

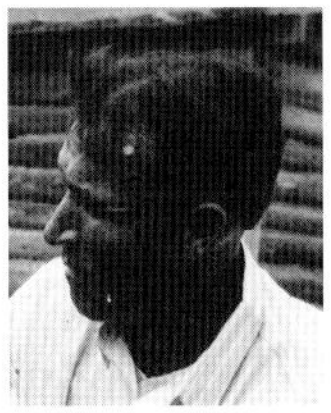

31. Tom Woodenlegs and Son

INFORMANT: JOHN WOODENLEGS

31a. This is my father Thomas Woodenlegs and one of my brothers. It's by a log house where they were living at the time. They built it themselves. This boy is about two or three years old. My mother passed on when I was about six years old and my dad remarried and this is one of my brothers, Joe. Later he was adopted by Frank Waters and used that name. He grew up there but he still knew all of us–he came back and forth.

My dad was a hard worker. He tried hard to have me get education. He sent me away to school. He worked for the cattle program on the reservation when they had a lot of cattle. He was a line rider. He worked there when I started school. He went on his own later and had cattle and horses. He was a good bronc rider and foot racer. He went to school and he could read and write, because when I went away to school he used to write to me. My mother could read and write also. Then I had stepmothers.

My dad was named after Richard Woodenlegs' brother, Twin. I didn't really know him, but I knew where he lived and I saw his cabin and some of his horses. He had an older half brother named Seminole. He was quite a lot older and he was a carpenter. They tried to make me a carpenter when I went away to school, but I didn't quite like that way. I wanted to be a stockman and be around cattle, but I thank my dad for trying to help me and sending me away to school.

My dad was a cowboy too and he and I roped calves and steers together. He had good horses. Everybody knew him. He got to be adopted over at Crow too. One Crow man looks like him, so his relatives kind of adopted my dad. He had race horses and he rodeoed. He always was a hard worker, he always worked. He was a very strong man. I guess his dad Richard was a strong, husky man. My dad wasn't as tall as Richard, but he was tall enough. And we prayed together. He belonged to the Native American Church. He never went to any other way of worship. He danced and he sang. His

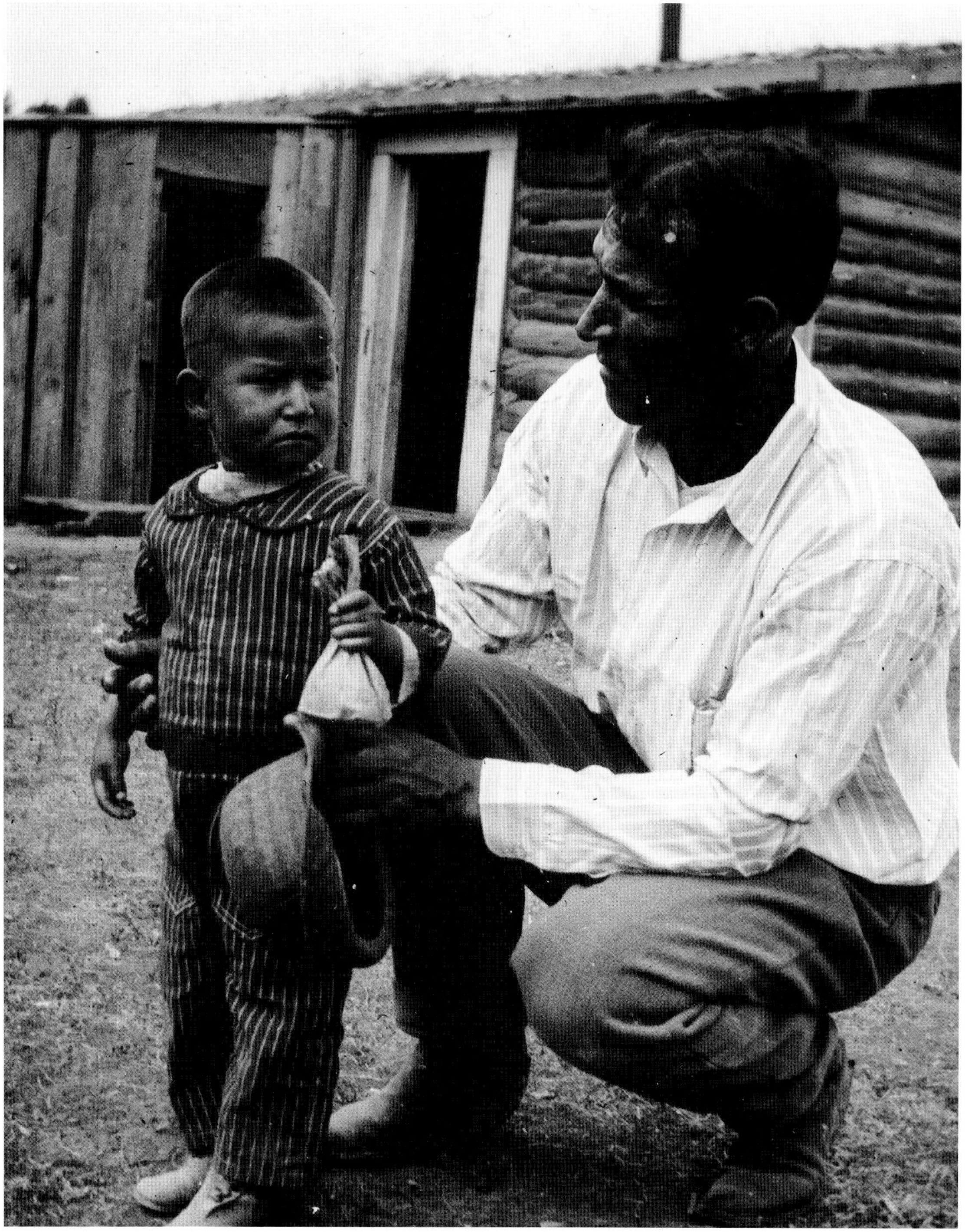

father knew the songs and I learned them from my dad, so I thank them for that. They are wolf songs and they are good songs.

Thomas took care of his father, but he died before my grandfather did. We worked in a coal mine, my father and I. The powder exploded and burned him. He died later. He lived seven or eight hours after it happened. It burned us; I was there with him.

Yes, we rode together and we trained our horses together and we raced, rode broncs and rode some good horses. He got some good horses from me. He was good to people—he learned from the old folks those real good Cheyenne ways. Each generation seems to lose a little as time passes on, but we hang onto some of it—the good way of life. To be good to people—our way of life was to God. I worked with my father and my grandfather and some of this I am passing on to my children—some of these good ways. I want to help children learn the good. Also my dad was a policeman, worked for the government. They liked him because he was a hard worker and he didn't give up. That was the same way Richard was. So I appreciate and I am thankful that I came from a good family.

31b. This commentary by John Woodenlegs concerning his father reflects Cheyenne pride and satisfaction in reservation cowboy life during the cattle period.

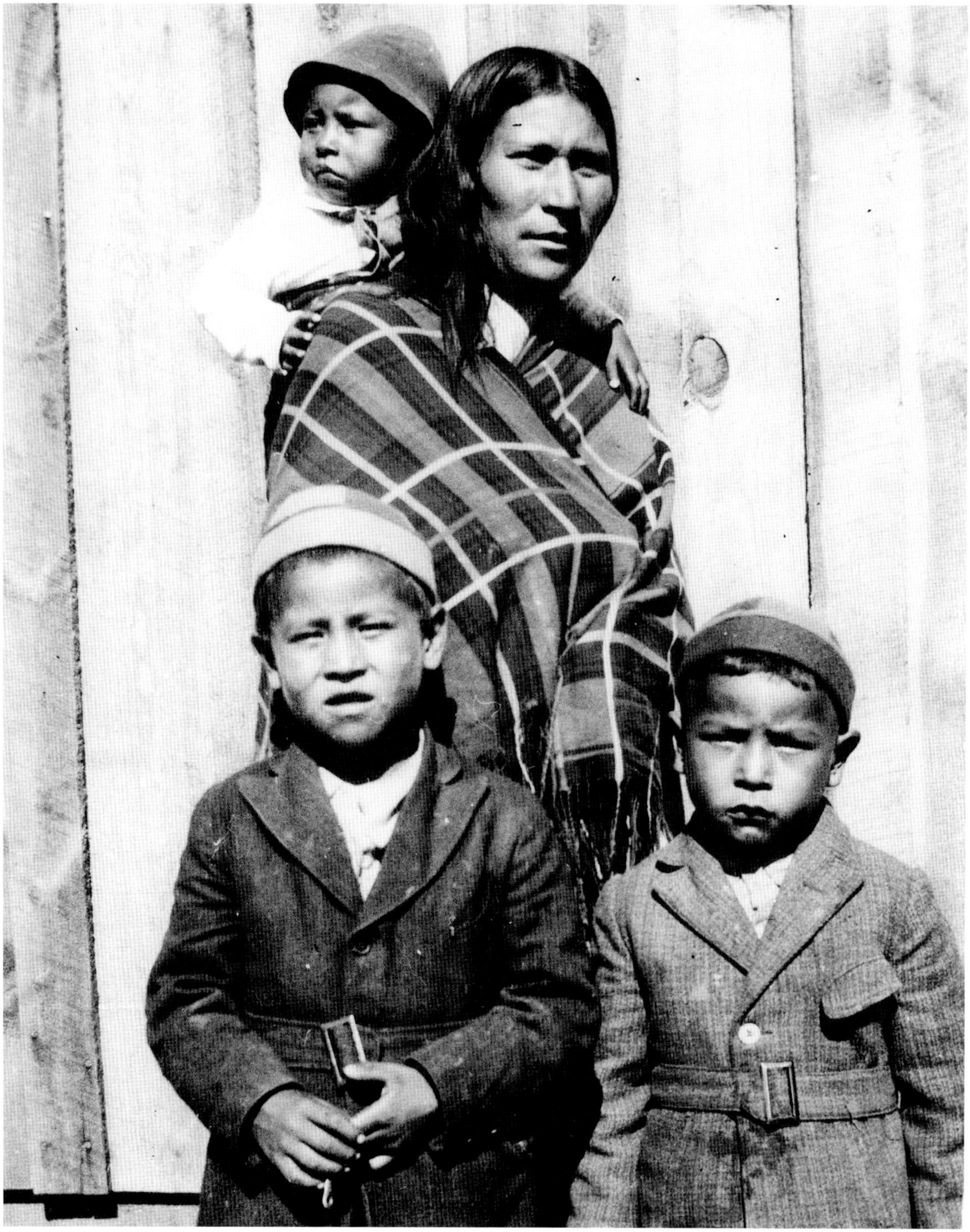

32. Ethel Shoulderblade and Children

INFORMANT: JOHN WOODENLEGS

32a. This was taken in Lame Deer in 1922. This is my aunt, my dad's sister. They have the same mother. My aunt married Pius Shoulderblade from Ashland, but they lived in Lame Deer. Pius had an education. He seemed like he had a high school education. He talked good English and interpreted. He was a government interpreter for the Cheyenne people for quite a long time. They lived at the agency in employee's quarters.

Her name was Ethel and they had more children than these three. These are Thomas, Francis, and Wendell. Wendell is the baby. Part of the time I lived with them and they were like brothers to me. My dad and his brother-in-law Pius all kind of lived together after Pius quit being an interpreter. He was a good Native Church man too. His folks didn't use that way, but he did and his uncles and his relatives did. He liked that way of worship. They homesteaded up on top of the divide—they had 320 acres and they fenced that in and they took half and half. They put in a partition fence. They put in grain and raised hay, and they camped up there in the summers. We children all kind of grew up together. They are younger than I am. They all grew up. Francis and Wendell went to the Army. Francis became a wrestler when he went away to school. He became a good wrestler, he weighed over 200 pounds. Wendell was called "Turkey." Thomas Shoulderblade's Indian name is "Yellow Bear," and Francis' is "Hawk That Speaks," and Wendell's is "Turkey Legs." Wendell became a boxer when he was in school, and he boxed with Francis and he really beat him up. Francis almost got mad, he wanted to take him down! Wendell called himself "Kid Chocolate." It was a black man's name, a man who was a good boxer. Thomas and Wendell got married, but Francis died; he never got married. They have two sisters: Claudia and Fern. They had two other brothers that passed away very young. Wendell was on the Tribal Council for many years and also served as vice-president.

My Aunt Ethel and her husband were good people. They were always good to me. They were good to their mothers on both sides. Thomas and I were like brothers—we stayed with the grandparents some of the time.

32b. The Native American Church was a system of worship based upon Christian concepts and use of the hallucinogenic cactus peyote, obtained in the Southwest and in Mexico. John Woodenlegs was a prominent leader in this church movement and refers often in these pages to its values. It came to the Northern Cheyennes about 1900, and regular meetings were being held by 1903–1904.

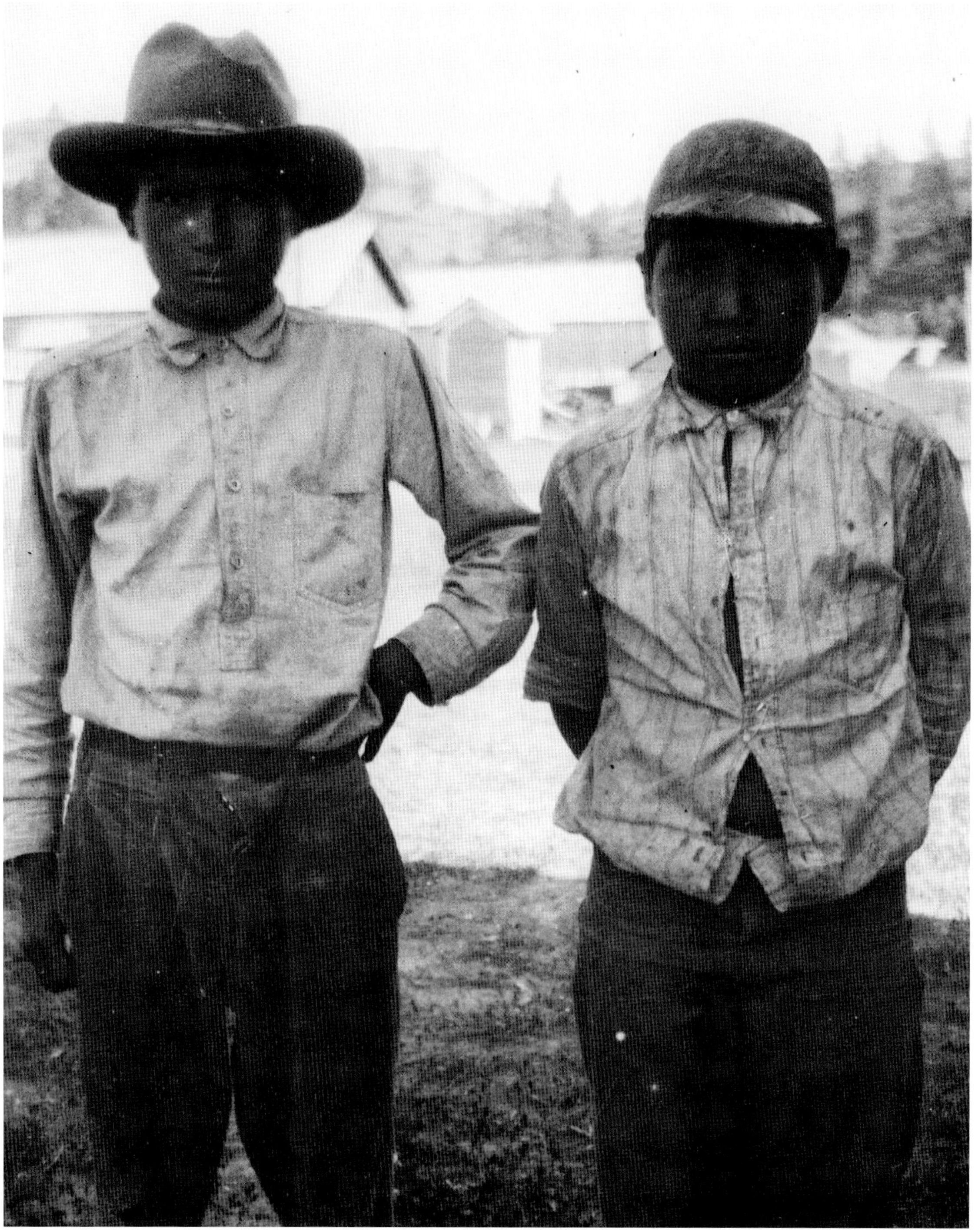

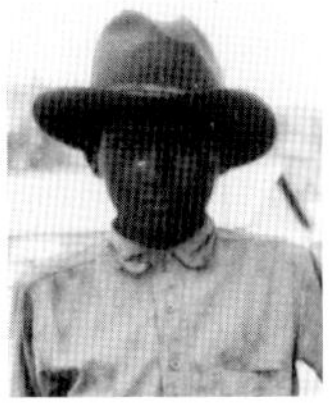

33. John and Frank

INFORMANT: JOHN WOODENLEGS

33a. This is Frank Little Head on the right and I am on the left. Our fathers were friends and so we got to be friends. We grew up together and we went to school together the first day of school. I told my dad to buy a new sled and get on his horse and drag that new sled to school so I could go to school. That was my last request! So Frank and I were in school together. It was kind of hard. It was my second contact with white people. This man had long whiskers, a great big guy. He talked kind of rough. I was really afraid of him. Frank was more afraid, and somehow during the day I must have done something wrong and that teacher whipped me. Boy, I didn't like that! My friend disappeared—he must have run home. This picture was taken by Dr. Marquis. Frank has on his baseball hat. This was the Lame Deer Day School. They gave us dinner and everybody liked the food. They had some good cooks. My father was a line rider for the Cheyenne cattle operation. The headquarters were right close to the Cheyenne Agency. This picture was taken close to the school there. It looks like the shirts we are wearing we had worn for about a week.

Frank Little Head got married down in Oklahoma to a Southern Cheyenne. He comes back and forth. He has a brother and sister.

33b. A line rider was a cowboy who patrolled pastures, repairing fences and caring for sick or injured livestock as well as strays.

34. Charles Spotted Elk

INFORMANT: JOHN WOODENLEGS

34a. This is Charles Spotted Elk. He was one of the Army scouts that soldiered down there in Miles City at Fort Keogh. As I knew him, he was single, but his wife had died. His children were August, Abraham, and Alex Spotted Elk, and he had a daughter, but I don't know her name. His second daughter was Jessie Spotted Elk. As an older man, I have known him. My dad married one of his daughters, and I have a sister still living who was their child. She's related to Spotted Elks. This old man lived just above Lame Deer. I guess a white fellow had settled there, but he was moved out so Charles took the place over. It had a big white house and an upstairs. He used to stop by and visit and that's why I know him and his sons. His daughter was my stepmother. Their place had quite a large area, they all lived there close together. When the allotment came I guess they were allotted close together there. They had horses and cattle and hogs. They raised quite a few hogs. Some of these soldier-scouts were quite good. They were trained about horses and cattle and hogs and about putting in grain. They could talk a little English because they learned it there in Miles City. I guess General Miles really liked the Cheyennes. This old man, Charles Spotted Elk, used to take a bunch of the Cheyenne people to Miles City to take part in the rodeos and the fair. They had to parade and take part in the celebrations. He was the leader of those Cheyennes at the time—to dress up in their Native outfits—bonnets, buckskin outfits, feathers, beaded decorations. Charles was a good old man, he always talked good to people. At the time I knew him he was getting a pension for being a scout. The scouts all seemed to have done real good. They were healthy and good people. One of his sons passed away recently, the other is still living. Abraham passed away quite some time ago, and also one of the girls. My sister Mabel is still living—she is his granddaughter. His sons were all good boys. Two of them were on the Tribal Council. I think he was one of the first Council men when it formed. They didn't get paid, they only got a dinner with their meetings.

There were quite a few of these scouts and everybody looked up to these good people. At the time there were hardly any jobs or anybody working for money. The scouts got pensions every month and they shared with their families and friends. Such a good thing that they had a pension from being a scout with the U.S. Army. Everybody seemed to respect them.

Now there were other soldiers that went in the Army in the First World War, and the Second one and later Korea and Vietnam. I guess the Army pays well and when you get older, you get a pension.

34b. Northern Cheyenne lands were allotted in severalty to individuals in 1930–32, much later than was the case for most tribes. Each enrolled tribal member received 160 acres or one quarter section. It was held in trust for twenty-five years, after which outside sale was permitted. Millions of acres of Indian lands were sold out of Indian ownership in this process on reservations throughout the country (Weist 1977: 190–91).

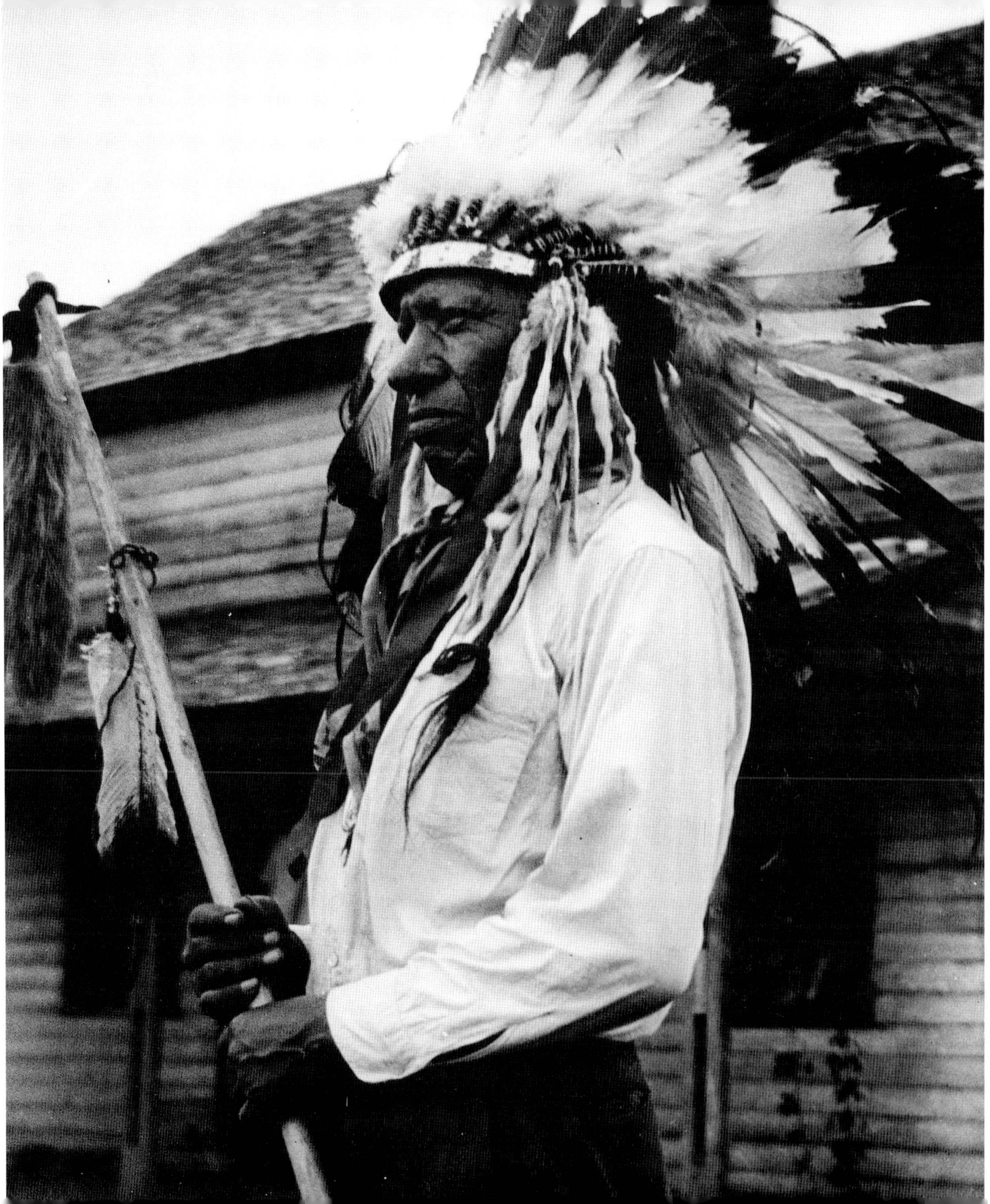

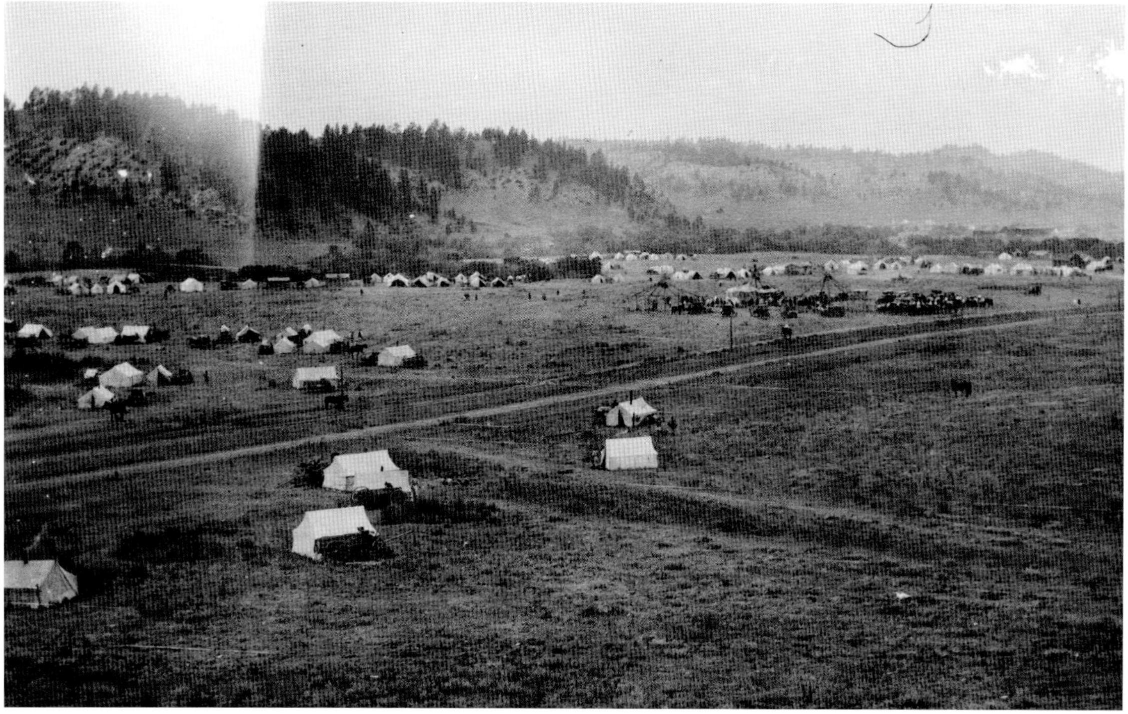

35. Sun Dance Encampment

INFORMANT: JOHN WOODENLEGS

35a. This shows all the people who came to camp while the Sun Dance is being held. The place is south of Lame Deer.

35b. The Sun Dance was also called the Medicine Lodge in English and sometimes the Willow Dance because of the use of willow wreaths in the ceremony (as well as to confuse whites who were anxious to suppress it). "Sun Dance" is a misnomer, because sun worship is not included; but the term has gained universal usage. The dancers line up at the eastward-facing door of the lodge at dawn during the last two mornings and dance until the rising sun is visible. This may explain the term's origin.

The Sun Dance was shared by more than twenty of the equestrian, buffalo-hunting Plains tribes. It was prohibited by the government for fifty years (1883–1933) but was kept alive by hidden or underground performances by several tribes, including the Northern and Southern Cheyennes. The reason for prohibition lay in the spectacular feats of self-torture that took place during the ceremonies of some groups, especially the Sioux.

The encampment shown here at Lame Deer in 1929 took place during one of the forbidden years. It approximates the striking mile-wide camp circle of earlier years. The Bureau of Indian Affairs agency was only a few miles away, so active suppression was obviously not taking place at this time.

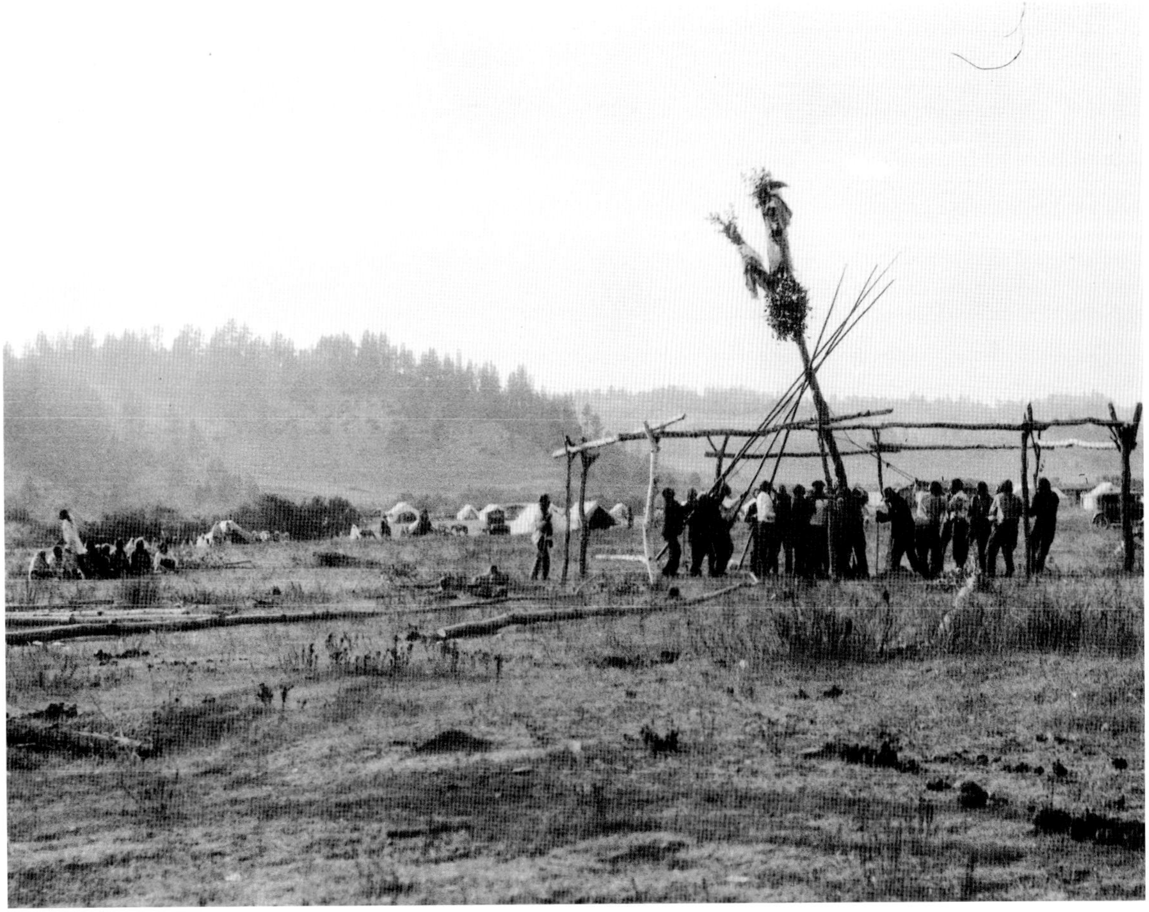

36. Raising the Center Pole

INFORMANT: JOHN WOODENLEGS

36a. This picture shows the raising of the center pole of the Medicine Lodge. This Sun Dance was held September of 1929, according to Dr. Marquis' notes.

36b. It is likely that the Sun Dance developed from the Mandan Okipa, an intricate week-long ritual first recorded by artist George Catlin in 1833 at Fort Clark on the Missouri River. The ritual probably originated among the Cheyennes and Arapahos during a time of epidemics that decimated the Missouri River tribes, including the Mandans, before they were visited by Meriwether Lewis and William Clark in 1804.

Construction elements of the Missouri River earth lodges are clearly seen in the nomadic Medicine Lodge structure, as shown here.

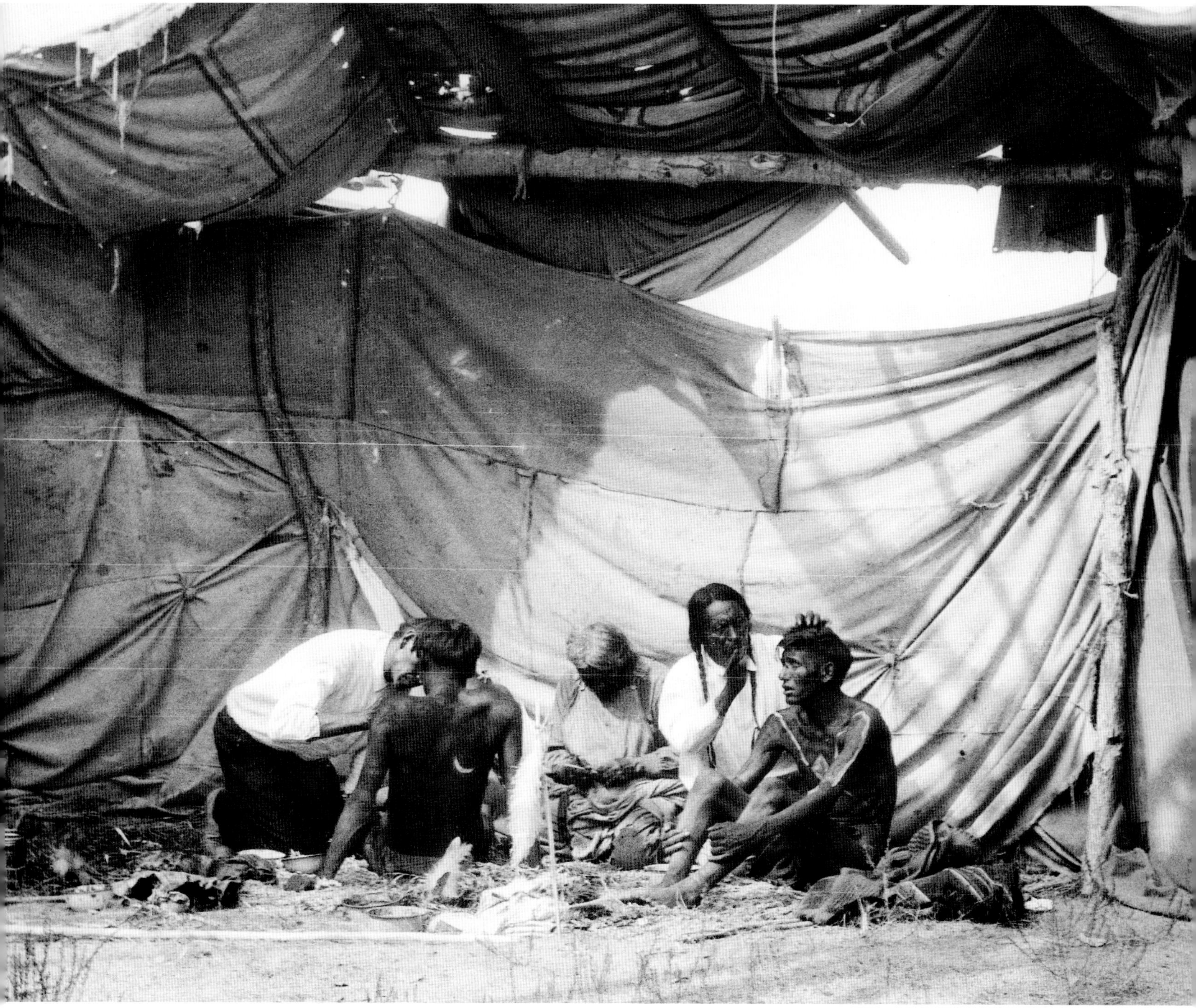

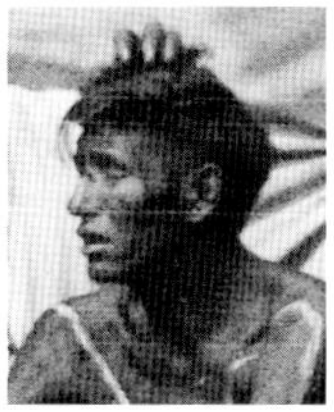

37. Painting Sun Dancers

INFORMANT: JOHN WOODENLEGS

37a. This is inside the Medicine Lodge. These men are helping paint two of the dancers.

37b. Special body paints were applied to Sun Dance participants or dancers by experienced instructors whom they chose for this role. An instructor remained with his pledger or dancer throughout weeks of preparatory activities as well as during the four-day ceremony itself.

The use of canvas tepee covers for the Medicine Lodge is clearly seen here.

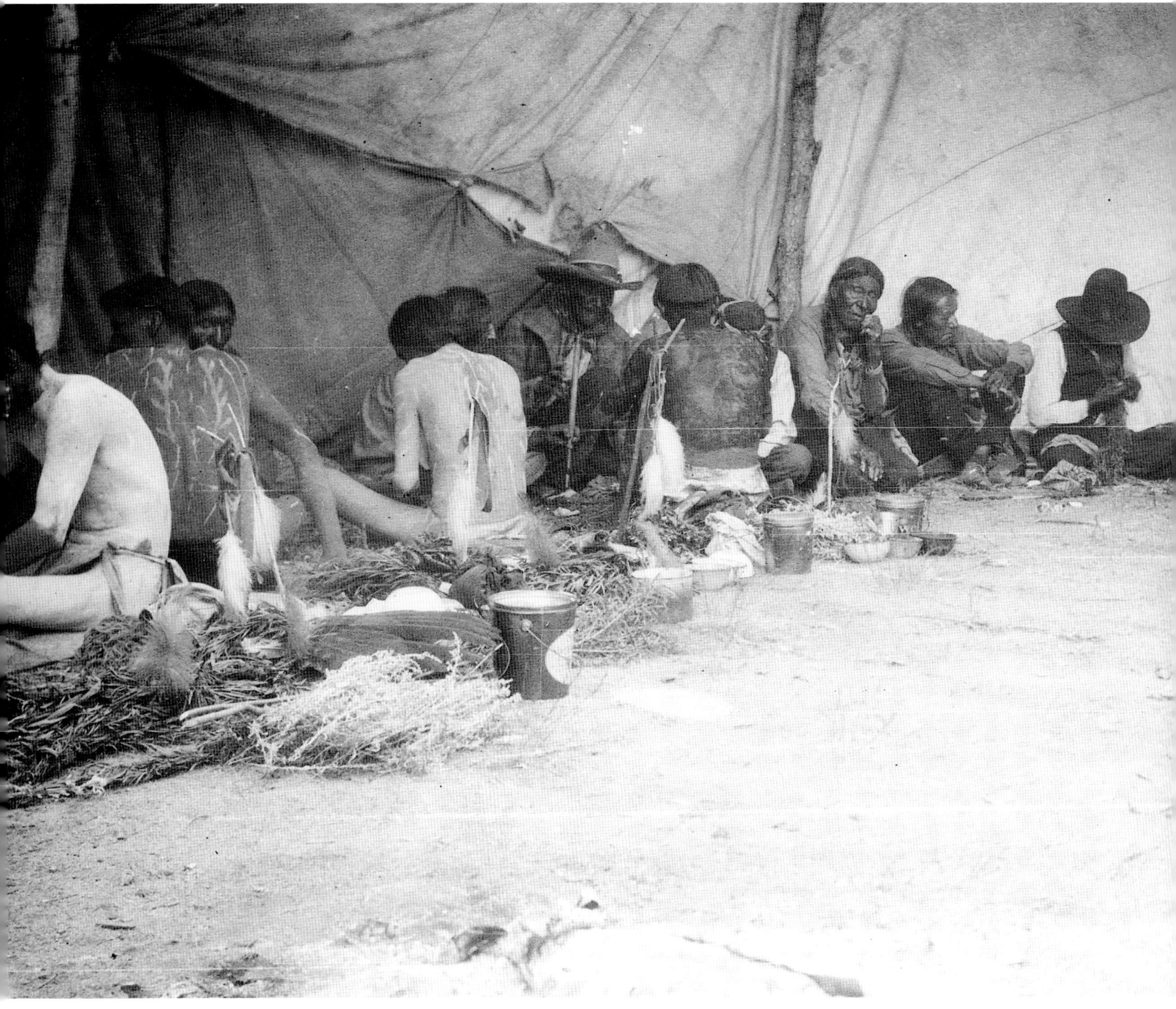

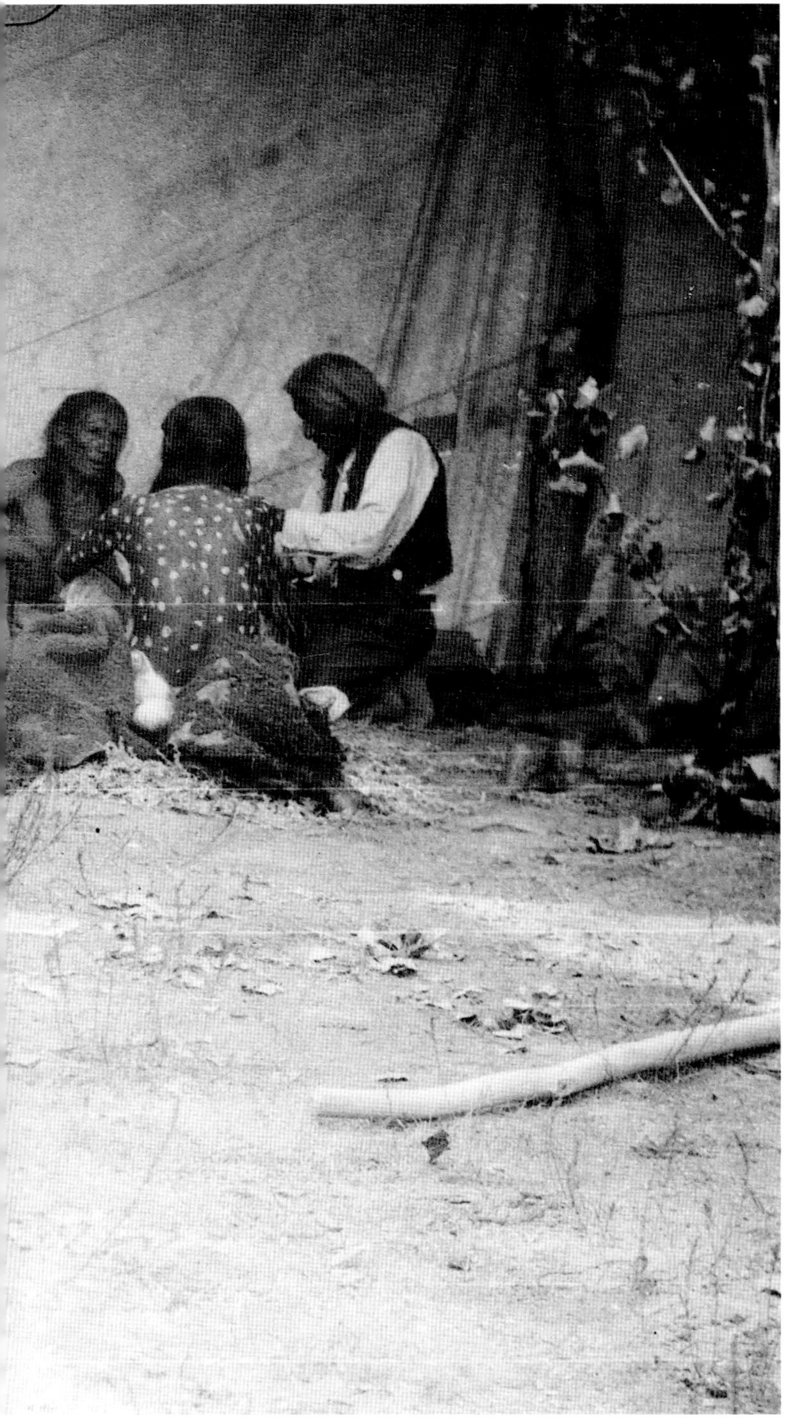

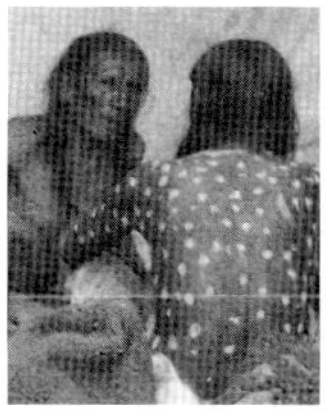

38. Inside the Medicine Lodge

INFORMANT: JOHN WOODENLEGS

38a. This is a picture of the painters and Sun Dance priests getting the dancers ready. Left to right (starting with the man in the big hat): Grasshopper, Limpy (by pole), Pine, unknown, unknown, Clubfoot (painted), and Wolf Chief.

38b. Dancers are again shown here with their instructors during the painting process. Such paints are changed several times throughout the ceremony. Limpy, identified above, was prominent in the Rosebud fight of 1876 (Stands in Timber and Liberty 1997: chapter 11). Limpy's wife was wounded in the Custer fight (see figure 22). Pine and Grasshopper, identified here, were tribal chiefs. Since these pictures were taken, restrictions on such photography have been enforced by most tribes.

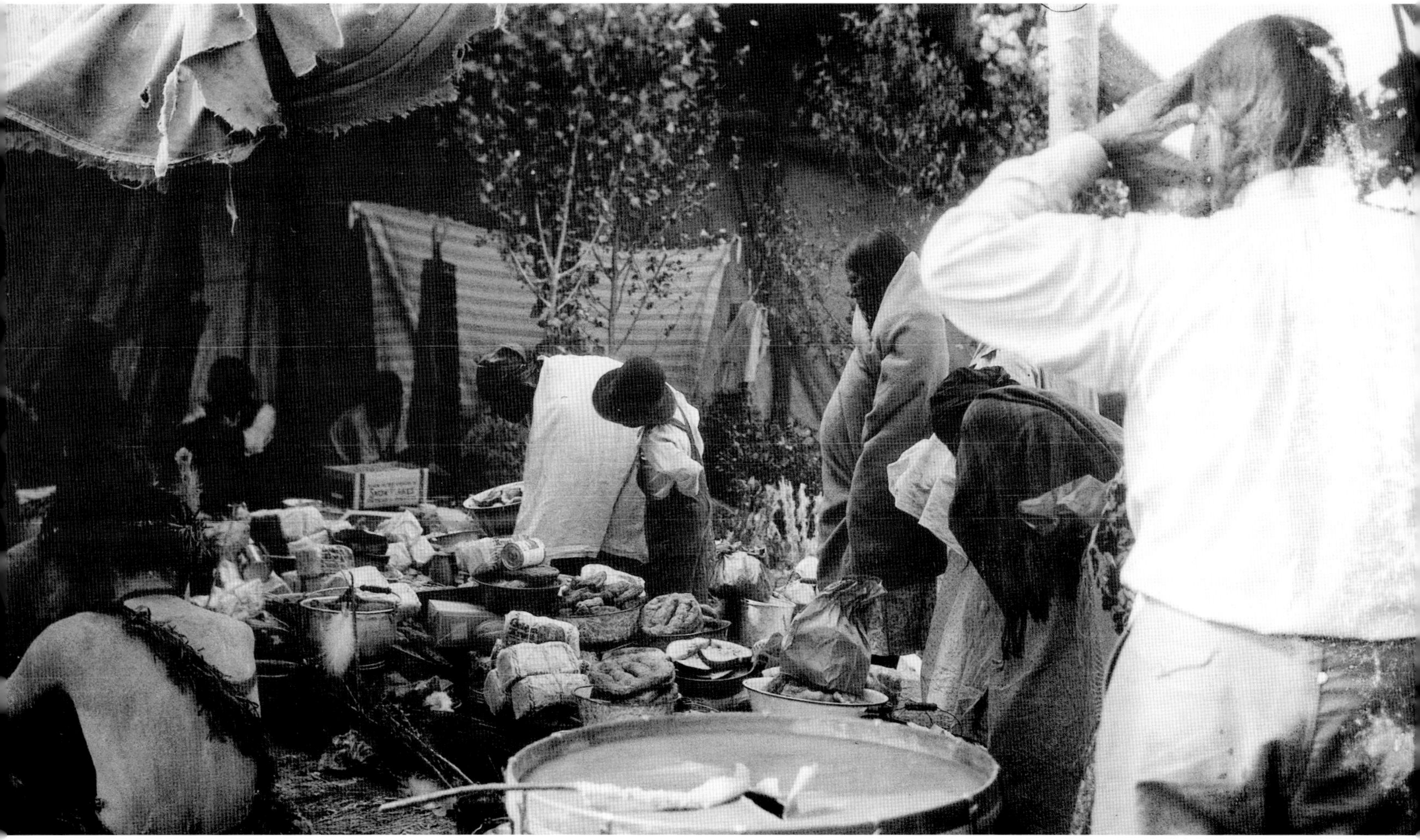

39. Food Offerings in the Medicine Lodge

INFORMANT: JOHN WOODENLEGS

39a. On the second and third days of the Sun Dance, the family and relatives of the dancers bring food offerings into the Medicine Lodge. Some is given to the Sun Dance priests who are helping, and then to other people who have helped the dancers at some time. The dancers do not eat or drink anything.

39b. The drum used during the ceremony can be seen here in the foreground. Music for dance sequences consists of special Sun Dance songs by changing groups of singers. This music is often available today on tape recordings, where the eagle-bone whistles used by the dancers are clearly audible.

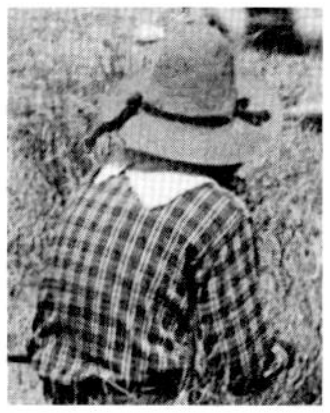

40. Sun Dance Medicine Lodge

Informant: James Limber Hand in 1978

40a. The Sun Dance, this picture I'm looking at—I was called in there. There used to be a lot of good older men at these ceremonial doings—they are all invited to come. They all wanted to be a part of it. It seems like I remember this Sun Dance. These are good old men; they were invited to sit there. One is Black Coyote, Buffalo Hump and Grasshopper, Turkey Legs [or Flying], Stump Horn, and Spotted Elk.

We were over to the Rees, my brother Richard and Mamie, and we came back to Northern Cheyennes. I'm 77 years old at this time, 1978. A lot of older people have passed on and a lot of the younger people are dying too. Young ones are dying because we are not taking care of our way of life and ourselves. Our way of life—traditional way—that the Spirit has given us is still with us, but we are not taking care of it. We don't follow it. There are good ways God or Spirit has given us—it's good. So it almost is gone. Now we're trying to put up these ceremonial things and they're not complete and they're doing things different. I went to Oklahoma and I was looking on when they were having a Sun Dance. They were not taking good care of it. When they were setting up the center pole, it fell back down. It broke some of the poles. When it fell back down, they hollered and yelled. I don't know why. It seems like they shouldn't do that. We depend on our worship ways when we are troubled; that's where we go for help. It seems like they shouldn't abuse it. When we go there for help for our problems, if we're doing it right and the people are right, we get help through that way from God. So if we don't listen and don't do right, we don't get help—we leave it and go away from it. Those were good ways of worshiping and today I have grown up to be one of the elders and there's no more of those good old men. Nobody is trying to set an example or say the good things—there's no more of that. It seems to be not good anymore—it was good, but now it's not being done right, so that's why it isn't good anymore. Now some of us have grown to be the older ones. We know some of the good. It seems as though Spirit is trying to tell us or show us not to do the things anymore that are hurting us. He's telling us not to mess up our way of life. When we don't do right and don't listen, we leave that good way. We should go back to that Spiritual way of life, that peaceful way that Spirit is trying to show us. Cheyennes a long time ago had this way of worship—the Sun Dance. At that time that way of life, that Spiritual way, was good. Spirit led us in a good way, and it was really good. It seems like we don't do right by it anymore, we have left the good way. It seems like we don't even believe in God anymore.

At the time that these people were alive, they were leaders—like Robert Yellow Fox, Robert Little Wolf, and Eugene Standing Elk. Things were good at the time. I have explained some of the good ways of the past. Young people today are growing up and destroying these ways, or neglecting them or covering them up. The way of life today is just like the wind—blowing away. About two years ago, Spirit talked to me at my house—late at night. He said, "Alright, Limber Hand, I came here to tell you something so if somebody asks you, try to tell them what I'm saying. I want to tell you about the way of life; I'm going to change the way of life. I am going to take the people away from you that are not treating you right—those that are misusing the traditional ways or the medicine ways. I'm going to tell you, Crooked Feather, that when you die, Spirit is going to take you to a high mountain, this big white mountain. There's nothing else there—that's where Spirit is."

I've been thinking this over and I don't go to dances or gatherings anymore. These ceremonial ways aren't right, like I said earlier. Some of these younger men don't really know. I'm old enough and I've had some experiences with these older times and I know the difference. The right way is a good way and it's true, and that's the way Spirit had taught us. So Spirit is with us today and when we pray in a good way, he answers us. Some of these good ways, we are leaving behind. We're doing something else phoney or not right. For the past year I've been thinking these things over. I'm not too old—I can still think clearly. The worship ways are true and they're good. I've been thinking about all this and I'm learning and realizing this. I'm happy and I feel good that I'm talking to you this way.

40b. Limber Hand was born in 1901. Despite his pessimism, Cheyenne ceremonies have continued in a more traditional fashion than those of most Plains tribes. His mention of the Southern Cheyenne Sun Dance in Oklahoma points to continuing performance in both locations.

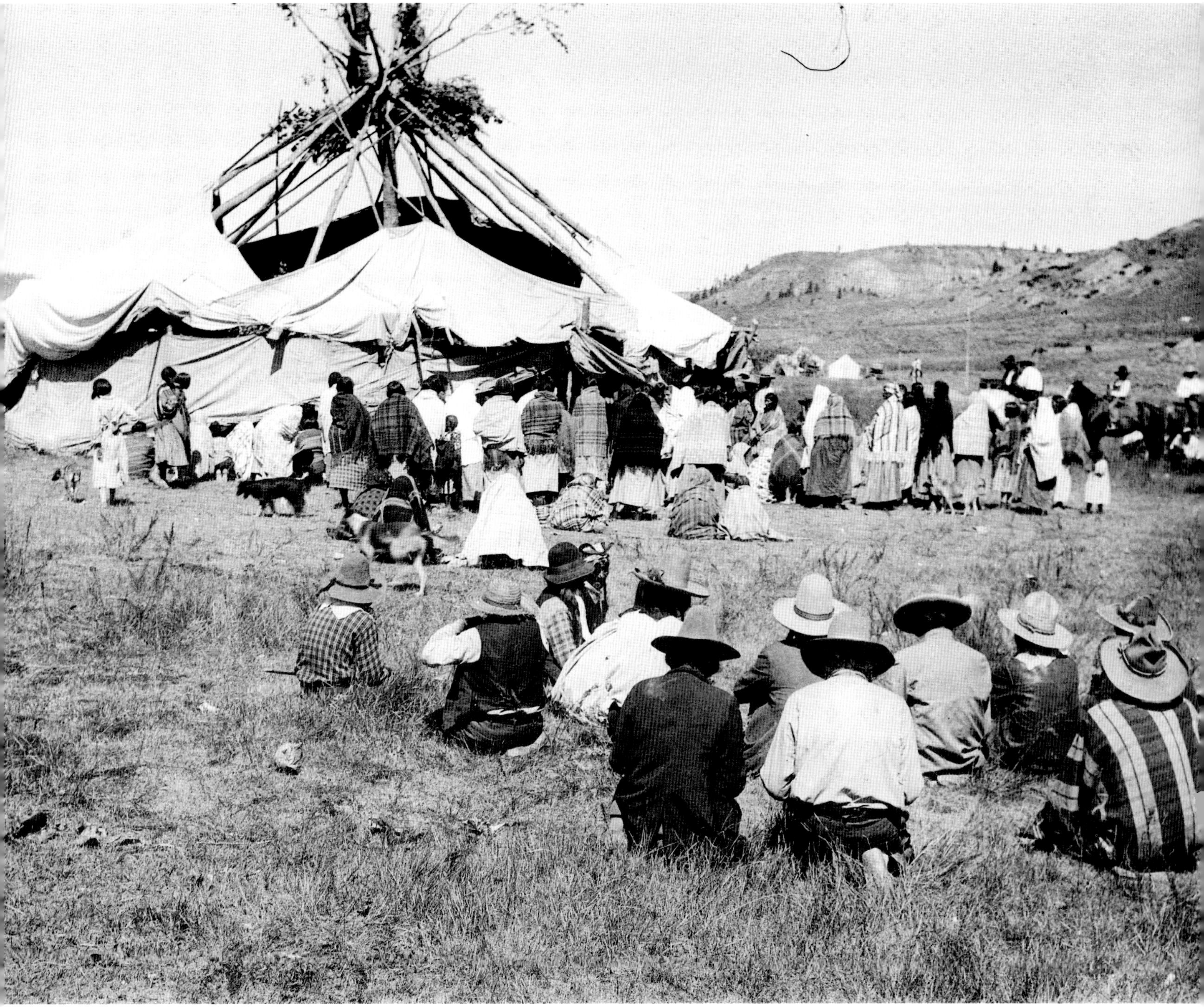

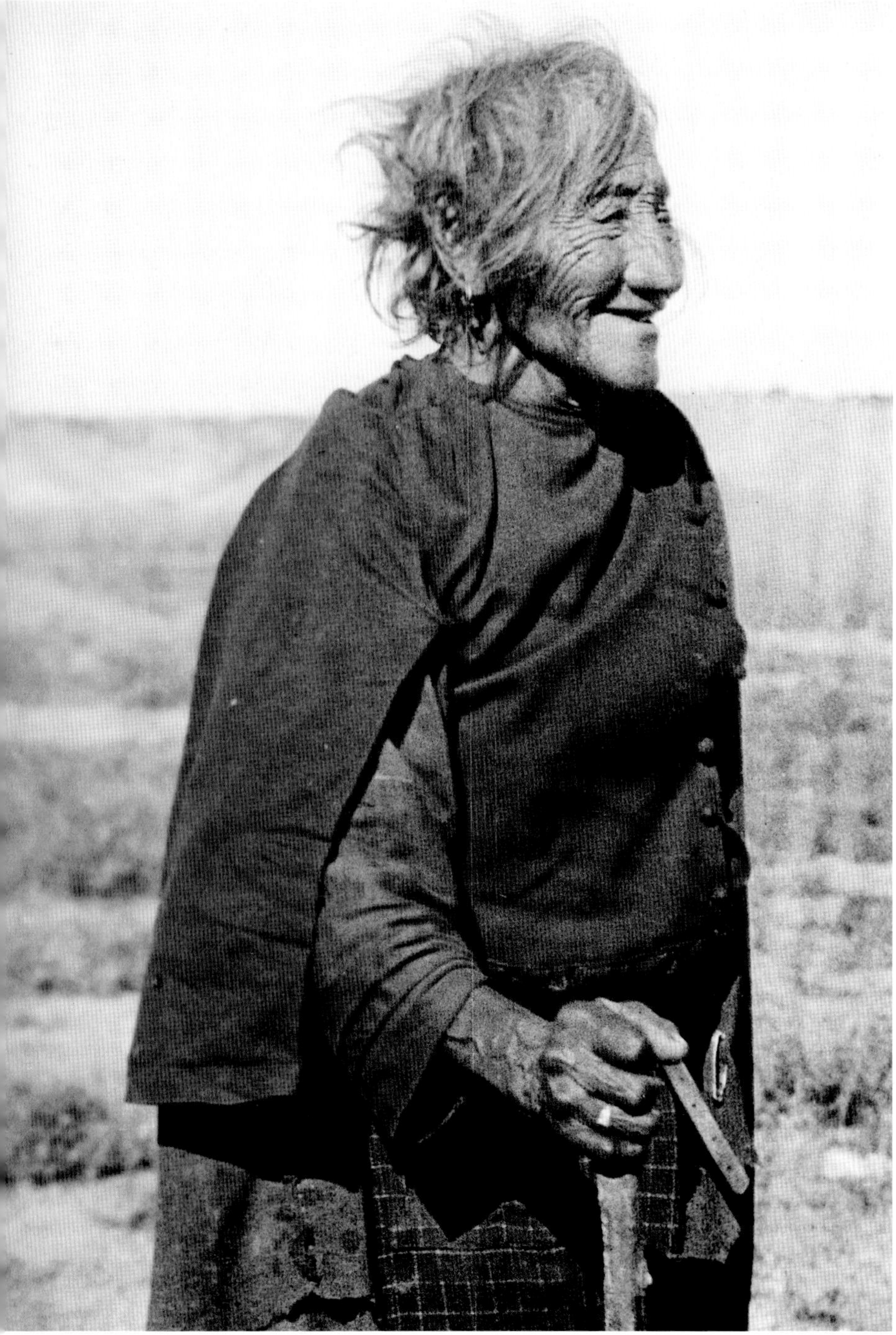

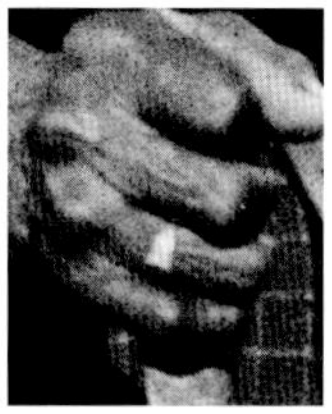

41. Susan Iron Teeth

INFORMANT: NOTES OF DR. MARQUIS

41a. Susan Iron Teeth, the oldest woman of her tribe at age 92, in 1926.

41b. Susan Iron Teeth was born in 1834. She would have been 42 years old when her husband was killed at the Dull Knife fight on Powder River in November of 1876. This was the fourth of four major battles fought by the Cheyennes and their Sioux allies in 1876. It ended disastrously for them, with the destruction of their village by the soldiers. The others were the Reynolds fight on the Powder River on March 17, the Rosebud fight on June 17, and the Custer fight on June 25–26, 1876.

The amazing story of this woman's life can be found in The Cheyennes of Montana *(Marquis 1978).*

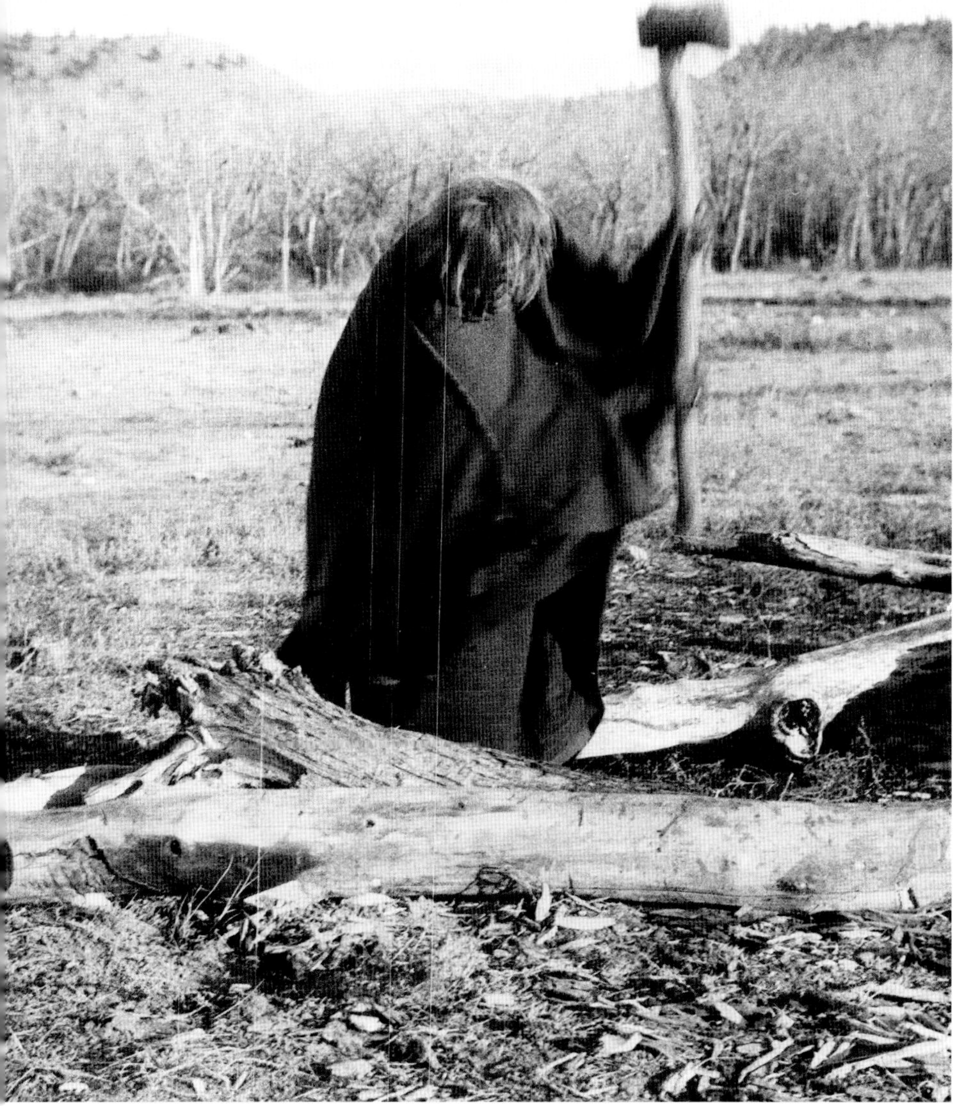

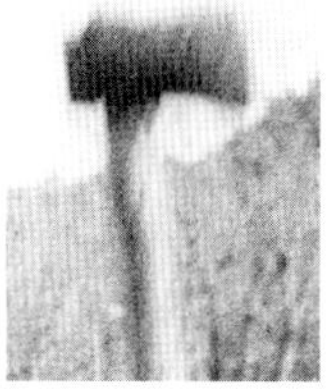

42. Chopping Wood at 92

INFORMANT: NOTES OF DR. THOMAS MARQUIS

42a. Susan Iron Teeth chopping wood at age 92, 1926.

42b. Women did most of the heavy work gathering and cutting firewood, as well as preparing food and preparing leather for clothing and tepees. They also did the main work of setting up and moving camp. Men were responsible for hunting and warfare, and much of their time in their later years was spent in ceremonial activity—learning about and preparing ceremonial regalia and medicine. Men also took turns as camp police.

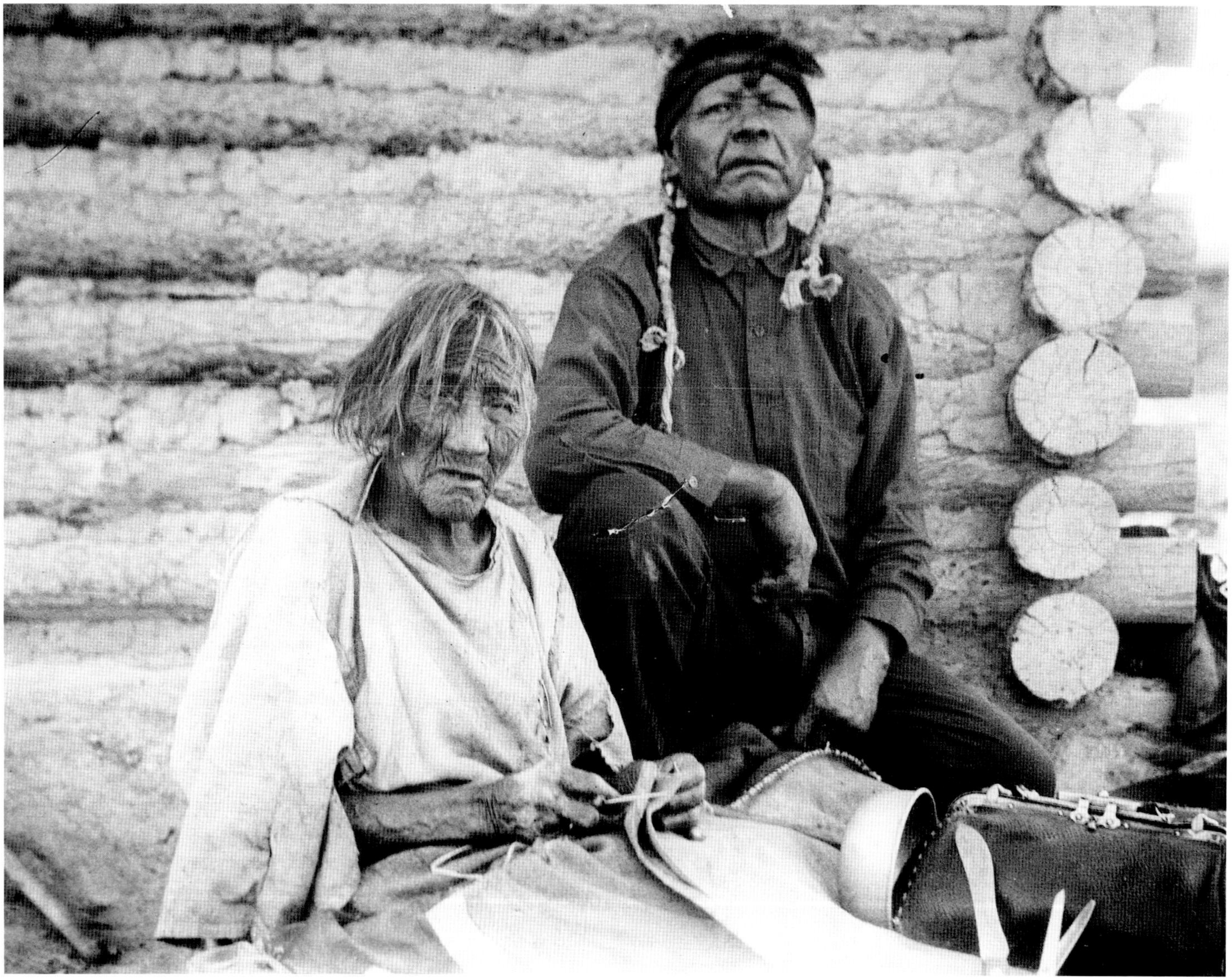

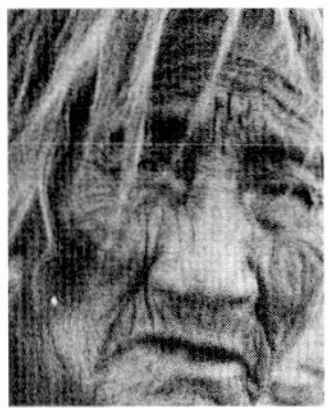

43. Sewing Buckskin

INFORMANT: NOTES OF DR. THOMAS MARQUIS

43a. This is Susan Iron Teeth and Shoulder Blade. She is sewing some buckskin together. She lived over in the area of Ashland. She really had a hard life, but she was a hard worker.

43b. Tanning and sewing of buckskin and other leather goods for clothing and lodging was a major responsibility of Plains Indian women. The work was extremely time consuming and arduous, so cotton and woolen woven goods were gladly adopted when they became available, as was canvas for tepee covers. For a picture of Susan Iron Teeth with the cherished elkhorn hide scraper with which she was buried, see The Cheyennes of Montana *(Marquis 1978: 81).*

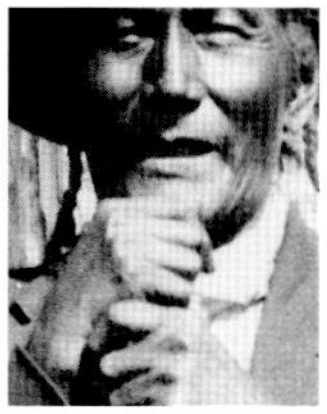

44. Four Good Cheyennes

INFORMANT: JOHN WOODENLEGS

44a. Laban Little Wolf, Hairy Hand, Porcupine, and Big Beaver are posing here. This is a picture of four Cheyenne older people, taken in 1922. At the time they were almost great-grandparents. There's Laban Little Wolf and Hairy Hand. Laban has his hat on and his braids, and he has a cane. Hairy Hand has his hat off, a big hat, handkerchief, and braids. The other man is Porcupine, Heskovestse. He's got his cane and hat. Looks like he's got a black suit on and he's using a cloth for his belt. They were all good Cheyenne people. And Big Beaver, he's got a little grin on him, smiling. He has Bull Durham in his pocket, you can see the string hanging out. Now these men were probably sitting around talking and Marquis came along and took their picture. I think he gave Porcupine a dollar to take his picture; he wanted to divide that and give them a quarter apiece, but one of them said, "I should have it all, I need it." But they're happy and they're smiling. They're good old men, if someone says, "Do this or do that," they're willing. They listened to one another and worked together and cooperated together. Big Beaver, as a small child, was kept two or three years by Catholic Missionaries, and he could speak some English and write his name. They took him to Newcastle, Wyoming, and he stayed with those people over there. He would come back for a while and then go back to them. I guess he helped round up cattle or sheep when he was young, him and another Cheyenne named Wooden Thigh. As Big Beaver grew up he got to be one of the chiefs of the Cheyennes.

As a young man Porcupine was an instigator of the wreck of a Union Pacific freight train near North Platte, Nebraska, in 1867, and was later the "Messiah Preacher" who brought the Ghost Dance to the Northern Cheyennes.

44b. The Cheyenne system of chiefs or Council of Forty-four was unique among Plains tribes. It drew four tribal chiefs from each of ten bands, which ranged across separate hunting locations for most of the year.

When the people came together for the big ceremonies in the summer (primarily the Sun Dance or renewal of the Sacred Arrows), the forty chiefs met in council. Four "old man chiefs" were elected each ten years, bringing the number to forty-four. Little Wolf and Dull Knife (Morning Star) held two of these positions in historic times.

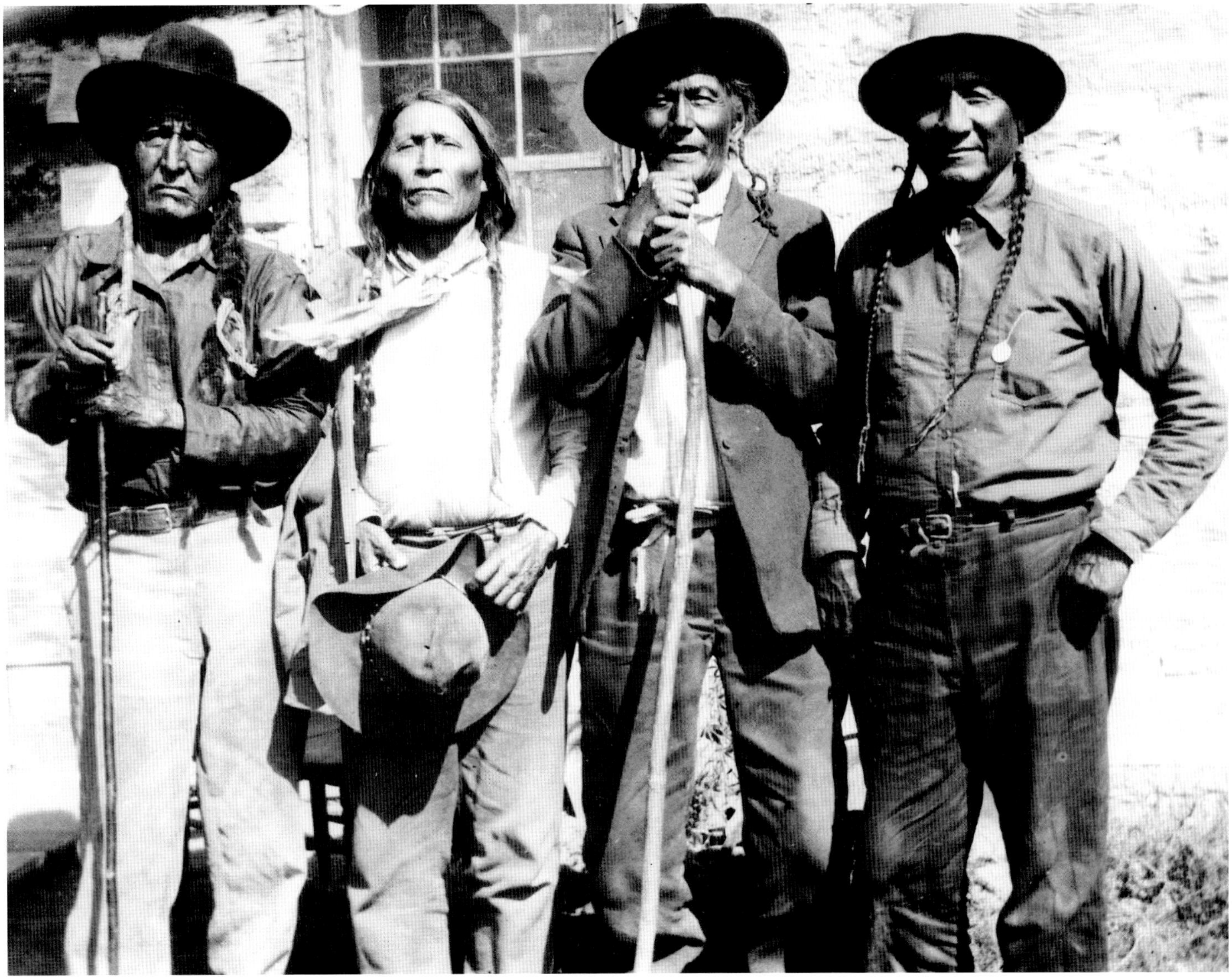

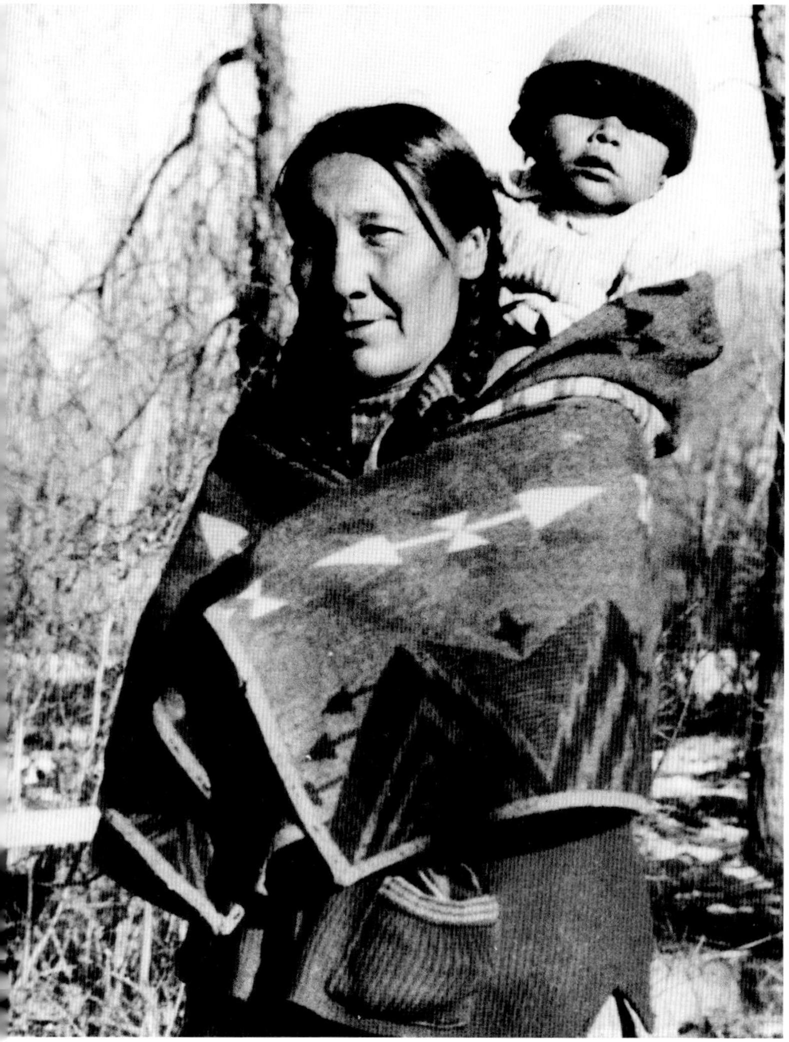

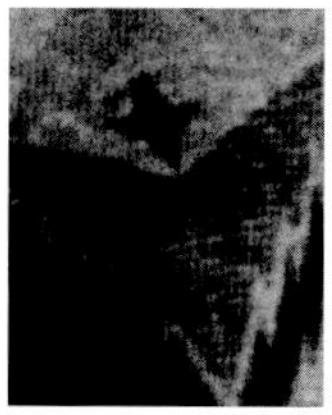

45. Bessie Twin and Child

INFORMANT: JOHN WOODENLEGS

45a. This is Bessie Twin, James Twin's wife, and a little girl on her back. She has a Pendleton blanket, sweater and dress, Cheyenne braided hair. The child has a stocking cap and it's over the eyes a little bit, but she's looking. The picture is taken alongside of trees and a corral. I know these people. I worked with James Twin. They are from Ashland. They were good people, hard working, honest, and they tried to live a good life. All the children died, got sick and then died. They were good to them and they were good to people. They talked real good to people. Bessie was the daughter of Big Beaver, a very kind man. He was one of the ceremonial people.

45b. Child mortality among the Cheyennes was extremely high during the years when these pictures were taken. Malnutrition and epidemics of measles as well as influenza were lethal in the closely settled, unsanitary communities that replaced the old nomadic camps. Tuberculosis also took a great many lives.

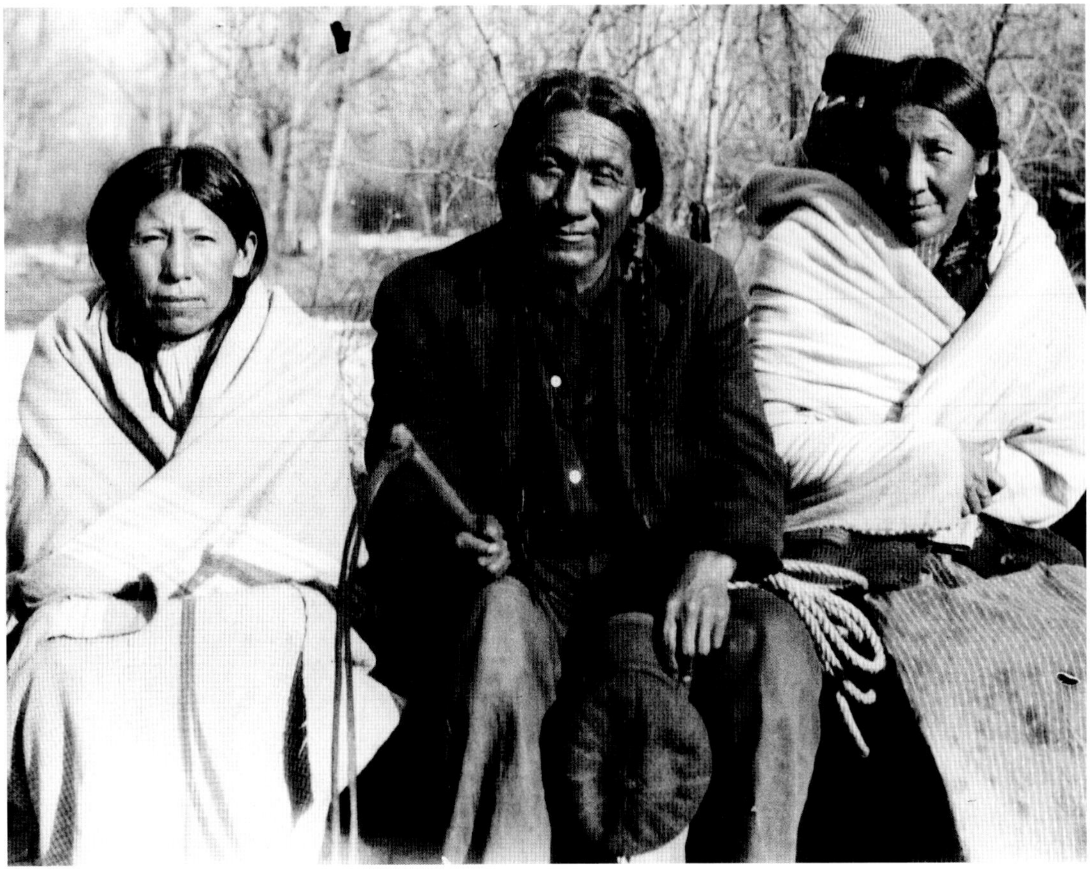

46. Mrs. Wooden Thigh, Big Beaver, and Bessie Twin.

INFORMANT: JOHN WOODENLEGS

46a. As a teenager, Big Beaver made the journey north from Oklahoma where many Cheyennes had been sent after the Custer battle. When Little Wolf and Morning Star chose to part ways, Big Beaver went with Morning Star's group to Fort Robinson. He survived the terrible fighting that took place when the Cheyennes broke out of Fort Robinson, and later with those who went to Pine Ridge Agency. Many of the men became scouts for the Army; Big Beaver was one of them.

46b. Big Beaver was 63 in 1926, so he would have been 13 at the 1876 Custer fight—an age when many Cheyenne males were becoming active warriors. Some of Big Beaver's ledger drawings are preserved by the National Park Service at Little Bighorn Battlefield National Monument in Montana.

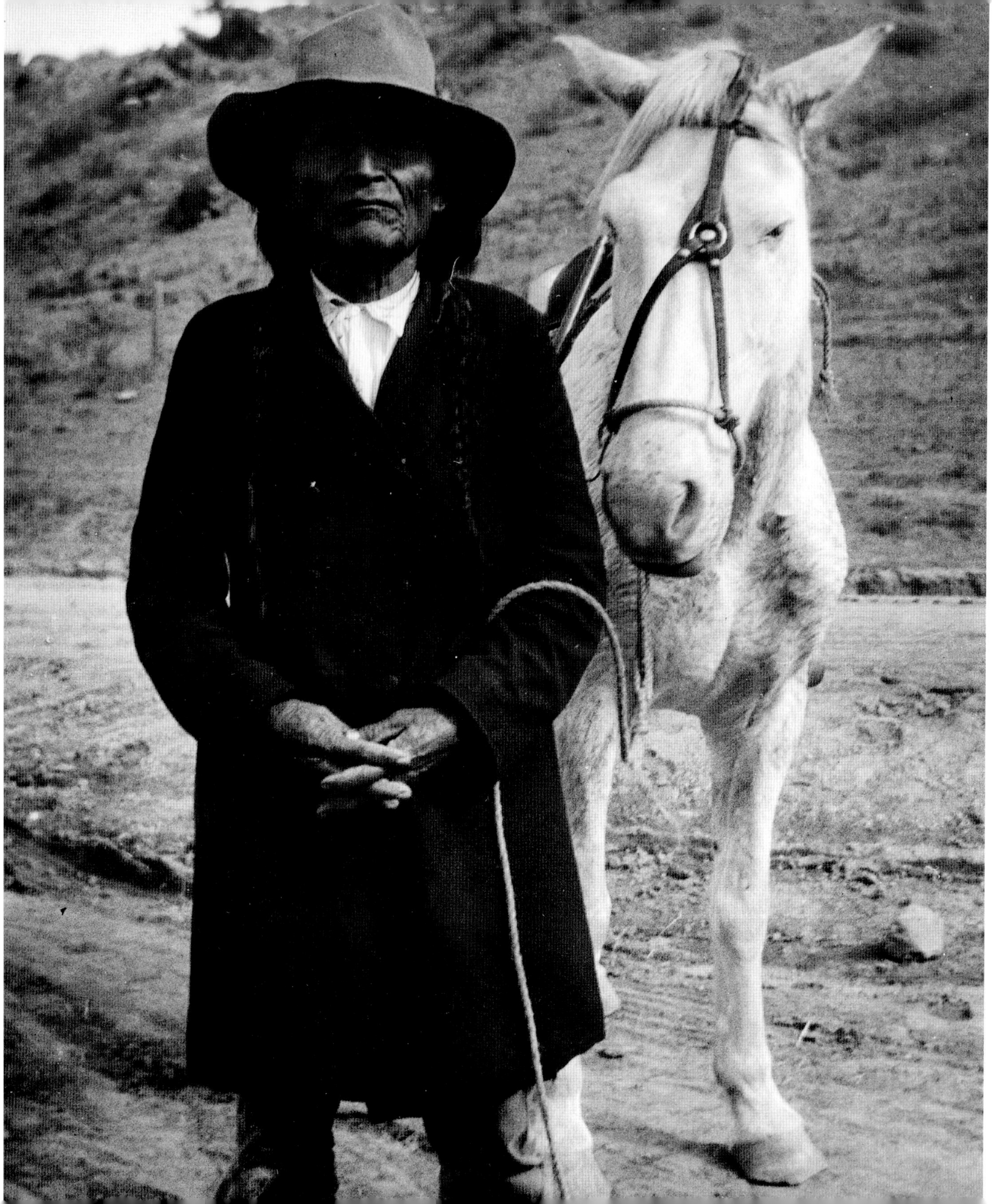

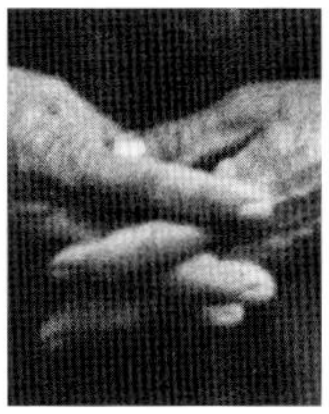

47. Hairy Hand

INFORMANT: JOHN WOODENLEGS

47a. In November 1876, after the Custer Battle, some of the Cheyennes were camped on the Powder River under their leader, Morning Star. General Ranald Mackenzie attacked and destroyed this camp, causing great loss to the people, almost total destruction of the camp and all the possessions in it. During this fighting, Hairy Hand rescued another wounded Cheyenne, Crawling, by returning to where he had fallen and carrying him and helping him back to the breastworks.

Hairy Hand later came to the Busby area with the Cheyennes who had been at Pine Ridge after the march north from Oklahoma.

47b. The reference to scouts for the military here and elsewhere in these captions indicates that a high proportion of defeated Northern Cheyenne warriors chose to accept the army's offer to assist it in pursuing as yet undefeated Indians such as the Nez Perces. The scouts received horses and guns and years later also received badly needed cash pensions. The scouts with their families lived at Fort Keogh on Tongue River near present Miles City, Montana, later returning upriver to join the rest of the tribe on the Tongue River Reservation.

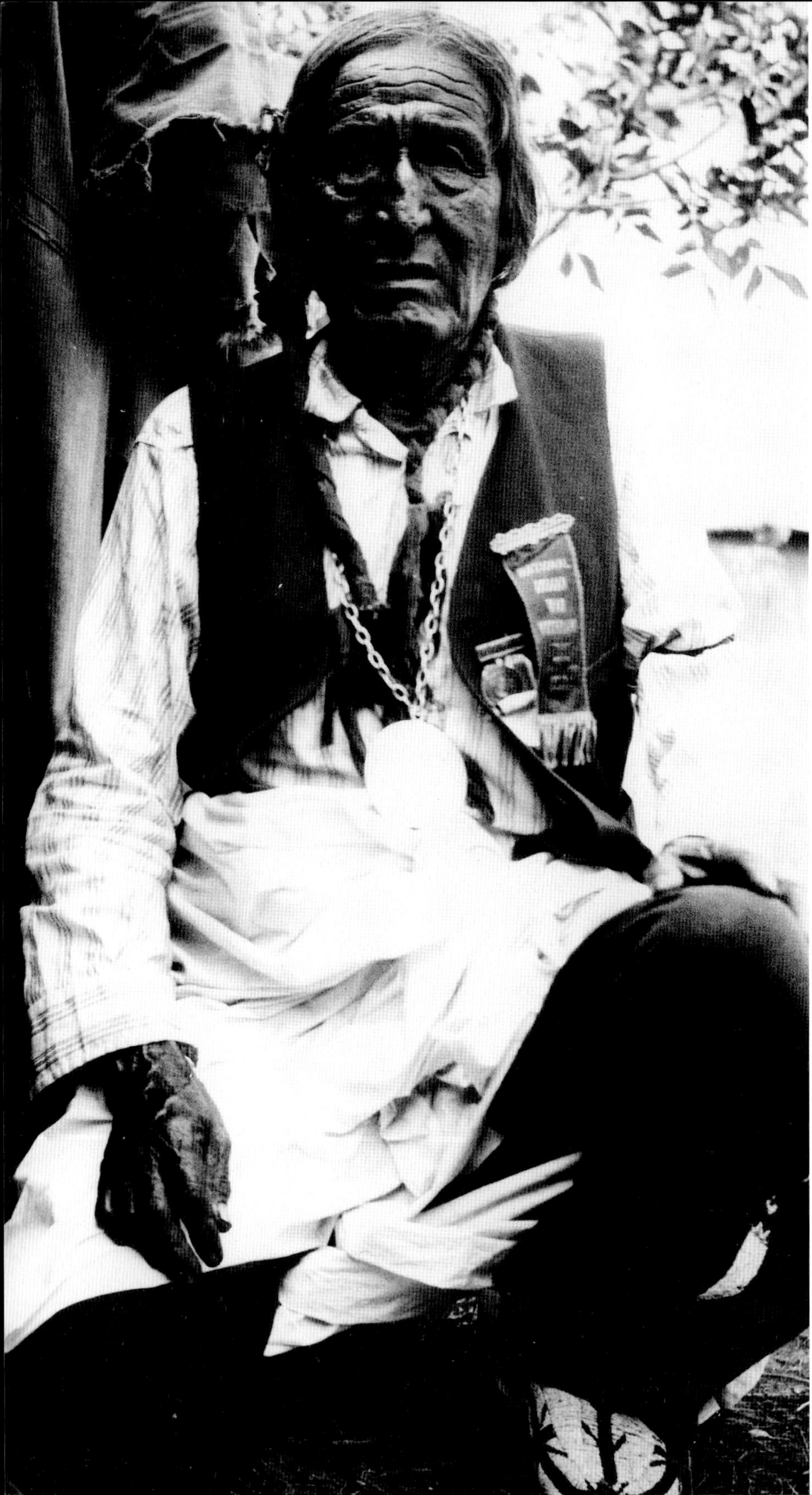

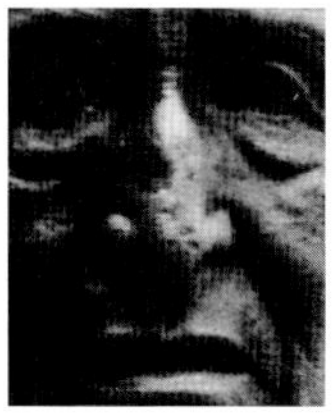

48. Laban Little Wolf

INFORMANT: JOHN WOODENLEGS

48a. Laban Little Wolf was a nephew of the Cheyenne old man chief, Little Wolf. Little Wolf was one of the leaders when the Cheyennes returned north from Oklahoma in 1879. Little Wolf had given his nephew his name following an early battle with the Shoshones in which the nephew had counted two coups and shown much bravery.

Laban died at the age of 77 in 1927.

48b. Laban Little Wolf was often confused with his uncle, the famous fighting chief, whose name was given him by the senior Little Wolf, as described here. John Stands in Timber gives an amusing account in Cheyenne Memories *(Stands in Timber and Liberty 1997: chapter 18) of how he coached the old man to please the crowd at some white celebration.*

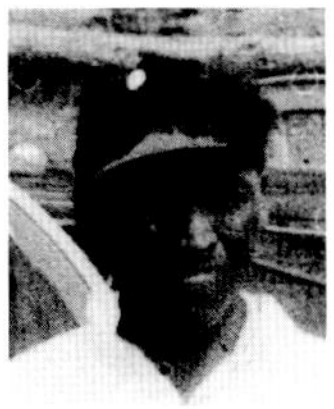

49. Wesley Whiteman and James Flying Bird

INFORMANT: WESLEY WHITEMAN AND JOHN WOODENLEGS

49a. **Woodenlegs:** Wesley Whiteman, my uncle, is going to talk about the time they used to farm. Wesley is on the left and the other man is his brother-in-law, James Flying Bird.

Wesley: I put up that place, my folks fixed it up. We used to live north of Lame Deer a mile or so and then we moved to this place east of Lame Deer about one mile. My grandfather and grandmother used to live where Sigfried's sawmill was. Mrs. Ford Wounded Eye and Mrs. Charles Whistling Elk were my aunts and my uncle was William Yellow Robe. I used to work hard at that time. My cousin, Hugh Walks Along [son of Yellow Robe], was a hard worker too. People used to see which of us could work the hardest. The garden I raised was sent to the State Fair in Helena to exhibit. The cabbages were that big! I had two of them to exhibit. It was dry land farming—if I had had irrigation on it, it would have really done good. The creek we lived on is Alderson Gulch, a dry creek.

This is my brother-in-law, James Flying Bird. I gave him one of the horses there. The horse was kind of mean, but after we got him broke good, he was really a good work horse. James lived on Rosebud Creek. James came and we were going to go play baseball, that's why I have my baseball cap on. We used to play baseball. We played a lot of white fellows.

We plowed early in the spring. Toward spring, we'd fix out our machinery. I had horses I used to get ready. This is a Belgian horse, we got it from old man Spang. Spang had a Belgian stallion. I had a team of gray mares. I used those mares and plowed with them. I had a bunch of horses and they all died. I had this sorrel horse. Alvin Parker came and wanted it. I used to run wild horses with this one, and my horse used to run so hard, he would quit running. So I would doctor him and then he got alright. We ran them in at Ed Harris' place at his corrals. These horses were hard to catch, they were mavericks. My garden won a prize at the State Fair. We planted wheat and oats. I even tied alfalfa and wheat

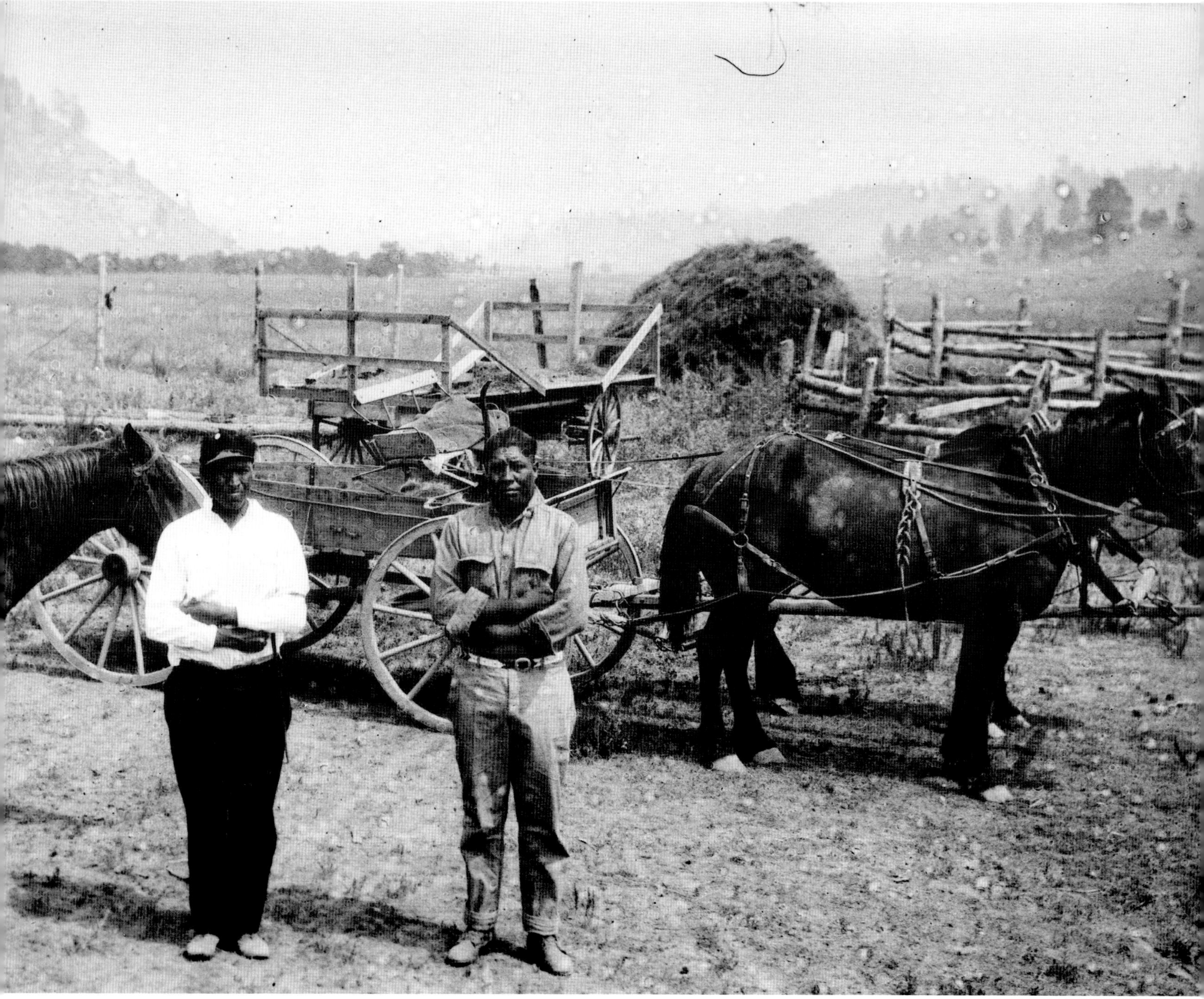

and oats together in bunches and sent it to the Helena State Fair. I won $221.00. I sent watermelon and squash. They sent all the stuff back to me. I had squash, the ones with big lumps on them, green ones. I planted all kinds of vegetables. I had seven gardens. I put the watermelon and cantaloupe on the side hill and when they got ripe, they'd come off the vine and roll down to a place where I'd pick them up. No irrigation.

We used to go to the Mennonite Church. They prayed for us and we prayed for each other—Yellow Fox, Standing Elk, and William Sweet Medicine. In 1910 they built the Mennonite Church. My grandmother, Traveling Wolf Woman, was the oldest of six sisters. Your grandmother, Elk Woman, was second to the oldest. The third one is Medicine Woman. She was the mother of Eagle Feathers. Another sister was Young Medicine Woman. Buffalo Woman was another sister [Mrs. Charles Whistling Elk]. Mrs. Ford Wounded Eye was another sister. There were two brothers: William Yellow Robe and Red around the Mouth, also called Red Sleeve. He got killed by electricity at Highwalkers'. [Red Sleeve had been a scout at Fort Keogh; early photographer L. A. Huffman took a fine picture of him that is still seen in Western collections and on postcards.] Red Sleeve's daughter was named Shell Woman. Carol White Wolf is named after her. Red Sleeve had a boy too, named "Man Bear" [Hetane Nahkohe]. His name was John Red Sleeve.

Coal Bear was Keeper of the Sacred Hat for the longest time. He was related to all these people some way. They all cooperated with him. We all fasted and prayed in the Sacred Hat tepee. My mother's uncle was Coal Bear.

49b. The early Cheyenne adjustment to farming and their remarkable optimism and good humor about everything from work horses to cabbages might not have been predicted—nor the fact that they won large cash prizes at the Montana state fair!

The following interview, which Woodenlegs recorded in 1978, discusses foot races, rain-making, the Sacred Arrows, prayer-offering ceremonies, and the Ghost Dance—winding up with an adventure that Wesley Whiteman had one Christmas.

Wesley Whiteman Interview (recorded in 1978)

Woodenlegs: This is Wesley Whiteman, who is 82 years old.

Wesley: My father, Little Whiteman, was married to a Southern Cheyenne woman and he came up here. His children were Milton, Stanley, John, Florence, and Jenny. My father could run a race. On the 4th of July at Fort Reno, Wyoming, they had a celebration and he was to run a race. He ran 100 yards in 8 seconds. He was a real fast runner. When he ran, he ran so hard, the bottom of his feet would peel. There were Indians from all over came and also white people. There was a man named Gary who trained my dad. The town of Gary, Oklahoma, was named after him. He was half-Indian. My father was given a horse and saddle and a bridle. A lot of people gathered to see this race and a lot of white people too. He tied the world's record. He told me, "I really run that time, just as hard as I could run." I don't quite remember when my father finished scouting in Miles City. It might have been after he finished scouting, he shot himself with a 45-70 soldier gun in the chest. Later you could see his heart beating in his chest, he had sort of a hole in his chest. If he had killed himself, my brother Frank and I would not be here because we weren't born yet. My father's Southern Cheyenne wife died when Jenny was born and he married a Northern Cheyenne woman, who was my mother. That book I bought from you [Woodenlegs] has a picture of four women and their babies—one of them is my mother. She is the one on the left. They were getting ready to leave Fort Keogh so they all dressed up to have their pictures taken. Yellow Robe and their wives were at Fort Keogh too at that time. Wolf Voice and Yellow Robe's wife are brother and sister. Yellow Robe and Wolf Voice's wife are brother and sister.

When my dad raced, it broke a banker. They all bet on someone else! I went over there one time where they raced.

Sun Maker was my dad's uncle. Where Old Bear lived, they lived below. His other name was "Dragon Contrary." He was kind of a spiritual man. One time, no rain, just dry, nothing growing, all burned up. Lot of white people came around asking why everything was burning up. The asked among the Indians, "Who could make it rain?" They went to the districts. They also went to the Kiowas and Comanches and Caddos seeking some man who would make it rain. They came to the Cheyennes asking. They said, "Let's go see Sun Maker and we'll give him $500 if he makes it rain." The Indian agent went with them. They had young people as interpreters and they kept some of the money. They only gave Sun Maker $200. He said, "I'll make it rain." He asked for his mirror; it was all wrapped up and put away. He unwrapped it and he blinded the sun with that mirror. After that he put water on the mirror. In the evening it started to rain and it just poured down. Sun Maker came and visited us when we were living where Fred White Wolf lives now, north of Lame Deer.

There was this Cheyenne named Lewis Little Man. His Cheyenne name was Grey Bird or he was called "Sand." He was in the First World War. He made a vow over there, "I want to go back home and I'll make the highest ceremonial doings." When he got back he put up an Arrow Worship ceremony. At the time I talked to him, he told me it had been thirty years since he had put up that ceremony. The year before when I was talking to him, he had put up another Arrow Worship. He said, "I almost died, and I was in a hospital and I was taken to the place where people who are dying were. I believe in this Arrow Worship so I prayed to the Spirit that if I get well, I would put up an Arrow Worship." And this Grey Bird was thanking me for the part I did in helping in the Arrow Worship. He said, "This way is real, it really helps. I was on my death bed, but Spirit brought me through." It's kind of special to me that I'm used in this ceremony. They take me to Oklahoma to help. It means a lot to me to be able to help this way. Some people there told me it's a special place where I am in this ceremony and that I should not tell stories and make jokes, but talk good and be good. I try not to joke or tell funny stories while I'm taking part in this ceremony. I've been to Oklahoma about eleven times to help with the ceremonies. I always try my best to go, but a year ago last summer, I started to have a stroke. It's too hot down there. I tried to get started to come home right away. I didn't go back again this summer.

Woodenlegs: Did your father take part in these ceremonies?

Wesley: Yes, he took part in a lot of things like racing and other things. He fasted out alone by himself and pierced himself. He believed in all the worship ways although he was half-white. He always told us to respect these worship ways and always talk good to old people and respect them, and not to make fun of the woman who takes part. "Don't act smart towards these old people. If a woman is used in a Sun Dance or in the Contrary ceremony, don't make fun of them. Respect them and don't try to make love to them no matter how much you might want them."

My brother, Frank Whiteman—people think he's not much of anything. When Frank was a baby our mother used to go to these different ceremonies. One was where they used prayer cloths. She took Frank with her. My mother and Elk Woman belonged to a ceremonial society—a prayer offering society. In this ceremony, the high priest said Frank had won the first prize as a baby to take part in this ceremony. He was blessed by Spirit as a baby. No matter what people say now or how much they get after him, he never says anything. He has that good way in him. The priest said Frank would live a long time and if people said bad things about him, it wouldn't throw him off.

My grandmother was married to Black Beaver. Your [speaking to Woodenlegs] grandmother, Elk Woman, and Medicine Woman and Young Medicine Woman were all daughters of Black Beaver. Charles Teeth was the son of Black Beaver. Teeth was my uncle. Teeth's daughter, Belle, married Floyd High Walking. Belle's half-brother was John Stands in Timber. They had the same mother, but different fathers. The mother's name was White Buffalo Woman. John's father was Stands Different. When the mother died they were very young. It's good I remember these people.

Porcupine and other Cheyennes had this ceremonial dance that was something like the ceremony Black Beaver performed and the Sioux made a big thing out of it. Porcupine was called a Ghost Dancer. The Sioux took some of this and misused it and changed it.

My mother took part in this ceremony that Black Beaver had. They build four fires in the four directions, and when all the smoke come together in the middle, it shows that Spirit is near. Porcupine took part of this ceremony for his Ghost Dance. They called him a Ghost Dancer.

When my mother was young, all of her family and relatives took part in these various ceremonies. They were all included, even the babies. Coal Bear, Black Beaver took part in a lot of this. In springtime, during the ceremony, we cut small pieces of our skin as an offering.

Black Beaver was going to perform this ceremony in the Big Horn Basin. A lot of people moved over there and camped. This ceremony is higher than the Arrow Worship or the Sun Dance. They build a fire in four directions. They cut up a lot of meat and they burned cedar and sweet grass to ask blessings for that meat. They took hooves of the buffalo according to their ages and stuck them in the mud near there. After all the meat was blessed, everyone was eating, and after that everybody left to go home. When all the smoke had come together it was finished. It was in Frannie, Wyoming, in the Big Horn Basin, close to Cowley. There were a lot of buffalo in that range so they could get a lot of meat to do that ceremony. They moved over there during the fall, killed a lot of buffalo and dried a lot of meat and made pemmican. They prepared for the winter so that they wouldn't have to go out in the deep snow. They got their winter clothing too—they tanned hides and got ready.

In the Ghost Dance, Porcupine used this ceremony of building four fires as part of it. He must have known something about this ceremony and included part of it in the Ghost Dance when he was doing that. One of Black Beaver's brothers-in-law went out hunting while this ceremony was going on, and you aren't supposed to be out doing that. He got a lot of meat and came back on horseback bringing a lot of meat. He stopped right in front of his tepee. He had an old time rifle and he let it down and the butt hit the ground. It went off and shot and killed him. My mother told me about that accident. All his relatives were crying during the ceremony. That man couldn't wait until the ceremony was over—he had to go. He didn't respect the ceremony, but wanted to show what he could do. My mother told me about all this.

When the Cheyennes were coming back to Montana from Oklahoma [1878–79], there was this woman named Northern Woman. She helped guide the Cheyennes back. She seemed to know when to go, or where the soldiers would be. She sometimes had dreams which helped her know. There was a song that the people heard and the people listened, "Northern Woman, where are you going, it's hard, difficult. But don't get discouraged. Try your best."

Grover Wolf Voice and I talked about this. There's a recording of this song at Busby School. A lady was singing the song.

Now I'm going to tell some other experiences I know. Long ago I went after some keys and somebody came over in a wagon. Eagle Feathers came down to my place in a sled or wagon and told us he was called over to Birney. They were giving away to him at the Christmas doings. So he borrowed a fresh horse to go to Birney. He got back early in the morning from Birney and he harnessed up his horses and left for Busby again. They don't leave home too long—they like to get back. He said, "Why don't you come along?" So there was this white horse he got from Frank Lightning at the dance hall, and he wanted me to ride it. I could never say "no" to anybody. So when we got to Eagle Feathers' home, the house was locked. They had some sort of doings above Busby at Trail Creek and Eagle Feathers' boy had gone and he had the keys. There was a big camp circle. They were having their Christmas doings. So Eagle Feathers told me to get this fast fresh horse and ride over and get the keys and come right back. I rode the big fresh gray horse, a fresh horse. "Don't be afraid to make him go. Don't stop for anything." When I got over there to the camp, the son had gone on, so I took after him. The road was kind of slippery, but I went on. When I got over there where they went, they were gone. Lodge Pole said they just left. They were going back to the dance on the other side of the creek. I caught up with them and told them about the keys. And this Eagle Feathers' son told me, "Why don't you stay overnight? There's an old lady just died, Buffalo Woman, and they have seen her. She might take after you." Willis Bad Horse said, "Take this stick and when you go by her place, go fast and don't stop. Just go ahead and stay with us overnight—they'll break a window and crawl in." "No," I said, "I've got the keys now and I'll go." I started out and I went across, on the old road along Rosebud Creek. When I got to the OD corrals, I saw somebody and my horse looked too. That thing must have come like a bullet and met me right at the crossing and tried to block me. It spooked my horse and it tried to jump on the bank. I passed it and it started after me. I looked back and she had a safety pin to hold her blanket on and she was coming after me. My horse got spooked and really took off, but she kept right behind me. At another crossing, the horse slipped and fell—he kind of sailed in the air and then caught himself and got up again and kept going. This old lady had hold of my horse's tail. I had that stick and I started to hit her with it. She said, "Nooooooooo." She kind of slacked off and then she held on. My horse was going as fast as he could go. At Last Bull's place, there is another dip. She quit chasing me then—I got through!

Right across from Muskrat's place, I met three boys

going to the dance. They were going to that circus tepee. They had a good place to dance. Paul Little Bear, Don Brady, and Jasper Yellow Robe were the boys. They had a lot of Indian perfume on. I told them that this person chased me all the way down. I told them to just shoot. My horse was just whistling. They said if they saw her, they'd shoot. Two of them had pistols. Where White Powder lived, my horse just wanted to go. When we got back, my horse just stopped in front of that house. I jumped off and pulled off the bridle. My friends had already crawled in the window. I run around the house, I thought that thing was going to get me. I couldn't sleep from seeing that person. That old man used cedar on me. We could hear the horses running. I was trying to sleep. An old man came to me and said, "If you listen to me, you'll live a long time. Look at me, I try to tell people up here that's living here to listen to me, but they won't and they're dying." This old man said, "One thing I want you to do." And I could see myself inside the Sun Dance tepee. "This is one thing I want you to go through." It was sort of like Spirit was telling me. So I do Sun Dance. I'm getting old now, but I never showed off in the Sun Dance. I didn't pretend or I didn't use it against anyone. I used it in a good way. I didn't abuse it. The Pines got scared up there and they moved to Lame Deer. They'd see a light that went across the valley and landed on top of those red hills. They really believed my story about that thing chasing me. This Spirit or person comes to me in my dreams. I went to the Mennonite Church and got baptized to see if it would go away, but it's still around me.

50. Thrashing Time

INFORMANT: WESLEY WHITEMAN

50a. These people are thrashing. The man on the left is Black Ree, the middle man is Williams, a white man, and Charles Yellow Robe [Davis Bailey] and Charles Teeth. The white man was the boss. Later after Williams left, another man named Mr. Ed Baldwin came. They were hired by the government. The superintendent was John Buntin. J. R. Eddy left. Red Hair was his Indian name. Then Buntin came about 1909 or 1910. We used to call him "Big Button." They all used to plow and have gardens. They went up on the divide and camped and plowed. I was still going to school. Then they moved down into Muddy—about twenty families plowed together, brought their walking plows and horses. It was community work. They didn't quarrel with one another. They did not kick on one another.

The government brought in a lot of white man horses, mares and studs, draft horses. Individuals bought them. There was a man named Selway who lived the other side of Sheridan, close to the Big Horn Mountains. He brought the horses. Also they brought cattle. Individuals got cattle—the ones that were not issued out were marked C.I.D., the government. The brands they used were numbers. My dad's number was 106—that's government cattle. There were a lot of wild animals—bobcats, badgers, wolves, fox, coyotes, deer, antelope. We didn't kill them for fun. You could hear them at night and see them. They must have a reason for being here on earth. It's good that they're here. Nobody was killing them to get rid of them. Even the prairie dogs, they were not poisoning them. All these animals were on the reservation and we had a lot of horses and cattle and nobody said "capacity." We used the whole reservation. We all got along together—no complaining. There were not any fences, just the reservation fence around the border.

They used to have Sun Dances and social dances. I witnessed Animal Dances. We hardly ever had the Arrow Worship up here, the Arrows were down south. They had the Animal Dance twice that I know, the Massaum. In these Animal Dances, they imitate the animals. The Contraries paint yellow and they shoot these animals with a bow and blunt arrows. They spit blood and blue and white flames-like. If a Contrary shoots one of the medicine men or medicine women, they have a spiritual power to spit out this way. Some of them have looking glasses too and they flash them when they're dancing. One represents a fox and he's leading the pack. They go in front of the tepees. Sometimes he charges back to the people behind. Some are painted yellow and their plume feathers are yellow.

We had a sawmill on the road to Ashland and we started to build houses and we were farming. The sawmill man was named David Winston. He was named after the cigarettes [joke]. He had one eye. From there I came down to Lame Deer to day school. No road and the snow was deep. I must have tried pretty hard to go

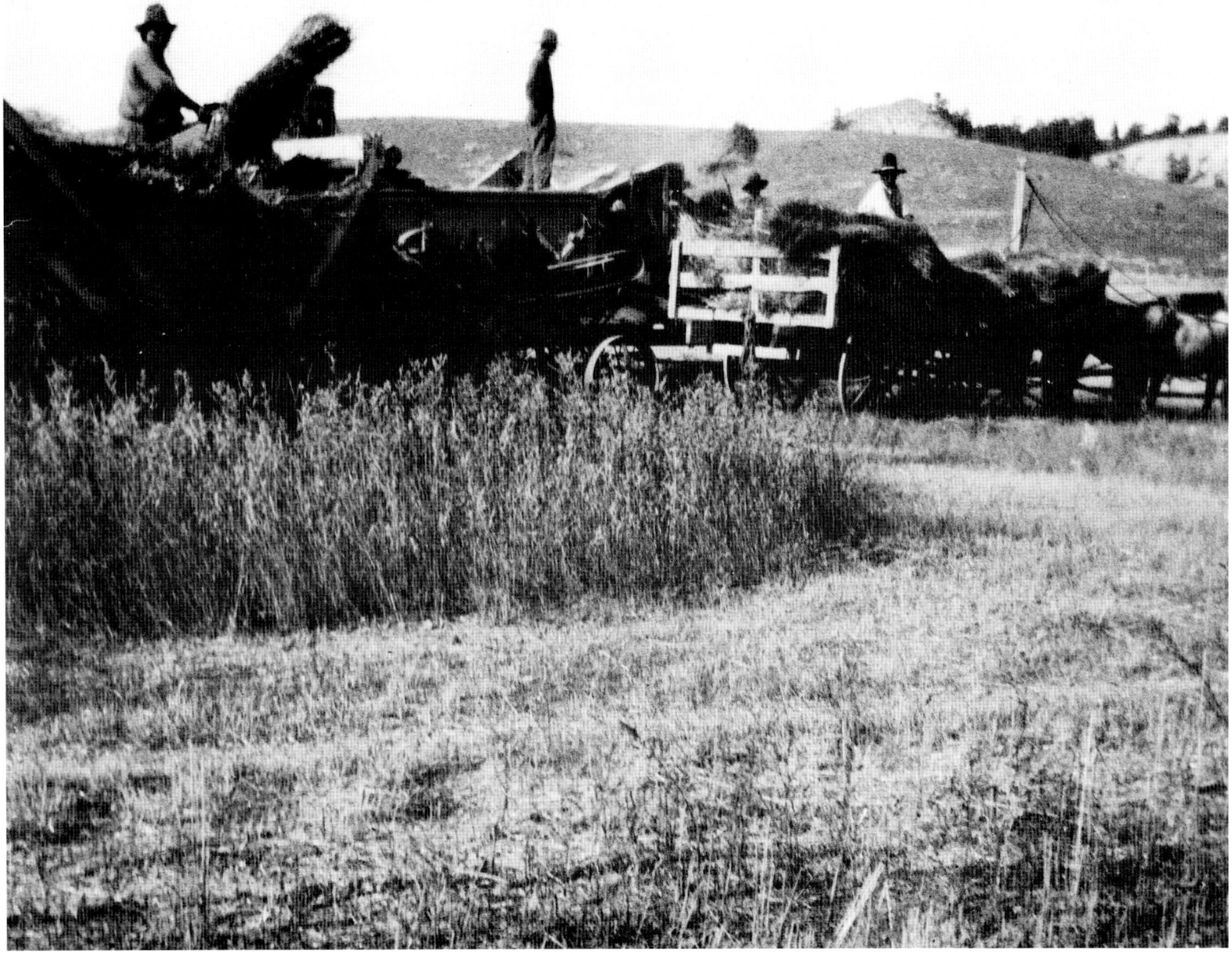

to school. I'm not educated. In my own ways, I'm telling a little of my experiences. I did go to school a little bit. I got as far as 6th grade and then the agent took me out of school. My father went blind so they wanted me to take care of him. His eyes were the color of yellow. So I quit school to take care of him. My dad shot himself in 1897 when he was a young man, but he lived. He was a part-blood. I have a brother named John. He was born at Fort Keogh. My dad was a scout for the Army. He shot himself with an Army gun. This was later after he was working at the Agency stable. Indian doctors doctored him. There was White Bull [or Ice] and Tall Whiteman and Lodge Pole. They used a snake and a turtle to help stop the bleeding. My dad worked at the stable. One of the bosses got after him and he took it pretty hard so he shot himself. He had a tough time when he was growing up. He only saw his dad once or twice at Fort Laramie. My dad was really little and they called him "Little Whiteman." His father told him, "I might see you at Fort Laramie." My dad could outrun a lot of people. He could run 100 yards in 8 seconds. It looked like he could fly. My dad's father was named Markis Whiteman. My dad's mother died in Custer, S.D., and she's buried there. She was buried on a scaffold. We went back and visited the place. In two or three years, it began to decay. My grandfather's half-brother named Lodge Pole visited there later. The bones were on the ground scattered. So he picked them all up and put them back together. Later when he was older, he got all shaky. If you handle bones, that's what happens. They gathered the bones and put them close to War Bonnet Creek in kind of a cave. That area was close to Newcastle, Wyoming. There was a Catholic Mission near there. They took two Cheyennes, Wooden Thigh and Big Beaver. They wanted to adopt them and have them go to school there. They kept them about three years and they were herding sheep and cattle. Those two boys seemed to have no home. They didn't seem to have any folks. They'd come to the Cheyennes sometimes, but then they'd go back to the Mission. They'd get hungry with no folks. They could speak some broken English and they could write their names. My dad spoke a little English. When he wanted to say "Thank you," he'd say "Much obliged." Wooden Thigh's other name was "Hair Curled Up" because he had curly hair. This name Big Beaver seems to be a part-blood name now, but Big Beaver was living with the Catholics and the white people before. Lodge Pole, Big Beaver, and Wooden Thigh became Chiefs, but my father was not a chief. He was one of the Dog Soldier leaders. There were different societies: Bowstrings, Crazy Dogs, Dog Soldiers. My dad is half white man. I have some kind of record of my dad's name and some of these crazy people today sure wanted that. I had this paper and these people are really after that. I lost track of it. I might have given it to John Toews. He was going to make copies of it—some kind of paper that belonged to my dad. It has a record of my dad talking to me about my grandfather being an offi-cer at Fort Laramie, about being in the Army and what he had to do. Also about Fetterman. They must have killed this Fetterman. [Capt. William Fetterman was killed in the Fetterman Fight in Wyoming in 1866, when Cheyennes and Sioux were defending their territory from encroachment of the Bozeman Trail.]

I rode there on a bus about three years ago, from Oklahoma to Fort Laramie. I had taken part in the Arrow Worship in Oklahoma, one of the only ones left.

50b. Wesley Whiteman was the uncle of John Woodenlegs and thus comfortable in giving him this information.

The Animal Dance he refers to (also called the Massaum) was one of four major religious complexes of the tribe, which also included the Sun Dance, the Sacred Arrows, and the Sacred Medicine (or Buffalo) Hat. The Animal Dance is now forgotten, probably because of the many highly specialized roles that had to be learned and perpetuated. The Sun Dance was the only one of the four shared with other tribes. For a concise overview of these ceremonies, see The Cheyennes *(Hoebel 1960).*

We do not know what story lies behind the statement that Wesley Whiteman's father's father was an officer at Fort Laramie.

The extended commentaries by Wesley Whiteman included here and above provide a number of details valuable to students of Cheyenne traditional religion.

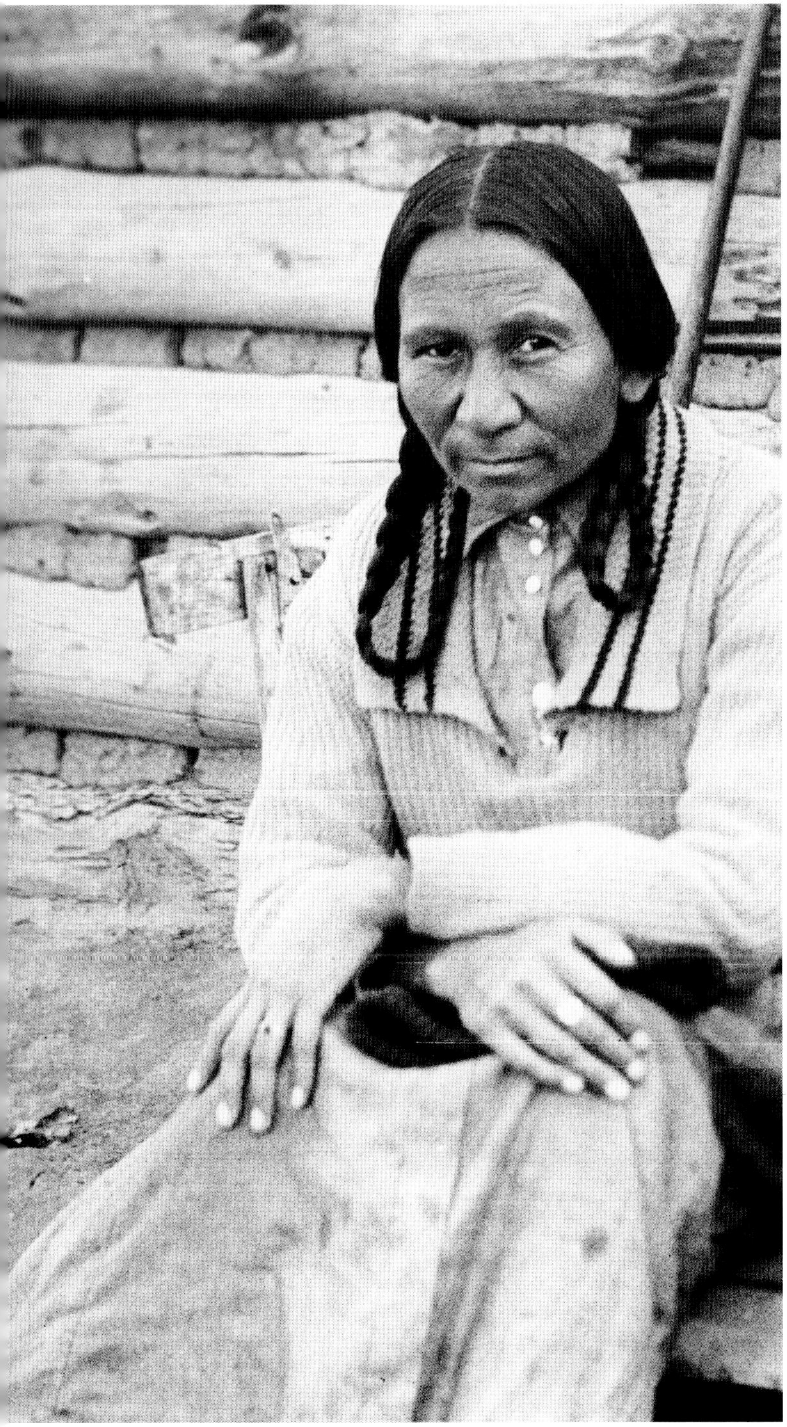

51. Jenny Little Whiteman

INFORMANT: WESLEY WHITEMAN

51a. This is Jenny Little Whiteman. My father and his Southern Cheyenne wife lived on Rosebud Creek between Lame Deer and Busby when she was born. She was the last one of their children because her mother died when she was born. When she was a day old, she was taken to Ashland to Shoulder Blades. They had a baby so both babies were nursed by Mrs. Shoulder Blade and they cared for her until she grew up. They adopted her and raised her, but there were no adoption papers. Jenny was raised over at Ashland and she went to the Mission school. We used to go over there and camp by the school just to visit her. They sent the Mission Children off to school at St. Peter's close to Great Falls. They went to Fort Shaw. Charlie Whiteman, my older brother, went to school there. He also went to Haskell and then to St. Louis University. He came home on vacation and he died. He had a good education and maybe could have been a leader.

Jenny married Albert Foote.

51b. The Last Contrary: The Story of Wesley Whiteman *(Schwartz 1989) documents the life of Wesley Whiteman.*

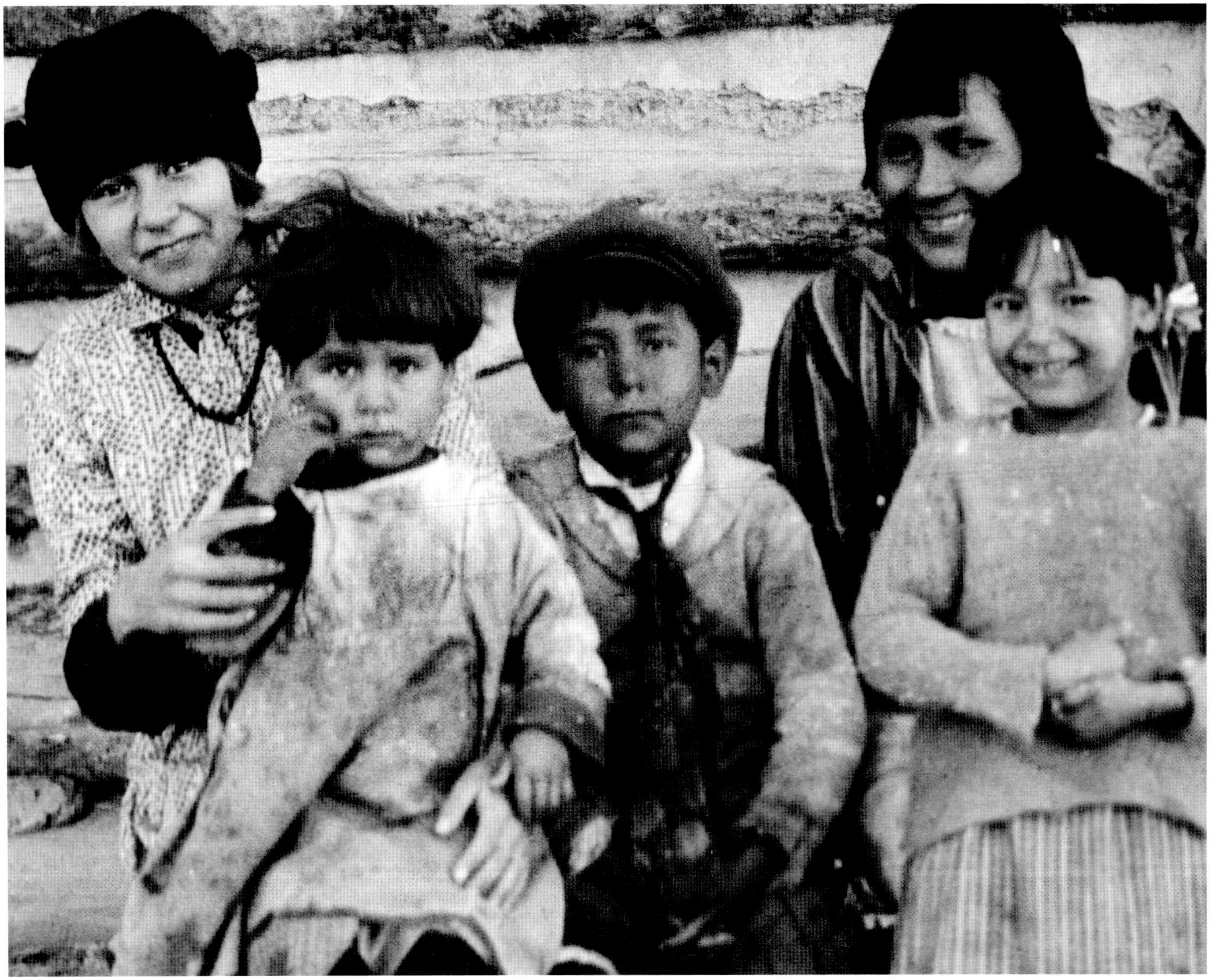

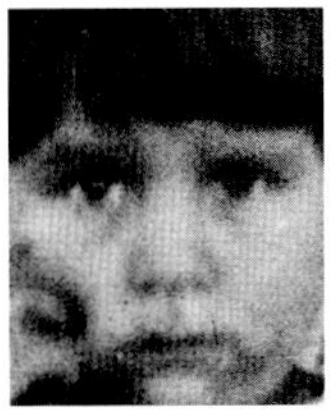

52. The Foote Family

INFORMANT: JOHN WOODENLEGS

52a. Jenny Little Whiteman married Albert Foote from North Dakota, a Sioux. They were married here on the Cheyenne reservation, and they lived here. Sometimes Albert Foote would go back home to his reservation, sometimes he took his family with him. He always kind of lived close to Shoulder Blades. My father, Thomas Woodenlegs, was a brother-in-law to Pius Shoulder Blade. They all kind of worked together, Albert, Pius, and my father. The three families would camp together, build fence or plow or cut down posts for timber. So they always kind of worked together and I knew these people. I know Jenny and Albert. Albert was a good dancer at the dances they had.

There were four children: Thelma with Eva on her lap, Eddie Foote is in the middle, and then Bertha. It seemed like their mother died kind of early and that Thelma kind of took care of these children. They called her "mother" because of the early death of their real mother. Albert didn't go back to he own reservation after his wife died. He stayed with the Cheyennes and with his children there. He married another Cheyenne lady, Yellow Nose, and he had one or two children from that marriage.

When Thelma grew up, she married a Sioux from South Dakota named Stephen Two Two. Bertha married Ray Harris from Muddy, and Eva married Allen Rowland. Eddie Foote married in Lame Deer to Margaret King. All of the Foote children are still living, they all have children and grandchildren now. They all went to school at the Mission school.

The other girl in the picture is Bernice Medicine Top from Birney. Later she married a man by the name of Charles Trusty.

52b. Charles Trusty was a black man with one leg who lived on the Tongue River north of the reservation community of Birney, where he operated a repair garage. There is also a white community of Birney seven miles away across the river. This led to a story in the Billings Gazette *a number of years ago titled "A Tale of Two Birneys," which might have amused Charles Dickens.*

The intermarriage of Sioux and Cheyenne tribal members remains common, as does the "matrilocal" residence pattern, in which the husband moves to join the wife's people.

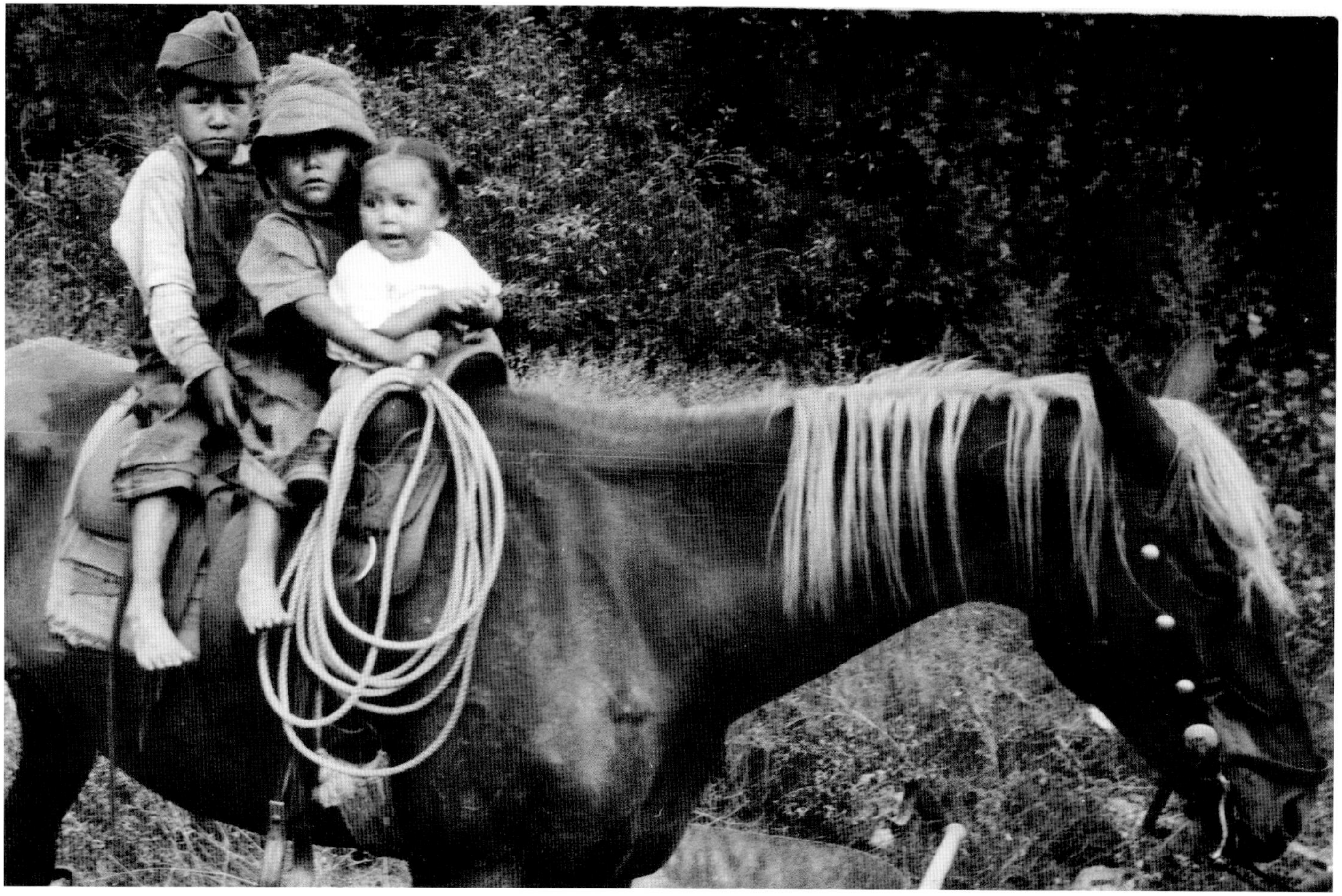

53. Three on a Horse

Informant: Wesley Whiteman

53a. These are the children of my brother Stanley and his wife Grace. Their names are Aaron, Willis, and Mary. The horse was named "Blondie." It belonged to Stanley.

53b. This original caption in particular led us to seek additional caption material for the pictures here. Many of these originals reflect important aspects of Cheyenne cultural emphasis: here, for example, the horse's name was as important as the names of the children. In this extended series of Whiteman pictures, the informants as well as the interviewer might have been getting somewhat tired—thus the brevity of the commentary in some cases.

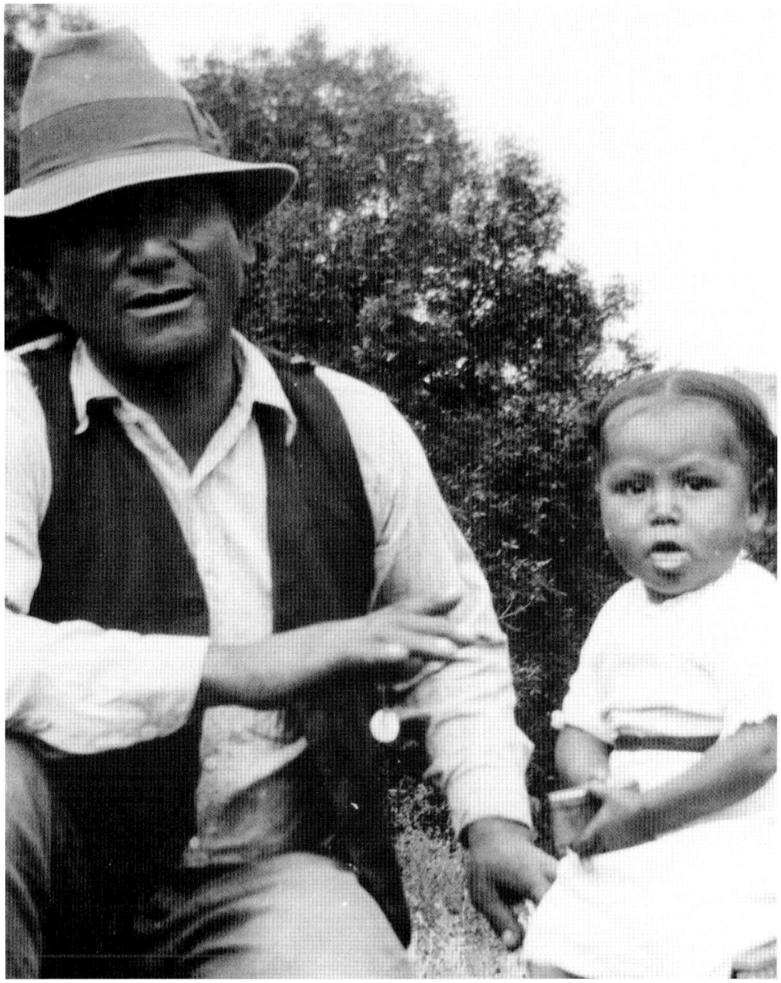

54. Stanley Little Whiteman and Daughter

INFORMANT: JOHN WOODENLEGS

54a. This is Stanley Little Whiteman and his little girl, Mary. Stanley was Wesley Whiteman's brother.

54b. In the intricate patterns of the Cheyenne kinship system, a father's brother was counted as a father and a mother's sister as a mother. This provided extra parent and child interconnections and responsibilities. The mother's brother would be called "uncle" in Cheyenne, and the father's sister would be called "aunt," in the fashion familiar in mainstream U.S. society.

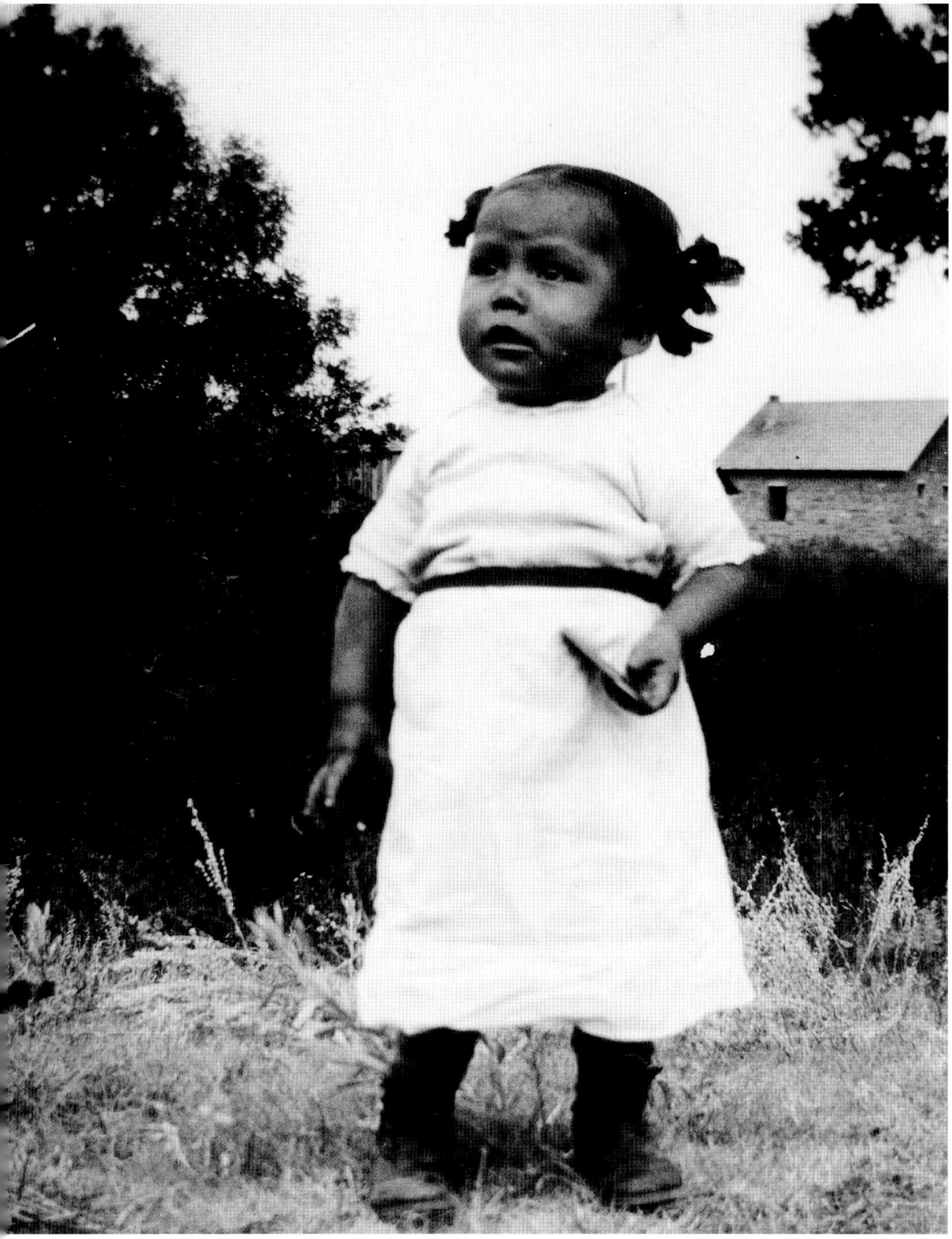

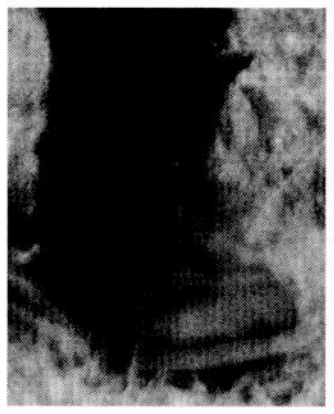

55. Mary Little Whiteman

INFORMANT: WESLEY WHITEMAN

55a. This is Mary Little Whiteman, Stanley and Grace's little girl.

55b. In traditional times Cheyenne girl children were brought up to respect a brother's wishes, especially concerning marriage, and in general to behave with extreme formality and chastity in relationships with men. In We Pointed Them North *Teddy Blue Abbott describes his rejection by a beautiful Cheyenne girl he wished to marry, who did not think he was good enough for her (Abbott and Smith 1939).*

Hanging Woman Creek near Birney, Montana, was named after a Cheyenne woman who committed suicide. This probably resulted from disagreement with a brother's marriage choice, though it might have been due to some other insult or perceived shame. Such suicides by women were not uncommon.

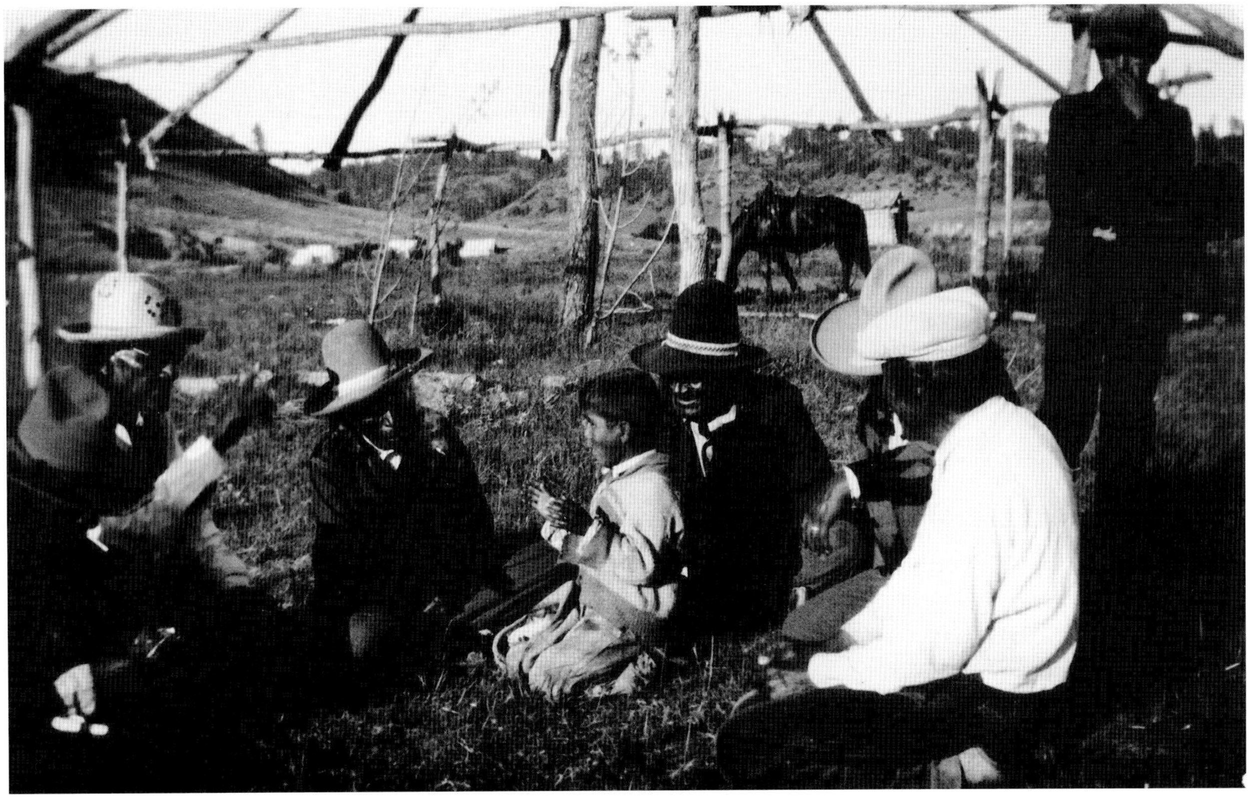

56. Making Sign Language

INFORMANT: JOHN WOODENLEGS

56a. The people in this picture (left to right) are: Charles Spotted Elk, Big Beaver, Grease Dog, Aaron Little Whiteman (boy), Charles Little Eagle, Killsback, John Squint Eye. I don't know the one standing.

After the Sun Dance people sit around and talk. Aaron's mother was mute so he learned sign language. Aaron is from Lame Deer. Spotted Elk and Squint Eye were also from Lame Deer. Squint Eye was an Indian Judge. He was a Southern Cheyenne married to a Northern Cheyenne. Grease Dog and Killsback were from Busby and Big Beaver and Little Eagle were from Ashland. These men must have liked to visit in sign language with this boy. They liked to visit after the Sun Dance—it's peaceful and good after the Sun Dance.

56b. Marquis attended four Sun Dances: September 1927 at Lame Deer, June 1928 at Lame Deer, June 1931 at Lame Deer, and June 1932 at Busby. All of these took place during the period when the Sun Dance was forbidden by federal decree (Weist 1978: 23–49).

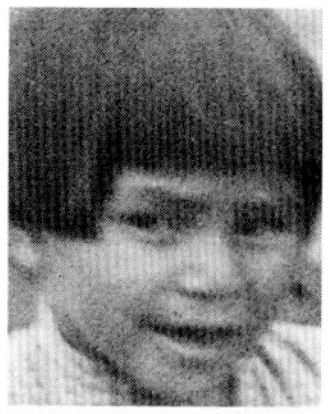

57. Getting Ready to Cook

INFORMANT: JOHN WOODENLEGS

57a. These two girls are Irene Sanchez and Florence Little Whiteman, maybe about six years old. They are sitting near an open fire with all the cooking pans ready. The lady sitting with the shawl, I don't know. These girls went to school in Busby. This picture is in front of a tent and there is a car alongside. Florence Little Whiteman is a niece of Wesley Whiteman.

57b. Reservation food supplies were different from the mostly meat diet of earlier days. Flour, sugar, and coffee had become familiar as treaty issue goods, as well as rice—given the Indian name "maggots" because of the obvious resemblance.

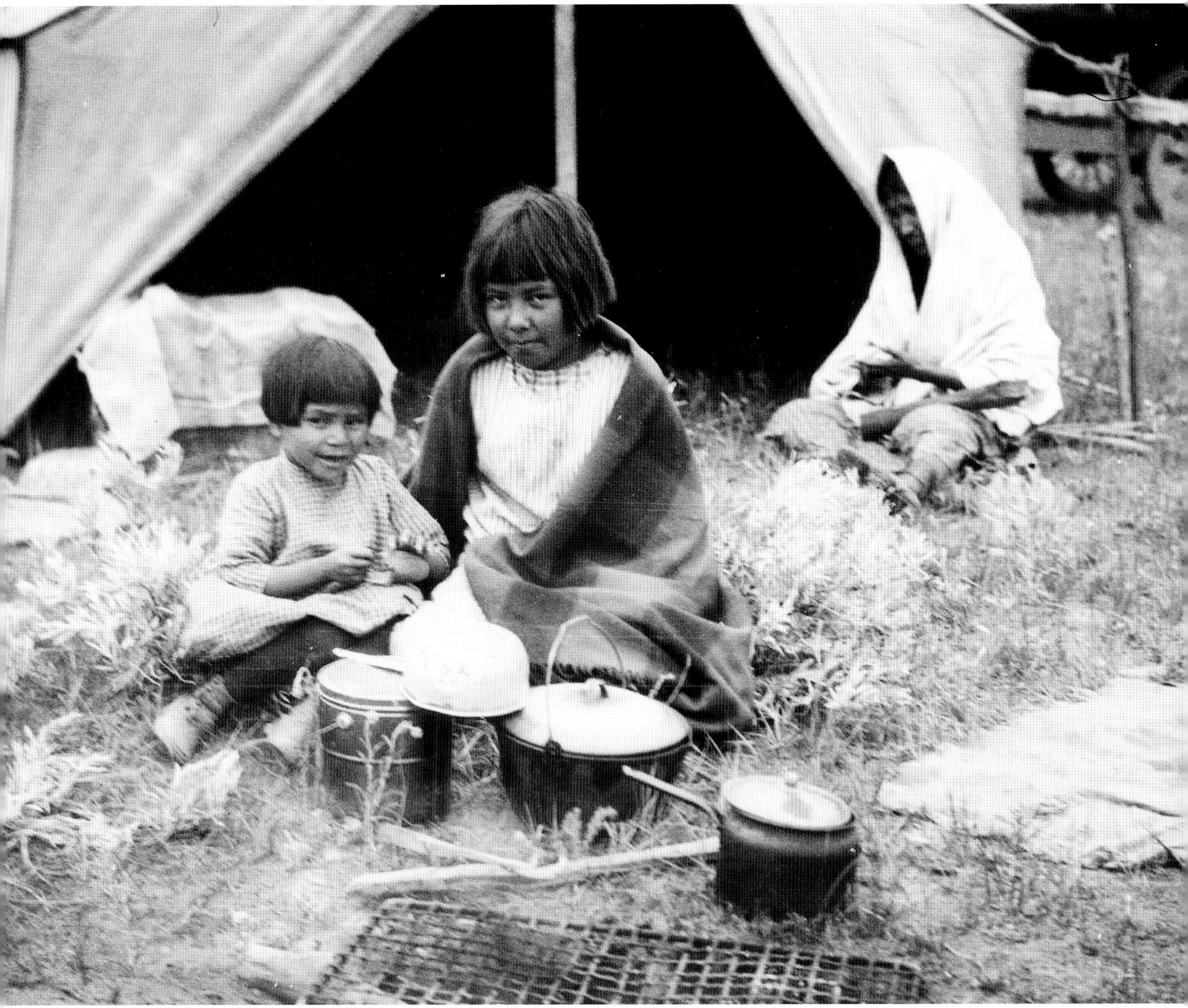

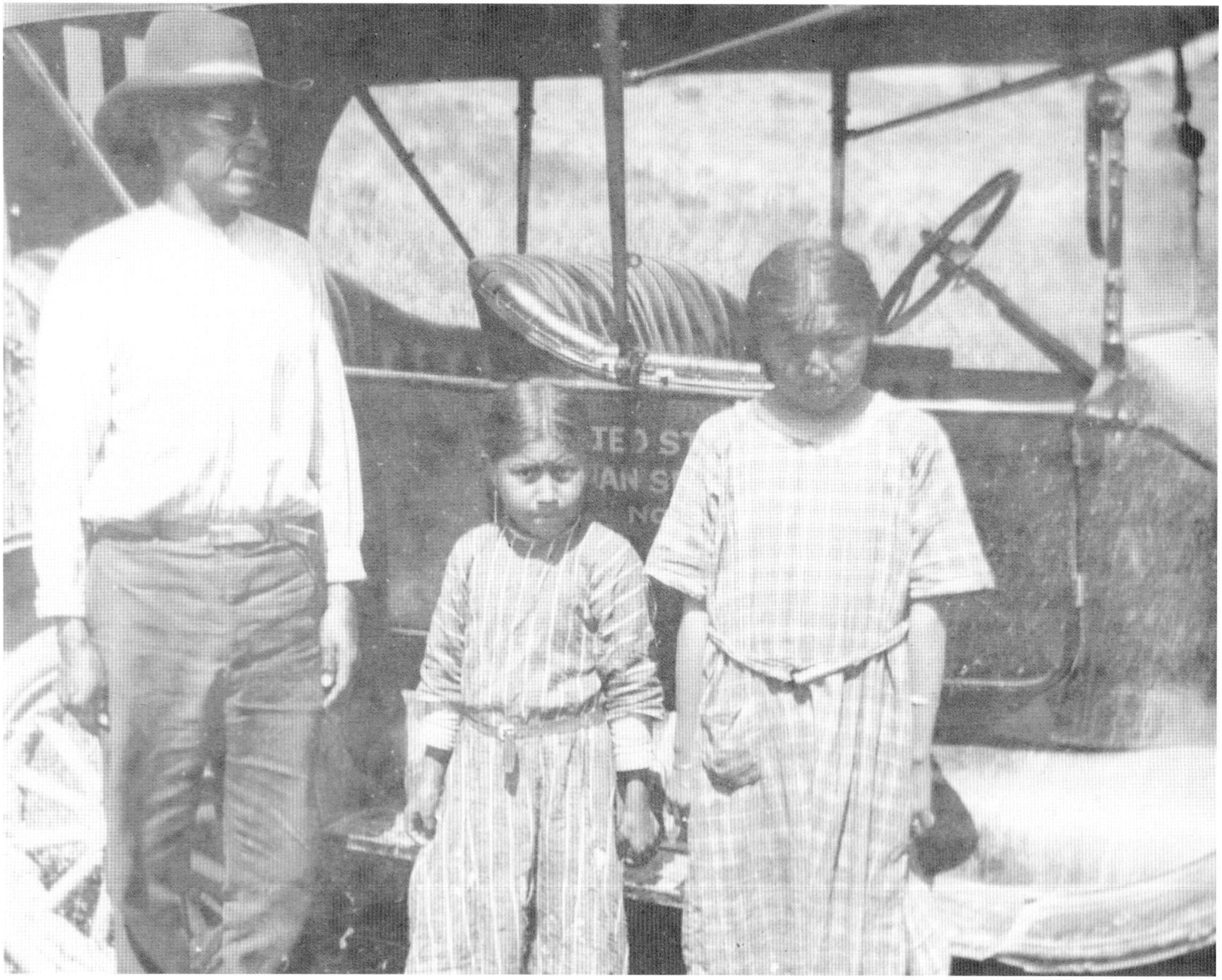

58. Frank Little Wolf and Daughters

INFORMANT: JOHN WOODENLEGS

58a. This picture is of Frank Little Wolf and family. His wife was named Shell Woman. They had three daughters: Mae, Susie, and Annie. These two are Susie and Mae. Frank was down to the Mennonite Church and I guess he had joined that church with Rudolph Petter. He was the judge of Indian court after John Squint Eye and some of the older ones had been judges.

His older daughter was Mae Little Wolf. I went to school with her, and also Susie. Frank could speak English. He was the one that put up the last Animal Dance on the Northern Cheyenne reservation. That dance I can just barely remember. Some of my relatives were in on it. I guess Frank left all the Indian ceremonial doings and went to the Mennonite Church. He was trained to preach the gospel. They had horses and wagon, but it seemed like he was one that owned a Model T Ford. The car had "United States Indian Service" marked on the door. Now they used to send him to Birney village to preach the gospel to the Birney people. He'd go over there on horseback or in a wagon or in his Model T Ford, maybe stay overnight or two nights. But these people were over there and I knew some of them, like Willis Medicine Bull. He thought it was something new that this man came over and he would like to go. He went to church two times and both times Frank would talk about black doings. What the Cheyenne meant was sinful doings—he called them black doings. And he talked about the Devil—he kept talking about the wrong doings, trying to caution the people. So Willis Medicine Bull, the second Sunday he went, took Frank aside and asked him, "I heard you came over to talk about God and the Bible and something good. Now two times I have come here and all you talk about is the Devil and the black doings. When are you going to talk about God?"

To change from one of the highest ceremonial ways of worship to God—the Animal Dance—where a lot of Cheyennes took part, and where the Contrary people take part—to change from that to go to church and be a missionary must have been quite a change. He was a kind man and he talked good to people. His daughters all got married and they had children. Annie was the youngest. Susie is still alive.

58b. I knew Willis Medicine Bull and his wife, Annie, in my days as a teacher at the Birney Day School between 1954 and 1958. They lived out on their allotment along Tongue River at that time. Medicine Bull was himself a Contrary and a participant in the Massaum or Animal Dance. His commentary here indicates typical Cheyenne tolerance for various religious traditions.

The Mennonite mission pressed more strongly for elimination of traditional Cheyenne religious practices than did the Catholics.

The Contrary group was a kind of clown society very important in Cheyenne tradition. It had a major role in the Animal Dance (for a concise depiction, see Hoebel 1960). Fear of the thunder and the "backward" performance of certain ceremonial activities were a part of Contrary belief and ritual.

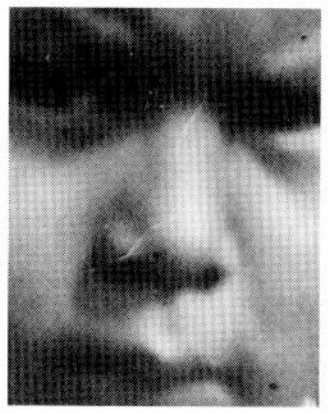

59. Mrs. Frank Little Wolf and Annie

INFORMANT: JOHN WOODENLEGS

59a. This is Shell Woman, the wife of Frank Little Wolf, with their daughter, Annie, whose Indian name was "Little Corn Woman." This picture was taken in 1925.

59b. Cheyenne Indian names (such as Little Corn Woman) continue within families, in addition to the usual non-Indian system of naming, which operates according to mainstream custom on all reservations today.

Mother and daughter are dressed up here for what might have been a picture taken on Sunday or at some special event.

The dress worn by Mrs. Little Wolf is the homemade type known as a camp dress, which replaced buckskin when cotton goods became available.

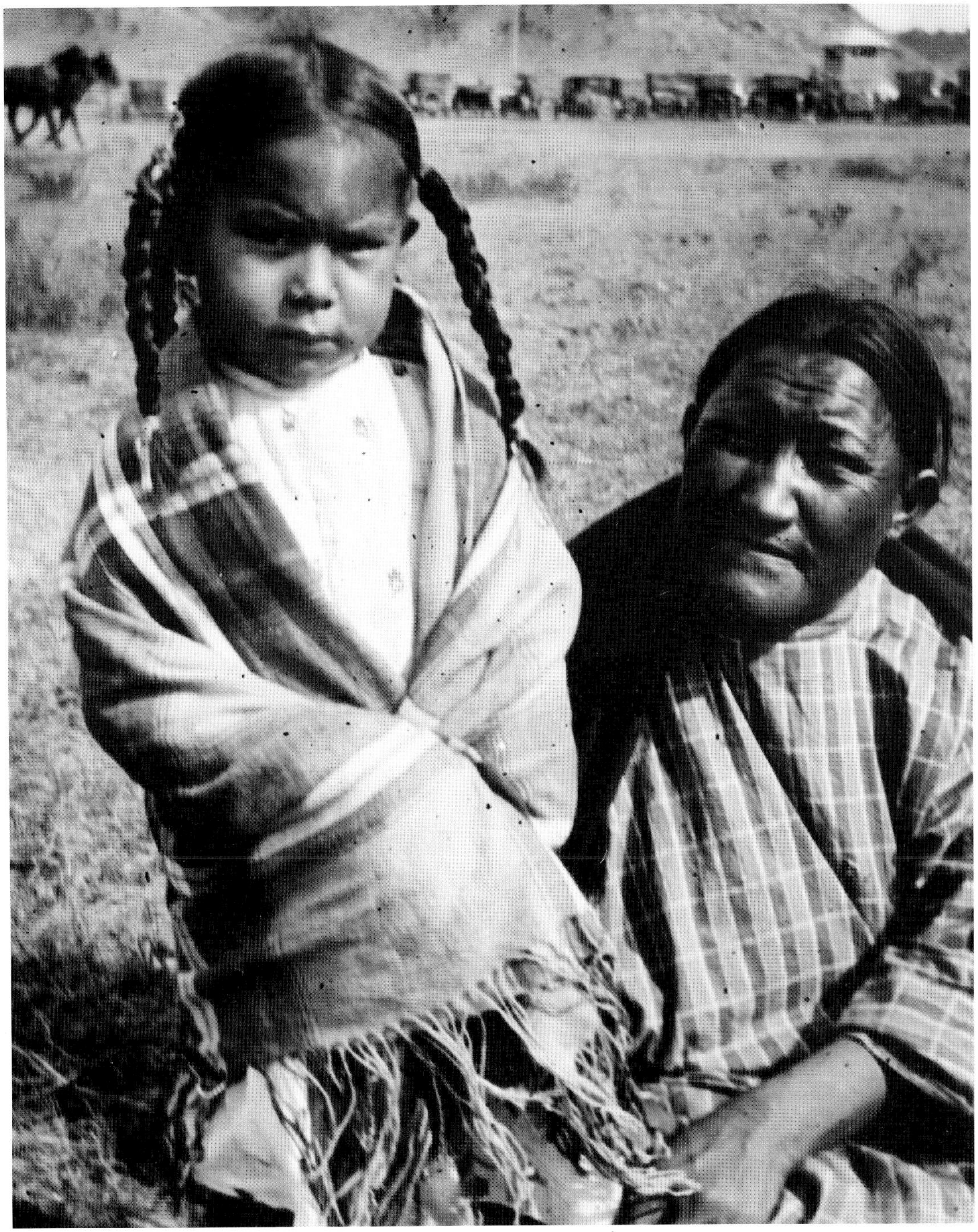

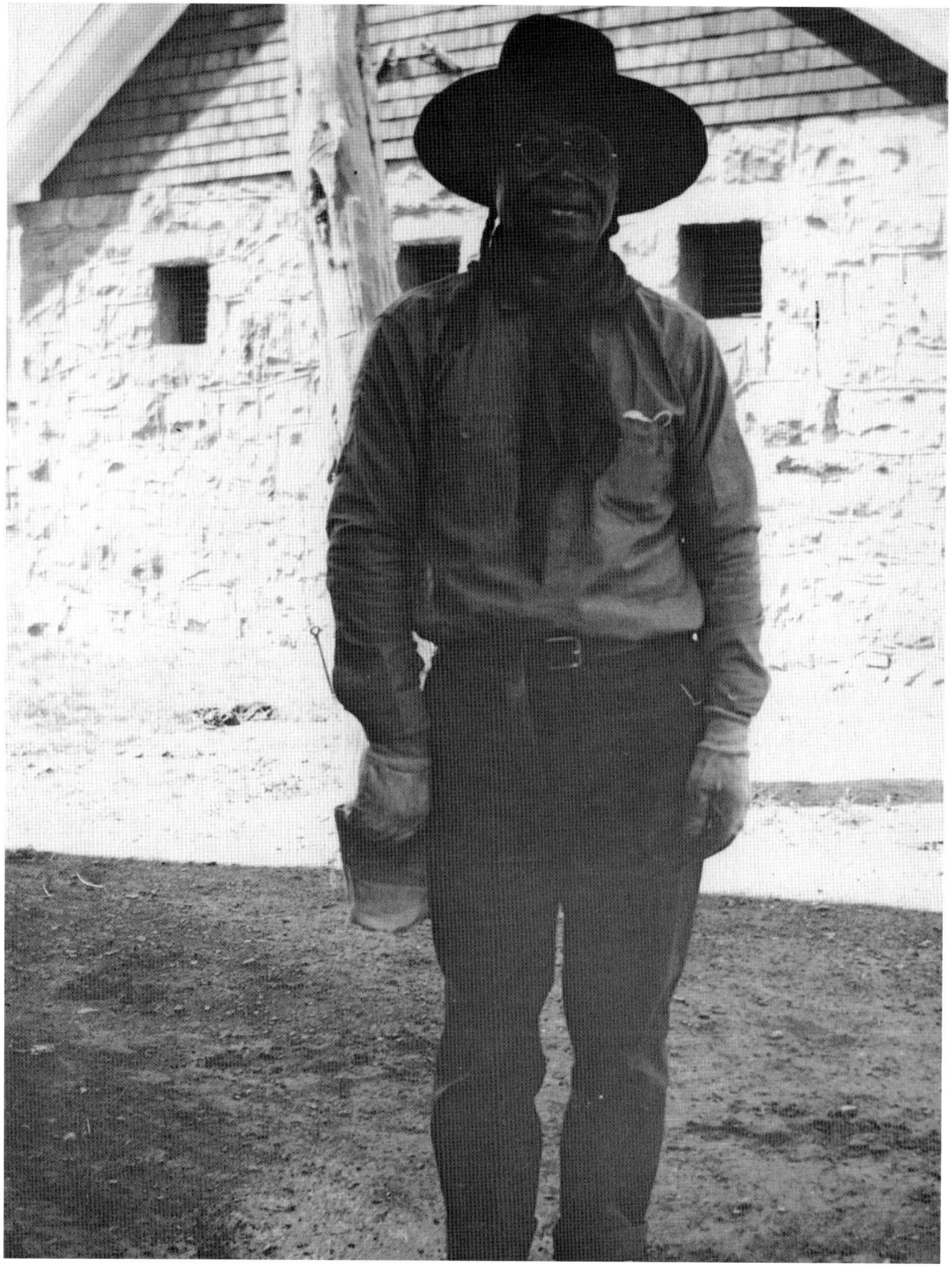

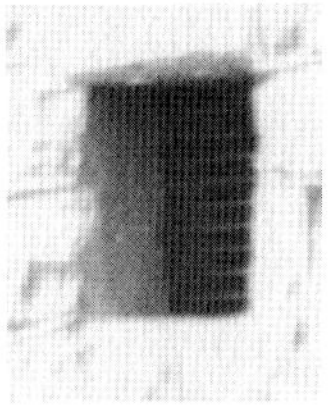

60. Charles Teeth

INFORMANT: JOHN WOODENLEGS

60a. This is Charles Teeth. He was one of the scouts at Fort Keogh. He lived on Rosebud Creek, close to Lame Deer. He got one of the places that white people had left–houses, barns, corrals. He lived there and had good horses and cattle. He had a son named John Teeth. When John was in school he played football. He was also a good runner. Then there was a daughter named Belle Teeth High Walking. She married Floyd High Walking. Charles always fixed up eagle feather bonnets and buckskin clothes. These old men always seemed to look good and dress good. They were always good to people, we all respected them. They shared their pension money with relatives and friends.

Charles had black and white pinto horses for a team. When they had harnyack races, he put them in and they always won. For an Indian to own a pinto team–they were a well matched team. They were not very heavy, they were to travel with. Charles lived on Rosebud Creek there close to his daughter. His son lived in Busby. His daughter, Belle, fixed up a book telling about some of her life and experiences. I am just kind of thankful that I knew these people. They had cattle and horses and put in a garden and wheat and oats. They worked hard. They done real good.

60b. Early white settlers–actually squatters on reservation land–were obliged to move elsewhere after legal designation of the reservation in 1884.

Photographs by Christian Barthelmess of the scouts who were stationed with the army at Fort Keogh can be found in A History of the Cheyenne People *(Weist 1977). See also* Photographer on an Army Mule *(Frink and Barthelmess 1958).*

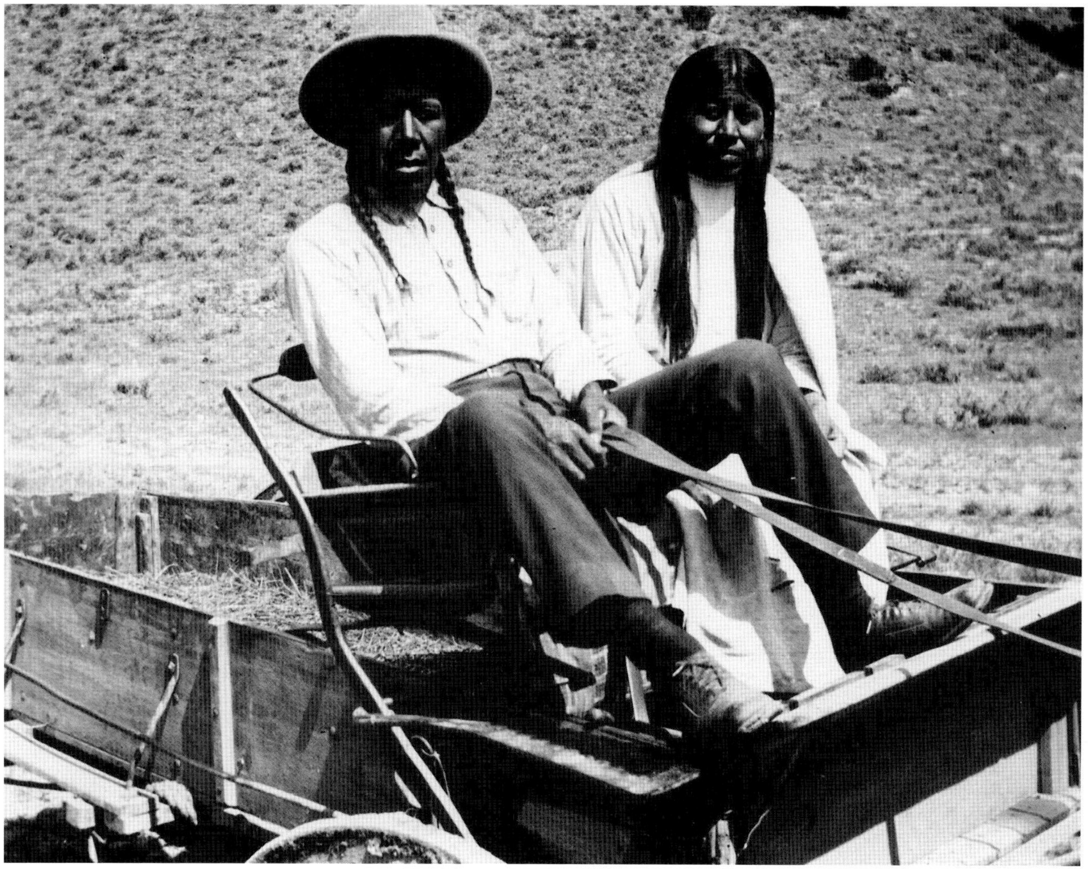

61. Floyd and Belle High Walking

INFORMANT: JOHN WOODENLEGS

61a. This is Floyd and Belle High Walking. I knew these people and I was a friend of their son. They really treated me good. They lived at the same place of his father. He always had a good team of horses, good wagon, and good saddle horses. He was one of the first cattlemen on the reservation, or the cowboys who handled the cattle. He didn't go to school but in his good Indian way, he had a lot of common sense. I learned a lot from these folks when I was over there playing with their son, George. Floyd had a good herd of cattle. His brand was 337. He had some great big cows, good looking cattle. He had a good house, barn, and corral. Good garden, grain. He lived on Rosebud Creek just below the mouth of Muddy Creek. His father-in-law, Charles Teeth, lived close there. Also Black Ree. They were all good people. Mr. High Walking was a good friend with

Peter Rising Sun. They always kind of worked together on roundups when the tribe had big herds of cattle, big herds of horses. In pictures of these old cowboys with long braids on, they have boots on that are up to their knees, really high top boots. They wrestle calves in a corral and Floyd High Walking is one of them. Being a good, sincere worker for the roundup, when they round up cattle, they cut out a cow and a calf to brand. They always got Floyd to do the roping. He hardly ever would miss a calf. He'd rope them on the head or heel them. He was noted as being a good roper. One place they thought they would have a contest with the Brown Cattle Company. They had 500 head of cows and calves and they were going to have Floyd and one of the Brown boys who was a good roper, a left-hander, to rope this 500 head. They were going to brand them. They would ride into the herd, rope a calf, and drag it out so it could be branded. I guess Floyd never did miss once and Mr. Brown, the white fellow from white Birney, missed one calf, so he lost. The Cheyennes won the contest.

High Walkings always abide by the rules and regulations. They sent their children to school. They had five boys and two girls, a big family, but he took good care of hem. One of the superintendents came to the reservation, John Artichoker, and he said, "Let's have a cleanup campaign. Everybody clean up around their homes, their ranches, the places where they live, and we'll give first place, and second, third, fourth, and fifth prizes." High Walkings were fourth generation people, and they already had great-grandchildren. They won the first prize, having their home neat inside and outside. Anything they had was piled up neat, they had a good corral, pasture, fences up, and the barn was in good shape, harness and wagons, horses and saddles. Everything had to be checked, and they won the first prize—these old folks. They knew how to take care of things. His wife had gone to school some, but he didn't, but he had good common sense and his good Indian way to do things right.

In this picture he's with his wife in a wagon with his horses. I always see him wearing boots, but here in the picture he's wearing oxfords. He has braids on and a big hat. His wife's hair is not braided—that's the way they looked if they lost a loved one in the family, maybe one of their relatives. Later on they braid their hair again. They are good looking people. They belonged to the Native American Church, and they did go to some churches other times, but they used the Native prayer way too. They belonged to different clubs and organizations. She did a lot of beautiful beadwork. They had good beaded outfits. She was one of the first members of the Northern Cheyenne Arts and Crafts group; she really helped out with it. She'd come to the meetings and encourage people. Her father was Charles Teeth, a good old man. She always kind of took care of her father. Floyd's father used to work down below along Rosebud Creek among the white people there, when they were farming. They all moved down there, camped down there to help with cleaning out the brush along the Rosebud Creek. I guess those people liked them, they were good workers.

61b. The commentary by Woodenlegs here gives some of the positive highlights of the Indian farming and cattle period. Cheyenne men made superb cowboys and remain nostalgic for the stock-raising way of life, which was promoted among them and then destroyed by white competition and adverse economic conditions.

For Belle's life story, see Belle Highwalking: The Narrative of a Northern Cheyenne Woman *(Highwalking and Weist 1991).*

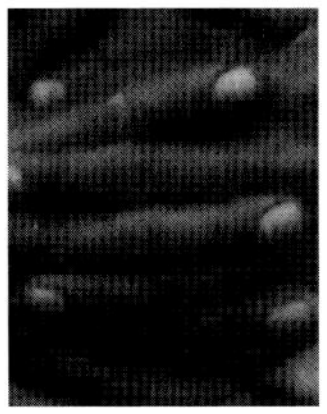

62. John and Josie Stands in Timber and Son

INFORMANT: JOSIE STANDS IN TIMBER

62a. This was taken at Lodge Grass. One of the Crows wanted to buy a race horse, told John to bring it there. They gave us a team of horses, harness, a brass bit, almost-a-brand-new wagon, and money as well, for that race horse. Sure wanted that race horse!

Burton is the baby. He was maybe three at that time. He died when he was four. Burton was the only one with us that time. The other children were at Old Lady's [Mrs. Ridge Walker, Josie's mother]. John Stands in Timber was born in 1884 and died in 1967. He was recognized as an historian and tribal leader among the Cheyennes.

62b. These pictures of a young John Stands in Timber and his family were taken by Marquis at the 1926 fiftieth anniversary commemoration of the Custer fight. John Stands in Timber was for many years tribal historian for the Northern Cheyennes. He pressed me into service as a writer of his historical memories soon after I met him while teaching at the Birney Indian Day School in 1955. Our co-authored book Cheyenne Memories *has remained in print ever since its publication by Yale University Press in 1967.*

Stands in Timber and Marquis knew one another, but each was doing his own investigation among old-timers during the 1920s and 1930s and may have felt that the other was unimportant as a source of information. Stands in Timber did not speak of Marquis to me.

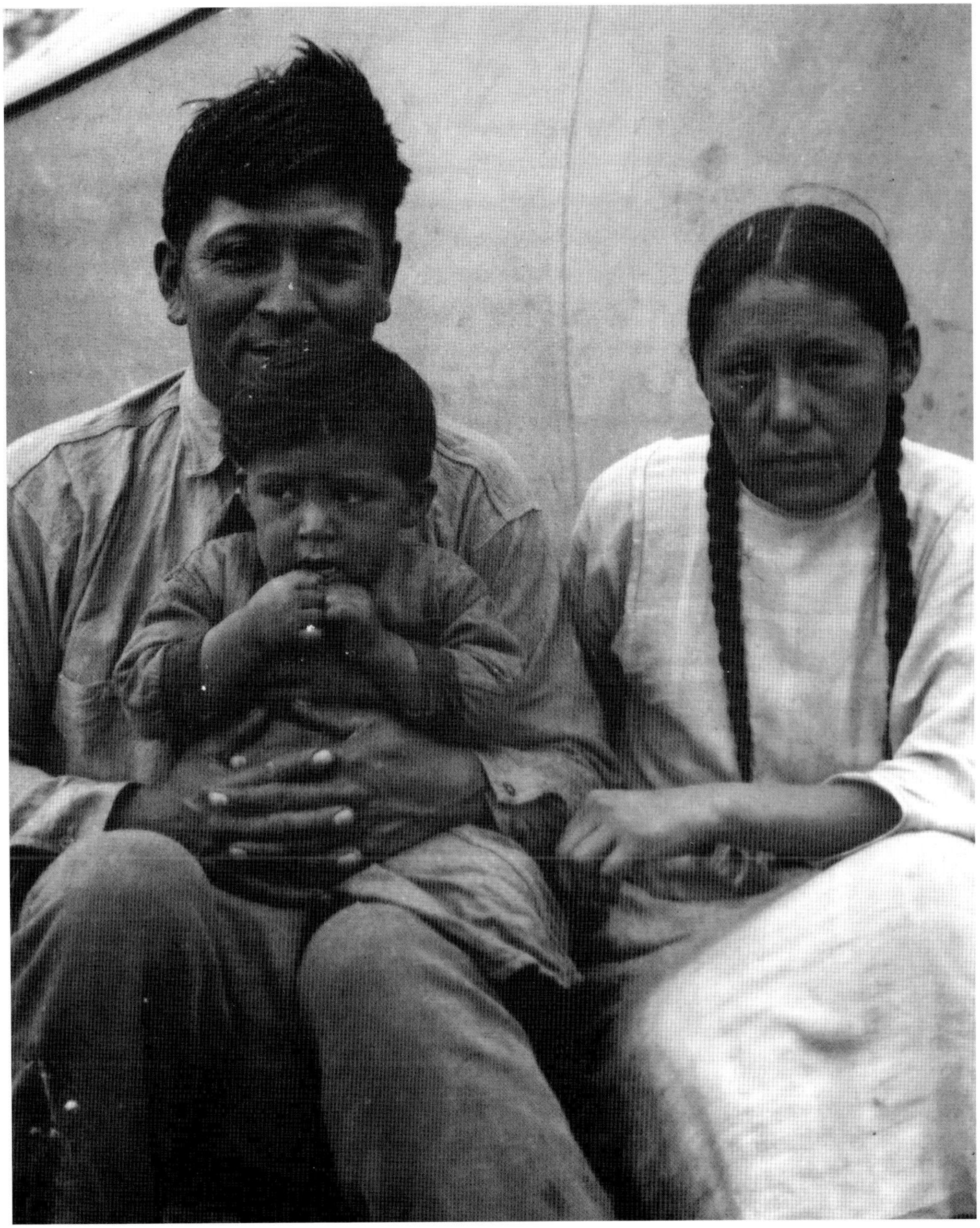

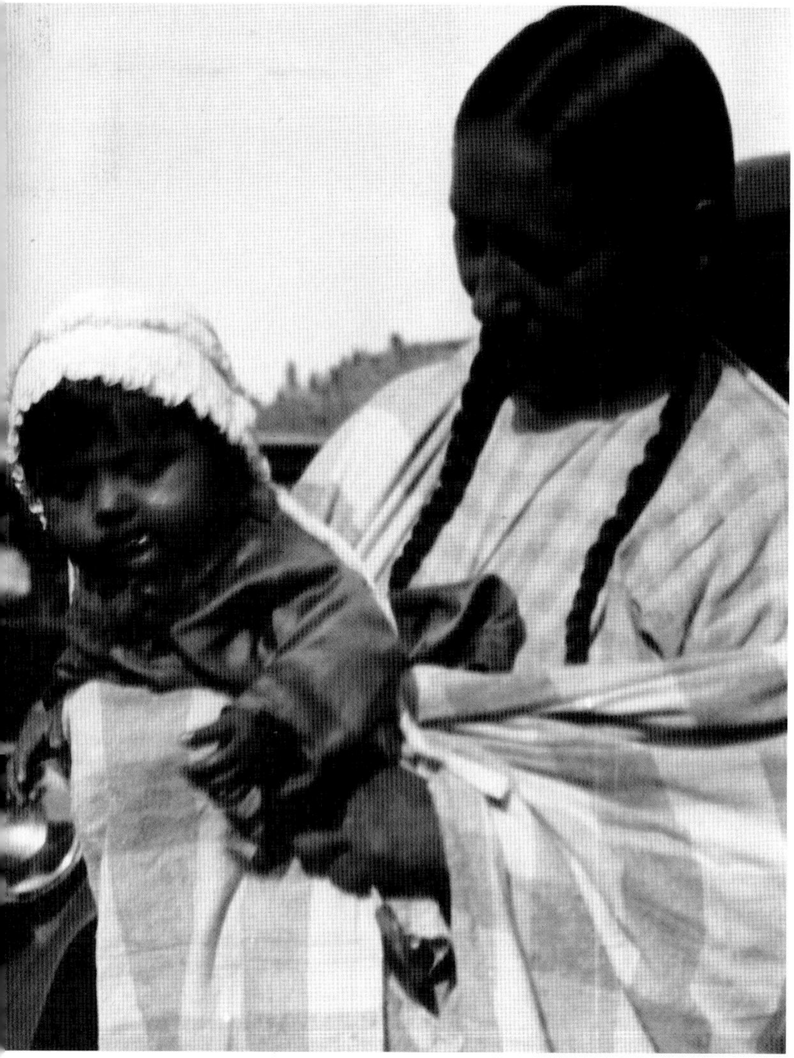

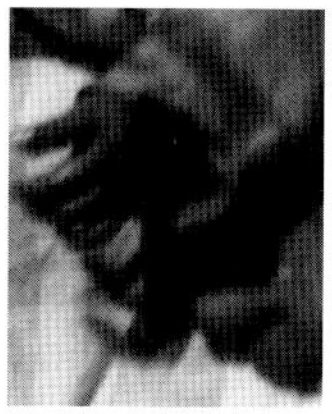

63. Josie Stands in Timber with Her Daughter Elva

INFORMANT: JOSIE STANDS IN TIMBER

63a. That's Elva! Elva Stands in Timber.

They need to have a race track someplace here at Lame Deer. Mrs. Willis Rowland was with us. We were sitting in a car and Willis' wife was in the back. A man called Marquis came along. Asked if he could take our picture.

Elva is our fourth child. First Josephine, then Burton, then Junior, then Elva—two years apart.

63b. Of Josie Stands in Timber's seven children, only Josephine, Elva, and their brother Emmett survived to adulthood.

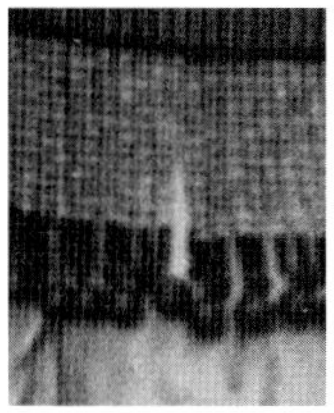

64. Josephine Stands in Timber Glenmore

INFORMANT: JOSIE STANDS IN TIMBER

64a. This is my daughter, Josephine. The picture was taken in 1926, at the 50th anniversary of the Custer fight. We were camping. Ethel Ridge Walker, my mother, made the dress and leggings. Josephine's Cheyenne name is White Buffalo Woman. She is married to David Glenmore.

64b. The ongoing use of Indian names is again documented here. As a grown-up, Josephine Glenmore performed outstanding work in Northern Cheyenne linguistics in association with linguist Wayne Leman of Hardin, Montana.

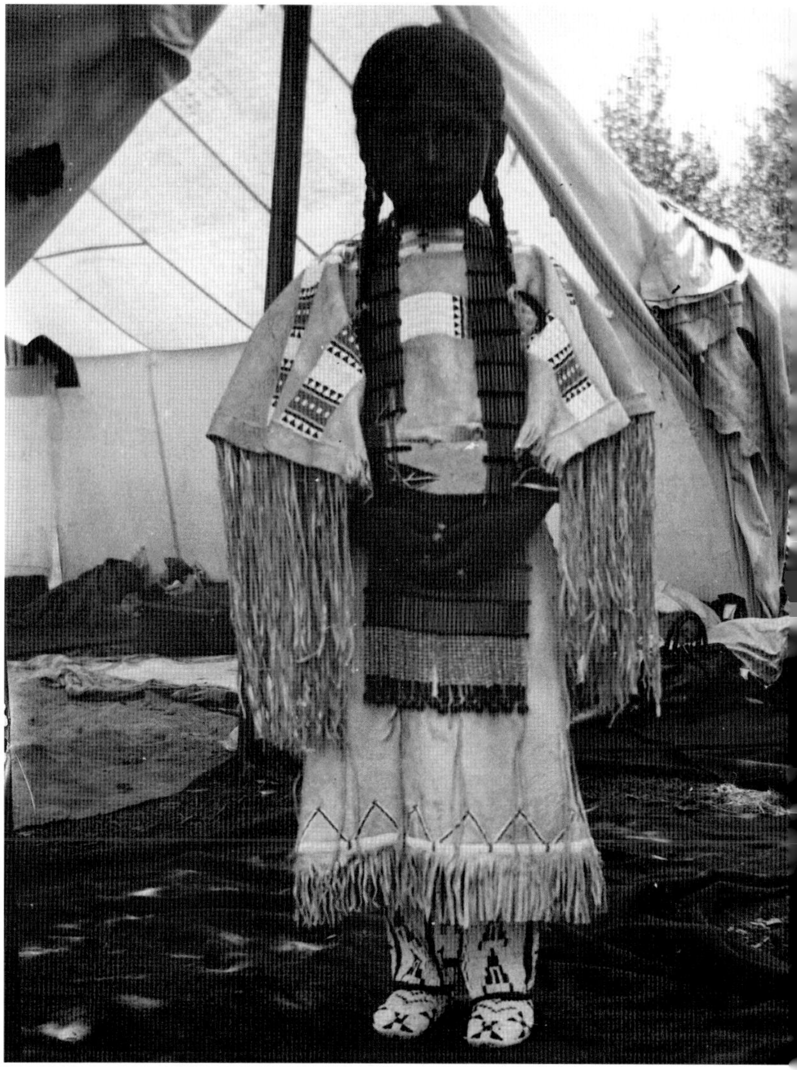

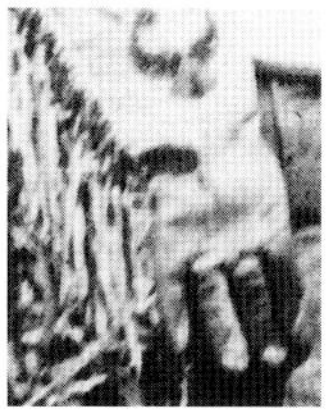

65. John Stands in Timber, Jr.

INFORMANTS: JOSIE STANDS IN TIMBER AND ELVA STANDS IN TIMBER FISHER

65a. This was taken in 1926 at the Custer Battlefield. They were celebrating. There was also a rodeo, horse racing going on.

John Jr. was about the same age as another boy, Frank Grasshopper. That boy's parents gave the outfit to Junior. I forget the boy's father's name, but he was the son of Grasshopper. So the boy was the grandson of Grasshopper. He is still alive—the son, Frank Grasshopper.

His mother made the vest and the cuffs. When Junior died, the beaded cuffs were given to Lee Lone Bear. He still has the cuffs. Burton, when he died, wore this beaded vest. He was buried in the beaded vest.

65b. Mrs. Stands in Timber and her daughter Elva most likely did not wish to speak further here to the interviewer (probably Woodenlegs) about their deceased son and brother.

Burial of cherished items of regalia with the dead is exemplified here.

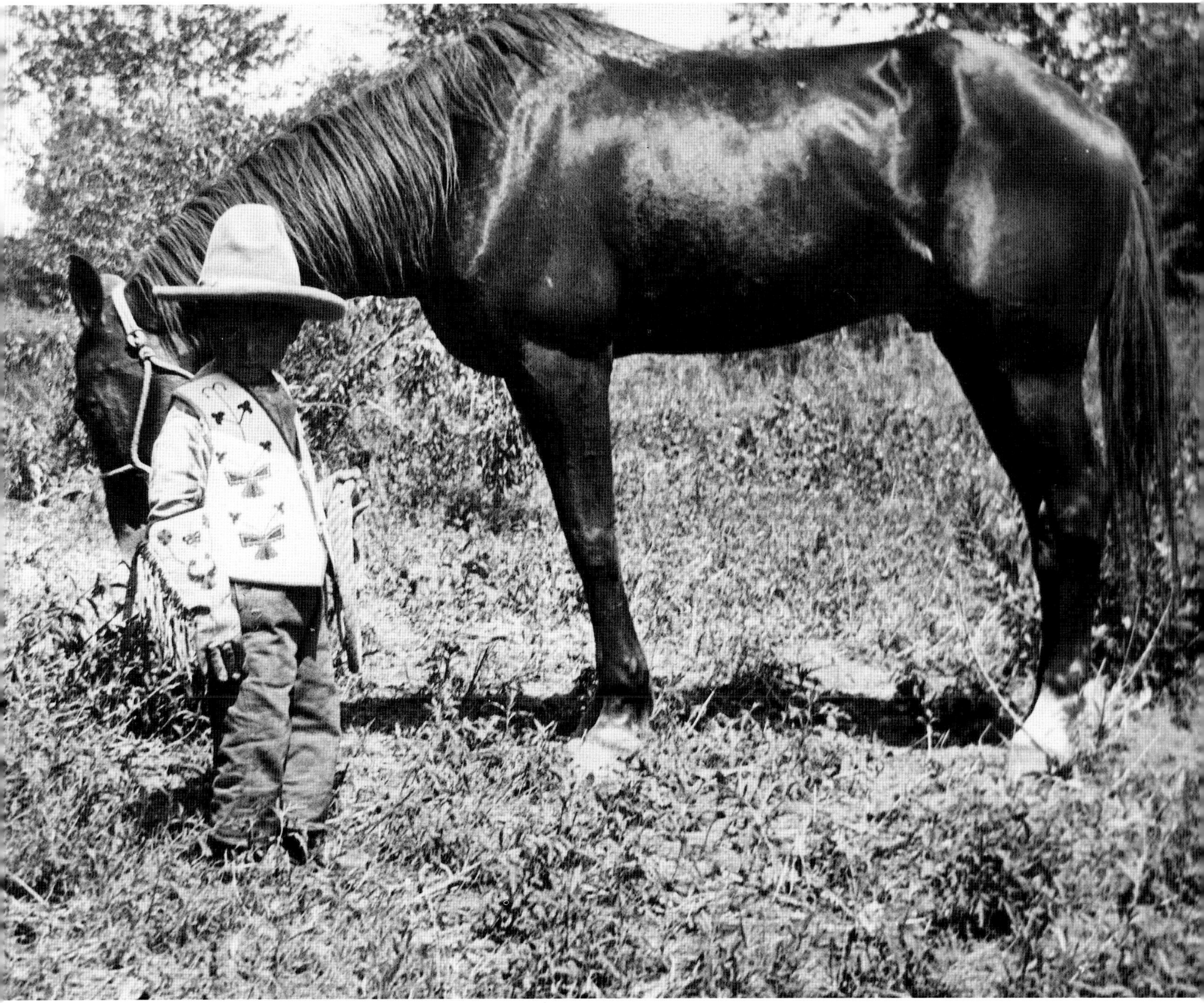

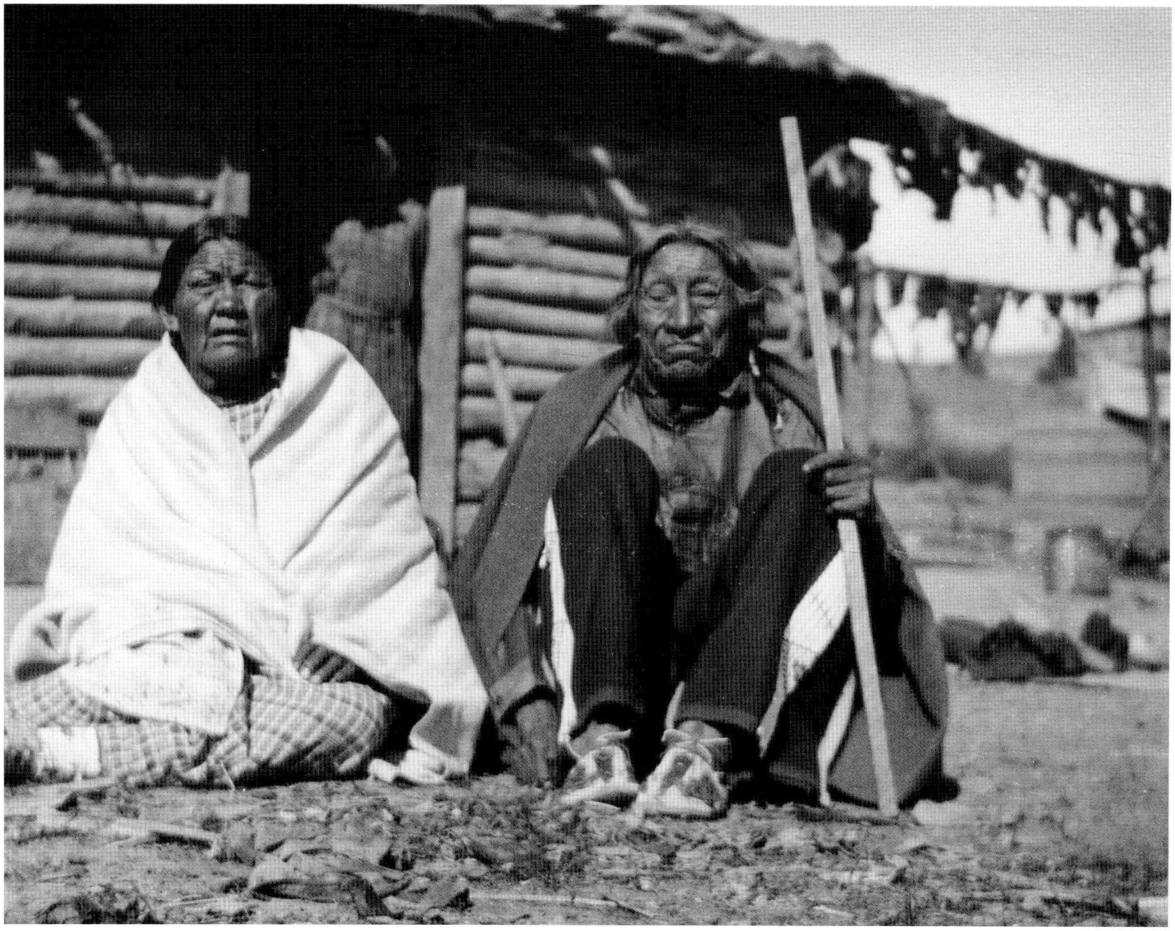

66. Arthur and Ellen Brady

INFORMANTS: JOHN WOODENLEGS AND JULIA WHITE DIRT

66a. **Woodenlegs:** This is a picture of Arthur Brady and his wife Ellen. The lady in the background is their daughter Mary. His Indian name is "Braid Locks." He was enrolled originally as Braid Locks. Later it was changed to Brady. Their children were Charles Whistling Elk, Appears in the Morning (one boy who died), George Brady, Alex Brady, and Mary Brady Tall Bull.

Arthur really knew how to butcher and he taught a

lot of people how to hunt and butcher. He hunted buffalo, deer, elk, antelope. He and his wife knew the old way of how to preserve food. This picture shows meat drying over poles that are used just for that purpose. After the meat got dry, it would be roasted over the coals of a fire or held close to the embers, or it would be boiled before it was eaten. Sometimes the dry roasted tenderloin would be pounded up to shred it and pulverize it. Then it would be mixed with fat and dried chokecherries or June berries to make pemmican.

Julia White Dirt is a granddaughter of Arthur and Ellen. Julia is my aunt. My mother and Julia's mother were cousins. Julia's parents were Charles Whistling Elk and Josie Whistling Elk. Julia is a great-grandmother herself now.

Julia: My grandmother's name, sort of nickname, was "Little Medicine Woman," but her real Indian name was "Hard Ear Woman." She didn't have her ears pierced, and she didn't want them pierced. My grandfather was wounded during the fight when the soldiers attacked Black Kettle's camp [Sand Creek Massacre, led by Col. John Chivington, 1864]. He got hit in the leg during that battle. After he got hit, somebody else shouted for the people to flee to the hills and my grandmother started to run. My grandmother had told me these stories of what happened there and a lot of things in the past. Their experiences she would tell her grandchildren. They lived on Muddy Creek between Busby and Lame Deer, going south on Muddy Creek on the right prong of the forks of Muddy. This picture shows their house and all the dried meat hanging. They always had plenty to eat. If they got too old to hunt, their sons hunted.

My grandfather was hit in the back of the leg. He was on horseback when the soldiers charged. He saw a child running and crying and he picked her up and put her behind him. He took her to the place where the others were running to the hills. The soldiers had charged on them in their camp even though they had put up a white flag. Black Kettle had been told his camp would be safe if he put up a white flag, and if the soldiers kept coming, put up an American flag, and they would be safe. Black Kettle had done this, but the soldiers kept coming. My grandfolks got away. They were already married at this time. After they got away from the soldiers, not long after that, my father, Charles Whistling Elk, was born. When they got up north here, he was still a baby. Another baby had been born during this flight north. That other baby was the mother of Josie Stands in Timber.

My grandfather was over 100 when he passed on. When he was 100 years old, he could see good, hear good and he talked good. He was not senile. He was still active. Even when he was old, he still rode horseback. That girl in the background of the picture is their only daughter, Mary. There were four boys and one girl.

66b. This picture was taken in 1925. The change of a translated Cheyenne name (Braided Locks) to a more mainstream-compatible English-language name (Brady) often took place when Indians were being shifted to the general U.S. naming system at the early agencies. See Cheyenne Memories *for a description of this process, in which the name of a household head was extended to all members, with English surnames added (Stands in Timber and Liberty 1997: chapter 16). For an overview of the very complex world of North American naming practices, see the* Handbook of North American Indians, *vol. 17,* Languages *(Sturtevant 1978).*

67. Charles Whistling Elk

INFORMANT: JULIA WHITE DIRT

67a. This is my father, Charles Whistling Elk. He belonged to the Crazy Dog Society. They lived in log houses. They were warm. Some of the new houses today are not warm. These houses are made out of boards, you almost freeze to death.

The way my folks and grandfolks lived was peaceful and they all got along good. They were healthy and didn't get sick. They ate jerky meat—about all they went after was flour and coffee. They didn't have all this white man food like today. They never were sick or diabetic either. People at one time started to move into the communities. They didn't stay on their places. When my folks were older, sometimes at night they would tell stories of the past. We children would all sit around and listen. They never told anything bad or gossip about people. They only talked about good things. We always liked to hear the stories. We never made fun of anyone—even older people—we respected them. If some older person came, we invited them to sit down and we would give them a cup of water. We never made fun of anyone—we were taught to respect people. We really respect old people. You didn't run back and forth in front of them. Now the kids just hop and jump and run by them. We seem to joke about our older people now—the children don't seem to respect them. Younger people seem to be forgetting the Spiritual ways. At our home here, we try to carry that on—to tell our children and grandchildren to respect that Spiritual way of life. I believe in Spirit and the Spiritual way of living—the Sun Dance and the fasting on the mountain. I believe in these good worship ways. I have my own children and my grandchildren. There's a big family of us. We also travel to Bear Butte to help people and to pray. I take prayer cloth offerings and I pray. I pray for people who are ill and for soldier boys. My father always talked to us in a good way—to respect the worship ways, to respect people and to be good to people.

67b. The Crazy Dog Society referred to here was one of the three original military societies or soldier bands of the Northern Cheyennes. The others were the Elks and the Swift Foxes. According to John Stands in Timber, three similar societies among the Southern Cheyennes were the Red Shields, Bowstrings, and Dog Men (Stands in Timber and Liberty 1997: chapter 4).

Confusion exists in contemporary popular use of the term "Dog Soldiers" to mean any warrior group pledged to particularly heroic rear-guard action. Marquis believed the correct usage of this term was for whichever military society was acting as camp police at a particular time. See his chapter "Indian Warrior Ways" in Keep the Last Bullet for Yourself *(Marquis 1976).*

Bear Butte is the Cheyenne sacred mountain near present Sturgis, South Dakota, where the people believe their culture hero Sweet Medicine brought the Sacred Arrows to the tribe and gave them rules to live by, including the strict law against intratribal homicide. Pilgrimages are still made by Cheyennes to worship at this place.

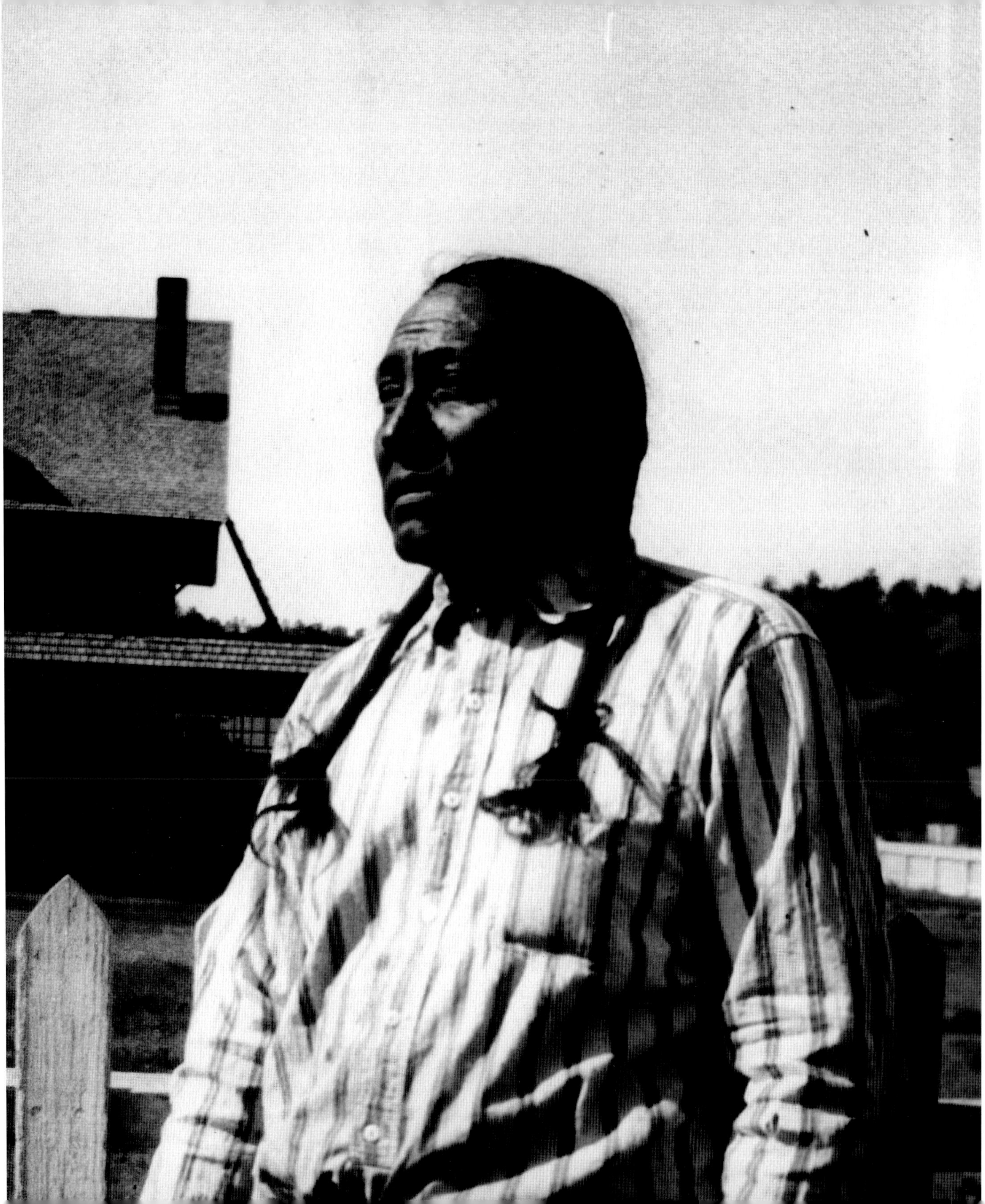

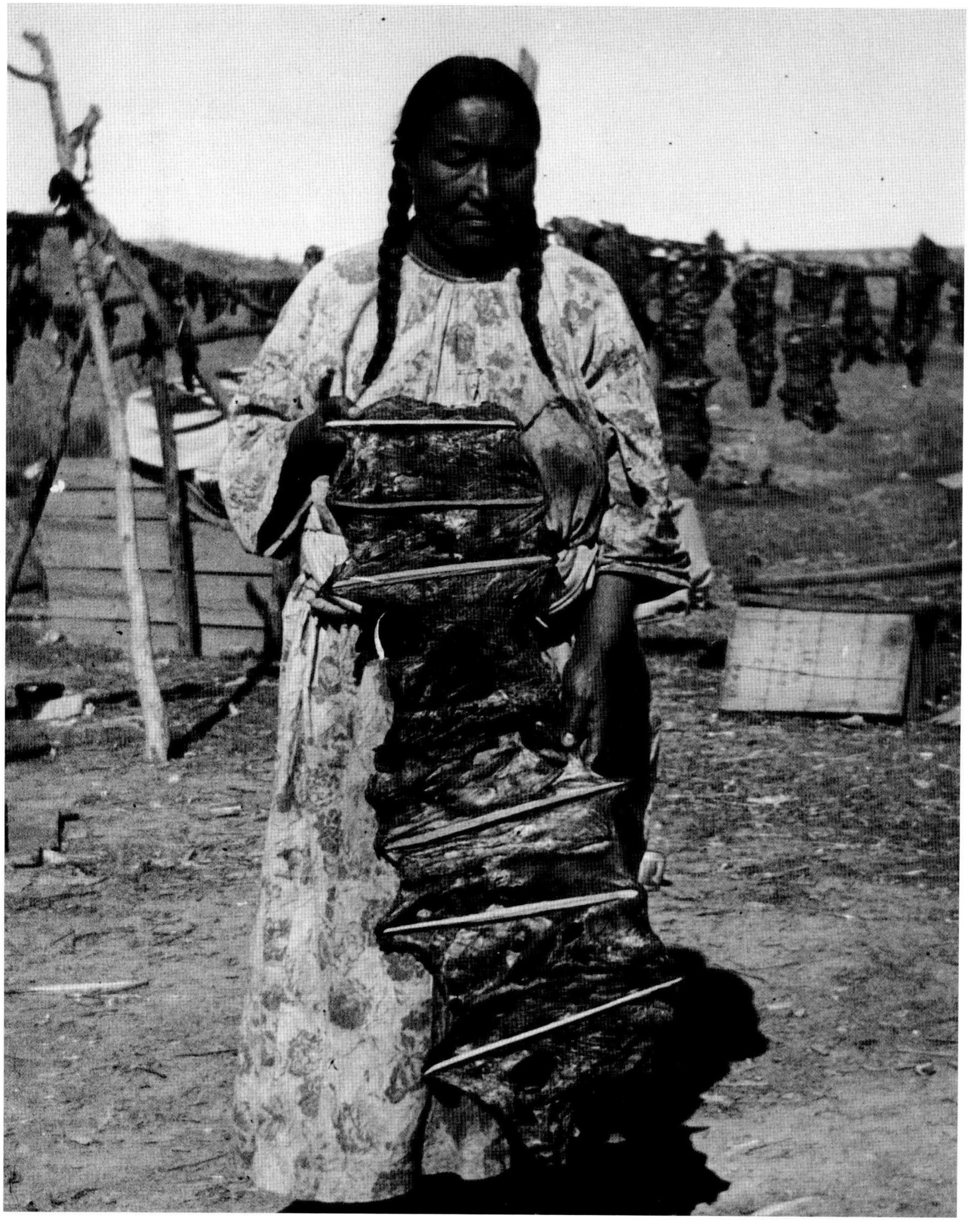

68. Josie Whistling Elk

INFORMANT: JULIA WHITE DIRT

68a. My mother, Josie Whistling Elk, really fixed meat good. She could fix buckskin and moccasin soles. She used all the parts of an animal. My father was a good hunter, like his father. My father used all game: pheasants, prairie chickens, sage hens, squirrels, porcupine, deer, antelope, elk. My mother knew how to take care of all of it. We never did eat the white man food and we got along alright. We grew up and we were healthy. My folks all lived on Muddy Creek. The brothers and sisters and old folks all helped one another. My father was a spiritual person—he believed in all these worship ways. He pierced his flesh and fasted four different times and broke away. He went to Bear Butte and fasted. He got some instructions there on how to paint and how to help people when they fast. The way he painted people, he passed that on to his son-in-law, my husband.

My father put up two Sun Dances and had his wife be the Sacred Woman. Four times he put up the Odd Dance. He was called a Contrary. When he pierced his flesh, his mother fixed the rawhide thongs that he used. It took two deer hides to make the thongs. They braided four strands together. This braided rope was strong, it never broke. My father helped a lot of people. He prayed for them. He painted them when they fasted. His brother-in-law called him "Contrary," but his name was Whistling Elk. He helped a lot of people and he belonged to the Dog Soldier Society and he never quit. After he died, sometimes I hear different ones say my father told them certain things, but I don't believe them. I hear people say, "Whistling Elk taught me," but we all lived close to him and I never saw some of these people ever come.

Now my mother's first child, Blue Wing [a boy], died. Next came Feather on the Head Woman [Mary Black Horse], Spirit Bird [John Whistling Elk], and me. Alice and Alfred are the youngest.

My grandfather on my mother's side was Strong Left Hand. A horse was running by and he was sitting on a little knoll. Someone hollered, "Strong Left Hand, hit that horse!" He picked up a bone and threw it at the horse and hit him in the ribs. It broke some ribs and the horse spit blood and later it died. The fellow who had hollered said, "I didn't really mean for you to kill him!" So the old man said, "You told me to hit him and kill him, so I did."

I used to go to school in Lame Deer. I rode horseback from Muddy to Lame Deer. Later they build a school here at Muddy and I went there. Mary went to school at Busby. There were Long Jaws lived up Muddy—they rode horseback to Lame Deer too, also Joe Tall Bull and Lucy Little Chief.

68b. As shown here, meat was cut away from the bone and sliced paper thin for drying. When dry it could be kept indefinitely. Marquis discusses Cheyenne rules of etiquette (such as the sharing of particular parts) during the butchering and distribution of meat in his chapter "Food Habits" in The Cheyennes of Montana *(Marquis 1978).*

For the role of the Sacred Woman in the Sun Dance and for the athletic feats of Strong Left Hand, see Cheyenne Memories *(Stands in Timber and Liberty 1997).*

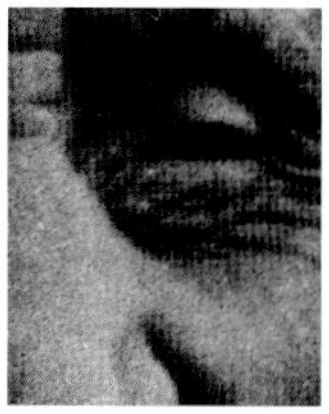

69. Sun Road

Informants: John Woodenlegs and Charles White Dirt

69a. **Woodenlegs:** This is a fine picture of Sun Road. Marquis took this picture in 1925. I know Sun Road and his wife, Buffalo Calf Woman. They lived on Muddy. Their grandson is Charlie White Dirt who is still living. They had a daughter who is Charlie's mother. They always lived there at Muddy and Charlie's folks lived there and now Charlie is living on the same place. They were all traditional people. They were kind people and that's how their daughter was and their grandchildren. They had two grandchildren, Charlie and his sister. The sister passed, left Charlie. I knew their daughter and son-in-law. Other relatives lived there too–they all seemed to live together there, close together with their houses and tents. Sun Road liked to have sweat baths and I used to help him with that. I got to know women of these older people. Sun Road was just a kind man, a good looking man and he got to be a four generation man before he passed on. They used the old Indian ways of taking care of one another–medicine men, doctoring. They helped with that. They believed in the Sun Dance and the Arrow Worship and took part in those ceremonies.

Charles White Dirt: I want to tell something about my grandparents on both sides of my family.

The ceremonial worship ways of my grandparents were really good. They all kind of lived those ways. Sometimes I remember about my parents and where I came from. I want to remember my father and mother and their mothers and fathers. A lot of people know my father, White Dirt, as a Chief. People know my father and that's why I am a son of a Chief. One of my grandfathers was Crazy in the Head, and he was a Crow. Crazy Head had two wives. They were sisters. My father was one of their children. Yellow Eyes was one of their children, also Elk Woman, who married Charles Sitting Man, Sr., and my father, White Dirt. His Indian name was "Travels with the Wolf." One of the four children died. The other woman had four children: Fingers, Turtle Woman, Buffalo Woman, and Traveling Woman. That's Crazy Head's two wives and their children.

Now on my mother's side, there's my mother, Kills at Night Woman, and her brother, Blind Bull. Another boy child died. Their father was Sun Road and their mother was Buffalo Calf Woman.

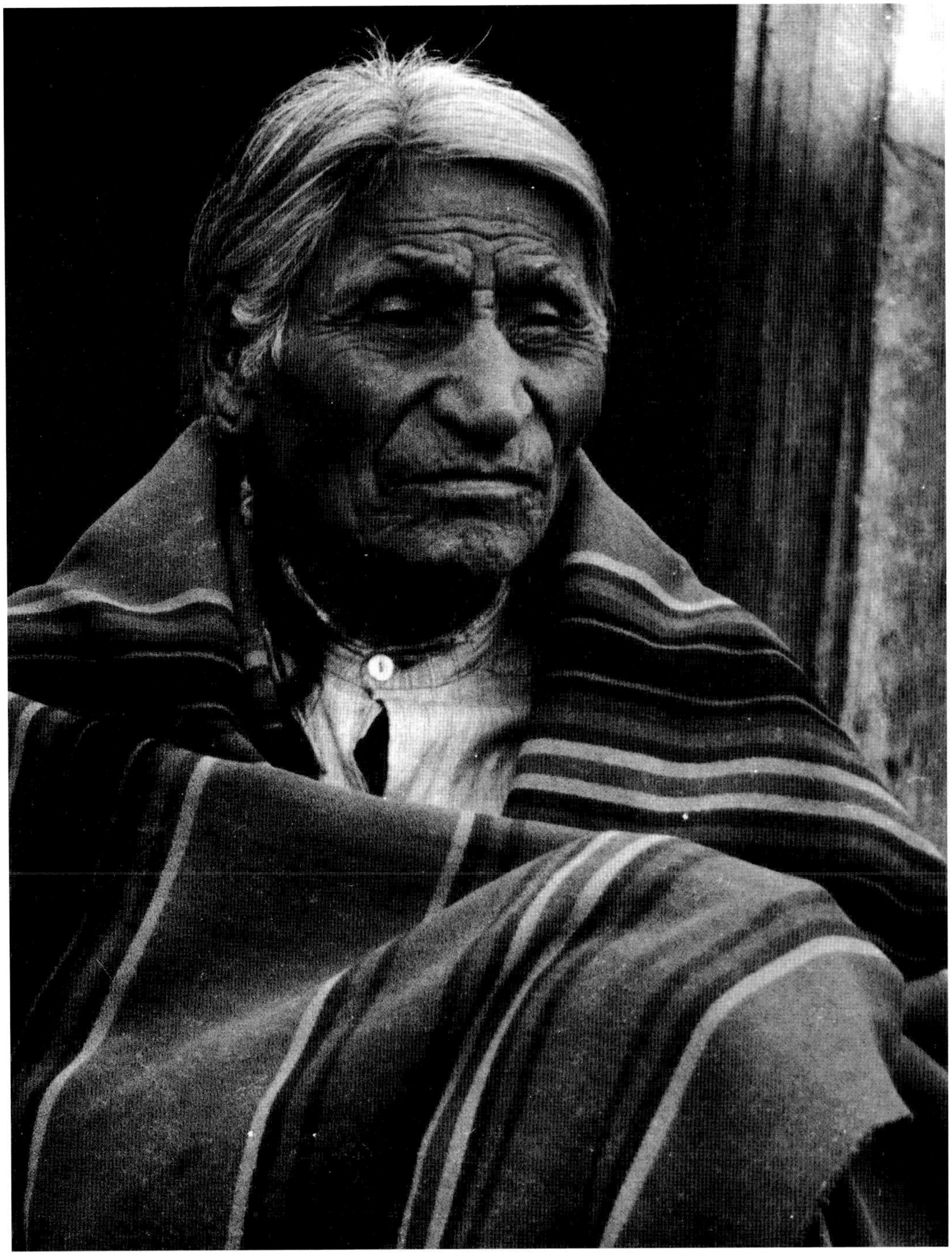

These people kind of all lived near each other and I knew all of them. They all got along good together, no fighting. Everything seemed to go along good, they all worshipped and prayed—took part in different ceremonials. It seemed like everything was easy and in harmony.

My folks lived on this place [Muddy Creek] and they really loved me. My grandparents too. If anything went wrong, or I got a little sick, they put up a ceremonial doings—like a sweat tepee, or they would go fast. They prayed for me to grow up as a teenager and man and that I would be healthy and that I would grow up and get married and have a good marriage and have children. My folks really like the prayer ways, the Native American Church. At that time it was such a real good thing. It seemed like Spirit listened and granted our prayers. When there were Prayer Meetings here, everyone was anxious to come. They would come on horseback and in wagons and camp. They were all interested to come. At these Prayer Meetings, everyone came together and we all went in together. Nobody was ever late. People really believed in that way of worship at that time. Nobody stood outside listening in, they all went in. I have been in meetings where the one who ran the meeting said no one should be outside listening or talking or joking. My folks used to give me peyote when I was four or five years old, and I began to come into the Prayer Meetings. I have used peyote for a long time. The way I look at it, I grew up with this way of worship. Now as I look back on the way they took care of me and taught me good things and loved me—my mother and father and my grandfolks, Sun Road and his wife—they told me I would learn to make my own way.

My mother got sick as we were all getting along. At that time there were lots of Indian medicine men and Indian doctors. Even with these doctors helping, my mother did not improve, and the white man doctor said that she would only live a few days, that she would die in a few days or maybe after midnight around 2 A.M. It seemed like people would use peyote as a last resort, when everything else failed. So they sent a word to Ashland [about 30 miles] to get Yellow Eyes, for him to come over. Snow was deep and cold. Whenever they called one another for help for doctoring or to have a Prayer Meeting, they would come. So Yellow Eyes came and ran a meeting and Little Chief drummed for him. Ernest King and Marion King were there too. They put up this Prayer Meeting asking that my mother would recover. Her husband and her brother, Blind Bull, put up the meeting. She was just skin and bones. When you looked at her, you would think she could not get well. Now they started the meeting. At that time, this peyote was a good medicine, Spirit could use it to help people. Even if you take just a little of it, it could help. And it did help my mother. They gave her one peyote and they gave her peyote tea. She looked pitiful—she was dying. At that time, these peyote people were really sincere, and they really tried to help through prayer. When they all cooperate and worked together in there—singing and praying, and taking peyote, their prayers will be answered. It must be that prayer is really good. After midnight, people began to realize what the white man doctor had said—that she was going to die after midnight. About 2 A.M. Tom Curly wanted to sing. He was a really ugly man to look at, and he couldn't sing very well, but he wanted to sing to help out. Some of the people hesitated because he was a poor singer. Ernest King drummed for him. After he was singing awhile, the sick lady sat up and she asked, "Who is that young man singing? He is singing so good! I started to feel better." And she sat up. After she said that, she fixed her hair and she said, "What a good looking young man!" She said, "I want to eat, I'm hungry." She asked an old man,

Samson Medicine, "Give my your feathers so I can fan myself." So the cedar man threw cedar on the fire and she fanned herself [a way of asking God's blessing]. The people began to realize that she was still alive. This peyote must be a good medicine when it is used in the right way.

Broken Jaw and some of the other medicine men were around outside. Broken Jaw danced to the drumming. He was making fun of this service. He was a medicine man and he had doctored her before. He said, "This way can't help her. Even I couldn't help her, and I am one of the best medicine men. I have spiritual powers."

This peyote service must be real good when everyone works together, thinks and prays together in one way. After she said she got all right, the other people noticed that she was getting better. Some of them made a vow that they would put up a thanksgiving meeting for her, giving thanks for her recovery. Six of them made a vow—that would be six tepees, to thank God for her health. As a young man, I often think of how that way of worship helped my mother. I could have been without a mother way back then when I was young. It's hard for children to be without a mother or father. It must be good to worship God and believe in Spirit—to be patient, no matter what gets in the way—to keep living that Spiritual way of life.

Now I grew up and I went to these meetings and I see my mother carry water in and pray—and I remember how she almost passed on. They used to pray for me, they helped me—that I would grow up in a good way and make a living. It seems like those prayers have come true. I got married to Julia Whistling Elk. My wife's father is Charles Whistling Elk. He is known as one of the Spiritual leaders—he and his whole family. It was so good that I married into that family. The prayers that were said for me—that I would get married and have children and that they would have children—those prayers all came true. I can see that now. I am a four generation man. It's good the way those prayers were said to God, and I'm always glad about this. Now I have thirty or so grandchildren. I'm using peyote services. I am 67 years old now [1981].

Just recently I started to get sick and I wasn't feeling very good. I had not gone to a Prayer Meeting for a long time, so this sickness chased me back into this prayer way. The Southern Cheyennes were all there and Leslie Howling Wolf ran the meeting. They prayed for me that I would get well again. So I am well again, I am alright now. I respect peyote and that way of worship—I try to take care of the way in the right way—my wife and I go to these prayer services. At the meeting when they prayed for me, I told them I had not been for a long time. I found it was still good, it renewed my memory of how good it really is. At that time I ate about fifty peyote because I wanted to help the people who were trying to help me. I know in the past how that way of worship has helped people. I got well, I came through. At that time the doctors had told me I had gallstones. At the Prayer Meeting, they prayed I would not have that sickness. The Chief running the meeting asked Spirit to make me well, and I am all right now. At that time my wife and I put up a Prayer Meeting. Just lately, my daughter put up a meeting. Her boy was sickly, and she wanted him to have good health like the other children. She was praying for her son and vowed to put up a meeting and ask people to come and have you [Woodenlegs] run it. At that time it was storming so we had the service in a house. You were praying in there. We were all glad—my wife is related to you. And I am related to your wife, so we are all kind of related. Altogether we liked that way of worship. I and my wife realize that we are the old folks now—we are the ones. My family prays together for help to keep on the right track. We try to live that way. The prayer is our way of life. Our prayers last a long time, from our grandparents on up to today and we are trying to do the same way—to live that way. We think of those prayers of our grandparents and we pray for our children that way and they will use that for their children. So it passes on. Sometimes I notice right here on this place the different places where we set up a tepee for prayer service, or a sweat tepee. It reminds me of those prayers and helps me live that way. People visit me here and I like to tell the stories of those tepees and the prayer times. It makes me feel good to tell of them. It's good to share the good things. We pray for people having problems and hard times. We pray for soldiers. One of my sons joined the Army and I put up prayer services and I went to Bear Butte and fasted four times to try to help my son and the other soldier boys. So I prayed over there at Bear Butte four days and four nights, and I prayed for them and also for the Cheyennes. I pray for everybody and asked for blessing for our health and our living conditions and any problems we might have. I often prayed that our tribal self-government would lead us in the right way, that it would help us. That's the way I live and the way I worship. I talked with Father Powell and he liked the way I talked about the Spiritual way of life. He made friends with me and he asked me that we would both go to Bear Butte and pray over there. He said, "My friend, let's you and me go to Bear Butte and pray over there together. When we go over there, Spirit must be all around there, and we will get good blessings. We'll help the Cheyenne people here and all people when we pray." We went over there and the man who is Keeper of the Sacred Arrows down south came there at the same time. We were up there fasting and praying four days and four nights. Charles Brady and Alex Brady were with us when we were there. These prayer worship ways are good. It helps people.

Last night we just heard Jasper Red Hat had a prayer service and you [Woodenlegs] ran the meeting. The prayers that were said for them included everybody. I just feel good about that. So all these ways try to hold us together. I really like that way, helping one another and thinking of each other in a good way.

Drinking is a problem we keep running into and it's no good. There should be a certain way we get away from this problem. We just heard another young man died. Some hard problems are really breaking us down, maybe there should be some way it could stop now. A lot of people have passed on now. One of my in-laws just passed on. If our relative passes on, we don't feel very good, we feel lonely. We don't let the Devil get the best of us, we keep praying. We should faithfully stay with these prayer ways—just keep thinking that Spiritual way. We should keep the peyote organization going for a long time. Almighty God would help us, using this peyote in a good way—to respect it and not abuse it. It's such a good thing to have, we should have it for a long time to help guide us in a good way. I'm coming to the end of my talk now. Lots of times I have thought about all this. Sometimes when I think about these things or talk about it, I start to say a prayer. I have said prayers for a lot of people and I want to keep helping and praying.

69b. This 1981 interview of Charles White Dirt gives a good idea of his values concerning family life and religion, especially the use of peyote for healing and in the Native American Church. The trouble with alcohol use addressed here is also discussed in The Road to Lame Deer *(Mader 2002).*

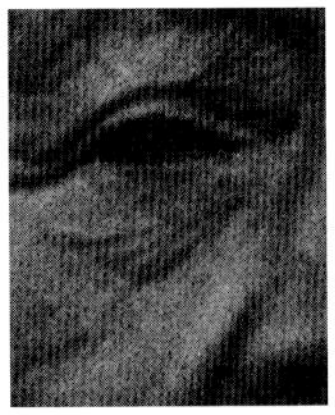

70. Buffalo Calf Woman

Informant: John Woodenlegs

70a. This is Buffalo Calf Woman, the wife of Sun Road. She was a kind, good person.

70b. Sun Road's wife, Buffalo Calf Woman, is not to be confused with Buffalo Calf Road Woman, the famous warrior woman who saved her brother at the Battle of the Rosebud in 1876.

After the reservation was established, the lives of women underwent less change than did the lives of men, which had been focused upon hunting and warfare. Women retained their traditional activities of food and clothing preparation and the care of children, whereas men were expected to make the transitions to stock-ranching, farming, and then wage work—transitions that became increasingly difficult and unsuccessful. Men retained ceremonial and healing roles and activities, but the missionaries wanted them to abandon these as well. It is no wonder that some found alcohol a serious temptation.

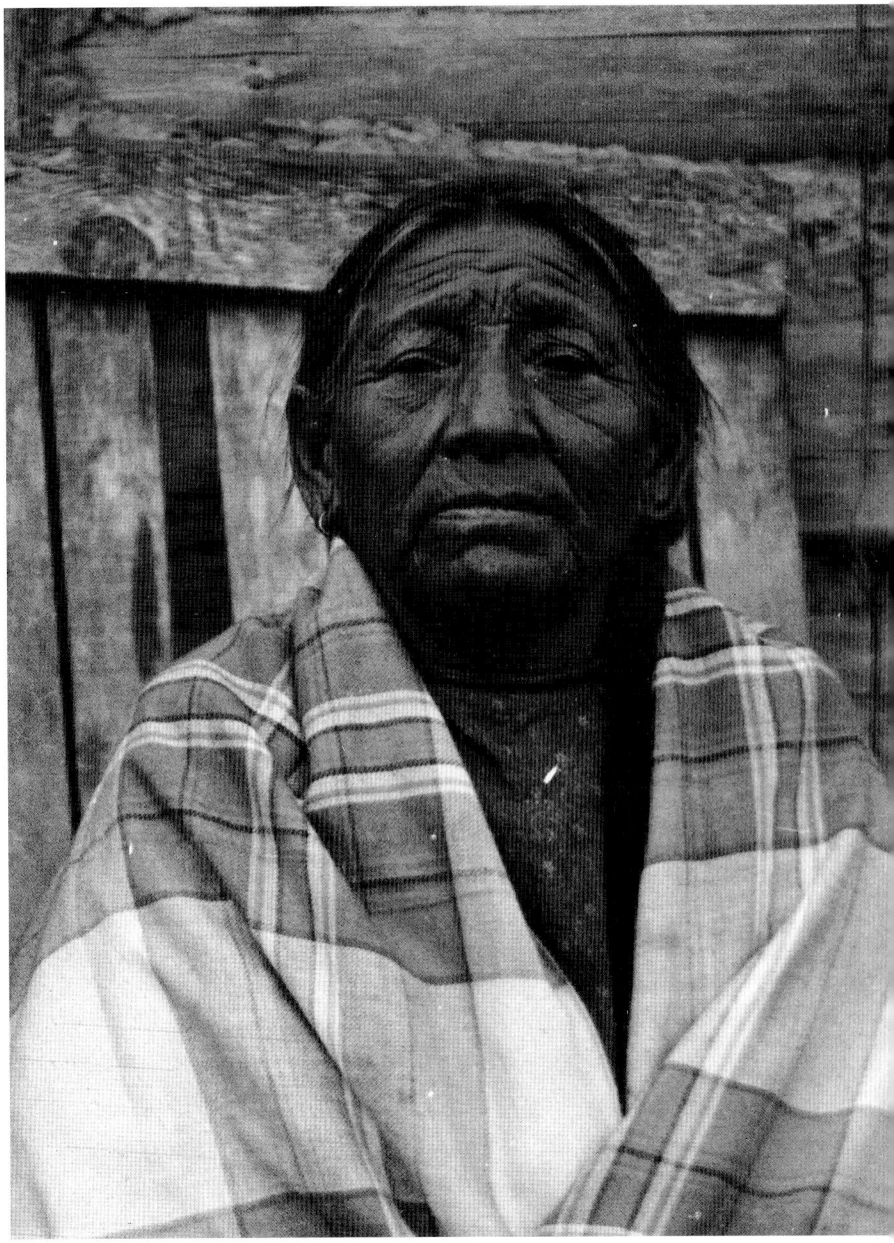

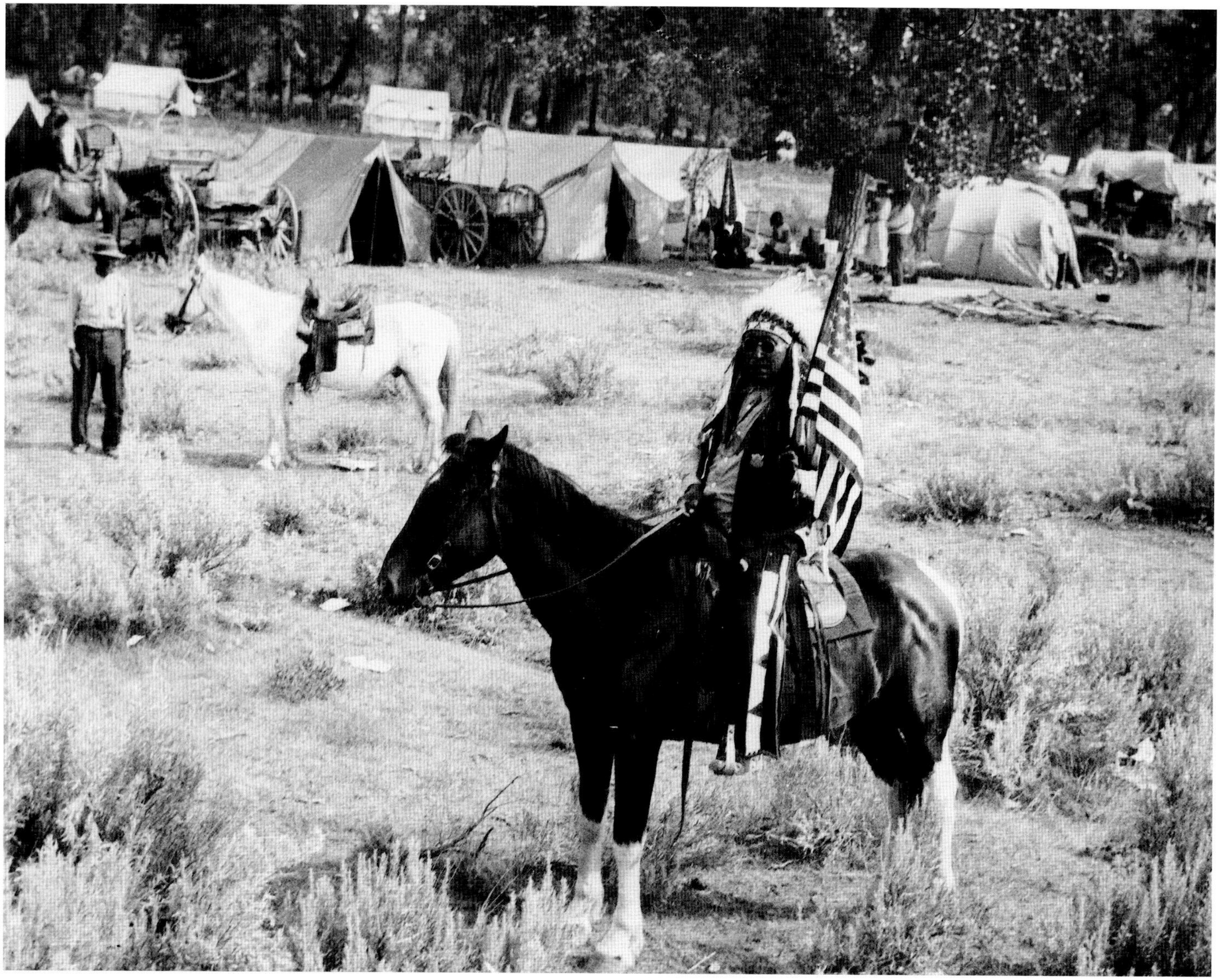

71. Charles Sitting Man, Sr.

Informants: John Woodenlegs and Charles Sitting Man, Jr.

71a. **Woodenlegs:** Charles Sitting Man's father used to be a leader of the Cheyennes at Miles City when they had celebrations there. The Cheyennes camped near the Tongue River.

Charles: It's been quite awhile back my father, Sitting Man, would go to Miles City. He was head of the group that goes there for a celebration. People from Miles City asked him to bring the Cheyennes. They went down in wagons.

Woodenlegs: What was the name of the man they worked with there? This man had a buckskin tie with rattlesnake rattles on it. The Cheyennes called him "Wearing Snake around His Neck." Sitting Man Sr. had the name of "Wolf around His Neck."

Charles: They used to dance at night on the main street of Miles City. Miles City people brought a lot of groceries to the Indians. They brought the beef out and let the Indians butcher it themselves. They cut it up and distributed the groceries among themselves. When they danced down there, people collected money in their hats and they took the money to the store and they counted it there. They equally divided it up right there. They took part in the parades; some were on foot, some on horseback, and some in wagons. Some Miles City children would ride in the wagons too. Some of this is not going on anymore, it's been awhile back. By taking part in Miles City, they got food and money and the people treated them good. We're forgetting those things and getting away from them. It seems like liquor is really bothering us. It would be hard to get people to cooperate now. Liquor is destroying these things. One day I sobered up and I wanted to stay sober, so I prayed to God. I promised God that I wanted to quit drinking, and if I drink again, it will be up to God whatever you want to do with me. I was always afraid to break my promise. If some good friend asked me to drink, I'd explain my promise and I got completely away from it—I forgot it and I found a lot of good things and that's the way I'm living. I help people and I pray for them. When I'm traveling in my car, I pray for people and at night if I wake up, I pray then. I'm telling some of these good things—a lot of young people don't understand Cheyenne and don't know, but it's changing some. We're trying to remember Native ways.

In Miles City, the leaders before my dad were Charles Spotted Elk and Spotted Hawk. They used to take care of it. Later my dad took care of it.

Talking about some of the older people—for instance, Richard Woodenlegs lived right across here [about six miles west of Ashland]. And then his brother, Twin, had a house right across the creek. His house had two rooms. Both of those houses are gone, but I know they lived there. A lot of these people used to live on their places and they traveled in a wagon. At that time they mostly lived on meat, beef and animals and birds, but now beef is really high. I know Richard Woodenlegs—he's a tall man. Woodenlegs lived here and stayed here all year—he took part in the Miles City doings. He was mostly self-supporting.

My father and my mother, when she was cooking, her heart stopped. We lived down there by the Church [Ashland] and she was cooking and then she died. After that I seemed to be kind of an orphan. I never said, "my mother" anymore. Mothers are very important. My dad married again, but he was afraid of his wife. He used to Indian doctor and he had blankets and a lot of good things he was given. He gave all that to his wife's folks. He never gave me anything. When he got old, I was the one that took him in and took care of him. He belonged to different societies—the Horse Medicine Society, but he never put up a Sun Dance or Arrow Worship, but he did Sun Dance. I did because he did. I know most of his painting for the Sun Dances. He taught me most of his ways. Now I teach some of that. I know some of those things at the Sun Dance.

Some of the things that I know from my father—and others have told me, so I know some of those things of the past. The Indian ceremonial ways—I know some of that and some of the ways that we lived at the time. I am 78 years old now [1978]. People have come to me and asked questions, also white people, but I don't tell these stories for nothing. So when they pay me I tell them. I tell them these stories and some of them make money on what I tell them. At this time I'm telling some of these stories and this is my relative here and he's asking me to tell some of these stories. He [Woodenlegs] hauled me over here to the house so I am telling some of these stories. I've told about going to Miles City and the parades there. I was willing to tell some of these stories and about ceremonial ways. Some are just using it and talk about it, but they don't really know. There's a certain man that I know. He seems to be just using these ceremonial ways and he doesn't even respect them. He's just destroying them. This person is a very young man, just growed up. His father died and no one told him anything. He went away to school and he's been in the Army. So he's been away and he never learned anything from his father. I know the person and he just does whatever is best for him and he stole a lot of money. On the silver dollar, it is written there that we're to respect that money. I guess he went away to school, but he never read that. So I respect that money and older people and I respect those good ways. It seems like I have grown up now and I respect people and the ways. When I was young, I didn't seem to care. I didn't respect nobody or care—I just done any old way. I didn't think right, I didn't respect anybody. But God knows what you are doing because Spirit is everywhere and you can't cheat him. He knows everything. I hear about that from older people.

Woodenlegs: How were the people treated in Miles City—your father was the leader—were they honest? They must have gotten food and money and divided equally among themselves. I always hear about my older people that you could trust them. The white people said that too. If you get to be a leader and misuse it or abuse it, it's not very good.

Charles: I went to school here at the St. Labre Mission. We used to call it the "white building school," but after we started to learn, it got a different name. Of the people I went to school with, I may be the only one left. There was John Gray, Alfred Sponge, Chasing Bear, George White Bird, Oliver Yellow Eyes, Leo White Crane, White Wolf, Martin Two Bulls, Eugene Tangled Yellow Hair, David Tangled Yellow Hair, One Little Bird Woman, Tangled Hair Woman, my wife that died, Mrs. Two Bulls, and Kingfisher Woman. She had a hard time. They would bring her there and she would run away. They tried to chase her on foot. She was a fast runner. Also Eugene Standing Elk. I'm the only one left from that school—they're all dead. Some went away to school at Rapid City. The people here lived on their places and planted gardens and grain. They had horses and cattle. They had wagons and a team and that was their transportation. They had horses and they rode them. You could hear some of those young men out riding and they'd be singing. If you heard that today you'd think somebody was drinking. At that time, hardly anybody drank. But today it's terrible. The women folks are just as bad as the men. In the past the men used to go after the girls and they were hard to get. The mother or chaperone came out of the house to see if anyone was around. This woman who looked around didn't look very good, but when they came back, a young man might grab the girl. Then the mother would say, "How come you're so brave to grab this girl? Why don't you be that brave over there fighting the enemy?" It really hurt the boy's feelings when he was told that. He went up on the hill and cried. It used to be hard to get a girl, but now they come after you—they knock on your door.

One thing here, Richard Woodenlegs had a home here with his wife. He had a wagon and she had a buggy. Woodenlegs' brother, Twin, had a house here too. Old Wolf used to live here too and also White Crane. Over toward Greenleaf, Whirl Wind lived and Yellow Hair and Little Eagle and that man Issues lived on Greenleaf. Some lived on just the other side of Ice Wells—they stayed there, it was their homes. Now they're bunching up in the communities together—they're not living out anymore. One thing we're doing is sending people away to get an education. He has a new house built in some community—not on his place. He doesn't have any hay or cows—all he has is a house. Now a young person who has some education and is living right—like your daughter—she's living on her place here. Some have education but they are not using it—they have nothing. The old people in Ashland lived on their places and had cattle and horses.

Woodenlegs: About the Sun Dance, did they make it once a year or more?

Charles: They could have it twice—in the spring or early summer and in the fall, if somebody made a vow. They used to gather and collect for the Sun Dance, do it themselves. Now they go to the Tribal Council and get the money.

There was some group of people who were really afraid of the Cheyennes. They caught one boy and his two friends went looking for him. They found this group of people camped during the day. They decided to go in at night. Everyone wore robes. They said, "They won't know us." They slept during the day. Toward evening they went down toward the camp. They got in. There were a lot of people in there and they were just right with them. They were having a Sun Dance and they went right among them. They heard something like somebody groaning. It was high up the center pole. "Maybe that's our friend tied up there. I'll climb that pole." There was hardly any light—just the fire near the door. This boy that went up had a knife and he cut him loose and he must have had spiritual powers because he had him on his shoulders when he came back down. He got down and they took him back home. These people that had this Sun Dance looked for him in the morning and he was gone. That's the reason why this group of Indians is really afraid of the Cheyennes. These people are from Idaho. The tribes in Idaho are afraid of the Cheyennes—the Nez Perces and the Bannocks.

71b. Miles City was known to the Cheyennes because some of them (under White Bull or Ice) surrendered there and also because of their subsequent service as army scouts at Fort Keogh. Details in Sitting Man's 1978 interview should be of interest to students of Cheyenne traditional religion, such as the tale that some Idaho tribes believed a live captive was once tied to the center pole of the Sun Dance lodge.

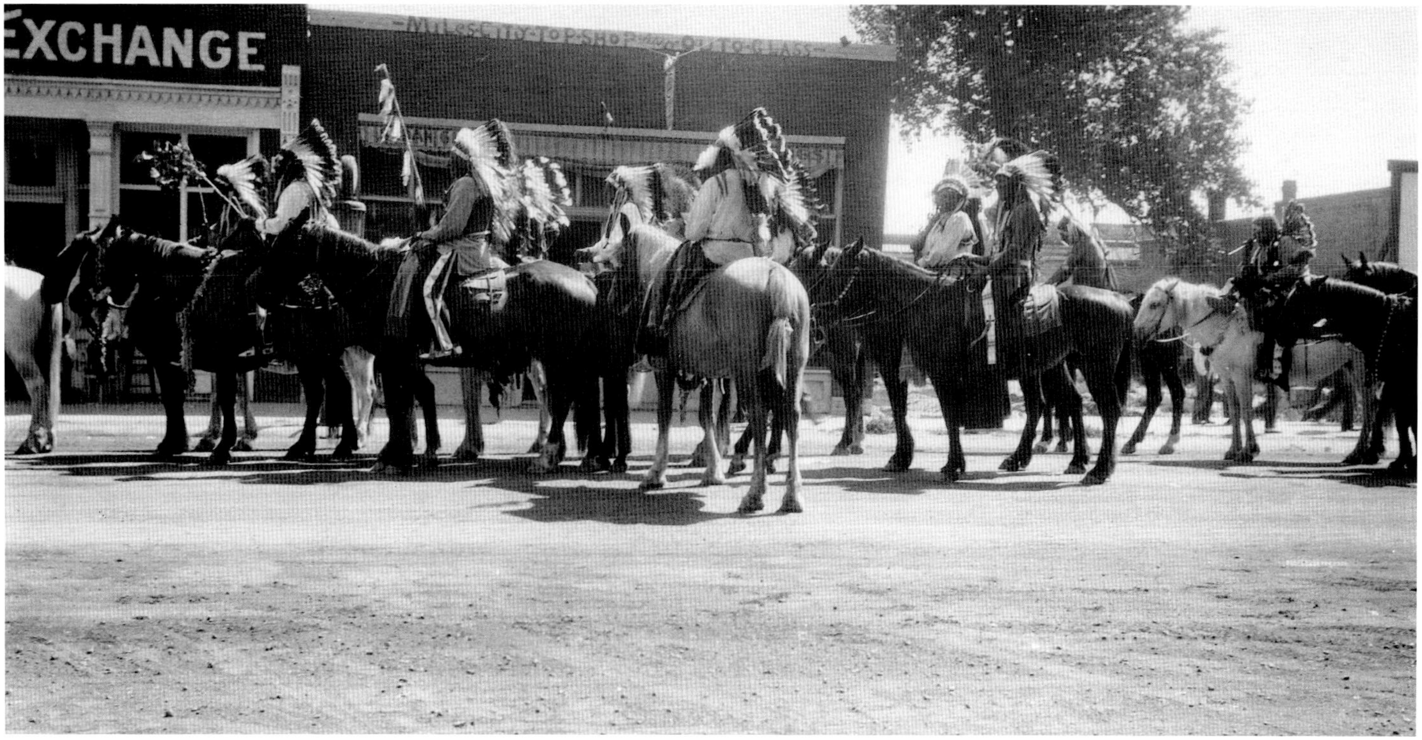

72. Parade at Miles City, July 4, 1930

INFORMANT: JOHN WOODENLEGS

72a. These Cheyennes are waiting for the parade to start. According to Dr. Marquis' notes, this was July 4, 1930, in Miles City, Montana.

72b. Participation in rodeos and celebrations at towns near the reservation was enjoyed by a number of Cheyennes through the years. All American Indian Days at Sheridan, Wyoming, now discontinued, was a major intertribal event organized some years ago, in which the crowning of a Miss Indian America took place.

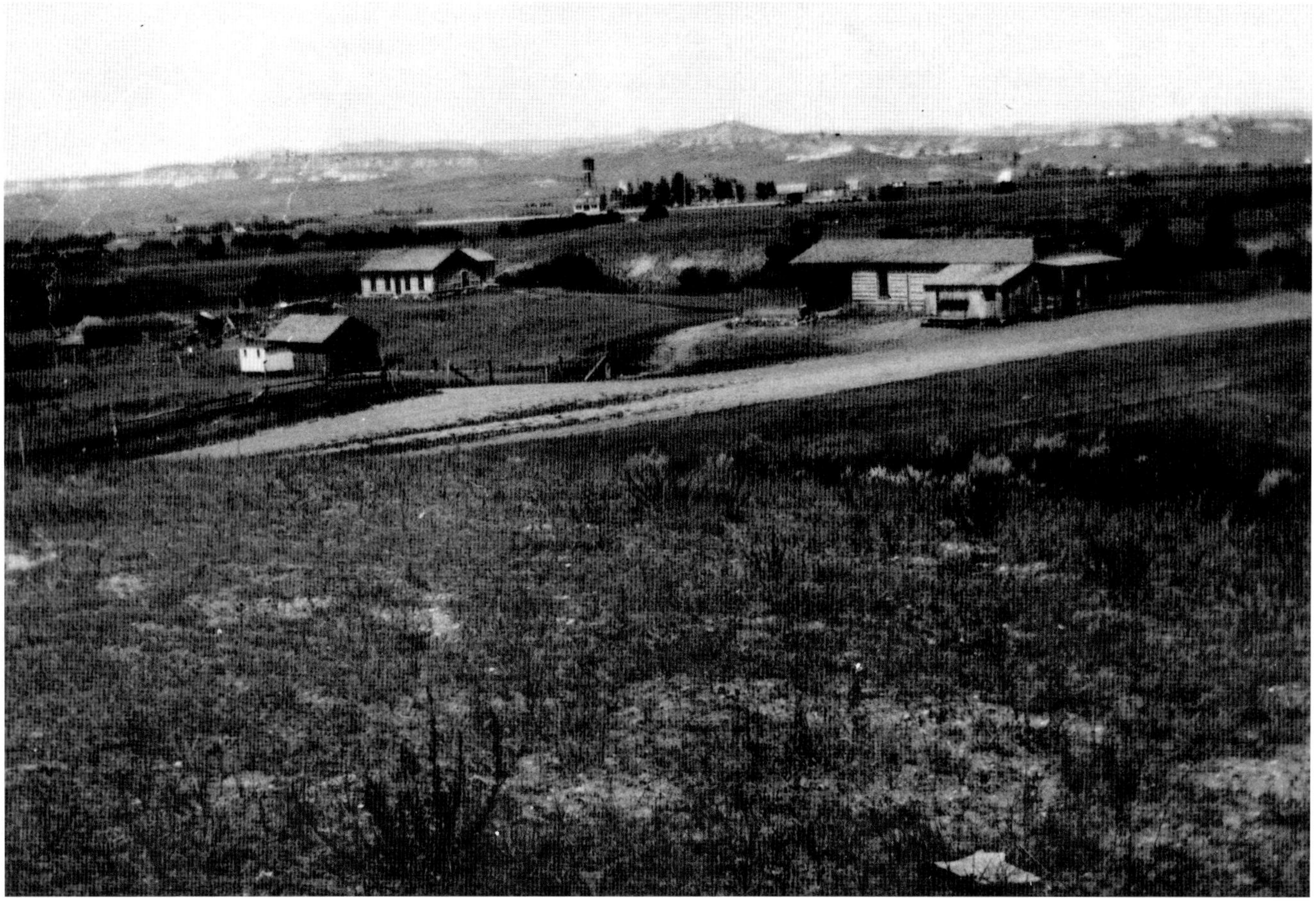

73. Busby Village

INFORMANT: JOHN WOODENLEGS

73a. This is the town of Busby, on the west side of the reservation. The dirt road is now U.S. 212. The building on the road is the old Busby store. Way in the background where the trees and water tower are is the school. It was a school run by the government. It was called Tongue River Boarding School, or the "government school."

73b. Busby is the westernmost Northern Cheyenne community, close to the border shared with the Crow reservation. An early trader there, W. P. Moncure, encouraged Cheyenne traditionalists to write down elements of Sun Dance ritual. This happened about 1930 and may be one reason why the Cheyenne ceremony has survived into modern times (Stands in Timber and Liberty 1997: 94). Moncure also built a stone memorial there in honor of the warrior leader Two Moons.

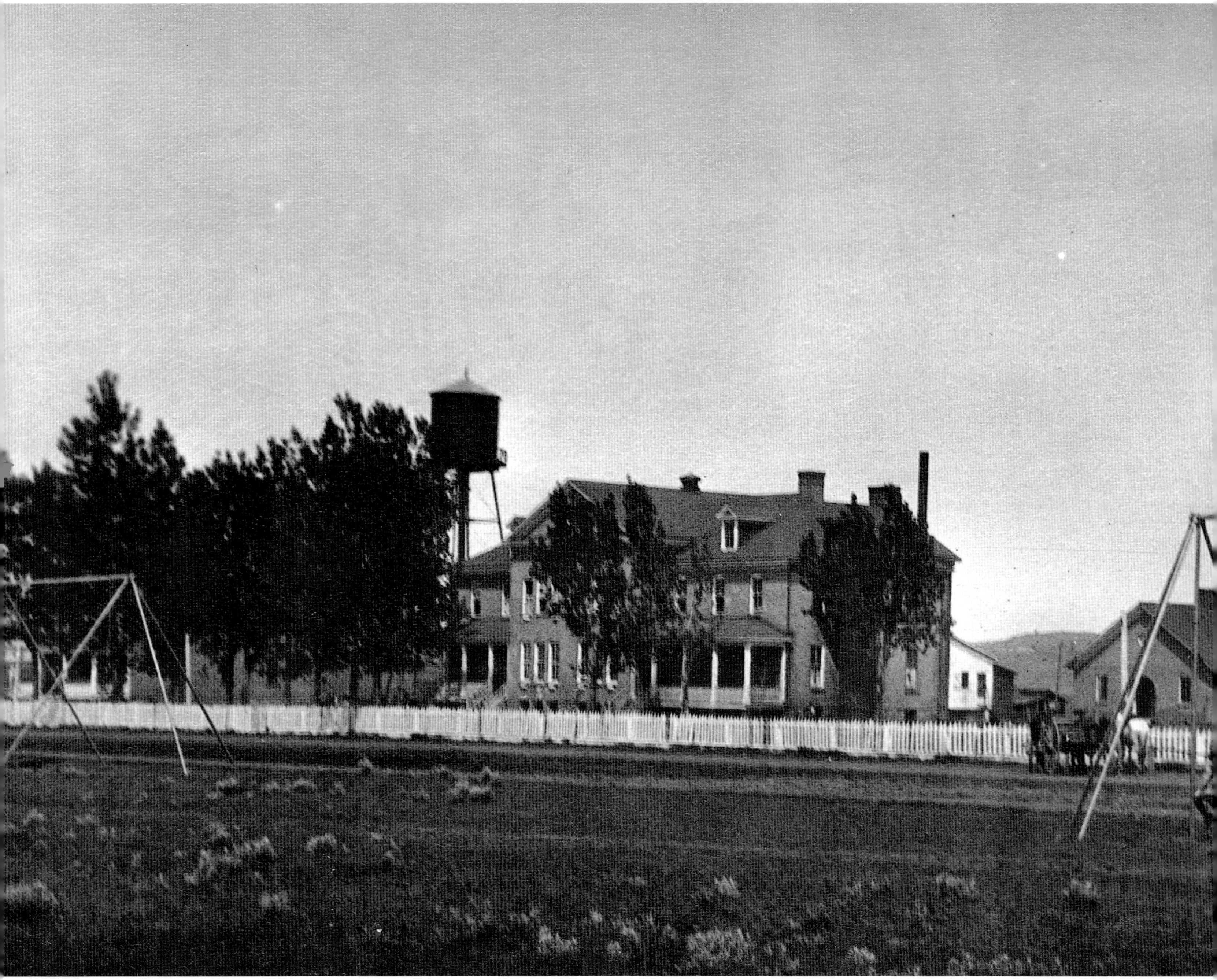

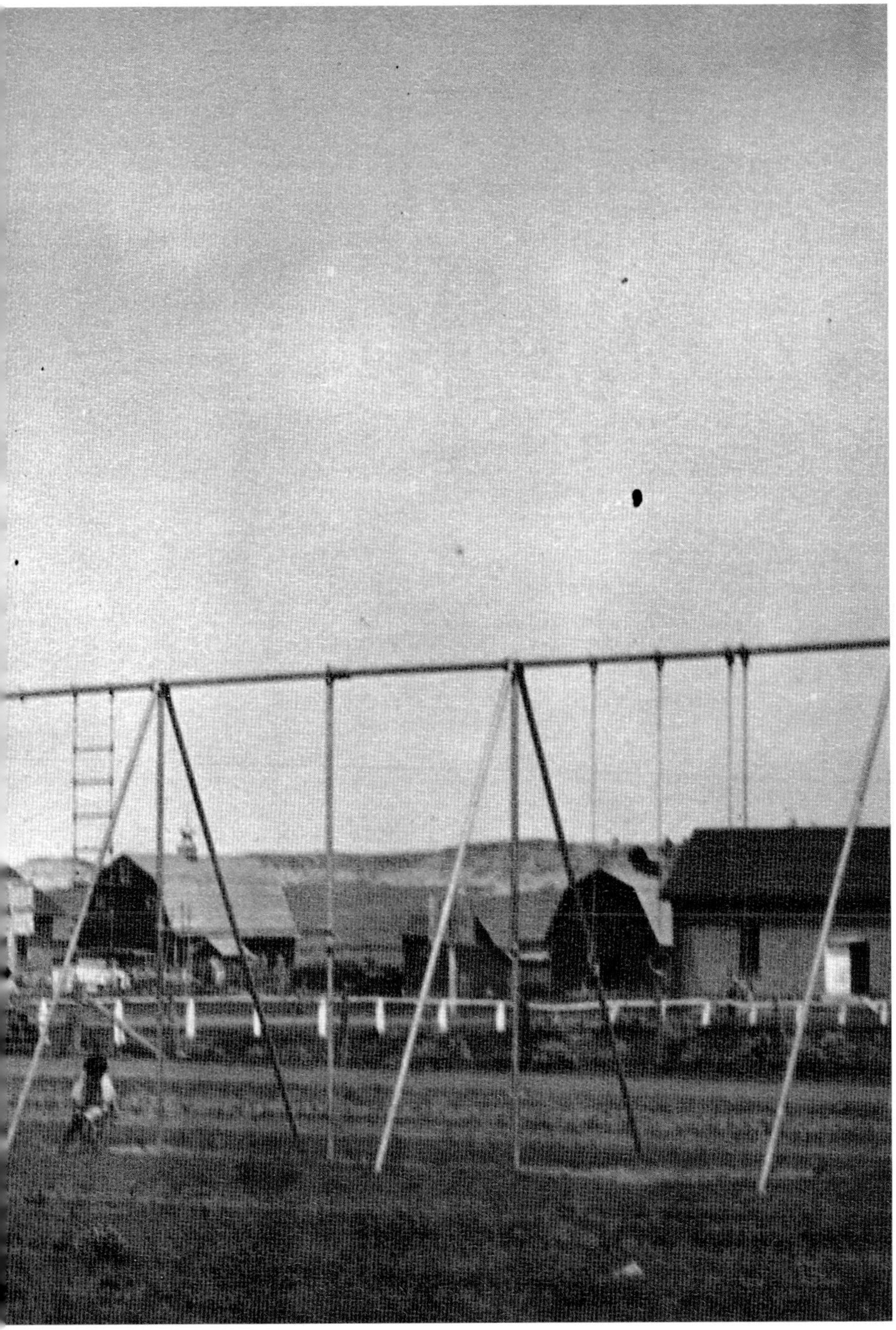

74. Boarding School at Busby

INFORMANT: JOHN WOODENLEGS

74a. This is the boarding school at Busby. The main building had classrooms on the main floor and dormitories upstairs, one side for the girls and one side for the boys. In the basement there were playrooms and bathrooms.

The building in the center was the laundry. The students helped do the laundry. There were some kind of laundry machines. Clothes were hung outside in back of the building. The barn on the left was the cow barn and the one on the right was the horse barn. In between there were pig pens. The building on the right was where the "boss farmer" lived, the man who was in charge of the livestock, the machinery, and overseeing the farming.

74b. The Busby school was built next to the last campsite or bivouac of George Custer and the Seventh Cavalry on the Rosebud, before they crossed the divide to defeat on the Little Bighorn in June 1876. A large wooden tepee structure, built to promote tourism after the 1926 fiftieth anniversary festivities, marks this area on modern Highway 212, which runs east–west across the reservation.

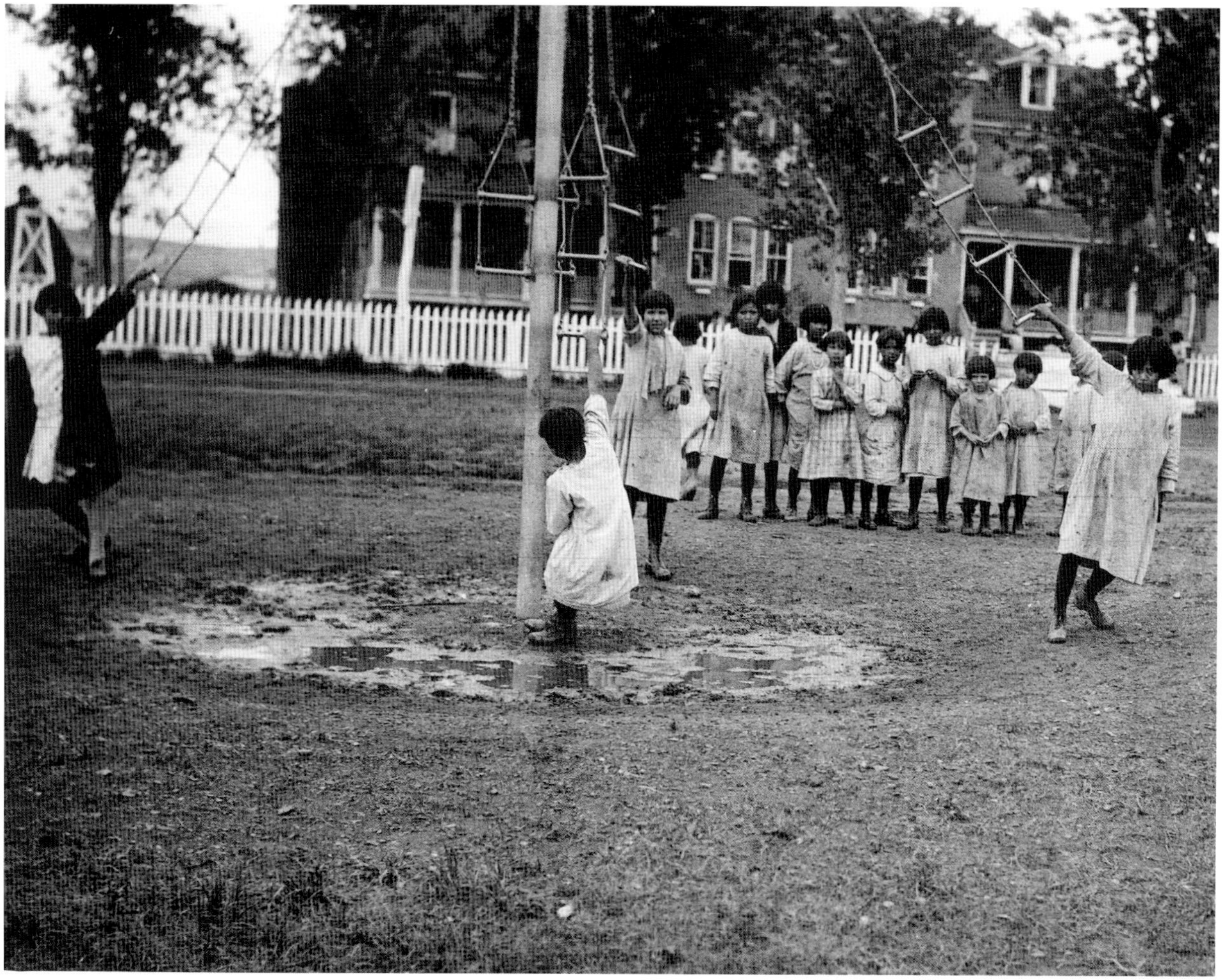

75. Busby School Girls

INFORMANT: JOHN WOODENLEGS

75a. Busby school girls at recess.

75b. The Busby boarding school was built in 1904. See caption 77a for extended commentary by John Woodenlegs (recorded in 1981) on the pros and cons of the reservation boarding school system and the frequent vacillations in government educational policy.

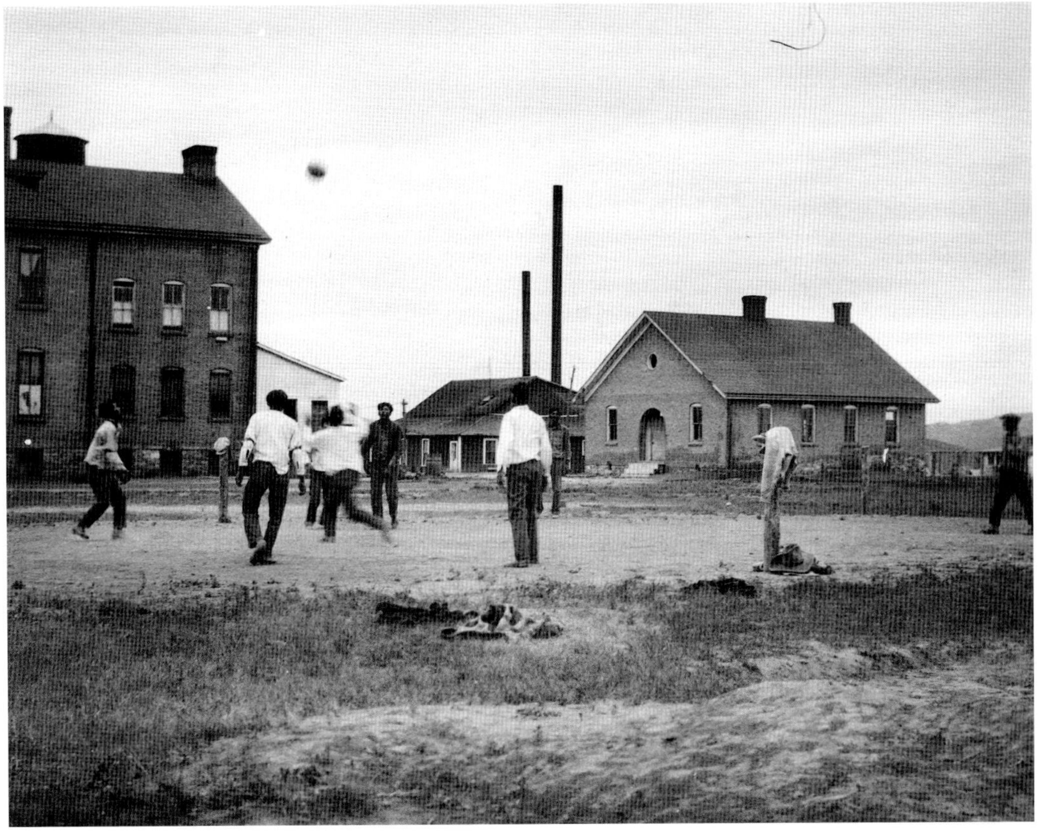

76. Playing Basketball

INFORMANT: JOHN WOODENLEGS

76a. This is a picture where we are playing outside. We were playing basketball. The school team is playing some of the outsiders, some of the older people who came and wanted to play. They like to play the school boys there. Stamper White and Deafy and Bearchum were not going to school there, but they liked to play the school team. That's what they're doing in this picture here. One of them must have a great big hat. It's lying there on the ground and also some shirts and jackets. In the picture, the one farthest to the left is me, then Sam Weasel Bear, Frank Bearchum, John Kills on Top, Stamper White, and the one coming in with the cap on is David Deafy. The man with arms up is unknown.

76b. Basketball has continued to be popular in most reservation communities. Football never took hold, and baseball is less popular today. For description of a modern Lakota basketball heroine at Pine Ridge, see On the Rez *(Frazier 2000). For a Marquis photo of a Cheyenne baseball team, see* The Cheyennes of Montana *(Marquis 1978).*

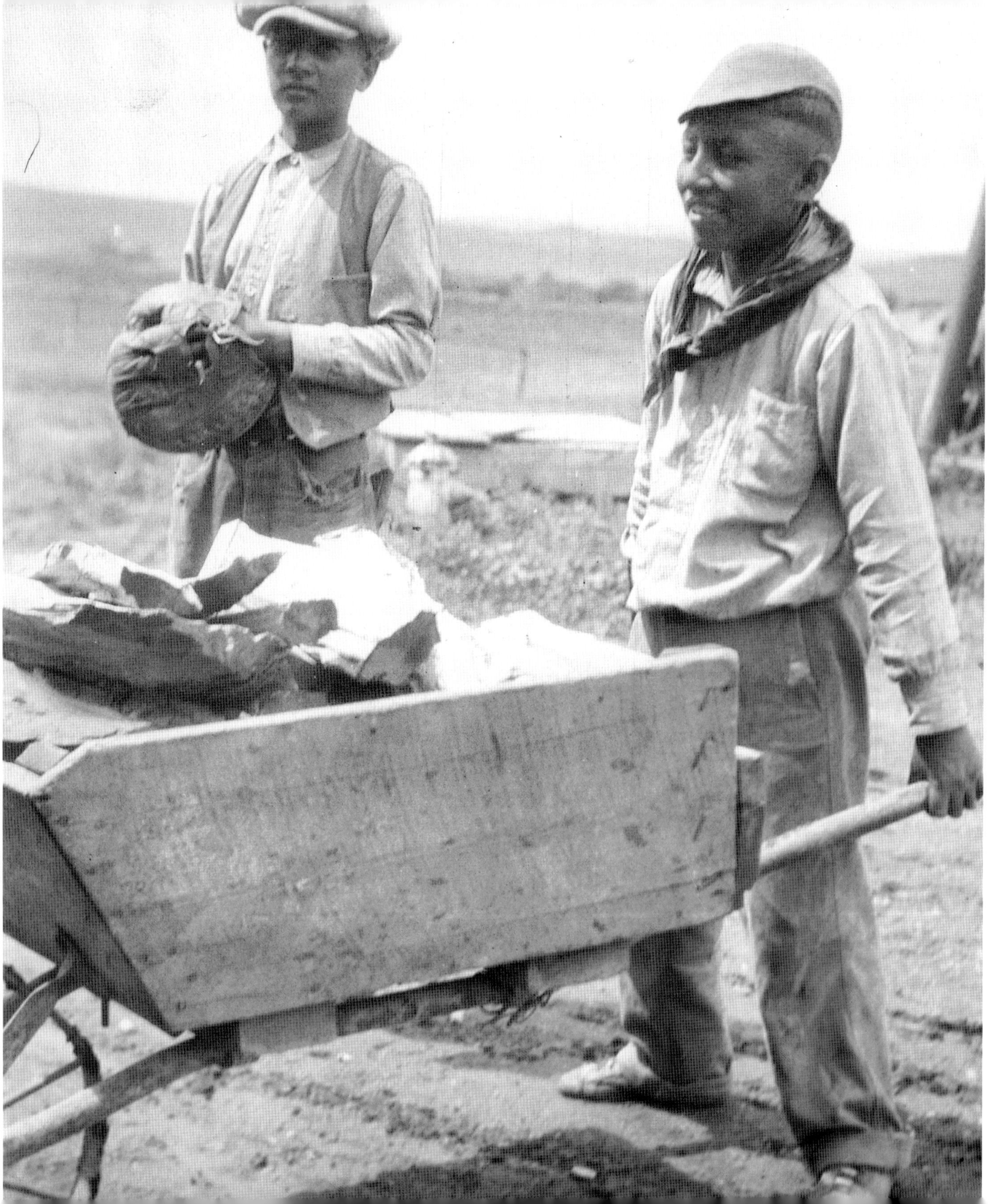

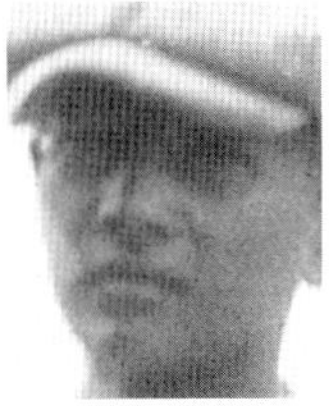

77. Two Busby Students

INFORMANT: JOHN WOODENLEGS

77a. This is Henry Sioux and Mike Bad Horse. They went to the Busby school. Baseball got to be a favorite sport on the reservation. Dr. Marquis mentioned that the Cheyenne men's team probably won as many games as they lost against off-reservation teams.

John Woodenlegs Recalls Busby School Days (recorded in 1981)

I want to talk about the time I went to school at Busby Tongue River Indian School. It is at Busby, Montana, on the Northern Cheyenne reservation. At the time it was called Tongue River reservation. I had gone to an Indian school away from the reservation in Idaho. I could hardly speak any English when I went to school as a young person. Among all the other tribes there, most of them talked English. I stayed there a couple years. Then I came back home, after maybe five years. When I came back home, I was in the seventh grade. I had passed the sixth grade while I was away. I had forgotten my Cheyenne language because I had nobody to speak to. So my friend Sam Weasel Bear said, "Come to school at Busby." That encouraged me and then I thought I would learn the Cheyenne language from other boys going to school. I took the sixth grade over, and I finished that one year. I got kind of interested with the people there. We worked half a day and we went to school half a day. It was kind of easy for me because I had already gone through sixth grade before. I could talk English then to the teachers and the employees. They kind of liked me because I could speak to them. I stayed there two years—I guess I was in sixth grade three years! I began to learn the Cheyenne language again, and we had to work—know how to harness and saddle a horse, plow and put in a garden. We had some wheat, oats that we planted. We had Holstein milk cows, quite a few, almost fifteen. We had beef cows and when the calves were born to the milk cows we had to teach them to drink milk and water so we could take them off the milk cows and have all the milk for the school. So we had to learn how to do that and also how to cut hay and put up hay in the barns for the milk cows, the horses, and the beef herd. We learned how to butcher beef every once in a while and how to take care of pigs, feed the pigs and know how to butcher them. We had to learn how to clean the barns and take care of the machinery. We had a manure spreader to put manure on the gardens, the wheat, and the oat fields. We learned to keep up the fences and the corrals. It was interesting to learn how to do those things. Once in a while they let us ride out where the beef herd was. A lot of us worked at the power house where they made steam to heat the school buildings. A lot of us worked at the school buildings, sweeping and doing the cleaning up of the rooms and the dormitories. We planted trees, we learned how. We learned a lot of thing in that half day. There was a church there and we went to Sunday School classes of the Mennonite Church. Mr. Habegger was there then. Some of the children kept running away from the school. Some didn't like to stay there, but later they learned how to stay because we made friends with them and tried to talk to them. They had the Busby store there and we could go there once in a while if we had any money. When school was going to be out, we had a big picnic. All the parents came to the school, and all the girls and boys rode horseback. We rode away from the school, someplace close to the Rosebud Creek, and we had a big picnic. We had races, wrestling matches, and different things that we did out there. It was a good thing to look forward to–everybody riding horseback and racing. Then we were through with the school, we could go home! All those things were kind of interesting to me so I went back again the next year to that school.

We learned how to do carpentry work, to fix windows that were broken, to fix doors. I never did like carpentry work. My father and his brother were carpenters. They earned good money. They tried to make me a carpenter, but I never did like to do that kind of work.

Busby school had dances Friday nights. Gee, I didn't know how to dance the two-step or the waltz or the Charleston. All my school buddies danced, and I just watched. I didn't know how. It seemed kind of interesting. A fellow played the saxophone. He was the "boss farmer," Mr. Scott, Frank Scott. His wife was a teacher. She played the piano. Then we had an Indian drum that we just beat that for a drum. The employees collected money and we got a bass drum and a snare drum, and whoever worked as a carpenter fixing doors and windows would get to play those drums. So I gave in, I was a carpenter just so I could get to play those drums. I played for the dances. After a while I got good at drumming. I made my own box things and then I fixed up bells off of cows or horses to use with the drum set. I really decorated my bass drum, snare drum, and the disks. I made the Busby students dance! There was one lady, Charlie Parker's wife, who was the cook and one of the matron. Charlie Parker showed me how to drum, the bass and the snare drum. He was working at the boiler house and I worked there for a while too. They had a ladies choice in dancing. Friday evening I was drumming and this lady, Mrs. Parker, came and said, "This is ladies choice and I want you to come and dance with me." She's the one who had tried to show me how to dance. I was always kind of afraid of ladies or girls. As we walked around she asked me if I liked chicken. I said, "Yeah, I like chicken." She put out her arm and said, "Here, have a wing." I put my arm in her arm. I was scared and my face got hot, but I did learn to dance from that lady. I was kind of thankful. So we had those dances on Friday nights. Some people could go home Friday night, but they had to be back Sunday night. It was easy to go away from the school and hard to be back Sunday night!

They tried to help us every which way. We got three good square meals a day, and sometimes snacks in the evening like apples or oranges or cookies. Once a week we'd have the drums, the bass drum and the snare drum. Some of the students could play mouth harps, so we'd go down in the basement and some of the boys would try to drum and play the harp. We'd all dance with each other. We played cowboys—we didn't have any handkerchiefs to tie around our necks, so we tied toilet paper on to look like a handkerchief! We'd dance around; one boy played the girl and one the boy, and we practiced. Once a week the girls got to practice on their side of the dormitory. We could hear the drumming over there—they were dancing and practicing. So that's the way we learned to dance. We could sure dance and sing that song, "It ain't gonna rain no more!" How did the old folks know that it wasn't going to rain no more? Sometimes the principal or superintendent of the school would dance and say, "Everybody sing." And everybody would sing. It was a lot of fun.

When I left there I went to school in Lame Deer for seventh and eighth grades. I was in eighth grade two years, then I went away to Flandreau Indian school in South Dakota. Toward springtime, I head home from there—I run away. When I got home, school wasn't out yet, so my dad sent me back to school in Busby. After I got done there, I didn't go to school anymore—I had gone to school eleven or twelve years.

At Busby school, you could not speak the Cheyenne language anymore. That's the time I really had a hard time. Maybe that's why so many kids were always running away from that school. If you got caught speaking Cheyenne, you were punished. Sometimes kids would be talking Cheyenne and they didn't know the disciplinarian came up on them from the back, and he would grab an ear and just twist it because the kid was talking Cheyenne. Sometimes they washed your mouth out with soap. They wanted us to talk English. I could talk English, but I wanted to learn Cheyenne and that's why when I was punished, I didn't take it so hard. You had to stand in the corner in the schoolroom if you got caught, or sometimes all those that talked Cheyenne had to march into the dining room saying, "We talk Indian, we talk Indian." We'd have to stand in the middle of the floor and mark time and keep saying that while everybody else was eating. After everybody got done, they would go out and then we would eat. Sometimes we would go without a meal. I know a lot of Indian schools were like that. Now after a while—I don't know who is saying it, government or the missionaries—I don't know who to blame, but now they are saying, "Talk Indian again." We have a bilingual program! We want to teach Cheyenne! So I notice this came back up again. This bilingual program is just in recent years. Now we have some white people learning different Indian languages and they can really talk good.

At this Busby school, they had goals outside so we could play basketball. They also played in the cow barn where we fed cows. They covered that over with boards. At that time Busby school had real good players—they were called "tigers." They played high school teams and they beat them. They played Hardin and Billings. They traveled a lot of places. At one time I was on the second team. We were called "wildcats." Now the people said there were really good basketball players at Busby. The students worked in the laundry, the boiler house, the carpenter's shop, so you got to learn different trades there—how to do some plumbing and a lot of good things there. I even learned to talk Cheyenne! One thing we learned too was about the fire drill. We had fire drills in case of fire. If you were upstairs you jumped into kind of a slide—it didn't have any steps—it was sort of an auger-thing that you came down on. You really came out of it when you got to the bottom! We learned to drill, to march and drill. The superintendent taught us how to drill, something like Army soldiers.

77b. This was one of the last interviews for this book, recorded by Tom Weist in 1981.

78. Turkey Legs

INFORMANT: JOHN WOODENLEGS

78a. Turkey Legs, also known as Flying, was a scout at Fort Keogh, Miles City. In this picture, he is all dressed up with beaded cuffs that have an elk and an eagle. The other bird must be a turkey. He has a beaded belt and his leggings. I knew this man. He lived close to Busby school. He had a ranch above there on Rosebud Creek. He was well known for taking part in the dances. He was a man that fixed flutes and played them. He had a son and a daughter that I knew, and I went to school with his grandchild. I knew his son Lawrence Flying and his daughter Jean Turkey Legs. She married a Crow boy, August White Shirt. Turkey Legs had quite a few horses, colorful horses—roans, grays, lots of pinto horses, palomino horses. He had a good saddle. I don't think he ever wore boots. He wore shoes or moccasins. He had a big reservation hat. He always had a good team of horses. He had cattle. So when he was a scout in Miles City, he learned to take care of horses, cattle, garden. He farmed on his place, a very good place. He talked real good to people, and he was always taking part in the different celebrations. His daughter and son went to school. His son Lawrence was a good basketball player. He went away to school at Haskell. They were good people—they fixed moccasin soles and beadwork and the flutes that he made. Sometimes he would come to Busby school and entertain the children with his flute and some stories.

This picture was taken in the 1920s. He was one of the scouts from Busby. Others were from Rosebud, Birney, Lame Deer, and Ashland. They got a pension from the time they were 62 until they passed on. All of these scouts could be buried at the Custer Battlefield, but they didn't want to. They did not want to be buried over there because they had fought the Battle over there, fought for their lives, so they didn't want to be buried there. Some of our younger people who are veterans have been buried over there.

78b. Cheyenne participants in the Custer fight generally chose to be buried on the reservation, not at the Custer Battlefield National Cemetery. See the picture of Isaac Black Bird (figure 25). At least seven Cheyennes died there. According to John Stands in Timber these included four suicide warriors—Little Whirlwind, Closed Hand, Cut Belly, and Noisy Walking, the son of White Bull—as well as Limber Bones, Roman Nose, the son of Long Roach, and the Southern Cheyenne tribal chief Lame White Man. Whirlwind the son of Black Crane may also possibly be added, as probably distinct from Whirlwind the suicide warrior mentioned in Cheyenne Memories *(Stands in Timber and Liberty 1997: 204).*

In keeping with the greater number of Sioux warriors on the field, Sioux losses numbered about sixty. Such numbers are difficult to confirm, because the Indian dead and wounded were removed from the battlefield by their relatives immediately afterward. The total number of U.S. soldiers who died at the Little Bighorn was 251: the 210 soldiers of Custer's five-company command and 41 killed from the Reno command.

Turkey Legs is shown talking sign language to Marquis in another photo from the Marquis collection included in Keep the Last Bullet for Yourself *(Marquis 1976: 156).*

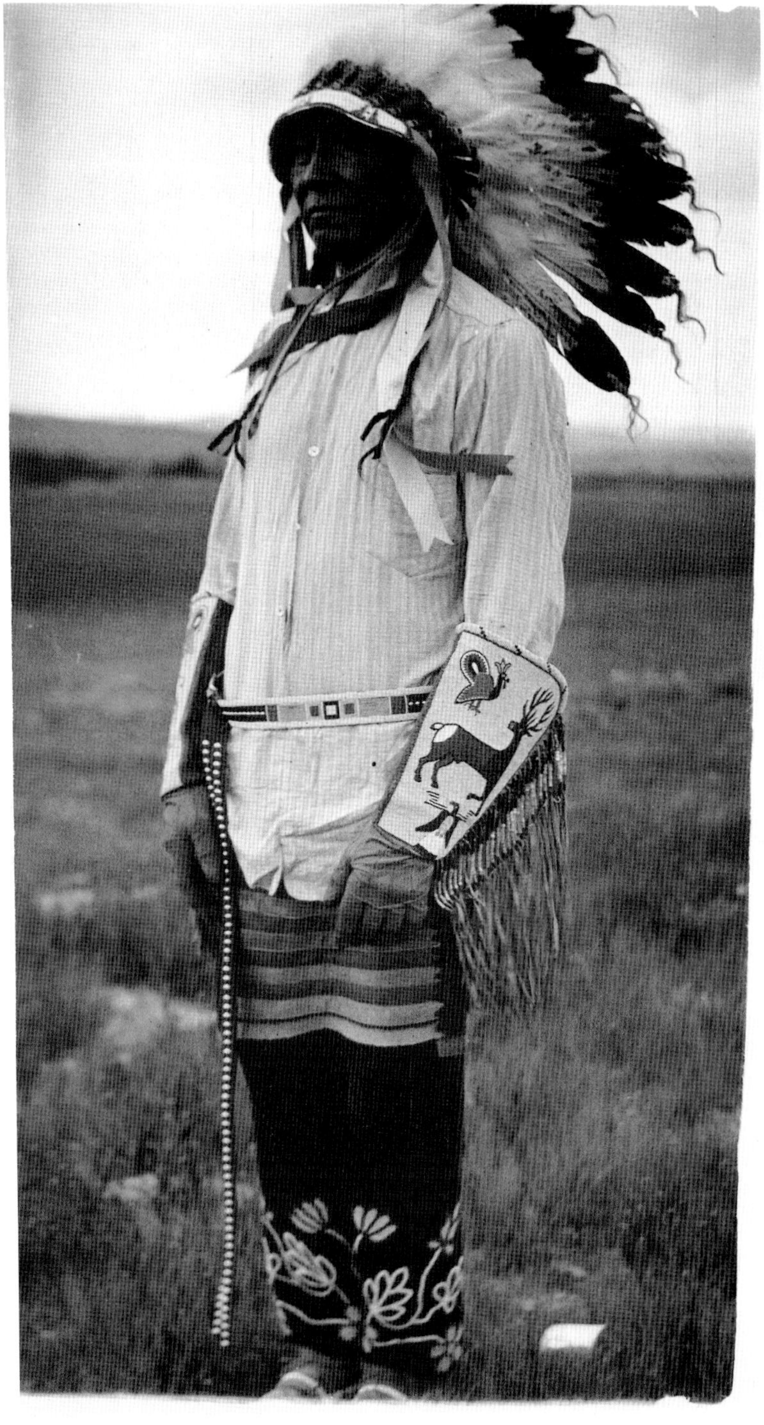

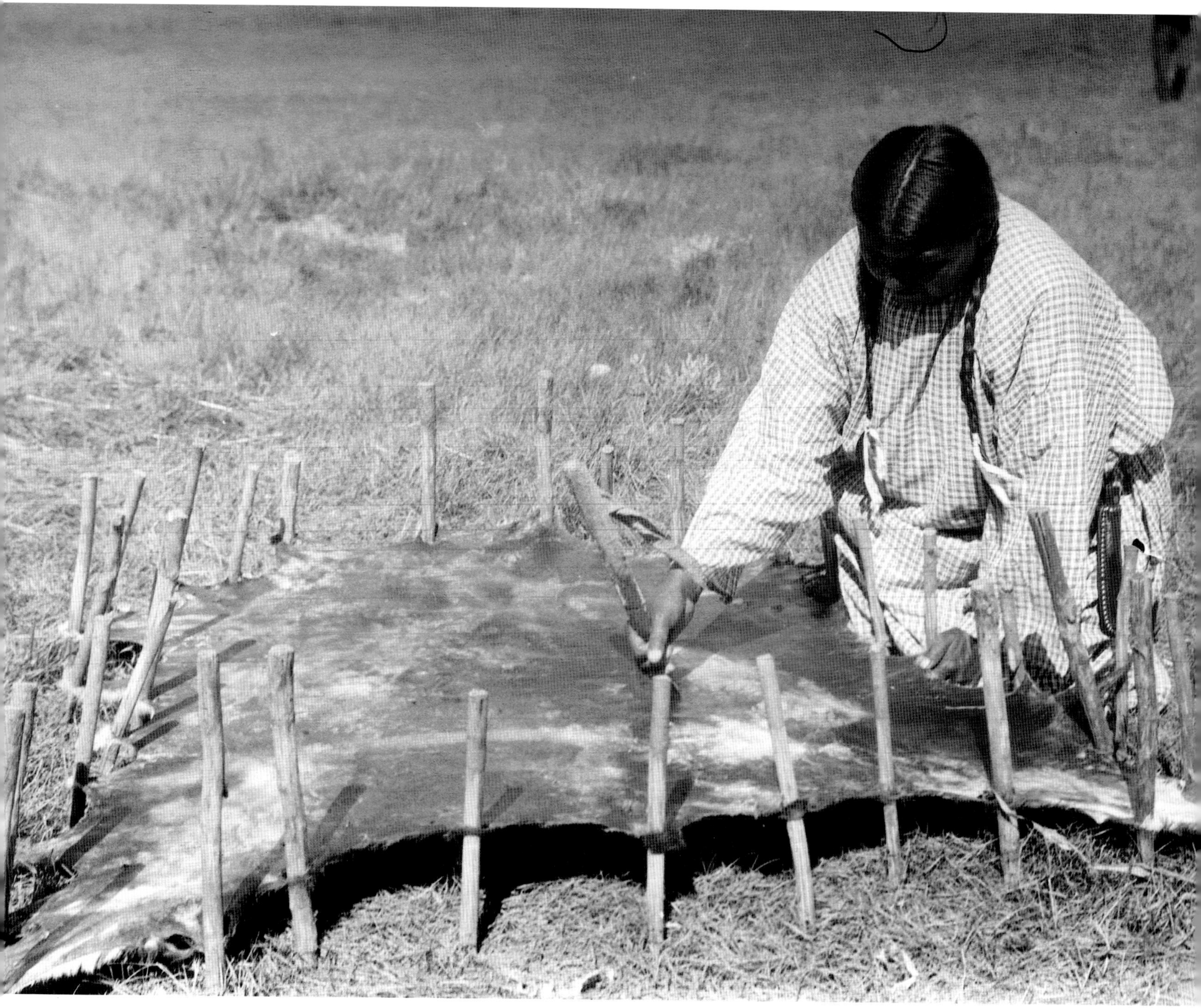

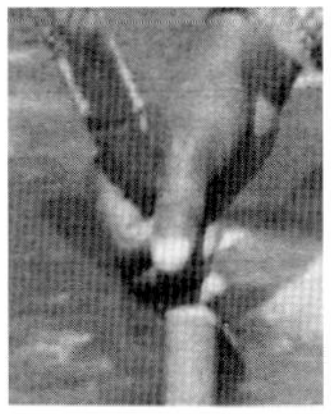

79. Fixing a Cowhide

INFORMANT: JOHN WOODENLEGS

79a. This is Turkey Legs' wife preparing a cowhide to be used for moccasin soles. She is scraping off the inside of the hide. It's quite a job to prepare a hide properly.

79b. Preparation of leather goods for a multitude of uses was one of the most arduous tasks performed by Indian women. In the decades before Cheyenne surrender, the number of workers required for tanning affected marriage patterns—a man often married two or more sisters. A humorous example of the duties expected of such a polygynous husband is found in the Dustin Hoffman film Little Big Man. *See also "Hell Came with Horses" (Liberty 1982) for an account of the changing roles and responsibilities of women—and their increasing hardships—throughout these times.*

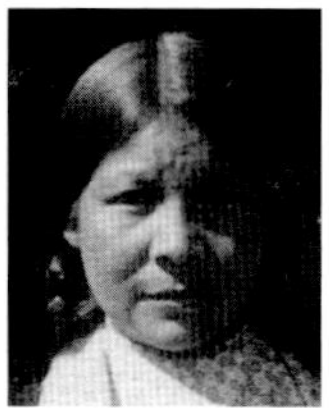

80. Visitors from Oklahoma

INFORMANTS: JEAN POITRA AND JOHN WOODENLEGS

80a. **Woodenlegs:** Jean Poitra is Turkey Legs' daughter. She was married to White Shirt, a Crow, and later on to Mike Poitra. She's quite elderly now and she is talking about the people in these pictures. Jean is standing in the center of the doorway.

Jean: These are Oklahoma people and my daughter Caroline White Shirt front right. The man on the left is Yellow Eyes. That's our house at Busby where this picture was taken. There was never a good picture taken of my father and my mother. Turkey Legs is wearing glasses, and his wife is next to him.

Woodenlegs: Are your father or mother related to these people?

Jean: These are my father's relations from Oklahoma. Carolyn White Shirt is my daughter. They just came and visited us.

Woodenlegs: Did your dad make flutes?

Jean: Yes, he used to go near Birney to cut cedar to make the flutes. I used to watch him make them. He had his own tools. He never used the white man's glue. He cooked pine gum to make the glue and he cut strips of buckskin to tie them together. He played the flutes and he really knew how. He sang love songs. Grover Wolf Voice must have watched him make those flutes and he learned how. My folks used to invite Southern Cheyennes and Sioux to come visit.

80b. Contact between Northern Cheyenne communities in Montana and Southern Cheyenne communities in Oklahoma has continued through the years. Intermarriage between Northern and Southern Cheyennes still takes place, with visits back and forth, especially in the summer ceremonial season.

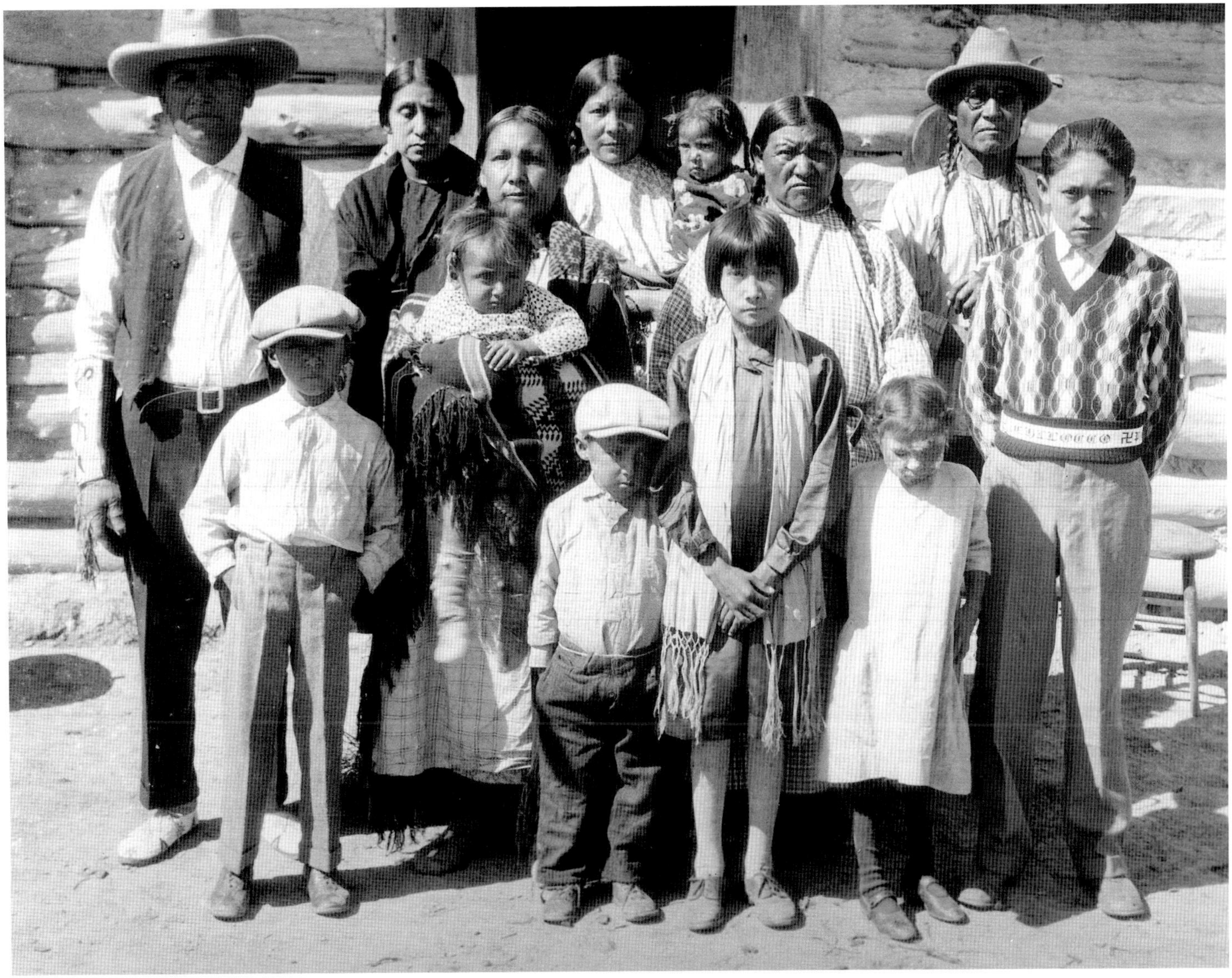

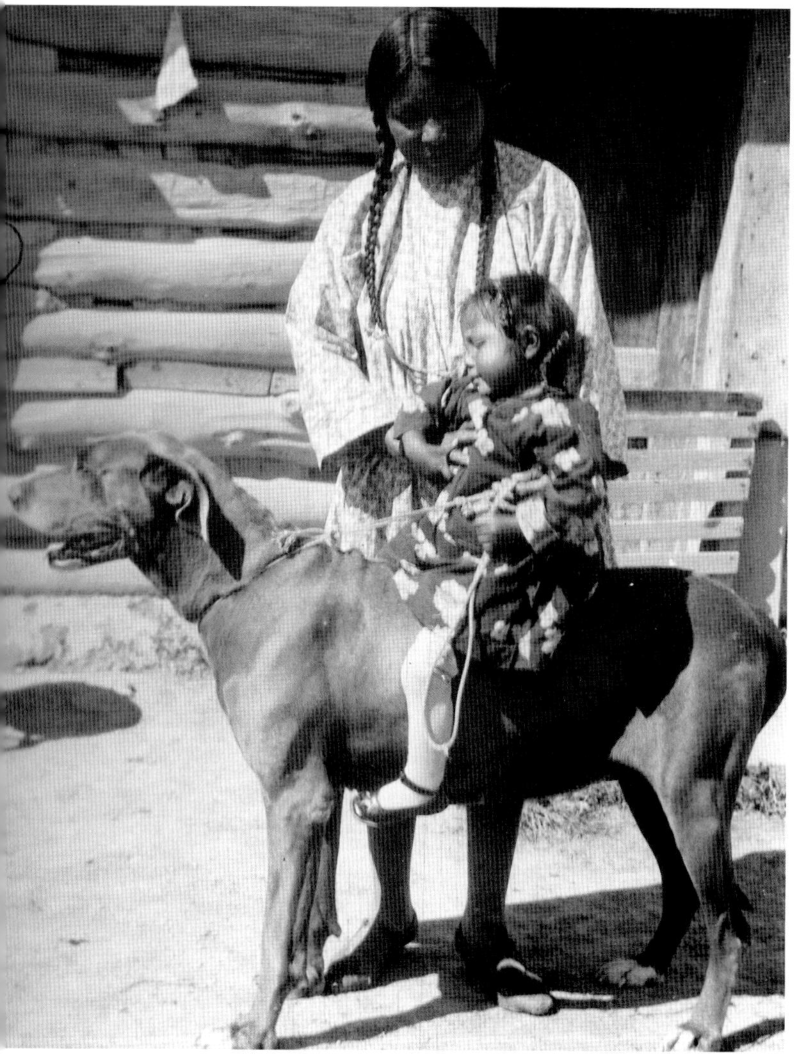

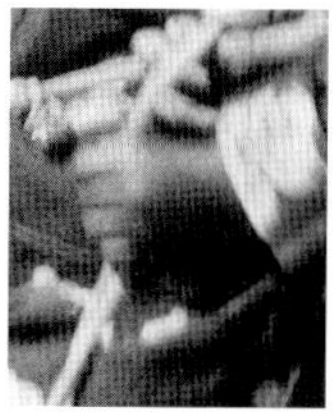

81. An Unwilling Rider

INFORMANT: JEAN POITRA

81a. This is my younger daughter sitting on that big dog. I'm holding her. That dog was really big. I don't know where we got the dog—some white man. We brought that dog a long ways. We hauled it in a wagon.

I went to school at Busby. I was in fifth grade two years. Busby school just started. I didn't go very far. I just learned to talk English anywhere. I don't know nothing. Half a day we went to school and half a day we worked.

81b. American Indian use of dogs, which were originally domesticated from wolves, reaches back thousands of years into the dawn of North American archeology. Dogs were the principal Cheyenne beasts of burden before horses became available about 1750. They also served as a source of food in hard times, as sentinels, and as camp sanitarians, who cleaned up human waste. According to A History of the Cheyenne People *(Weist 1977), some elders referred to earliest Cheyenne history as "The Time of the Dog," followed by "The Time of the Buffalo" as the prereservation period in the plains. "The Time of the Horse" referred to early reservation days before horse slaughter became adopted as government policy after 1920.*

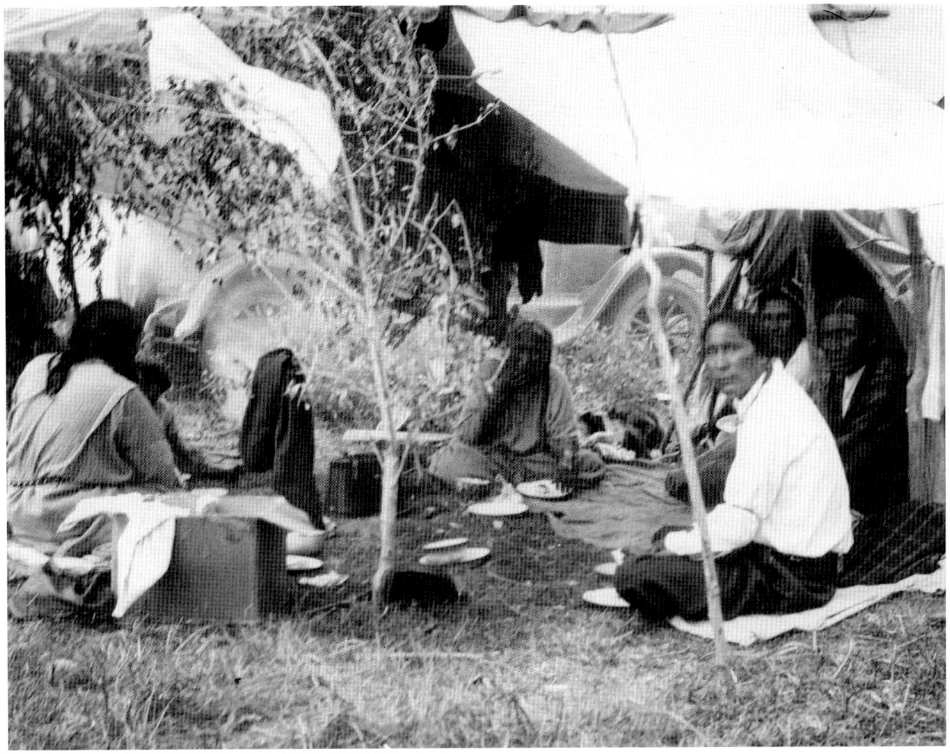

82. Camping at Crow Fair

INFORMANT: MARTIN ROUND STONE, SR.

82a. This picture must have been taken over at Crow. I remember the picture and the old lady that's facing this way. She is Morning Star Woman, Frank Waters' mother. Her English name was Braided Locks. The man in the back is Joseph Red Bird, my older brother. The next man is an Arapaho man. They called him Joe Coe and Joe Barron. Frank Waters [in the white shirt] and the lady on the left is Frank's wife, Sarah Waters, my aunt. They camped in such a peaceful place when they were invited over to the Crow Fair. The man in the white shirt is Frank Waters and my aunt was married to him. It looks like they are eating supper.

82b. Crow Fair, which has taken place annually for about a century, is held at Crow Agency, Montana, each August. Hundreds of tepees owned by Crow tribal members and visitors are erected for this week-long event, which features a spectacular parade on several mornings and dance contests and giveaways each afternoon and evening. The Cheyennes camp at a traditionally designated section of the grounds. Their own annual powwow is held for several days around the Fourth of July. Virtually every organized tribe holds such an annual event, which often functions as a homecoming celebration for members who have moved away from the reservations.

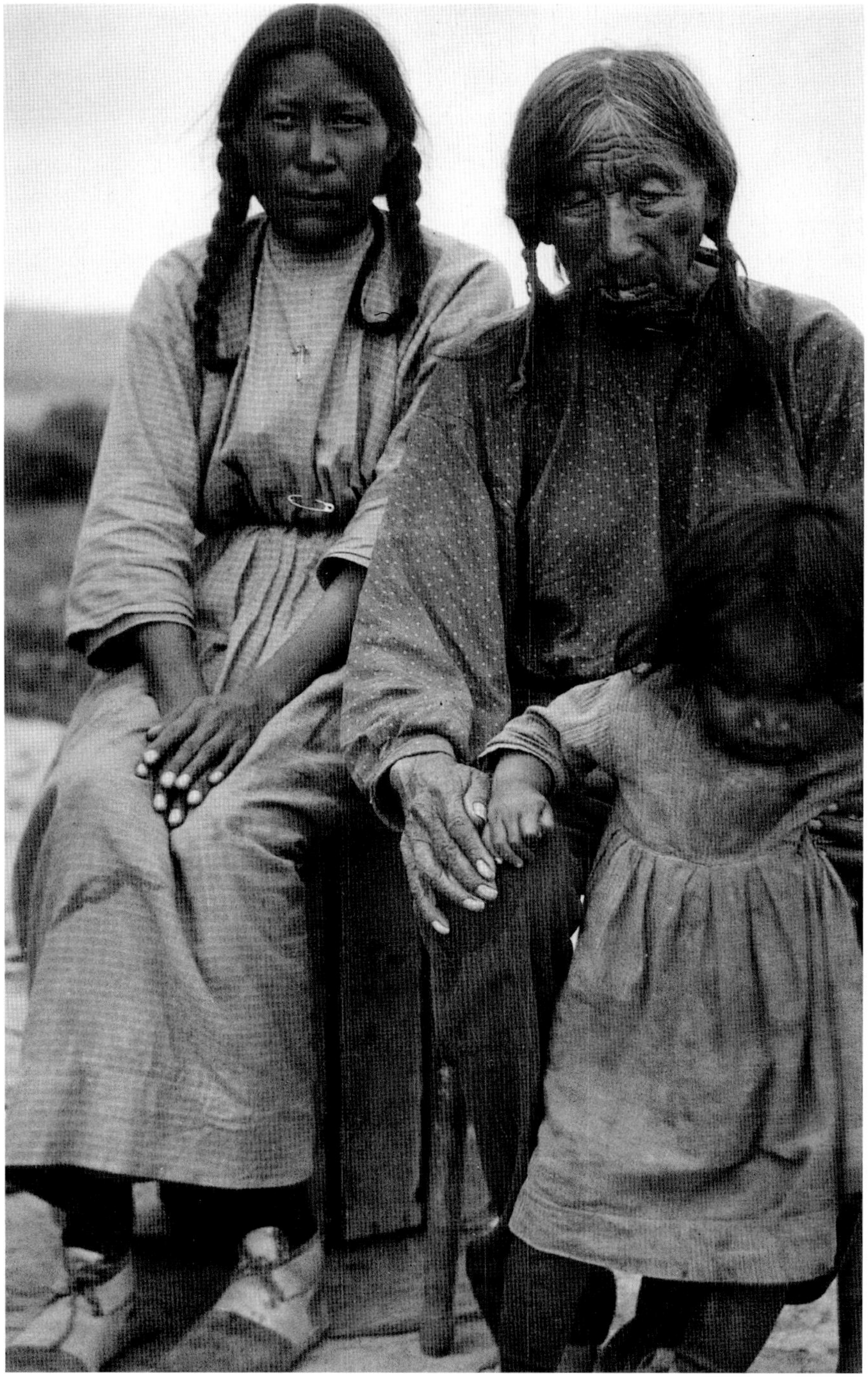

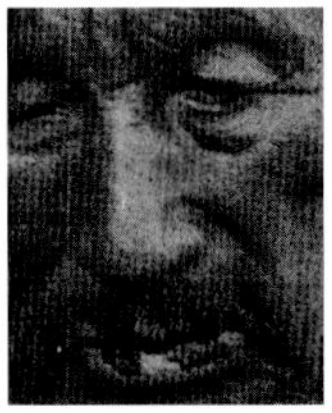

83. Black Whetstone and Medicine Woman with Child

INFORMANT: MARTIN ROUND STONE, SR.

83a. I know these people. They lived the other side of Busby. The lady's name was Medicine Woman. Her father, Black Whetstone, is sitting next to her. I really know that old man and his wife too. Her name was Crooked Nose, a great big woman. We used to visit back and forth, so I know them pretty good. Medicine Woman married Jasper Tall Whiteman. She had a son and daughter. I still think about them today when I go by their place. The little girl, Agnes, is full grown today, even a grandmother. In an Indian way she is my sister. Her brother was Antoine Tall Whiteman—he died a few years ago. Agnes married Clarence Medicine Top; they live over in Birney. Clarence used to work on the roundup with me and with John Woodenlegs.

83b. Marquis noted that this picture was taken in 1926. The roundup mentioned was part of the Cheyenne cattle program in effect on the reservation in the early 1900s. Cheyenne men loved their work as cowboys, which was facilitated by their long experience with horses. Marquis pictures of Cheyenne cowboys are found in The Cheyennes of Montana *(Marquis 1978: 163) and in* A History of the Cheyenne People *(Weist 1977: following 164).*

John Stands in Timber in Cheyenne Memories *also recounts some of his experiences as a line rider or cowboy (Stands in Timber and Liberty 1997).*

84. Bob Tail Horse

INFORMANT: JOHN WOODENLEGS

84a. This man is Bob Tail Horse. I knew this old man. He was such a kind man, jolly. He liked to dance. He was a medicine man, sort of a doctor to help the sick. I know he owned a white mare with a black colt, and also other horses and cattle. In the picture he seems to be butchering. He's always smiling. One time when he was old, a photographer wanted to take his picture, and he told that photographer that he would bet him ten dollars that his camera couldn't take his picture. So the man took his picture and when he got it developed, it was a blank. So Bob Tail Horse won his ten dollars. It should have been more, maybe a hundred dollars! To perform that—have someone take a picture but it didn't take. But he has had pictures taken riding on horseback. His son, Thaddeus Red Water, is a very big man. Bob Tail Horse was not very big. He lived over towards Ashland. He had a place over there along Logging Creek. He was one of the people I saw when he was dancing, he had a horse tail fixed that he used as a bustle. A long time ago some of the Cheyennes used those. There was a clan of them that used horses' tails for bustles. He was one of them. He's the only one I've seen that had that on. Bob Tail Horse's name came from one of his uncles, his father's brother maybe—he had the name "Owns Bob Tail Horses." They seemed to be good war horses, with their tails bobbed off. So his father or grandfather or someone had those kind of horses. They were good horses when the Cheyennes were fighting.

84b. Bobtailed Horse was one of the four Cheyenne warriors who rode out into the river to stop the entry of Custer's battalion into their camp at the lower end of the big village on the Little Bighorn River on June 25, 1876. The others were Roan Bear, Mad Wolf, Calf, and possibly White Shield as well. This delayed Custer's charge until sufficient numbers of additional warriors could ride into the fight and force the soldiers to retreat to the hilltop, where they all died.

Little recognized by Custer battle authorities, this may have been the single most dramatic and heroic event in the entire fight. See The Fighting Cheyennes *(Grinnell 1956) and* Crazy Horse *(Sandoz 1961: 328).*

Bobtailed Horse also served as a scout for the army against the Nez Perces in autumn 1877 at the Battle of Bear Paw Mountain. At the conclusion of this fight Chief Joseph made the famous surrender speech, including the words "From where the sun now stands, I will fight no more forever." Forced to settle in Indian Territory, the Nez Perces were returned to reservations in Idaho and Washington in 1883–84 (Stands in Timber and Liberty 1997: 227–28). For another picture of Bobtailed Horse (following his fifth marriage), see The Cheyennes of Montana *(Marquis 1978: 259).*

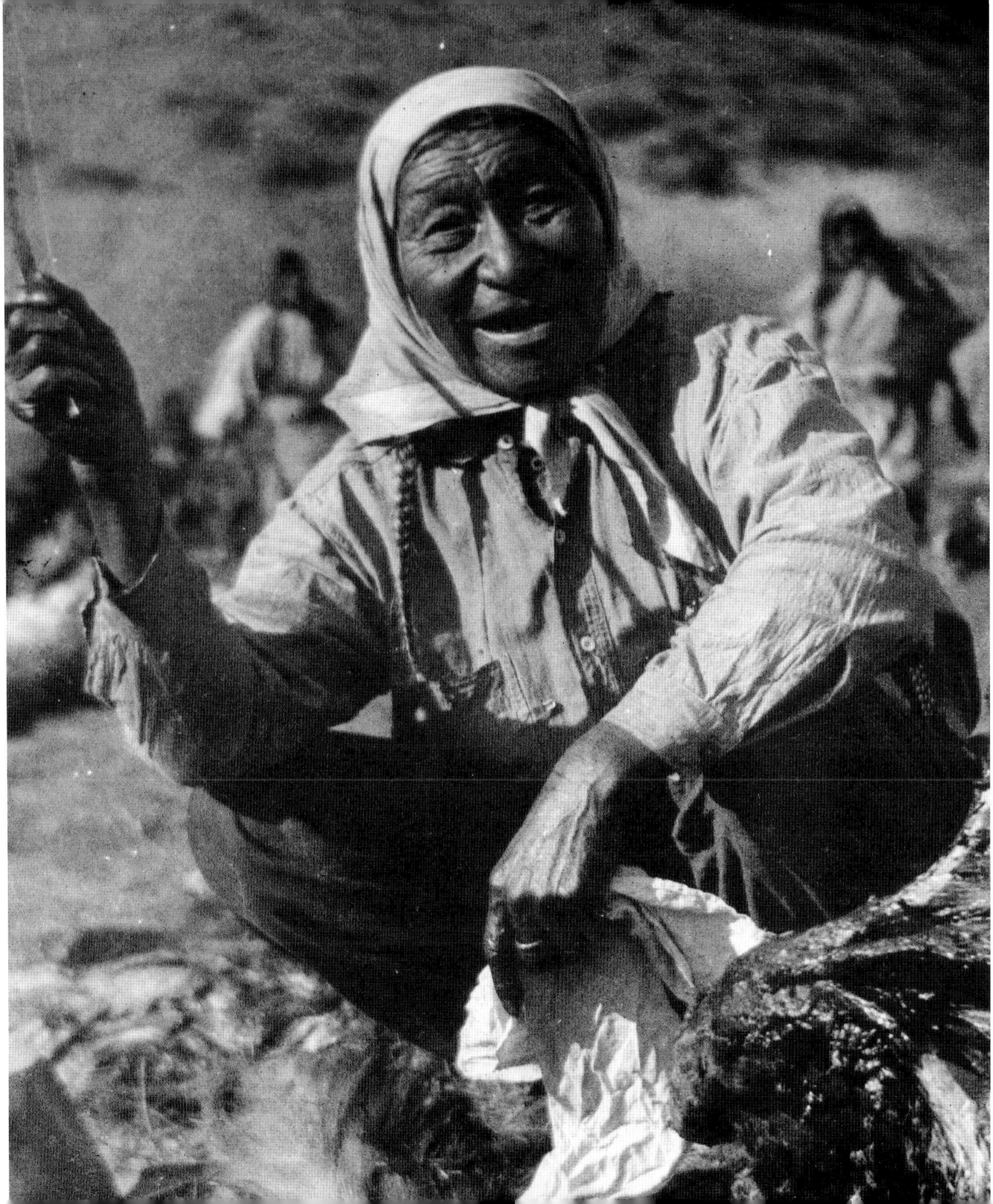

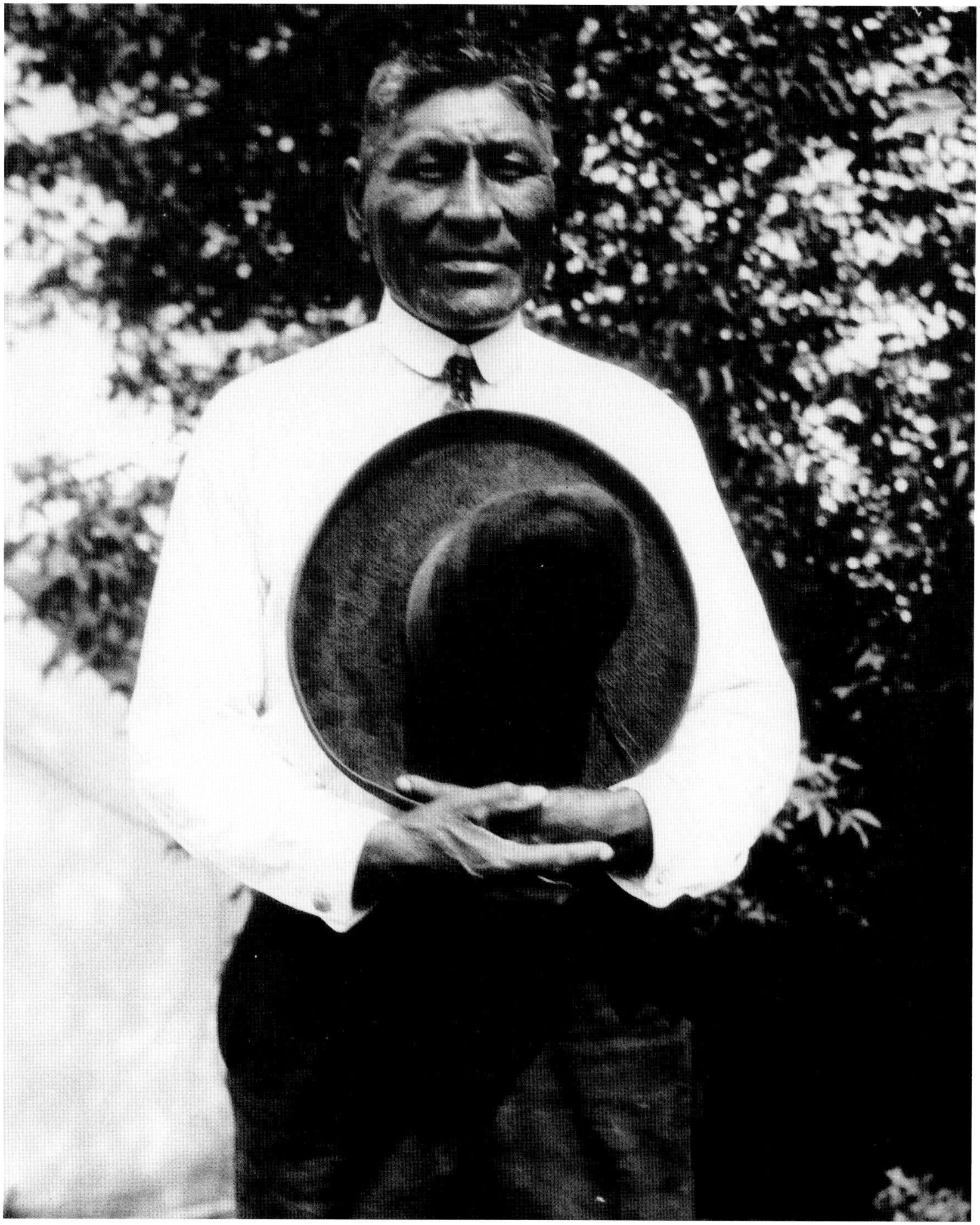

85. Thaddeus Red Water

INFORMANT: JOHN WOODENLEGS

85a. Thaddeus Red Water was a very tall, big man. He went to school at Carlisle Indian School in Pennsylvania. He was one of the football players. He could talk good English and good Cheyenne. He was such a strong man and he knew how to argue with people in English. He helped the football team one time when they were getting beaten. So they asked Red Water, "Can you tackle, we want you to tackle." He said, "Alright." He tackled the fellow running and just knocked him out. Somehow the ball went up in the air and Red Water caught it and ran and they made a touchdown. So he was a good tackler!

When he came back to the reservation, he worked as an interpreter and worked around the Agency. The Native Church people were going to have a Prayer Meeting. Red Water didn't belong to it and had never gone, but the people heard that the Agency police and the superintendent were going to go and catch these ones going to the Prayer Meeting. At the time, the government didn't like these Native ways of worship. So the church members asked Red Water, "Could you run the meeting for us?" He said, "Gee, I never did go in these Prayer Meetings. I don't even know one song, and I don't know what you do." "But you can talk English and when the superintendent or the police come to catch us and put us in jail, you can interpret for us. You can talk to them, and you'll be running the meeting." Now I think my father drummed for him, and he (my dad) did the singing. So they got Thaddeus to run the meeting in a tepee and nobody never came—no policemen, no superintendent, no missionaries. The Good Spirit kept them away, I guess. But that meeting got Red Water started and he thought it was a good way of worship. He finally joined the church. Later he got to run meetings and he sang songs. He got good. He felt so good in a meeting one time, people were just singing. Wild Hog happened to be in there and boy! He can just holler, war whoop you might call it. Red Water had his peyote feathers—"I was feeling so good and this guy must have hollered 'yeeeee.' I throwed my feathers in the air and then I jumped up and grabbed them! I thought they were going to go in the fire! Then I sat back down." To scare a great big man like that!

Thaddeus helped as a delegate to go to Washington for the Cheyennes. He had some education and could talk English, so that was good. He was married to Spotted Wolf's sister and later to an ex-wife of Little Chief. As I know, he never did have any children. He had lots of other relatives though. He always talked good—he was kind of a friend to my father, and that's why I know him. He used to visit us. He worked hard, he had a team of horses. He did a lot of interpreting.

85b. One of several periods of government suppression of the peyote religion or Native American Church is referred to here. For general accounts of the history of this religion, see the works of Weston La Barre, an anthropologist who studied and fought for its legality for many decades. The experiences of Thaddeus Red Water at the Ghost Dance and as a troublemaker in an early Cheyenne camp can be found in Cheyenne Memories *(Stands in Timber and Liberty 1997: 258, 276).*

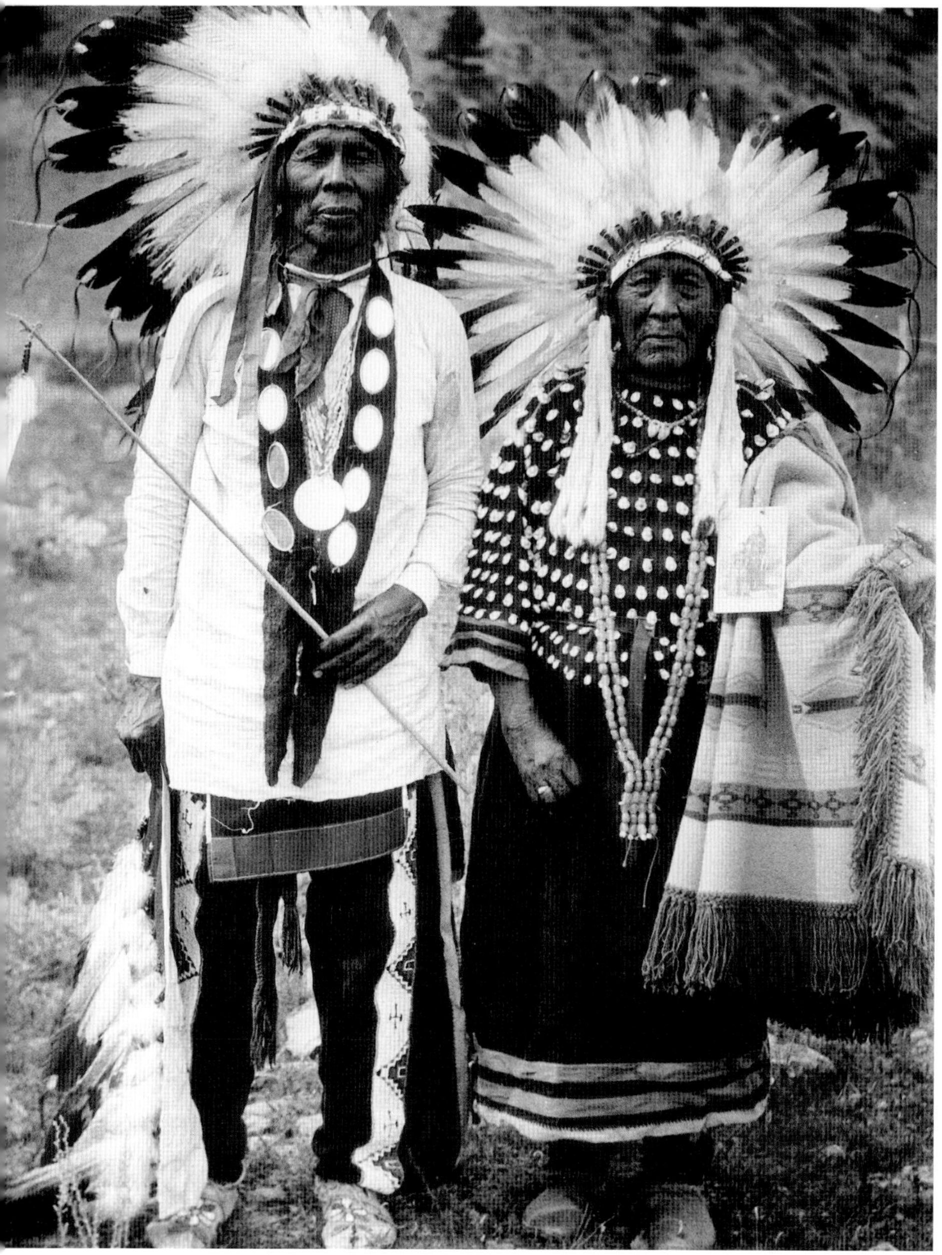

86. Hollow Wood and Wife

INFORMANT: JOHN WOODENLEGS

86a. This is old man Hollow Wood and his wife. He farmed and planted garden and had cattle and horses. He traveled clear to Miles City to parade and dance, and he liked that kind of life. Such a kind man, never spoke rough or anything to anybody. That's the way he made his living out there on Logging Creek. He was good to everybody—he wanted to be related to everybody, a grandfather or great-grandfather to a lot of children.

His wife was a Sioux. She could understand Cheyenne and her husband could understand Sioux, so each talked in their own language to the other, but he could not speak Sioux and she could not speak Cheyenne. They used to travel to South Dakota in a wagon with a team of horses to go visit her relatives. Marquis said that Minnie was the only woman in her tribe entitled to wear a war bonnet, because she had taken part in actual fighting along with the men.

86b. The communication process of Mr. and Mrs. Hollow Wood, who could understand the other's language but were unable to speak it, was surely unusual. Women warriors among the Sioux and Cheyennes were rare enough to be well remembered. Among the Cheyennes the most famous was Buffalo Calf Road Woman, who rescued her brother at the June 17, 1876, Battle of the Rosebud. Elsewhere Mrs. Hollow Wood has been identified by Marquis as a "favorite" of Gen. Nelson Miles when she was a Sioux prisoner at Fort Keogh (Marquis collection labels in Custer Battlefield archives).

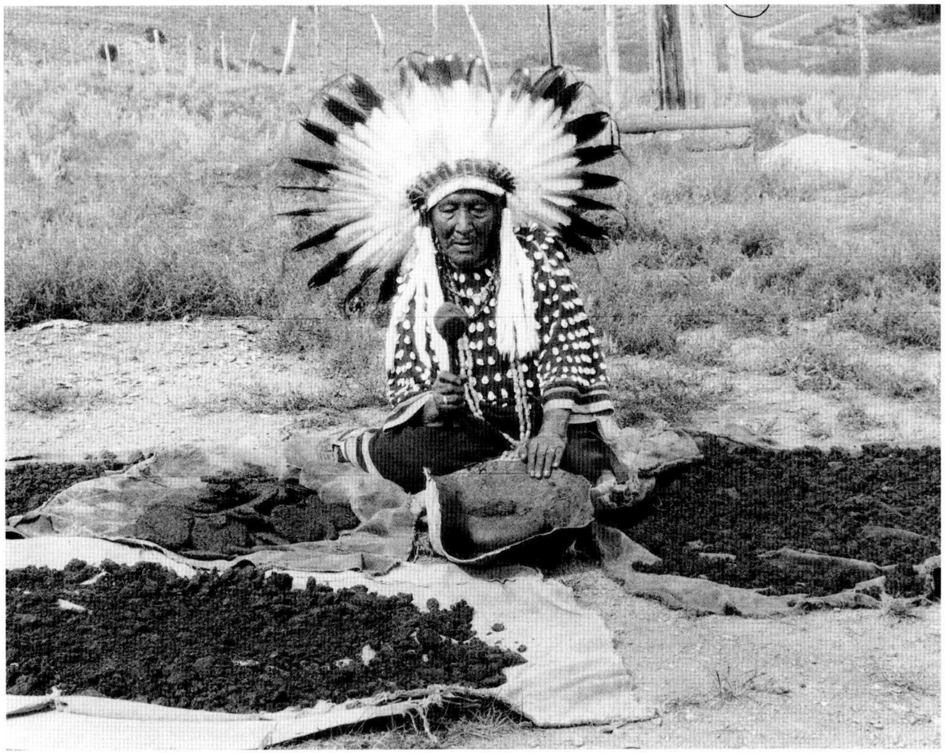

87. Pounding Chokecherry Patties

INFORMANT: JOHN WOODENLEGS

87a. This is Hollow Wood's wife, Minnie. She is showing how to pound chokecherry patties to mix with dried pounded meat to make pemmican. She has a rawhide plate and the rock to pound things together. She pounded up the chokecherries earlier and made the patties and let them dry. People dried them for use in the winter.

She has her bonnet on, elk teeth dress and moccasins, but you don't wear them when you are fixing pemmican or chokecherries. But she is working. I know people have work clothes they put on when they are working, but she must have put on this dancing dress, one of her best dresses, because someone asked her to do it. She must have cooperated with the photographer. Maybe he asked her to be dressed this way.

87b. As Woodenlegs suggests, Mrs. Hollow Wood's dress-up costume for pounding chokecherries was probably encouraged by the photographer.

Processed wild fruit, very high in nutritional value, was dried and stored for later use. The pits are included with the rest of the berries, so the resulting dish can be scratchy to swallow unless strained. It is usually cooked with sugar and flour to make a pudding.

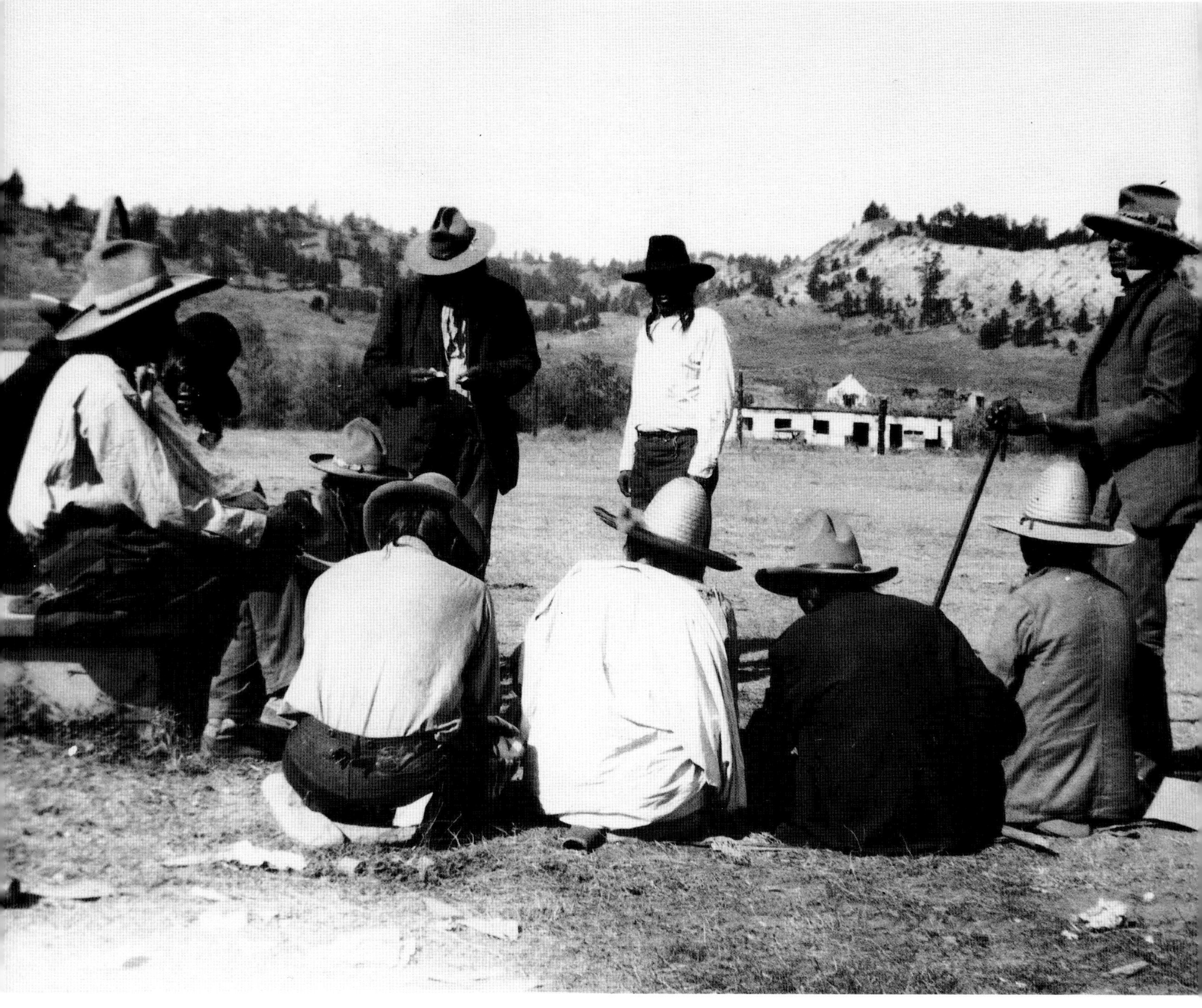

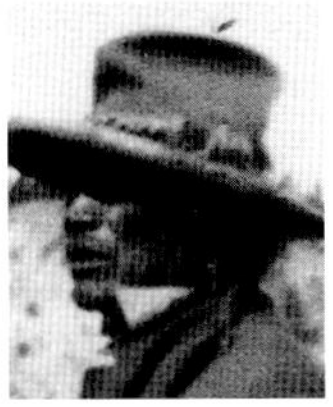

88. Talking It Over

INFORMANT: JOHN WOODENLEGS

88a. In this picture, standing is Richard Woodenlegs, Black Stone, and Spotted Black Bird (with cane). Cheyennes used to have lots of race horses. The race horse barns are in back. These men are gathered close to the Lame Deer fairgrounds. Sitting down is Grasshopper, Medicine Flying, Issues, Porcupine, and Otis Fingers. These older men talk about old times—maybe they were talking about the Black Hills claims. Some of these men were scouts in Miles City. They had their own places and houses and they lived on their places. They had cattle, horses, gardens, wagons. As a young man at the time I should have listened closely to these people. I have seen them sit around in a circle and talk about old times. It was a lot of good information. Spotted Black Bird and Flying were from Birney. Fingers was from Ashland, Porcupine from Rosebud, Issues and Black Stone were from Lame Deer.

At the fair, they had races and they exhibited garden stuff. There used to be a well there—these men are sitting on a platform that was there. Now today there's houses all over, offices and the Tribal Office. It's all changed. These good old men were willing to share their past experiences. The white people who came to trade there—like Mr. Stohr who ran the store—these people thought a lot of these older Indians. They said they were really honest people. So they must have got-ten that from their folks. There were a lot of them besides the few that had their pictures taken. This picture was taken in August 1928, according to Dr. Marquis' notes.

88b. At least five Custer fight veterans—Woodenlegs, Spotted Black Bird (Isaac Black Bird), Flying (or Turkey Legs), Issues, and Porcupine—from four different reservation communities are shown among the eight men identified in this picture. Spotted Black Bird is portrayed in figure 25, praying at the battlefield. Otis Fingers was one of the tribal chiefs, as was Grasshopper (aged 78 in this picture). Marquis comments most tellingly on the failed efforts of history-minded outsiders to gather information from such sources, saying that their haste, bad manners, and pushiness drove the old warriors into permanent silence (Liberty 1996: 125–38).

The race horse barns mentioned here are long gone, having been replaced by contemporary project housing needed for the growing Northern Cheyenne population.

89. Visiting Together

INFORMANT: JOHN WOODENLEGS

89a. This picture was taken at the Sun Dance in Lame Deer, July 2, 1928, according to Dr. Marquis' notes. These men are sitting around visiting. From left to right is Blue Hawk, a Spanish boy that the Cheyennes captured, and adopted him over in Birney. An old couple over there adopted him as their son. He lived over there and later he had a chance to go back to his people, but he didn't want to go. He raised cattle, real good horses.

The next person is Kills Back. He lived just below Busby, east of Busby on the Rosebud Creek. He seems to dress up and be a dancer taking part in these celebrations. He lived on his place there and farmed and ranched. He was one of the scouts for the Army. I knew Kills Back. He was a kind man. He owned a little brown race horse and he always won money. He had a good home, he took part in dances and celebrations, like Sun Dances and different Indian ceremonial doings. All these old scouts were good, they all took part. They were sincere about the Sun Dance and the Arrow Worship, but later some of them went to different churches.

The next person in the picture is Frank Red Woman. He was a good old man. He was younger than some of these older men, but he associated with them in these ceremonial doings. He practiced to be a medicine man. He was a goodhearted man, and he wanted to help in different ways. He helped with the Sun Dance. He also helped rodeo. He had a daughter named Flossie Red Woman, and two sons that I know: Eugene Red Woman and Joseph Red Woman. He lived with them and he worked and had cattle and horses. He took part in the singing at the powwows and dances. He was very good with the Sun Dance. He tried to take care of the things that they need for that—he tried to save them. He fixed porcupine headdresses and war bonnets and travois. He knew how to make those things. He gave me some cedar—I have that cedar. It was to ask blessings for the children. He called me "friend"—he was a very good friend.

The next man with the big hat, I don't know, but the next man to him is Starving Bear. He had a daughter Mary Starving Bear, and a son named Jack. The daughter married Charles Bear Comes Out. He was an older man. They had one boy named Joe Bear Comes Out. Starving Bear was a friend to my father and he was such a good, kind man. They were all friends. My father was good to them and they were good to him. That's how I got to know some of these older people.

89b. It takes a keen eye to discern the identities of the five men photographed here. The surprising thing is that Woodenlegs and his team could make as many positive identifications in these pictures as they did. Also note the keen memory for horses, as illustrated throughout this volume.

The Mexican captive Blue Hawk grew up Cheyenne and died in Montana in 1926.

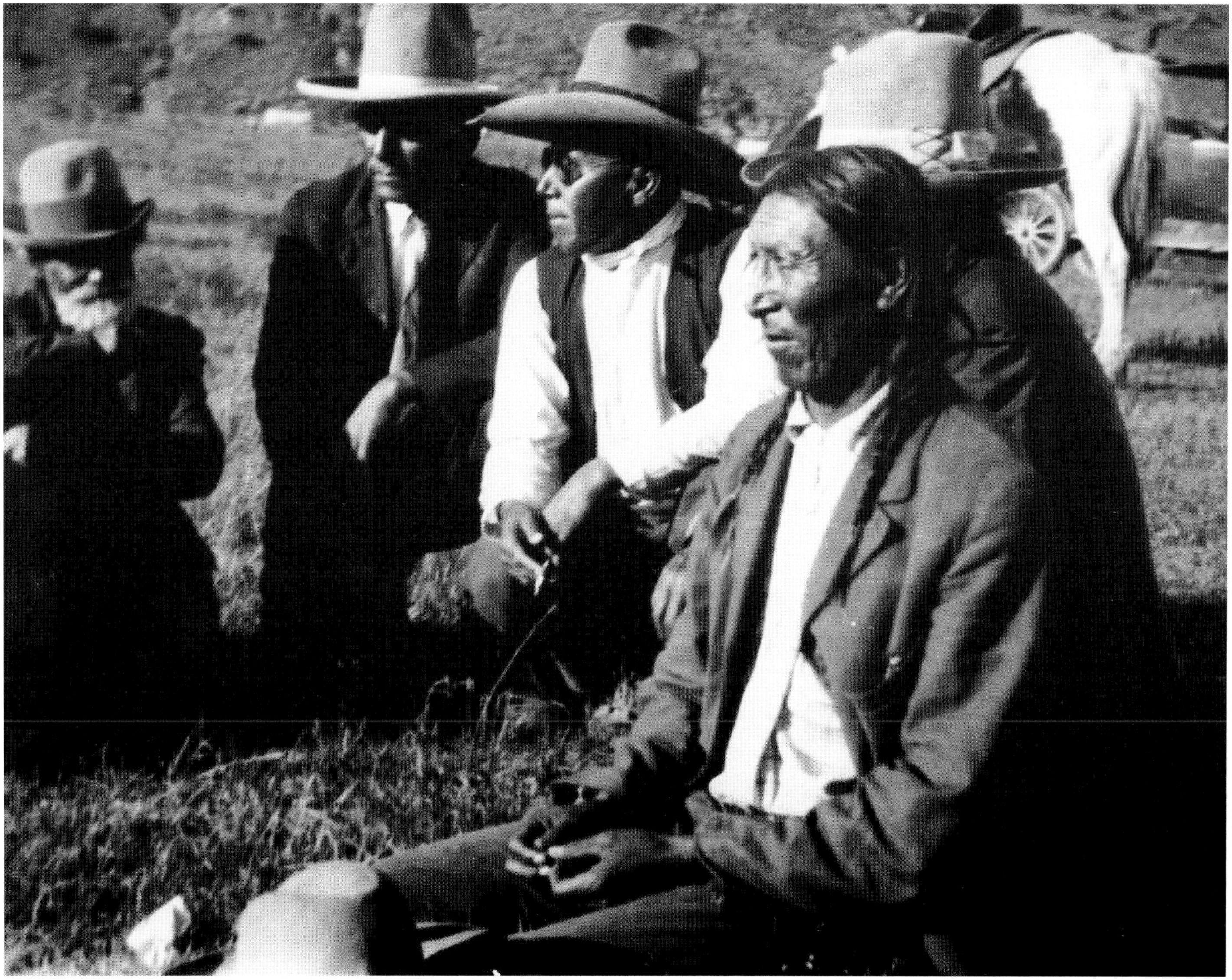

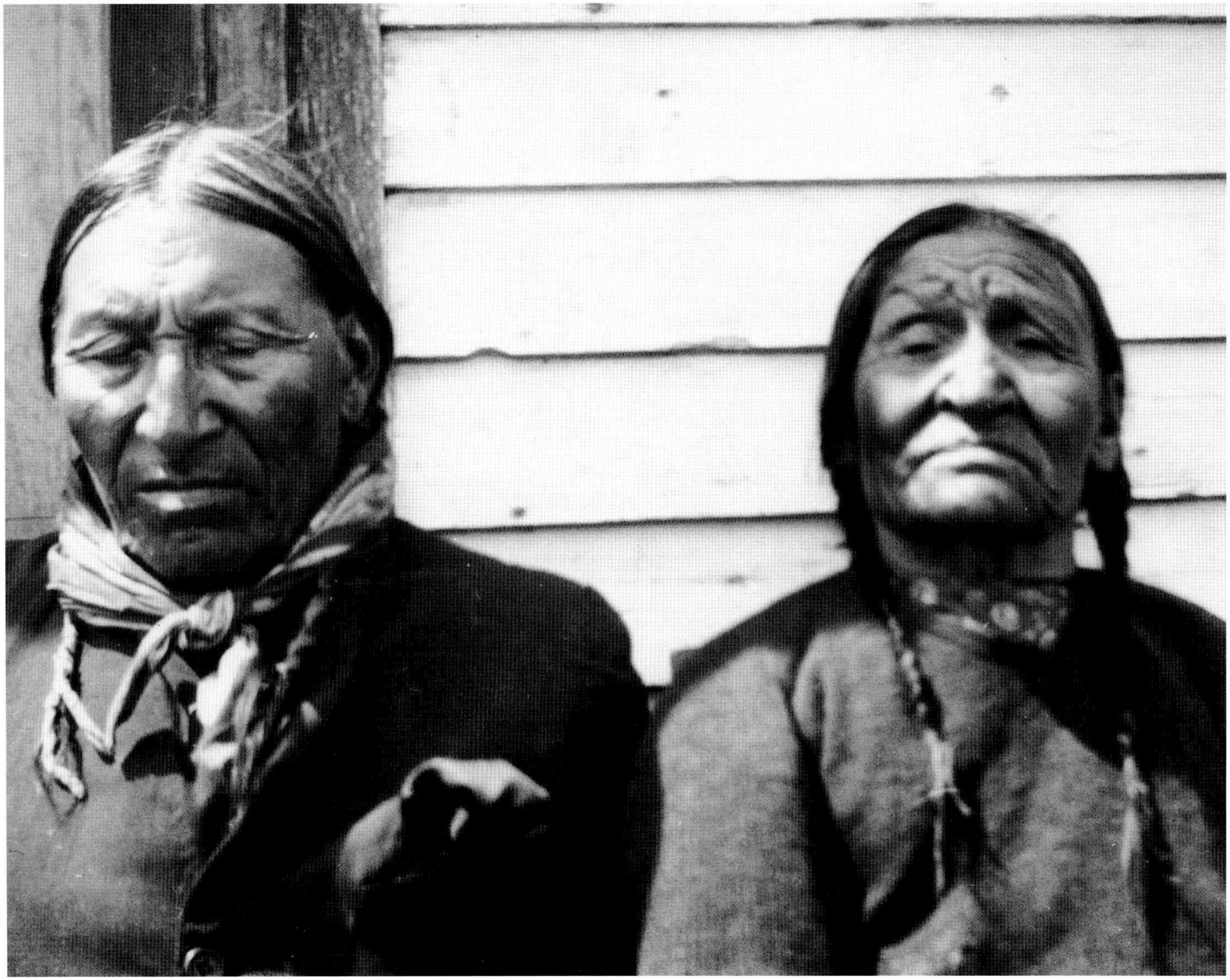

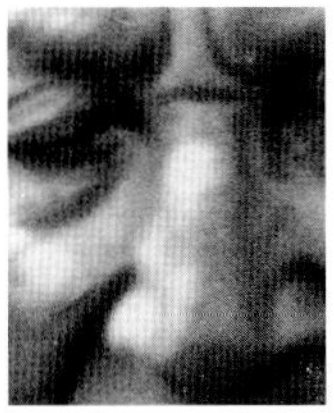

90. White Wolf and Wife

INFORMANT: JOHN WOODENLEGS

90a. This is White Wolf and his wife. He is from Ashland. He has a handkerchief around his neck and his coat on. His eyes are shut, but his wife is looking. I have known them because I know their son, Isadore. Isadore married one of Little Eagle's daughters and they had four boys: one of them died, one was Joseph, the second was George and then Fred.

Old man White Wolf was a scout for the U.S. Army. Now two of his grandsons were old enough to join the Army in the Second World War. Old man White Wolf lived below Ashland on a ranch. They were good people—the older people were good people, especially the ones who were trained by the Army. These old people had the cattle and the horses and the gardens—they did real good. They were quiet people, didn't say much but when they did say things, they talked good to people. I knew these people because of my grandparents. White Wolf worked hard around his place, he kept it up good and neat. They cut down timber to build their own log houses.

90b. White Wolf (also called Shot in the Head) was a Custer fight veteran who reported the gathering of soldiers' money scattered on the battlefield or found on the bodies of the dead after the fight. He said that some of it was cached in pockets in the sand rocks along Reno Creek (Stands in Timber and Liberty 1997: 206).

91. Black Ree and Wife

INFORMANT: JOHN WOODENLEGS

91a. This is Paul Black Ree and his wife, Strange Owl Woman, and a little girl who is either their grandchild or great-grandchild. I have known Mr. Black Ree for a long time. He always talked to people good and also his wife. He was one of the Cheyenne wrestlers. He wasn't very tall, he was short and blocky. He lived on his place and had a frame house. As big as he was, he still rode horseback and had cattle and he farmed with horses, thrashed wheat and oats, and put up hay. He shipped cattle. Being a wrestler, I guess he had to eat certain foods and have exercise and all that. I know he had two daughters. He knew my father and he said he wrestled with him once. The way they wrestled was to stand up to each other and get a good hold of each other. They tried to lift each other off the ground and swing the person around, round and round, and then slam him on the ground. They won when they slammed someone on the ground. But sometimes they could never lift anyone off the ground. They take sides too. When they're swinging one another, the one who is being swung has his legs out—spread out. If his opponent tries to throw him when his legs are out, spread out, he'll catch himself and swing the other guy. People would holler, "His legs has come together!" Then he'd slam him in the ground. That's how they won that. Then they had that Indian arm wrestle too, but this one was a good one where they got together and got a good hold of one another. They both had to say, "We're ready," and then they'd try to lift themselves off the ground so they could swing one another.

Now Mr. Ree told me he trained and just ate certain things. He said he would eat meat with a lot of fat, maybe dry meat with fat and bacon with it. "That's good food," he said. When he took that soup with fat and bacon, he put lard in it too. It was already rich with fat and bacon! He said, "Lately, I went to a feast where they had a prayer service. At noon time I went over there and they had such good food, and then they had something that looked like it was red and it kind of shook." It must have been jello. He said he ate that and he wondered and he asked the people if the white people who made that jello forgot to put something in it, "because every time I chew it, it disappears. There was nothing to it." He didn't quite like the jello. He liked the meat and the fat and the grease. That made him strong. He got to be a real old man. His wife died first. They both died of old age. In this picture they look real good and healthy. They are in front of their house. Looks like there is a stack of hay behind the house. He always worked with horses and cattle.

91b. Perhaps to the surprise of modern nutritionists, Mr. Black Ree appears to have trained on a regime of straight meat and fat with no harm to his health or any concern about cholesterol. His comments on the unsubstantial nature of Jello are some of the funnier observations on record concerning the qualities of white people's food. The Cheyennes also think it humorous that they originally tried to boil watermelon, as they did the squashes it resembled, but it disappeared into a pulpy broth full of seeds.

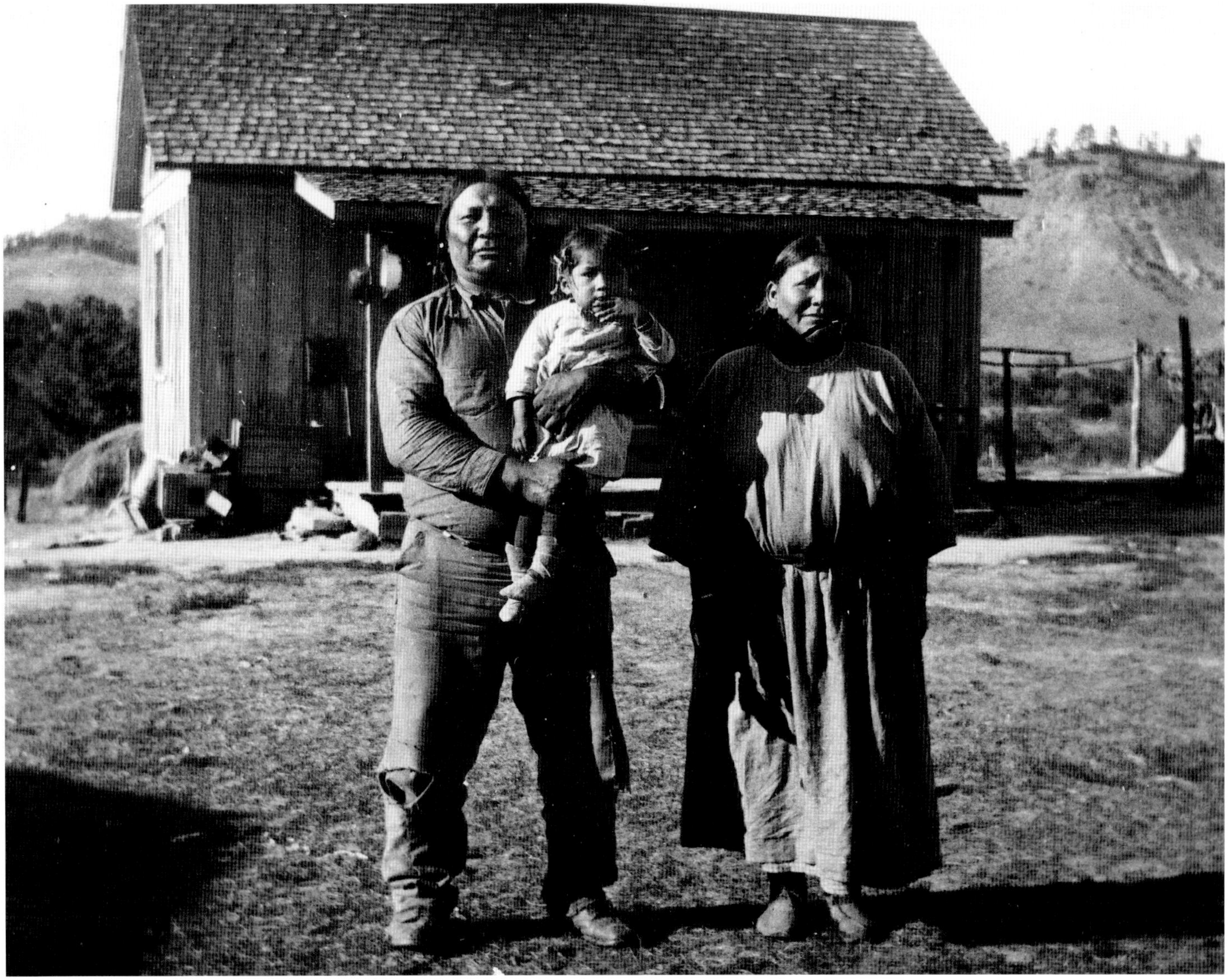

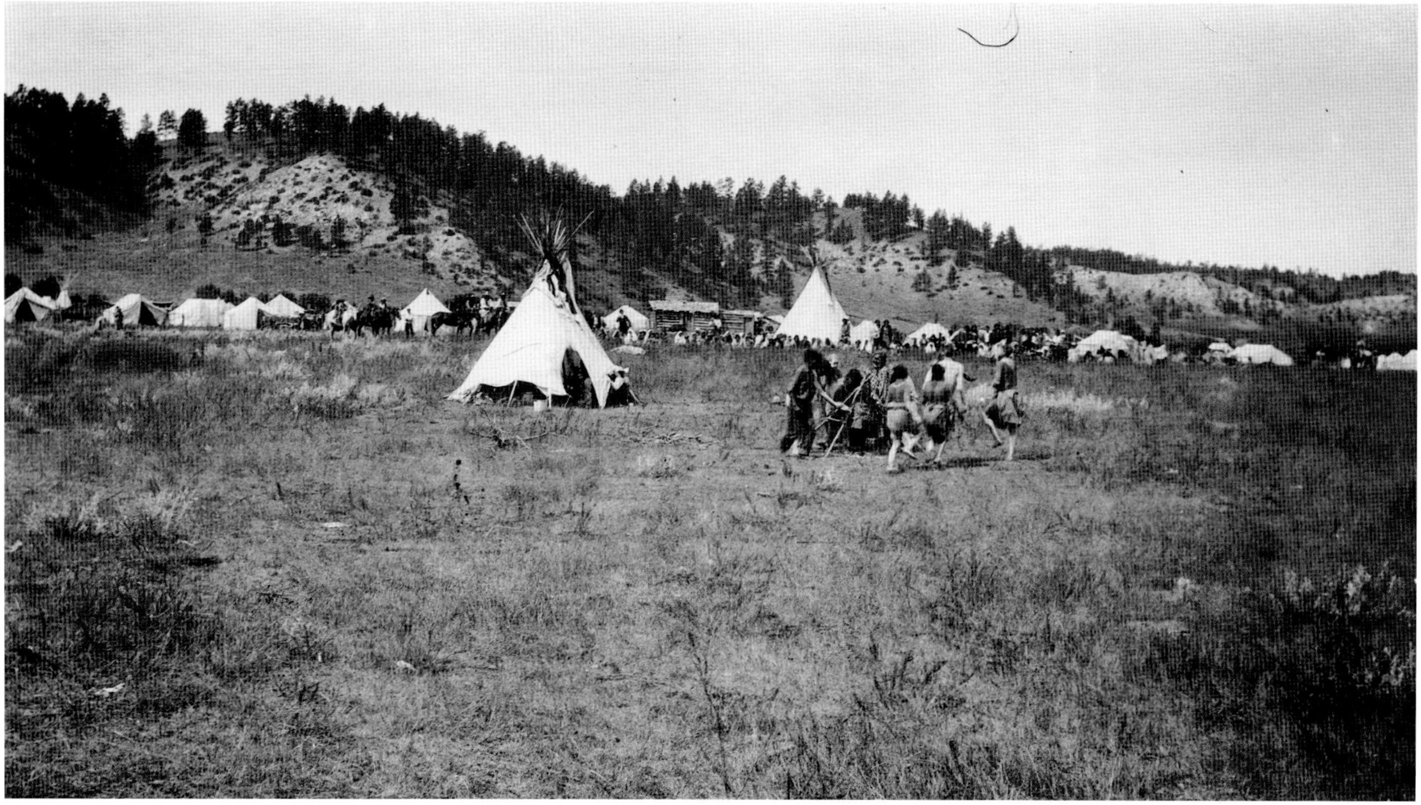

92. Contrary Dance

INFORMANTS: WILLIS MEDICINE BULL AND JOHN WOODENLEGS

92a. **Willis Medicine Bull:** I'm going to talk about the Contrary Dance or Odd Dance. I put one up. It's kind of a ceremonial dance. I used Broken Jaw as the High Priest. We had a tripod set up to hold a big cooking pot over the fire. Inside this tepee, we drew the thunderbird on the dirt and there were markings of lightning on four sticks. They have a pipe and they load it and smoke it. Instead of just passing it on to one another, they throw it to one another. After they fix the thunderbird and the lightning sticks, I had to look underneath the tepee to the four directions and each time I looked, I blew a whistle. We went outside the tepee and this old man sang a song. We stood outside in each of the four directions, ending up by the pot. He was singing songs. When he got done, he took my right hand and he was saying a prayer. He stuck my hand in the pot and stirred the meat with it. I never got burned or hurt. The leaders of that dance are all passed on. They are called kind of clowns too when they dance. They do things the opposite way or backwards and they make people laugh.

After I got my hand back out of the pot, we went back in the tepee, but we went in backwards. Now we're going to come back out and start to dance. Broken Jaw had a certain plant and the three of us each had one too. We went out and started to dance. We danced around the pot. We used that plant and some willow and sage and we'd stick it in the pot and sprinkle some of that hot soup on ourselves. The fourth time we scooped out some meat and ran to the four directions, each one to a person in a white shawl. We put some meat along side this person, on a corner of his shawl. One dancer had to go back for the fourth person.

Today there's just four of us Odd Dancers left: Wesley Whiteman, Swallow, Mrs. Benjamin Limpy, and myself. We have one leader, Daniel Old Bull, from Birney, who knows the songs and the ways of the Contrary Ceremonial. [Tom Weist recorded this interview in 1967.]

John Woodenlegs: The Cheyennes are performing a ceremonial dance. When I was a little boy, I saw one or two of these dances. They only have one tepee in the center, and the people are sitting all around, but not close. They sit quietly and listen. When the dancers go in the tepee, they go in backwards and they come out backwards. They are called Odd Dancers, doing things the opposite way. In front of the tepee, there is a tripod with a pot cooking, either prairie dogs or dogs. After they all get through dressing, they come out and they dance, sing songs and say prayers, both outside and inside. The head priests are inside the tepee. The dancers do different things different ways, like sometimes they lean against the tepee with their feet up. Sometimes they're wrestling with each other instead of just hugging and loving each other. Sometimes they're looking for something and they're going away from it. They have some good songs, and they dance around that pot that's boiling. You can see steam coming from it. They have some sage and willow branches and they dip them in the pot and sprinkle some of that soup on themselves. They really get lively. They're painted white and black spots. It's a ceremonial dance. I never got close to it because you have to sit way away from it. They kind of stir that meat with their hands and they don't get burned or scalded. When the meat is ready, there's people sitting all around, some with white blankets. One fellow takes a piece of meat in his hand and he runs east, runs just as fast as he can go. People sitting on the east side don't try to grab it. If you try to grab it, the Odd Dancer throws it at them. One goes to the south, and one to the west, and one to the north. The people that's sitting close and that get a piece of meat, they all share it. There's a lot of people standing around on horseback, but you never get close to these dancers. They seem to really kick up their heels, they get lively, even older ladies take part and they come alive. When they all get through dancing, they run down to the river to wash off. Some of the people go downstream from where they wash off, and they drink that water. This was called a Contrary Dance. It hasn't been put on now for a long, long time.

92b. The Massaum or Animal Dance (also called the Contrary Dance or Odd Dance) is relatively little known. It was one of the four great Cheyenne religious complexes, along with the Sun Dance, the Sacred Arrows, and the Sacred Medicine Hat. The Contrary Dance did not continue after the performance pictured here (Stands in Timber and Liberty 1997: chapter 6).

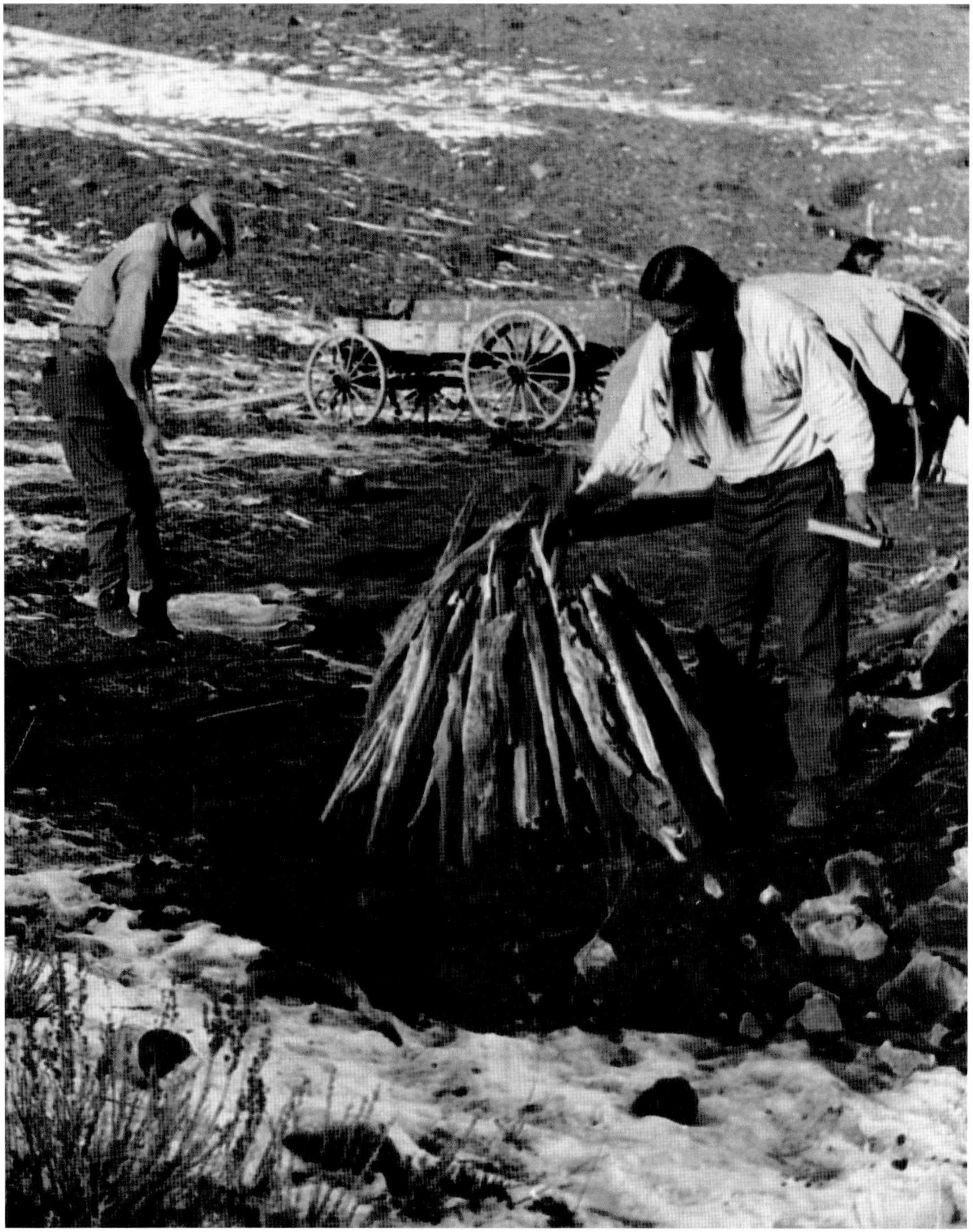

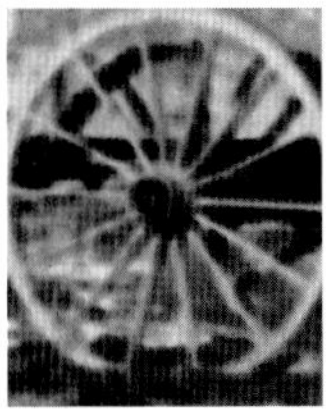

93. Preparing a Fire to Heat Stones

INFORMANT: JOHN WOODENLEGS

93a. This is Dallas Wolf Black chopping wood with his overshoes on and a cap. His cousin, Fire Wolf, is helping. They are fixing a sweat tepee. There's a wagon there by the tepee and a bucket and the wood is piled up, and the rocks. The wood is used to build a fire to get the rocks hot. The sweat tepee is ready there. Some people are covering it up with tarps. There's snow on the ground. These people are from Birney and the picture was taken in Birney. Fire Wolf is older than Dallas. They were both good people and took part in the various religious ceremonies. They talked good to people. Dallas was kind of a leader of the Native Church in Birney. Fire Wolf was a medicine man and doctored sick people. It doesn't seem like they're very cold; they are in their shirt sleeves. After they get the rocks hot, they put them in the sweat lodge and sprinkle water over them. They go inside and cover it over. They say prayers in there and they sing songs. Sometimes when a sick person is in there, they doctor him, but it's similar to a sauna. They have warm water there when they come out. Four times they lift the covering of the sweat lodge—the fourth time, they come out. They have water in there and they keep sprinkling it on the rocks. The rocks are in the middle. They sweat all their sickness out. A lot of people still take sweat baths today. One fellow sort of leads the service in there—he says the prayer and sprinkles the water. It's been done in a good way, but like everything else, we sometimes misuse and abuse it now. But it has helped people in the past; the old people seemed to be healthy and they used sweat baths. This picture was taken in 1926.

93b. Sweat lodges have been a common feature of Indian camps both before and after the reservation era. The use of sweat baths created by putting water on heated stones and praying in an enclosed space dates back many millennia. Modern visitors are sometimes honored by being invited to participate by contemporary reservation hosts.

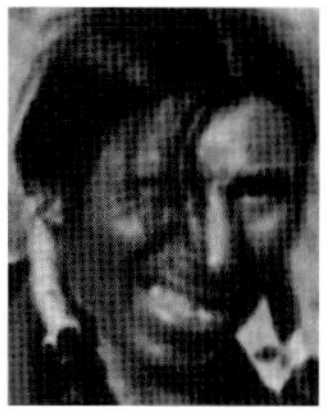

94. Black Eagle

INFORMANT: JOHN WOODENLEGS

94a. This is a good picture of Black Eagle. He's standing right alongside a sweat tepee ready to go in. He has his breech cloth on and he's wearing overshoes, overcoat and has his hair in braids. He's kind of smiling, maybe because the photographer said, "Look over here." There's a wagon alongside of it and a harness hanging there and two tents alongside of a hill, probably in Lame Deer, close to the place where the Tribal Office is now. Black Horses and Issues and different people lived close together near where this sweat tepee is. Black Eagle was married to one of Black Horse's daughters—they had one child. Black Eagle must have gone to school; he could speak English and talk to white people. He worked hard and he was a good Native Church man. He was from Birney too, but he married and stayed in Lame Deer. He worked in Lame Deer. He was a good honest man. These old people were really good.

94b. A completed sweat lodge or tepee is shown here, ready for use. The comment by Woodenlegs on Black Eagle's facility in English indicates that this was not common in Cheyenne reservation communities of the 1920s. John Stands in Timber in Cheyenne Memories *mentions Black Eagle's participation in the last Piegan raid against the Cheyennes in the 1880s, when a war party came south to steal Cheyenne horses. They were not successful (Stands in Timber and Liberty 1997). Nannie T. Alderson in* A Bride Goes West *describes the Cheyennes dancing and celebrating over a Piegan scalp that was taken on that occasion, several years after the reservation was established in 1884 (Alderson and Smith 1942).*

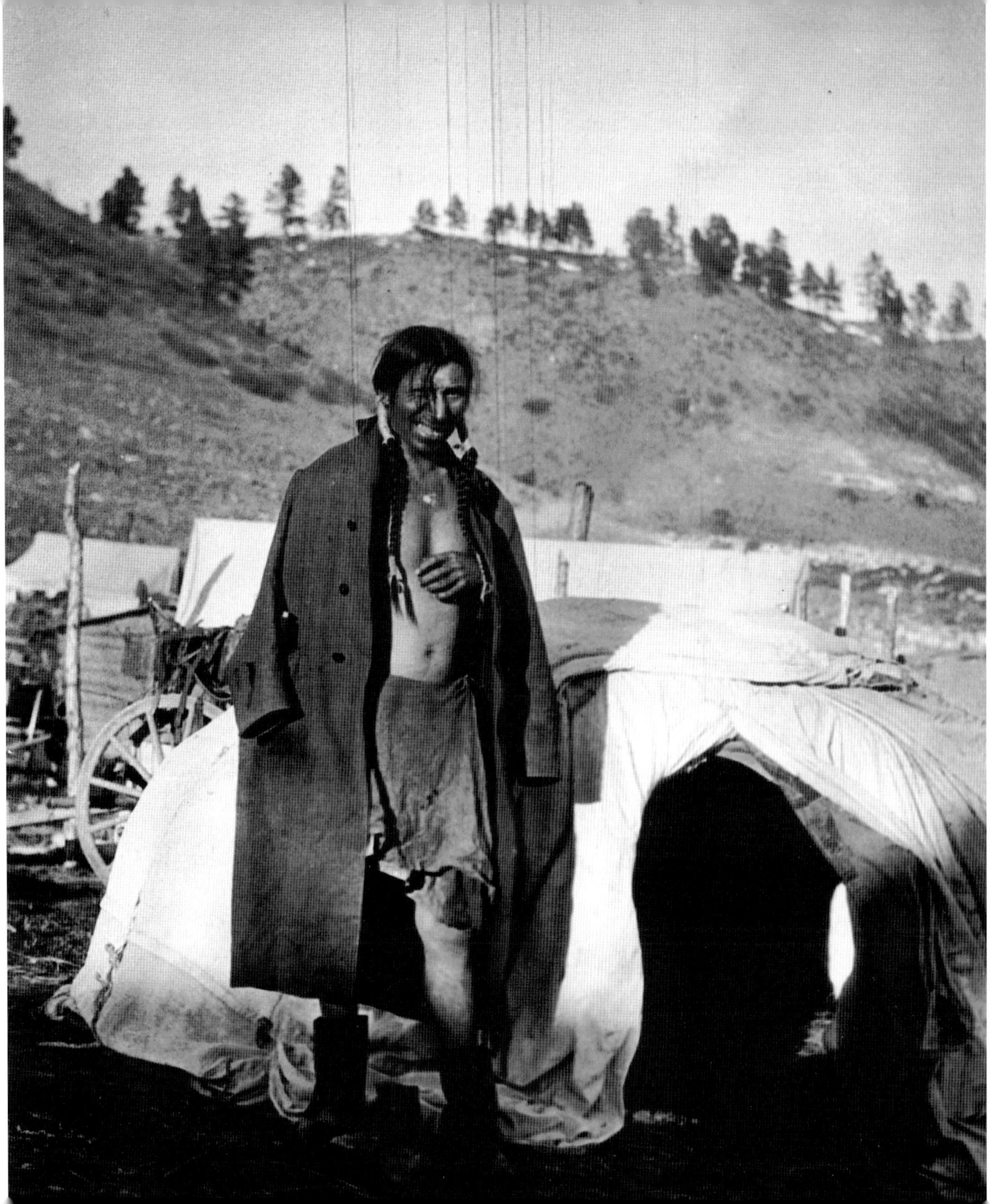

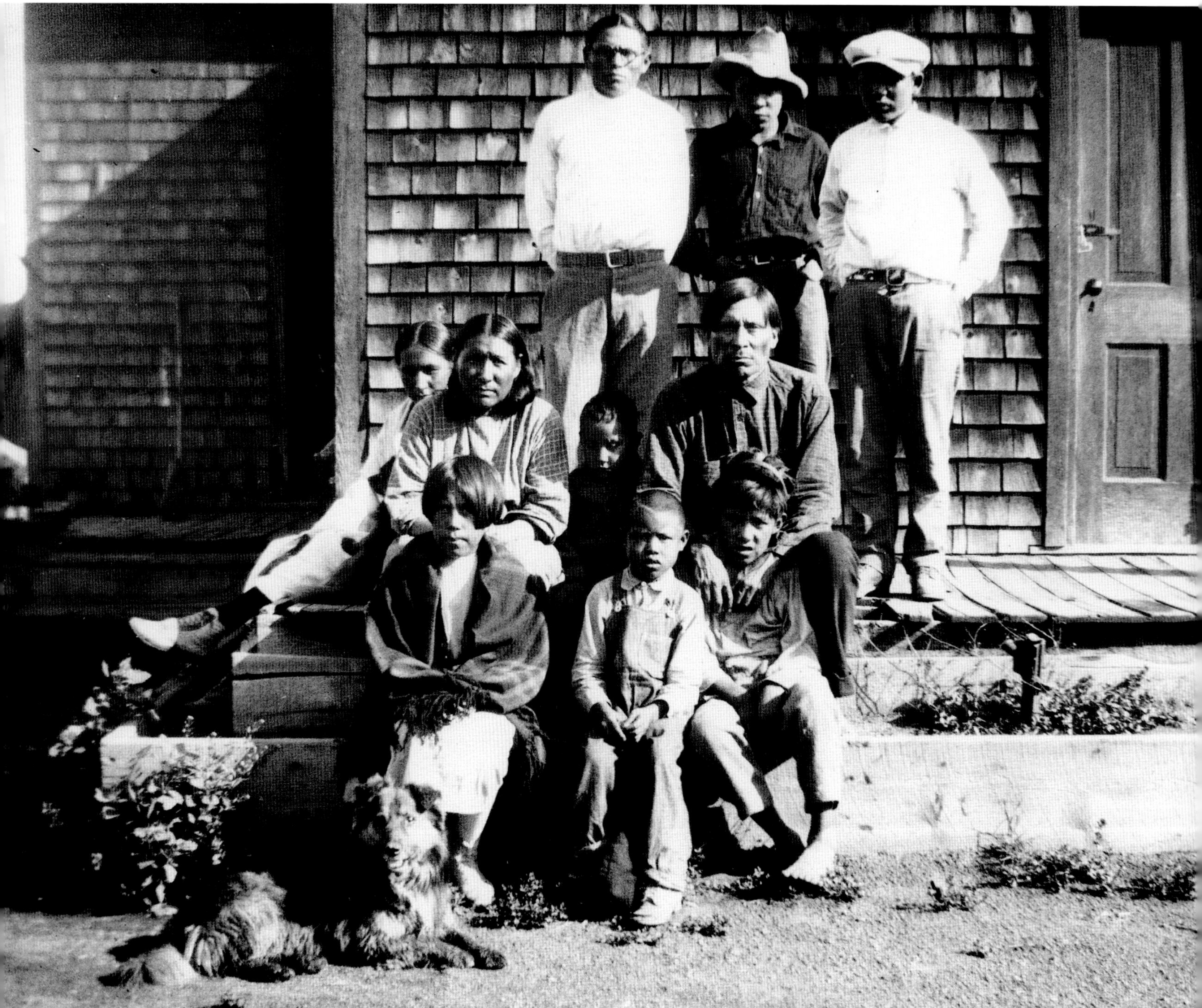

95. Iron Hand and Family

INFORMANT: JOHN WOODENLEGS

95a. In this group picture, the people are (back row, left to right): Charlie White Wolf, Henry Iron Hand, August Scalpcane. Middle row: Mrs. James Atwood, Mrs. Iron Hand, Waldo Atwood, Iron Hand. Front row: Mary Atwood, Henry Scalpcane, Willis Iron Hand.

Iron Hand lived in a government house close to the Agency and close to the barns where the government had a lot of work horses. The barn had hay inside of it and stalls, a tack room and granary, and Mr. Iron Hand took care of it. He was caretaker of this big barn. Winter time when it snowed, he had a white team of draft horses. He drove these with a snow plow that a blacksmith made. It was a V-shaped thing that he made trails for the employees and also for the schoolchildren.

They have a little dog there. He's really posing, looking at the camera man. I guess these Scalpcane brothers stayed there with Iron Hand for a while. Charlie White Wolf was a Southern Cheyenne who stayed with them some.

Iron Hands were just kind people, and he took good care of the barn. At dinner time, his wife prepared dinner and they fed everybody else who might be around. He really took good care of the horses and the milk cow they had there. He worked pretty hard. He went to the Mennonite Church—he was a good churchman. It seemed like he was related to Wolf Blacks and some other good people. His wife was a Lame Woman. He always tried to take care of his job and his family. He had two good boys that were going to school. When Willis Iron Hand grew up to be a teenager, he was such a kind boy like his mother and father. Iron Hand was still working for the government when he passed on. He had his own home too, but the government furnished this house where they were staying. He ran errands for the Agency also. Sometimes he helped out on ration days. He went to different gatherings and he always helped out. Something good that he did was to make those trails for the schoolchildren—day school and the public school. There was a lot of alfalfa hay to be put up and grain and he helped with that too. He was a good employee for the government. He and his wife were good looking people.

95b. The variety of wage work that Cheyenne men could perform, and perform with enthusiasm, is exemplified here. They learned to do all kinds of farm work on their own allotments, and many became expert cowboys or "line riders" when the cattle program was in effect between 1900 and 1920.

96. Cecelia Atwood and Baby

INFORMANT: JOHN WOODENLEGS

96a. This lady with her braids and her baby is Cecelia Atwood. She was married to James Atwood, who used to be called James Twenty Stand. James worked there with the Mennonite Missionary people, and also with this lady's father, Yellow Fox. They all joined in that church and they seemed to stay in a group. Cecelia had two brothers. She had four children: Mary, Waldo, David, and Rosemary. Mary and Waldo are not married. Waldo is a veteran. The other two have been married. They were good people, good members of that church.

96b. Rodolphe Petter, a Swiss Mennonite missionary and linguist, first visited the Northern Cheyennes in 1916 after having worked among the Southern Cheyennes since 1891. The Mennonite mission in Montana began its work under the direction of G. A. Linscheid in 1904. St. Labre's, the Catholic mission at Ashland, had begun about 1885 (Petter and Petter 1936[?]: 43). The Mennonites were active in suppression of traditional religious practice and the Native American Church.

Petter's great achievement was the compilation of a Cheyenne language dictionary (Petter 1913–15).

Of the language he says:

To dwell on the Cheyenne language would be a dry subject, however, a few remarks should not be left out. Although Indians are classed as primitive people, the Cheyenne language is highly developed, admirably descriptive, has an inexhaustive vocabulary with thousands of verbal forms, many of which are not found in modern languages, neither in Latin, Greek and Hebrew. Verbs will undergo as many changes as actions are done or compounded. Thus what is done or expressed or felt by mind, senses, words, motions, attitudes and postures demands different verbal forms. Further, what is done by means of head, eyes, mouth, teeth, arms, legs, bones, water, fire, heat, striking, cutting, or other instruments requires as many verbal changes. All these forms adopt thousands of other changes, according as they become compounded or affected by animate or inanimate subjects or objects.

The Cheyenne has five, whereas we have only three personal pronouns, four imperatives, and can conjugate the numbers "ad indefinitum." I have nearly ten large pages of different forms expressing "cutting" of course without including the thousands of forms that any of these forms can take. Then two or even three verbs can be compounded into a single one. (Petter and Petter 1936[?]: 47)

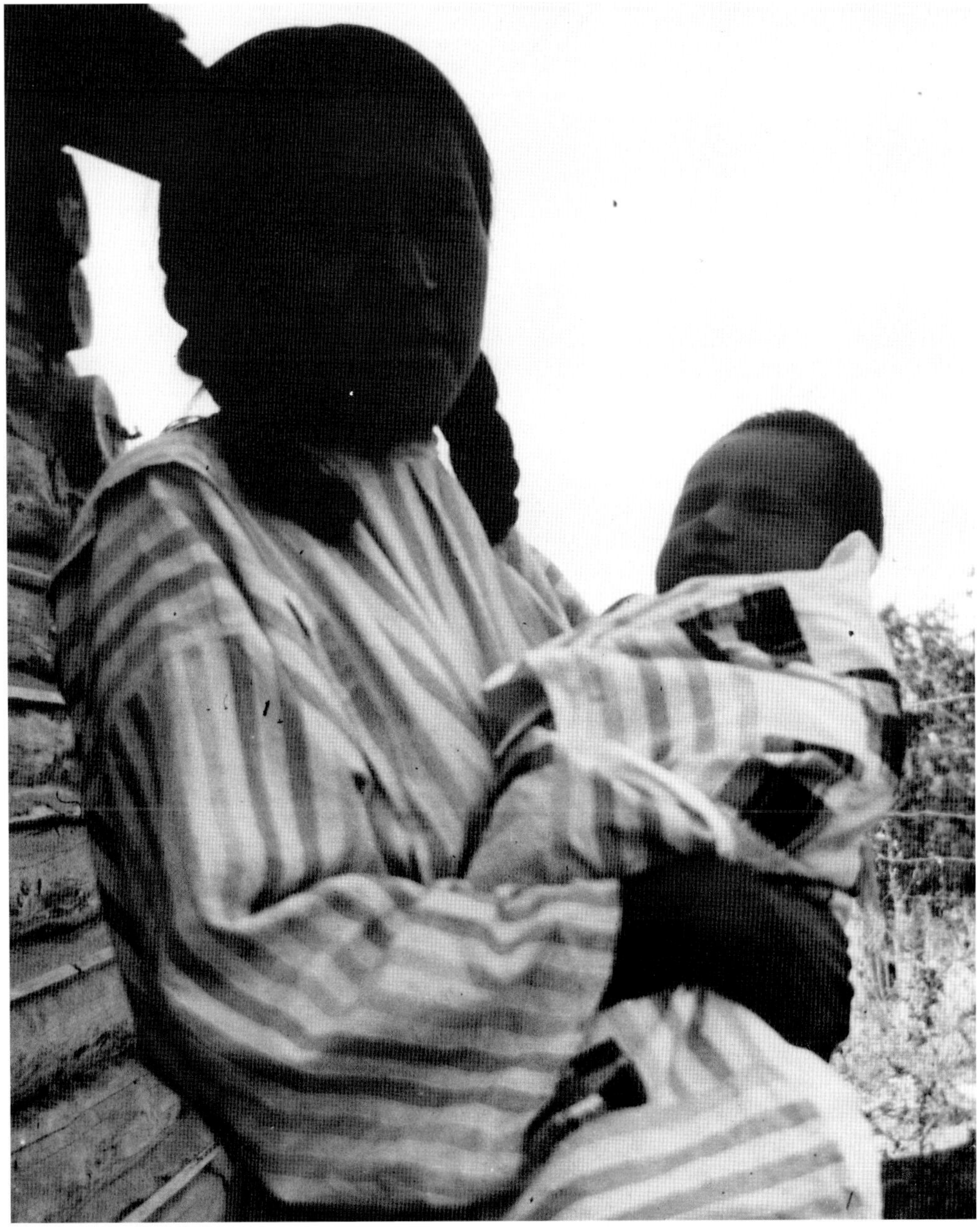

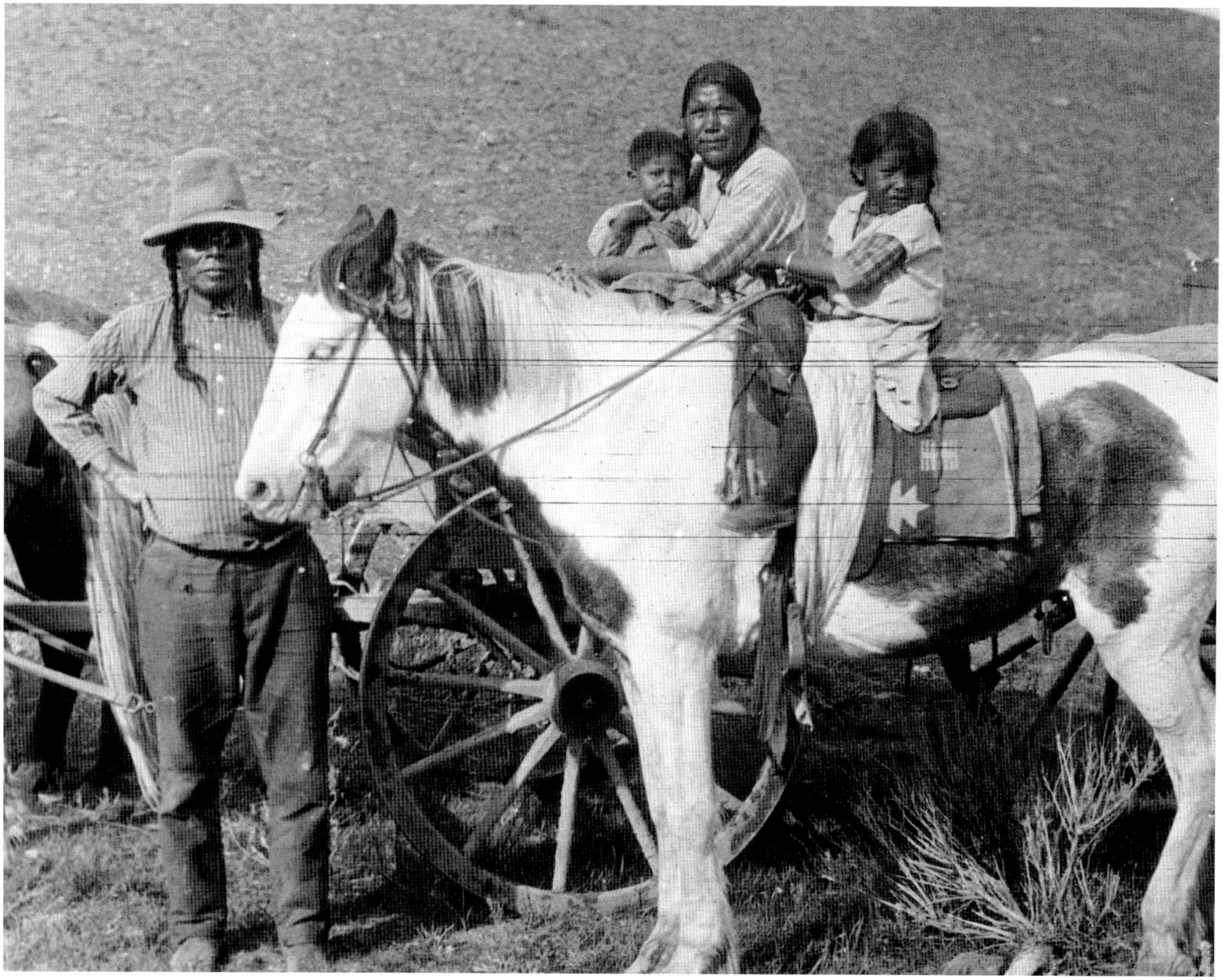

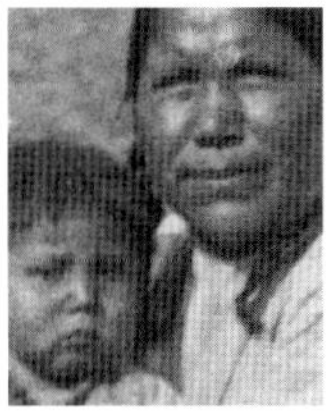

97. Peter and Rose Little Bird and Family

INFORMANT: JOHN WOODENLEGS

97a. This is Peter Little Bird with his team of horses and wagon. The little girl is riding. The mother, Rose Little Bird, has a little boy in her lap. That pinto horse was kind of yellow-eared, white and yellow spots on him. That little girl has a bracelet and they're all looking at the photographer. They were just kind people. Peter had a place up Logging Creek, a ranch, farm and he had cattle. He worked hard, very hard. He was one of the first Native Church people, the peyote people. The first meeting was held at his ranch—at his place. He took good care of old people, same way with his wife. They were just good people, kind and helpful.

97b. This picture shows another typical Cheyenne family group.

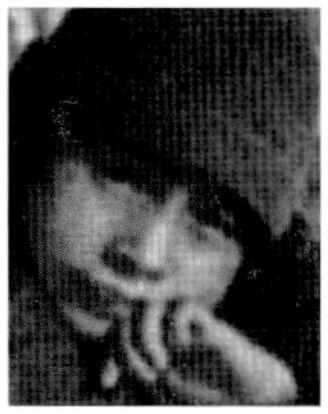

98. Traveling by Sled

Informant: John Woodenlegs

98a. This was taken in winter time with a sled and team of horses. You can't see the horses, but the harness reins show. Two women, one standing and one sitting, a man, and two boys. The lady standing was married to Charlie White Hawk, and later on she was married to Jerome Bear Tusk. She had children from both marriages. After Jerome passed on, she married William Hollow Breast and later they split up. Her Indian name would be Holy Standing Woman. The other woman is Mrs. Martin Two Bulls, wearing a wool blanket and a stocking cap. They lived at Ashland. Her son, Joseph, is the boy without a hat. Maybe they had gone to town to get groceries. The man looks like Oliver Sponge, but it might be Martin Two Bulls. Long time ago the women folks knew how to harness up the horses to a wagon or sled. They all knew how to ride. These two women were probably girlfriends when they were young.

98b. The expertise of Cheyenne horsewomen was widespread. When wagons and sleds came in with reservation days, skills formerly used with the traditional Plains travois or pony drag (in earliest times pulled by dogs) were easily transferred. The wheel was not known to North American peoples prior to European contact, except for rare and limited use as a toy. Items such as the bicycle were sources of Indian humor as well as astonishment.

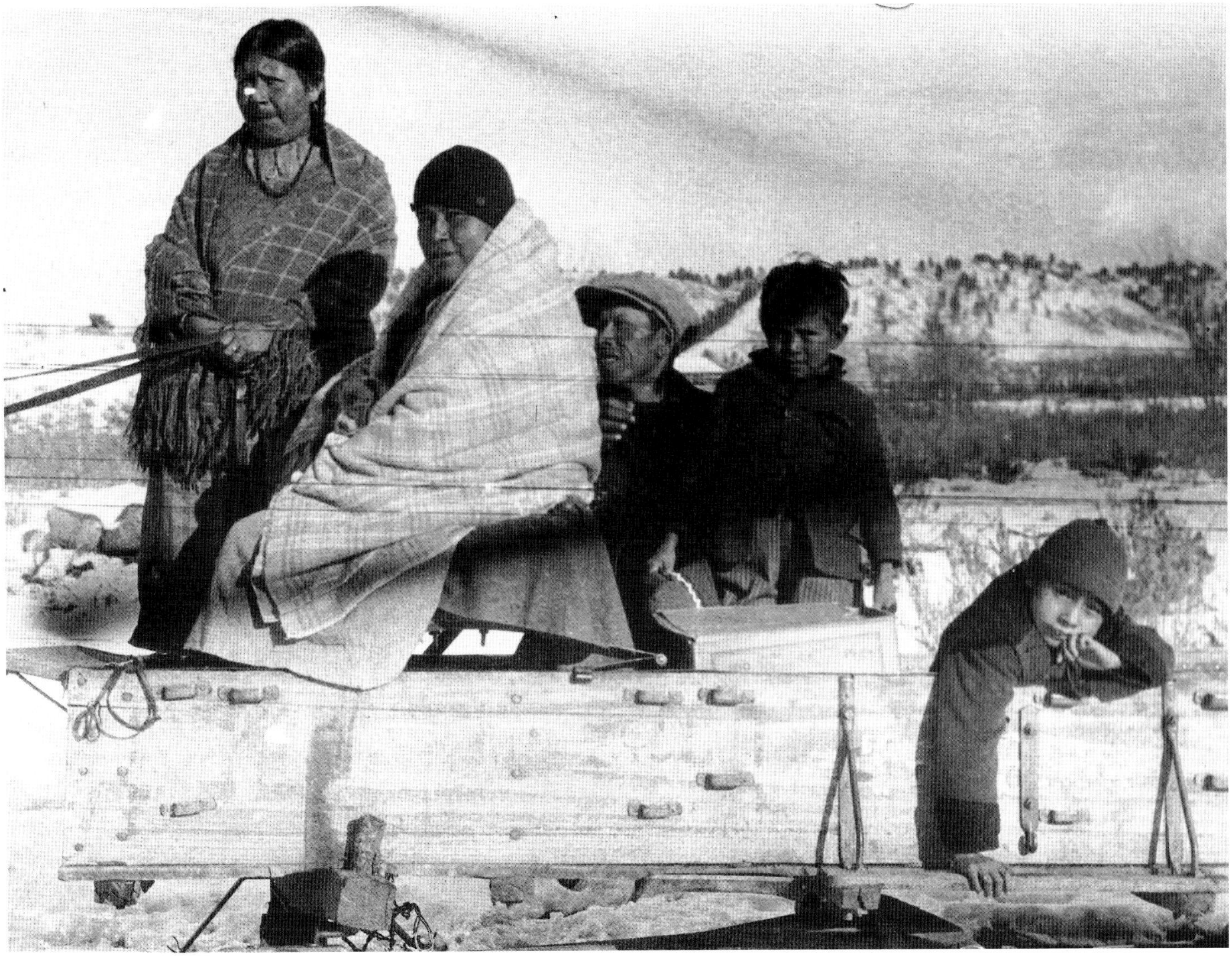

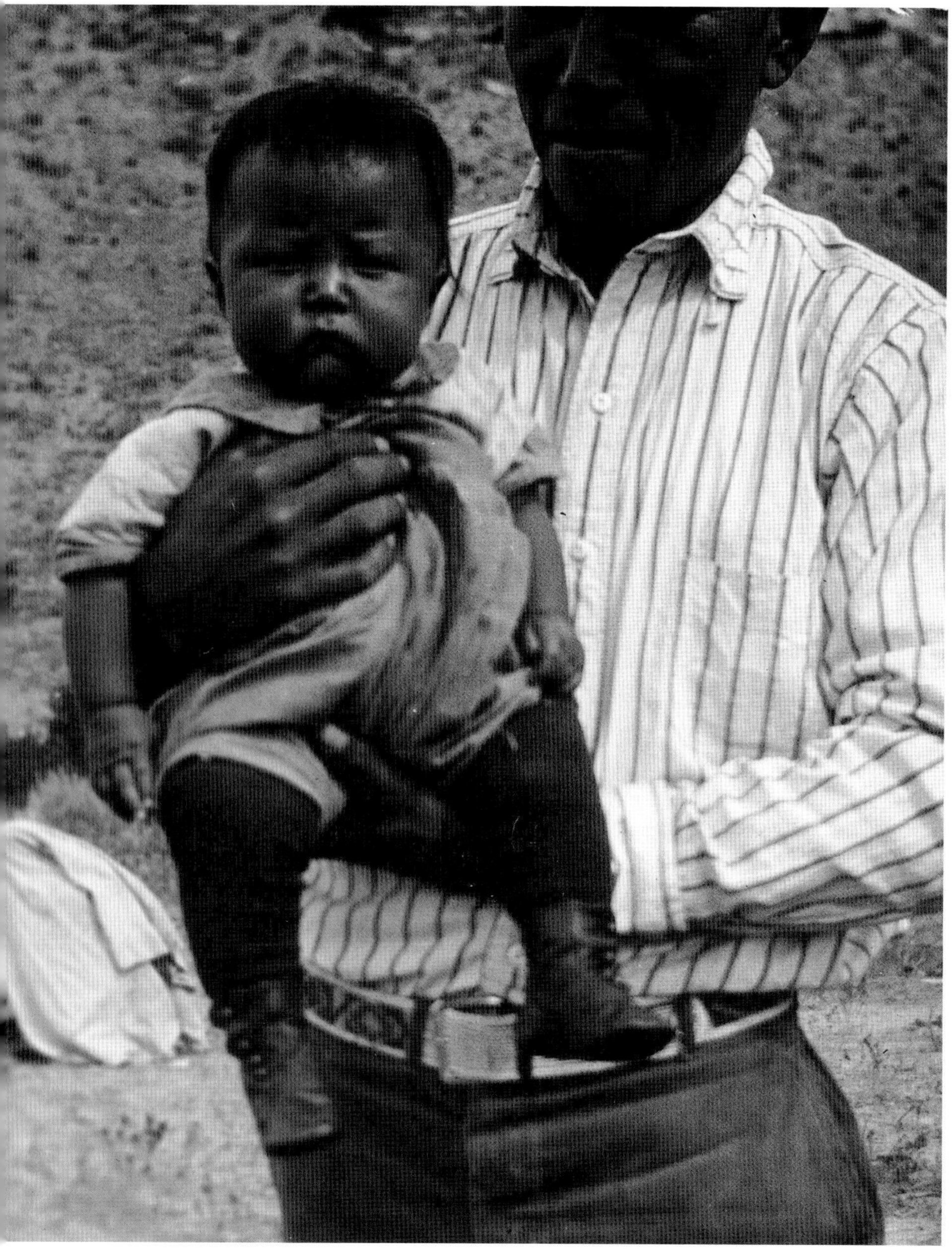

99. Oliver Sponge and Baby

INFORMANT: JOHN WOODENLEGS

99a. This is Oliver Sponge and baby. They lived at Ashland. His brother was Alfred Sponge. They were good people, talked real good. They were married and had children and they made their living. They all got along real good and worked hard. Oliver had thirteen children. Today he has passed on and some of the children, but his wife is still living. He's wearing a white shirt, striped with a beaded belt. He was such a good dancer, good stick game player, and a good singer. He and his brother were good dancers.

99b. The "stick game" or hand game is illustrated in figure 15.

The deliberate limitation of Cheyenne family size has not been widespread in reservation times. In earlier days, the wider spacing of births through sexual abstinence was believed to add strength and spiritual power to the fewer children born, and the "better" families practiced this. Throughout these photographs we see numerous pictures of men caring for children, a role not usually associated with their reputation as warriors.

100. Setting up a Tepee

INFORMANT: JOHN WOODENLEGS

100a. This is a tepee, partly up. They were putting it up either to live in or to have some sort of a ceremony. The ladies were the only ones that put up tepees, certain old ladies who were the experts. They know how to make them and fix them, with the decorations on, and how it's put up. They tie three poles together, and then put the fourth pole on to start with. These ladies I know. The one on the right is Mrs. Two Bulls from Ashland. The other one is Mrs. George American Horse. At the present time, boys and men put up the tepees, but at that time, the women really put it up good so it would not fall over. A tepee generally had 19 to 21 poles.

100b. As suggested here, the two Plains methods of erecting tepees utilized three versus four poles as a base. Tepees have many advantages as portable living space and are often favored today by Indians and non-Indians alike. The painting of tepee covers is enjoying a revival as a reservation art form.

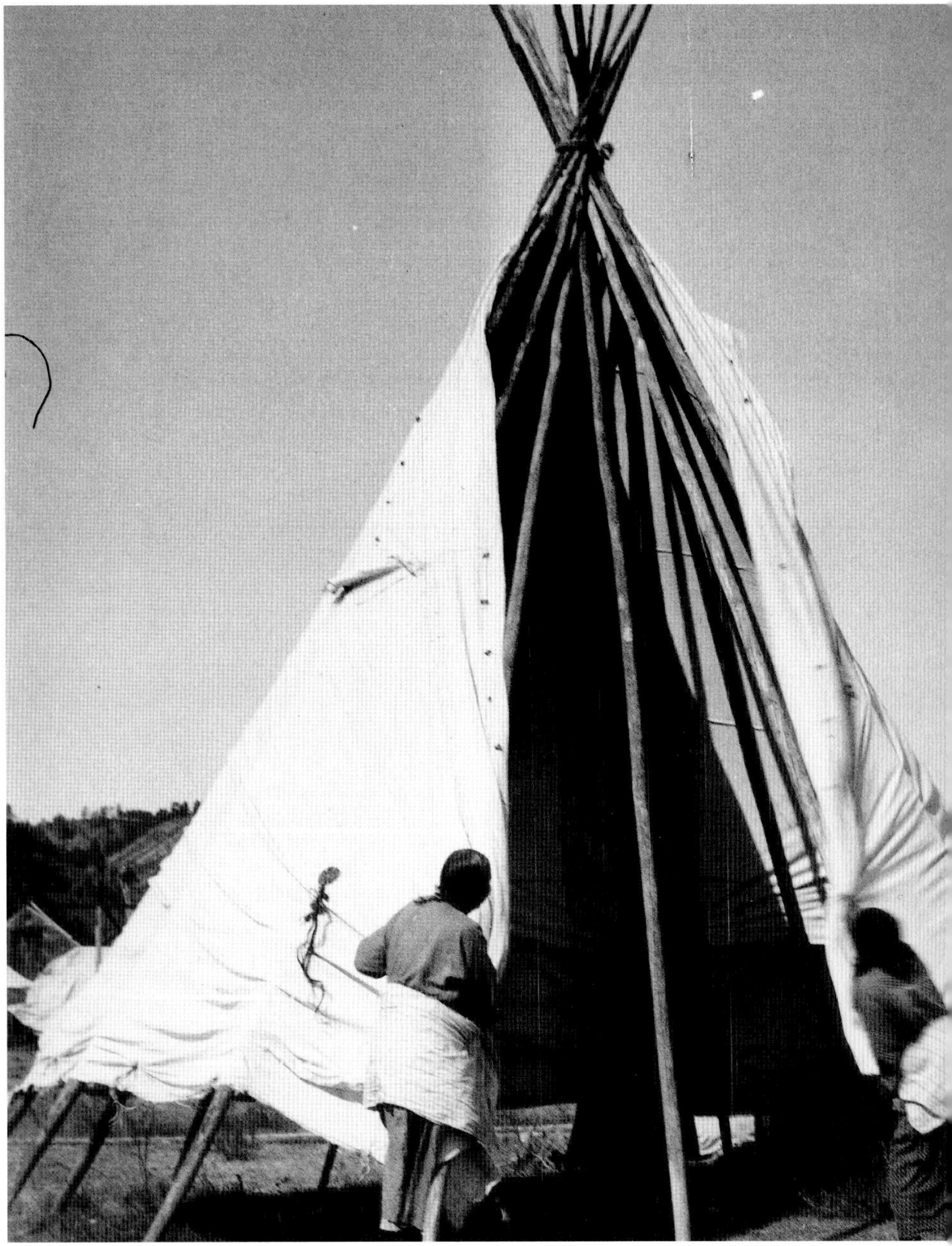

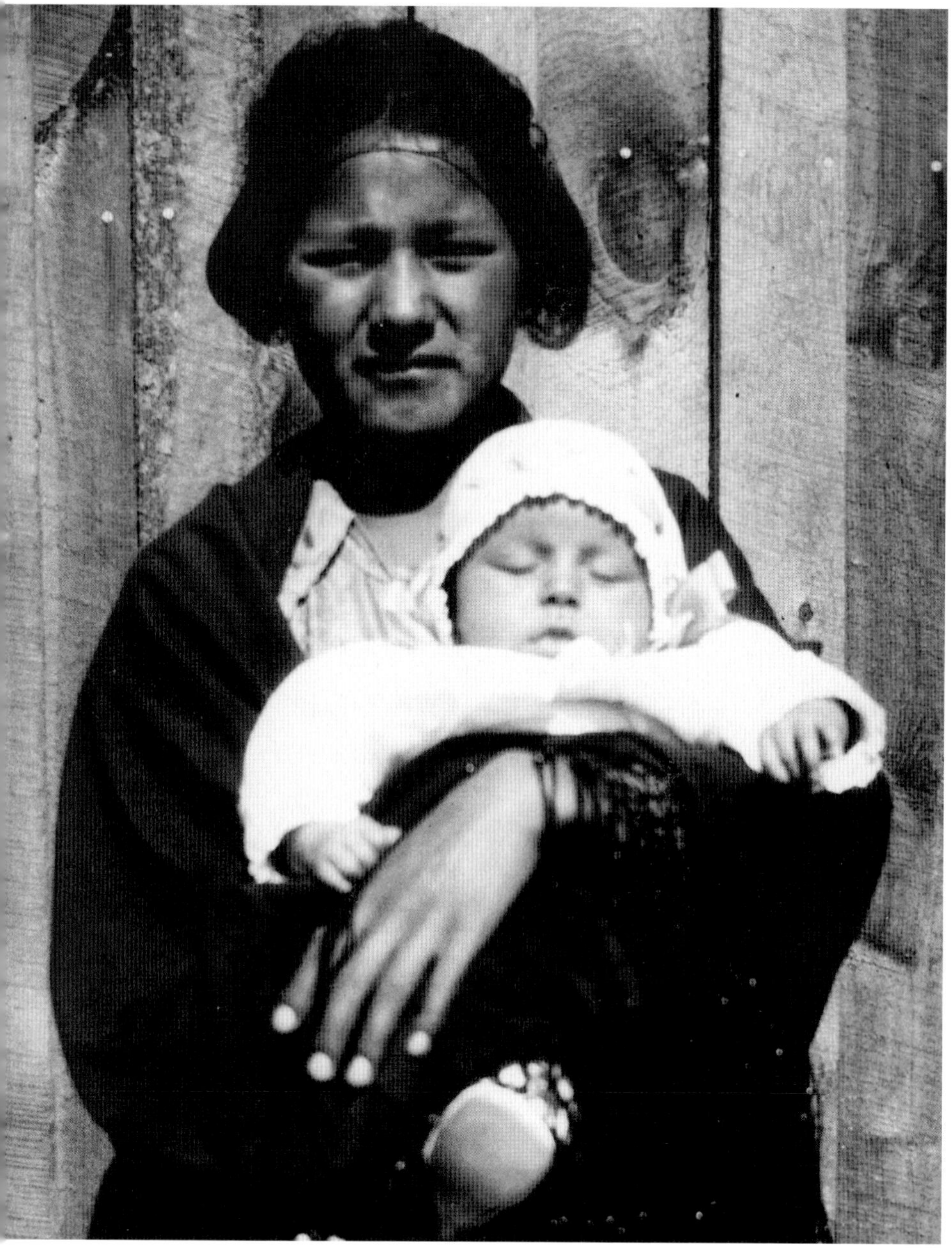

101. Jessie Roman Nose and Baby

INFORMANT: JOHN WOODENLEGS

101a. This is Jessie Roman Nose. She has a baby and a shawl. She married Roy Spang, and they had a boy and girl that I know. She was such a good looking lady. Her children are living–Lyman Spang and Virginia. Later she and her husband split up and she married a white man, Howard Vassau. This baby is Howard's baby. She grew up to be a grandmother, but she has passed on now.

101b. The best-known Roman Nose in Cheyenne history was the Southern Cheyenne leader who died at the battle of Beecher Island in Colorado in 1868, after he inadvertently broke the rule of his personal medicine that he was not to eat food cooked with metal implements.

Intermarriage of Cheyenne women with non-Indian men was common in early reservation days, although not always sought after by the women themselves.

Such intermarriage led to a mixed-blood population segment in many reservation communities. People of mixed blood enjoyed both tribal enrollment privileges (such as land allotment) and access to white institutions and technology (such as bank loans), which often made them a dominant force in tribal business and politics. The largest cattle-ranching operations on the Northern Cheyenne reservation in recent years have been run by such families.

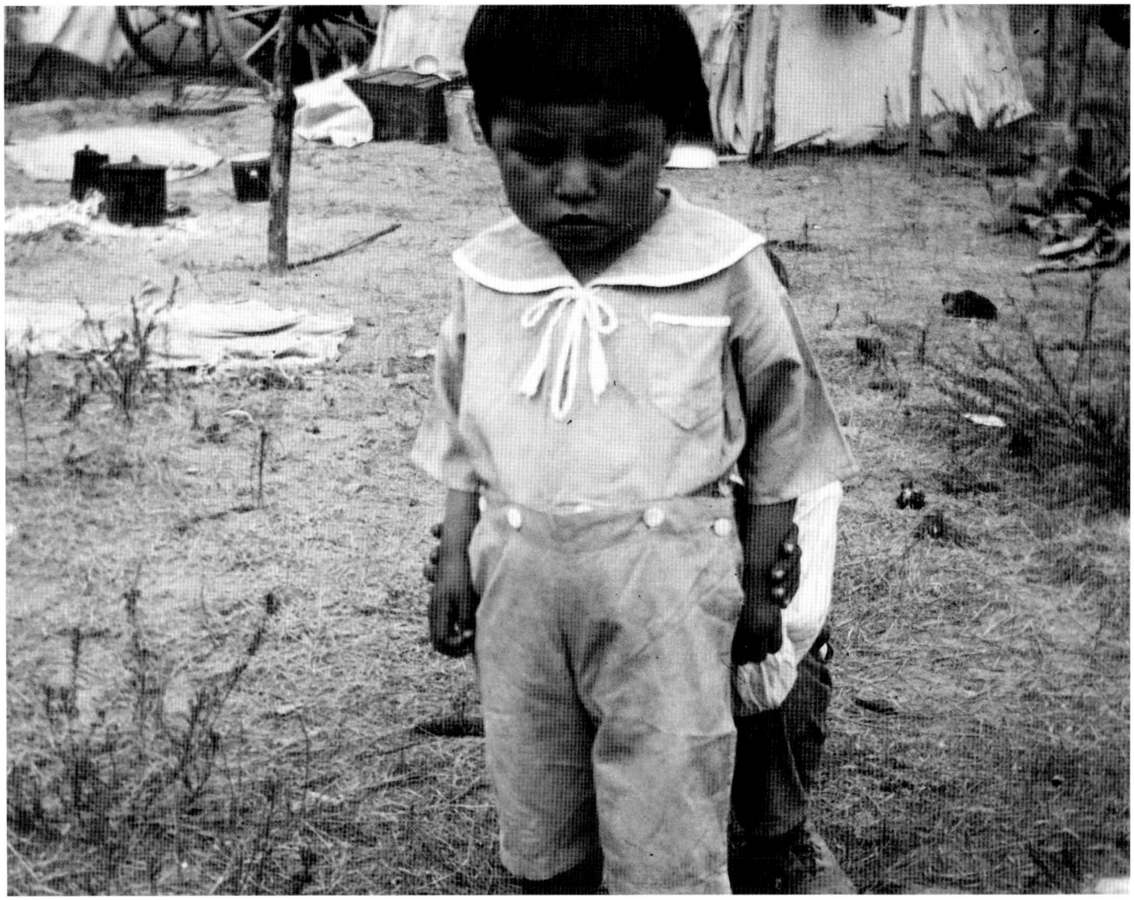

102. James Clubfoot

INFORMANT: JOHN WOODENLEGS

102a. Dr. Marquis took this picture of James Clubfoot in 1925. His mother was Alice Seminole Clubfoot. It looks like another child is holding James from the back so he could get this picture taken.

102b. Cheyenne child-rearing techniques included a minimum of physical punishment or restraint. Children were taught by example, and only as they reached adolescence were the majority of Cheyenne rules of behavior imposed. These rules were especially strict for young women in their relationships with men, which were usually dictated by family preferences (particularly those of brothers).

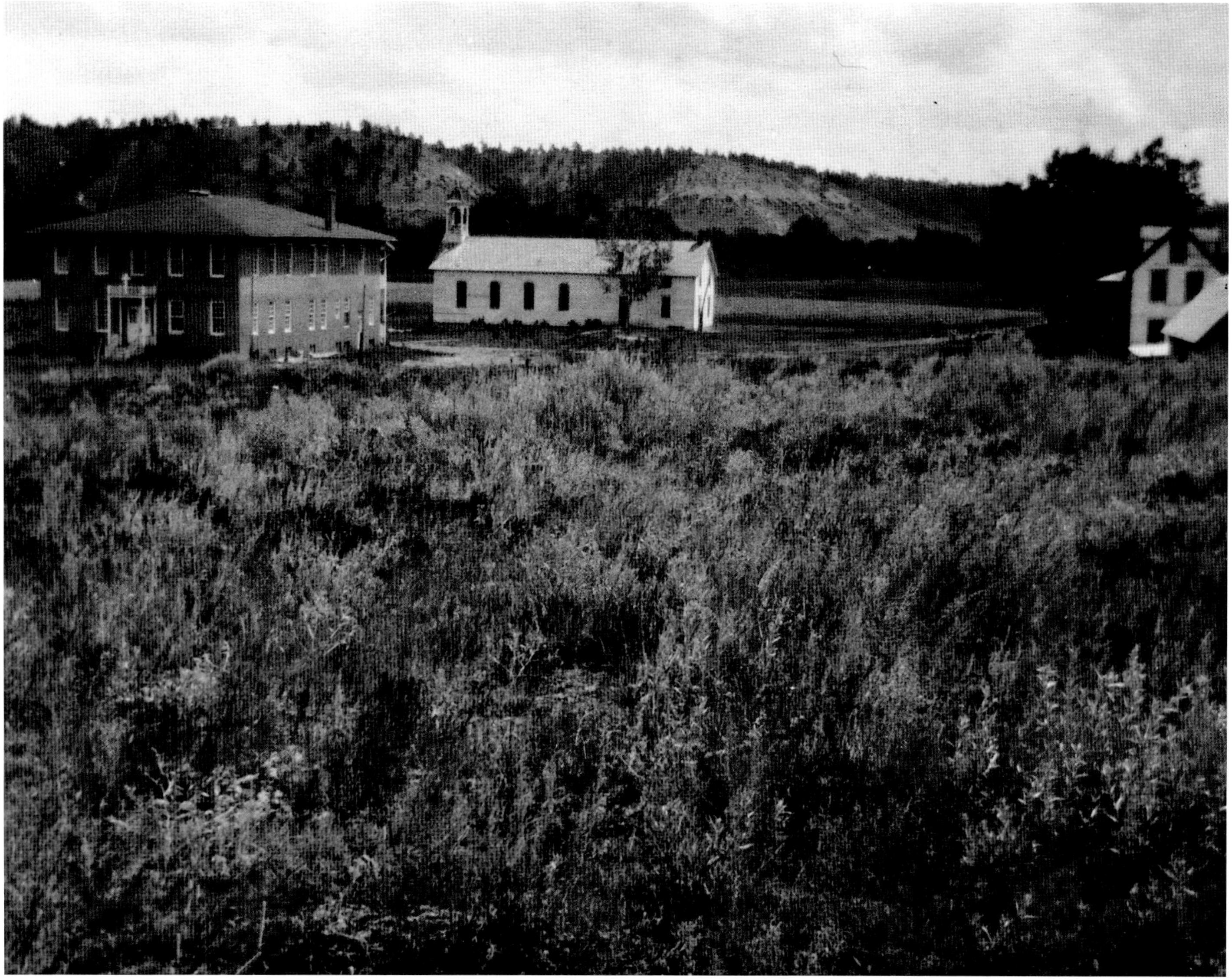

103. St. Labre Mission School

Informant: John Woodenlegs

103a. This is St. Labre Mission School at Ashland. The big building was for classes. The church is in back. The small building on the right might have been the boys' building. This was the early Mission, just these three buildings. Today the area is almost filled up with buildings and a football field and a landing strip for airplanes. I did go to school there for half a year. My older sister went there too. They fed us good. The Mission was close to the Tongue River in Ashland. It has grown a whole lot since those days, with buildings all over.

Cecilia Woodenlegs Interview:
Going to School at the Mission (recorded in 1981)

My name is Cecelia Little Eagle Woodenlegs. I am going to talk about St. Labre school at the time I went to school there. The school is in Ashland. I must have started when I was about seven years old, I don't really know. My father and mother lived below (north) of the school about seven miles. Then they would move close to Richard Woodenlegs' house close to that Mission while school was in session. One of the buildings is a gray stone (stucco) building—an old building, and that's where I went. Later they built a new school and we moved into that. Towards spring time that same year, that new building caught fire and burned up. It was in March. It was a big fire and we all had to move out. That was a dormitory and school together. Then they moved our beds into the church to use as a dormitory.

When I first went, I was a day student. My folks took me to school in a wagon and then they'd come back at 4 P.M. One day one of the nun teachers was going to keep me in. I was to board there, but I didn't know that. So I looked out the window and saw my folks coming, but the teacher had locked the door. So I went back in the room and saw a window open. I crawled out and jumped.

Later on I did board there and then in March, the building burned. My folks had gone to Lame Deer at the time of the fire, so I moved into the church with other children who couldn't go home. We had to move back into the old gray building and use the church for classes. We had to work half a day and go to school half a day. We helped clean up the various buildings, we helped cook and to make bread and learned to sew.

Old folks used to come and eat there. The nuns and the priests all tried to make friends with the Indian people. The nuns kept close supervision on the girls. We had to dress neat and clean. We had certain kinds of clothes to wear. The whole experience there was a change from the kind of life we had been living. In those days, the church expected people to kneel during prayer. Some of the girls ran away. They said they were tired of kneeling so much and their knees hurt. Probably it was really because they weren't too happy in school.

103b. Today St. Labre's Mission at Ashland, Montana, at the northeastern corner of the reservation is known worldwide for its fund-raising activities and its ministry to what it terms the Cheyenne "Race of Sorrows." An architecturally i mpressive church now incorporates aspects of Native American religion, such as the pipe, into Christian worship services.

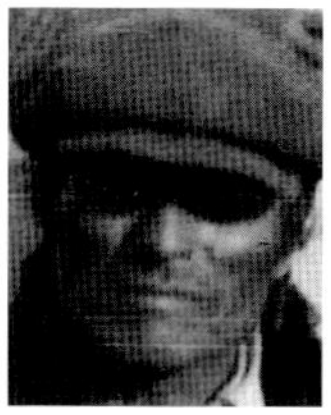

104. Red Bird Family

Informant: John Woodenlegs

104a. This is the Red Bird family taken at the St. Labre Mission School. The two small children are Lena and Frank, being held by the mother. They lived on a ranch and worked hard, sent their children to school. This Red Bird was such a kind man, talked good to everybody. He was kind of a crier in big gatherings, telling the things that should be done. He was a good looking man. His wife's name was Florence. She had two children from a previous marriage to Tom Rowland. They are in back. The one on the left is Rhoda and the other is Elizabeth.

104b. This Red Bird may have been related to a well-known tribal policeman of the same name but also called Big Ankles, who was killed in a butchering accident earlier in the reservation period (Stands in Timber and Liberty 1997: 266, 289).

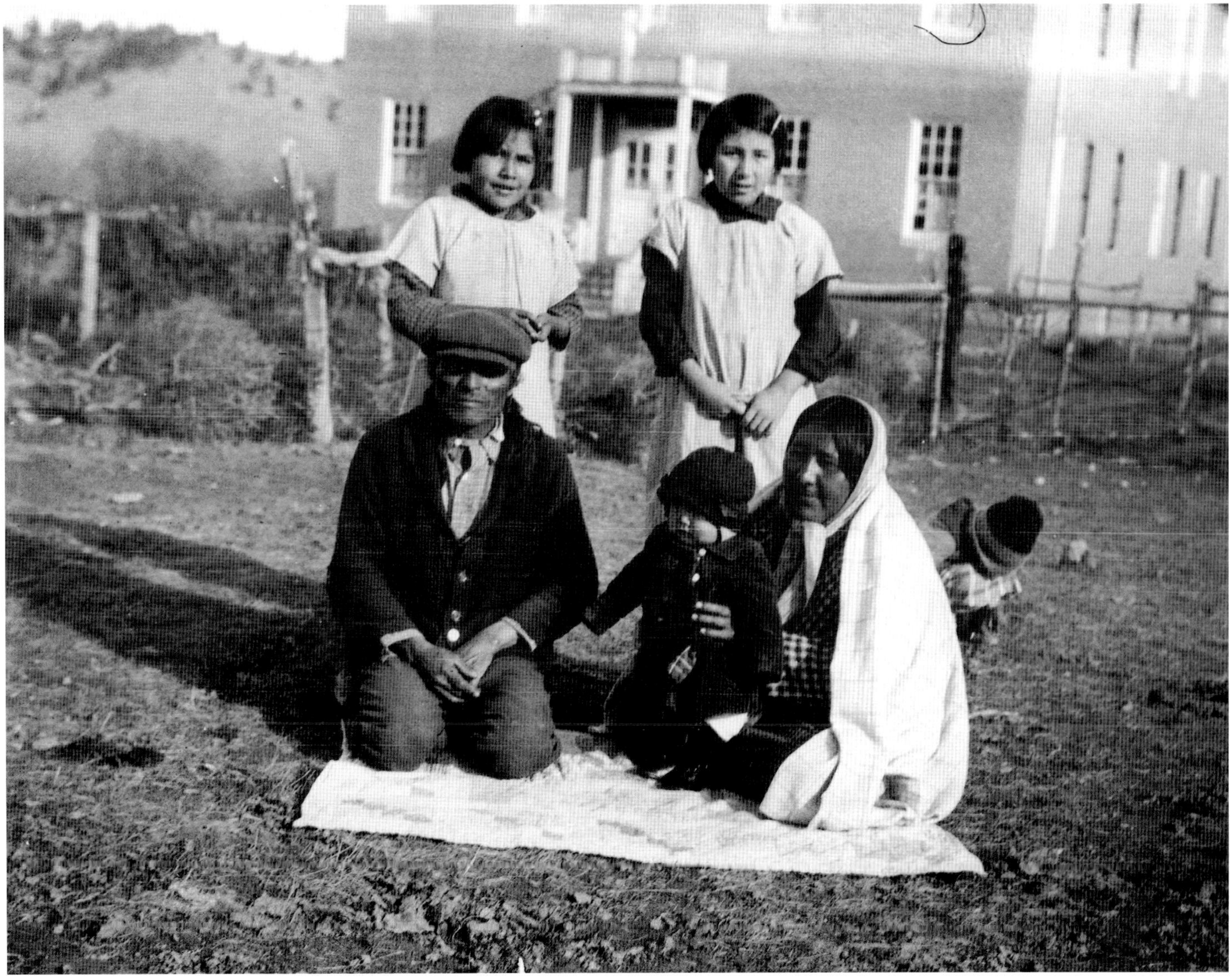

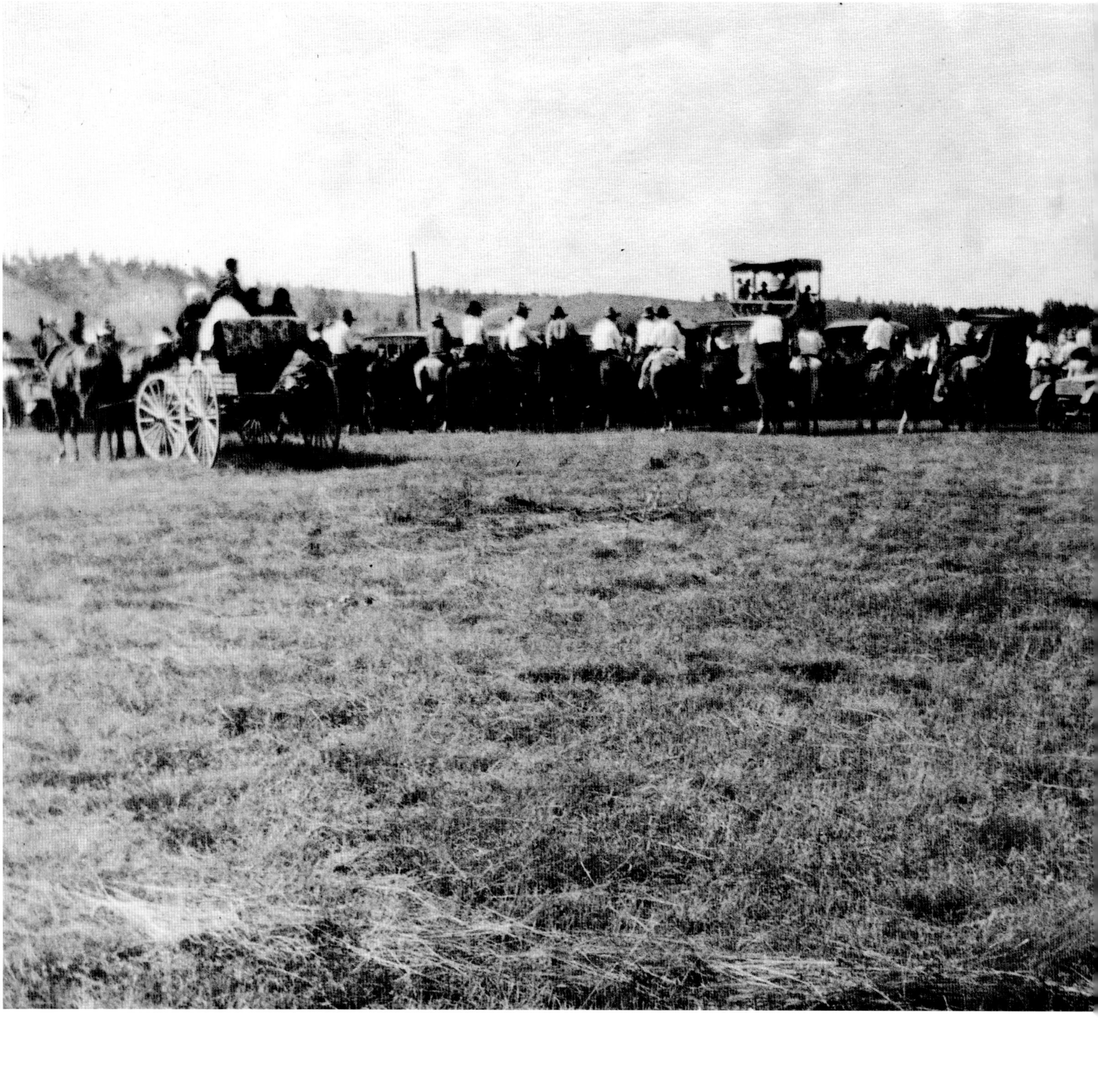

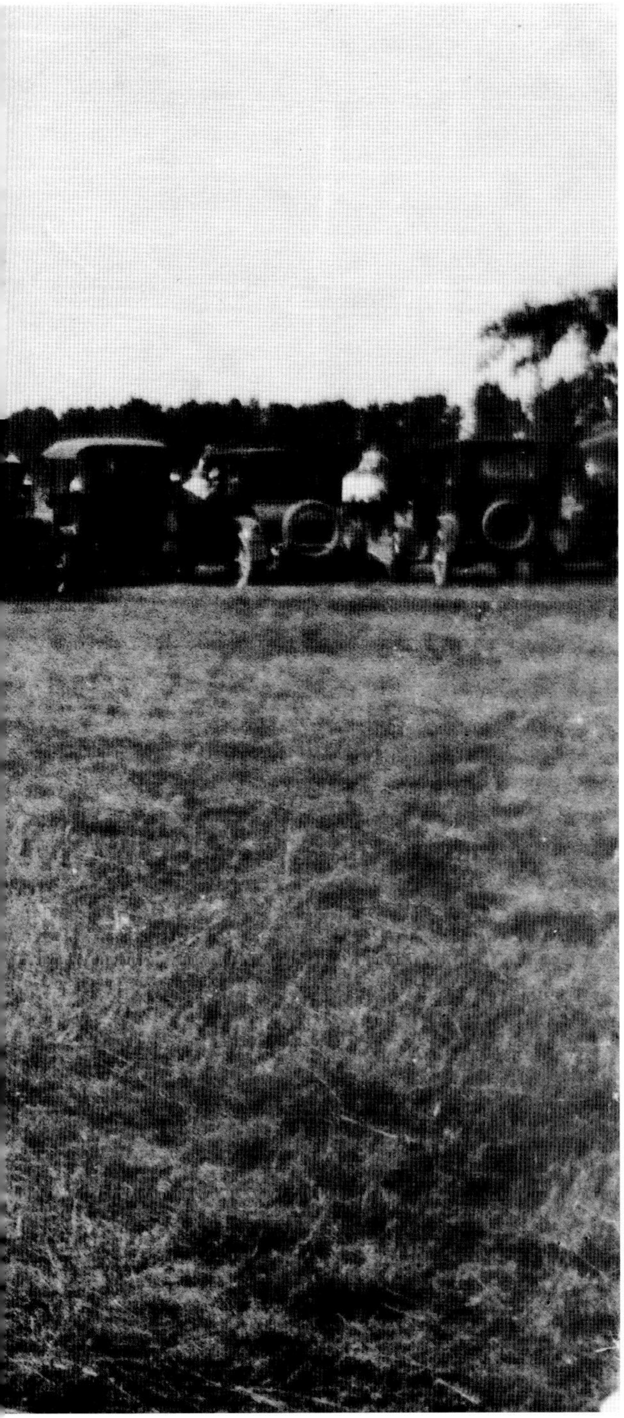

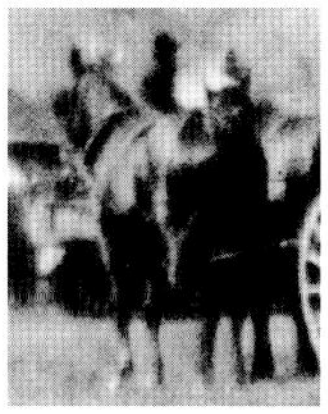

105. Ashland Races and Rodeo

Informant: John Woodenlegs

105a. This is a rodeo and races, taken from the back. There's a crow's nest where the officials sat. This is at Ashland along the Tongue River. There's a lot of people riding horseback looking on. There's also a line-up of Model T Fords. There's a buggy there with four seats in it with four Cheyenne women and children on it. They had good races and rodeos at Ashland.

105b. The Tongue River, which has been of major importance in Cheyenne and Sioux history, now forms the eastern boundary of the Northern Cheyenne Reservation. At roughly 450,000 acres it is less than a fourth the size of the two million acres belonging to the Crows. Both reservation areas contain some of the best grazing land in the short-grass plains. The Crows, however, have lost control of close to 80 percent of this original amount through sale and lease to outside cattle interests. Some of the biggest cattle outfits in the nation have operated here, including the Padlock Ranch, which until very recently continued the use of a roundup wagon on Crow leases.

Nearly 100 percent of Cheyenne land remains in Indian control, either as individual allotments or as reserves retained by the tribe.

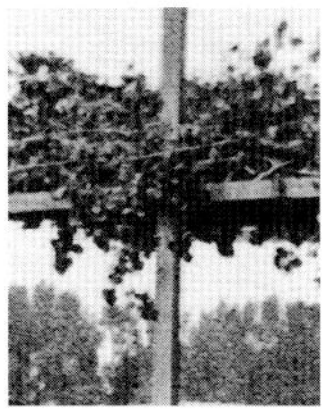

106. Refreshment Arbor

INFORMANT: JOHN WOODENLEGS

106a. This is at the Ashland rodeo and races, and there's a big shade arbor where they are selling refreshments. Indian women are standing around and also white people. Most of the Ford cars belong to the white people—a lot of them came to our celebrations. This shade is made of small cottonwood trees cut and put on top of the uprights. They all celebrated together and kind of worked together and were friends. Later on Cheyennes began to own cars too.

106b. The number of cars shown here reflects attendance by numerous whites at the Ashland celebration. Concerning Cheyenne-language terms for automobiles, missionary Rodolphe Petter wrote: "The language is so exactly descriptive that new words can be made with ease. So the Cheyenne has names for different parts of the automobile. An auto dealer told me recently that the Crow Indians must use the English to denote the car's parts, while the Cheyenne have the names of the parts in their own language" (Petter and Petter 1936[?]: 48).

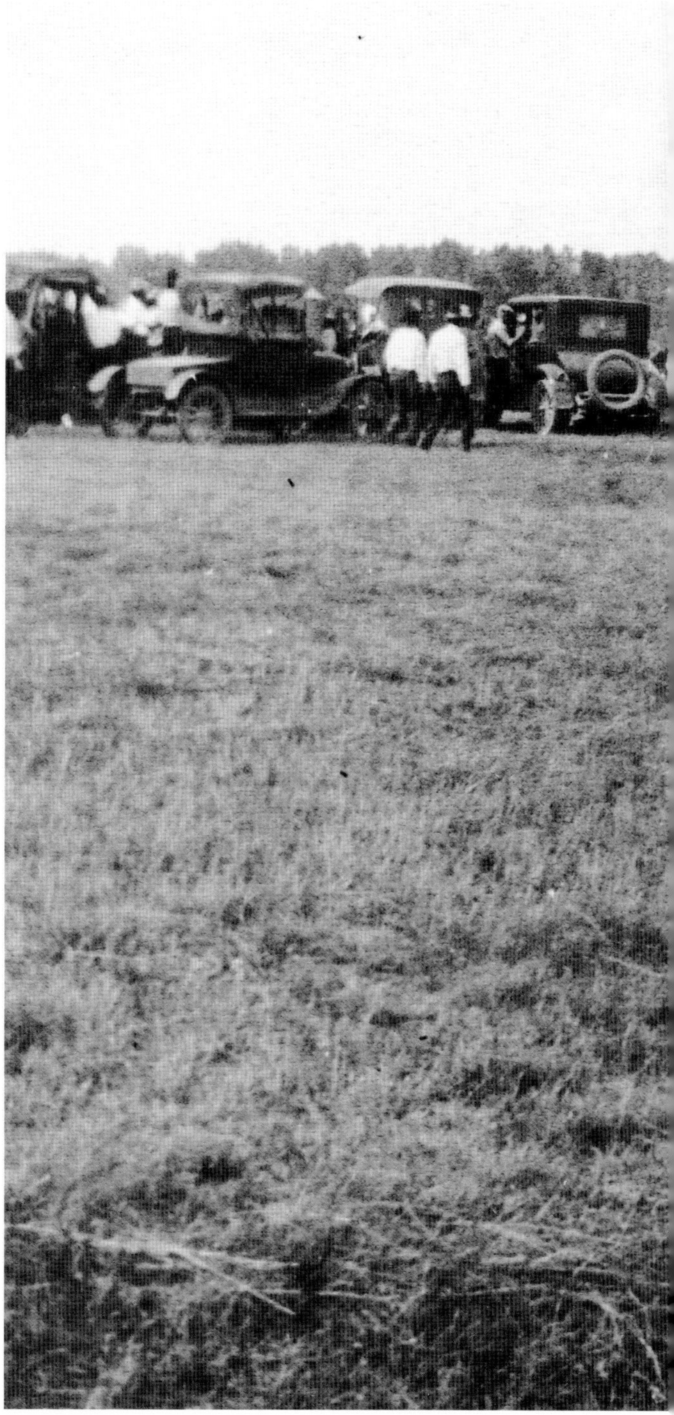

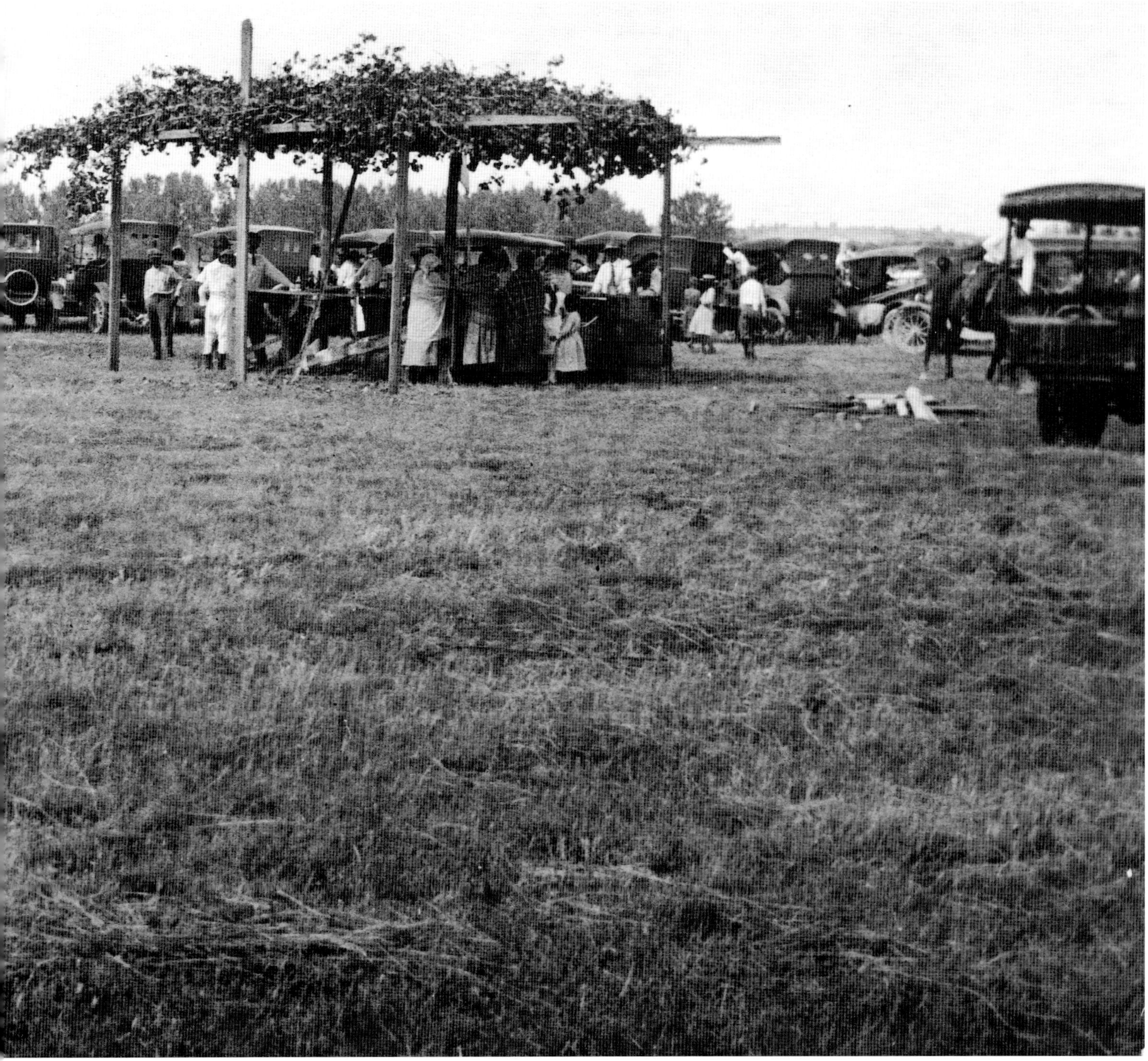

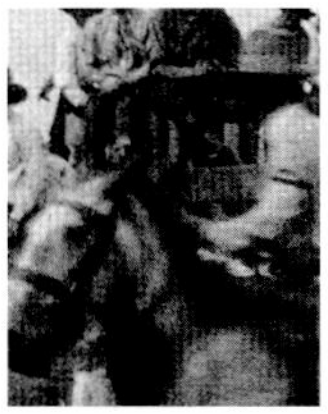

107. Bronc Riding

Informant: John Woodenlegs

107a. These are bronc riders at the Ashland rodeo in August 1927.

107b. Rodeo was becoming popular throughout the American West by the 1920s, when these pictures were taken. Early rodeos featured roping and bronc-riding events plus horse races, but not the more dangerous bull-riding contests of today.

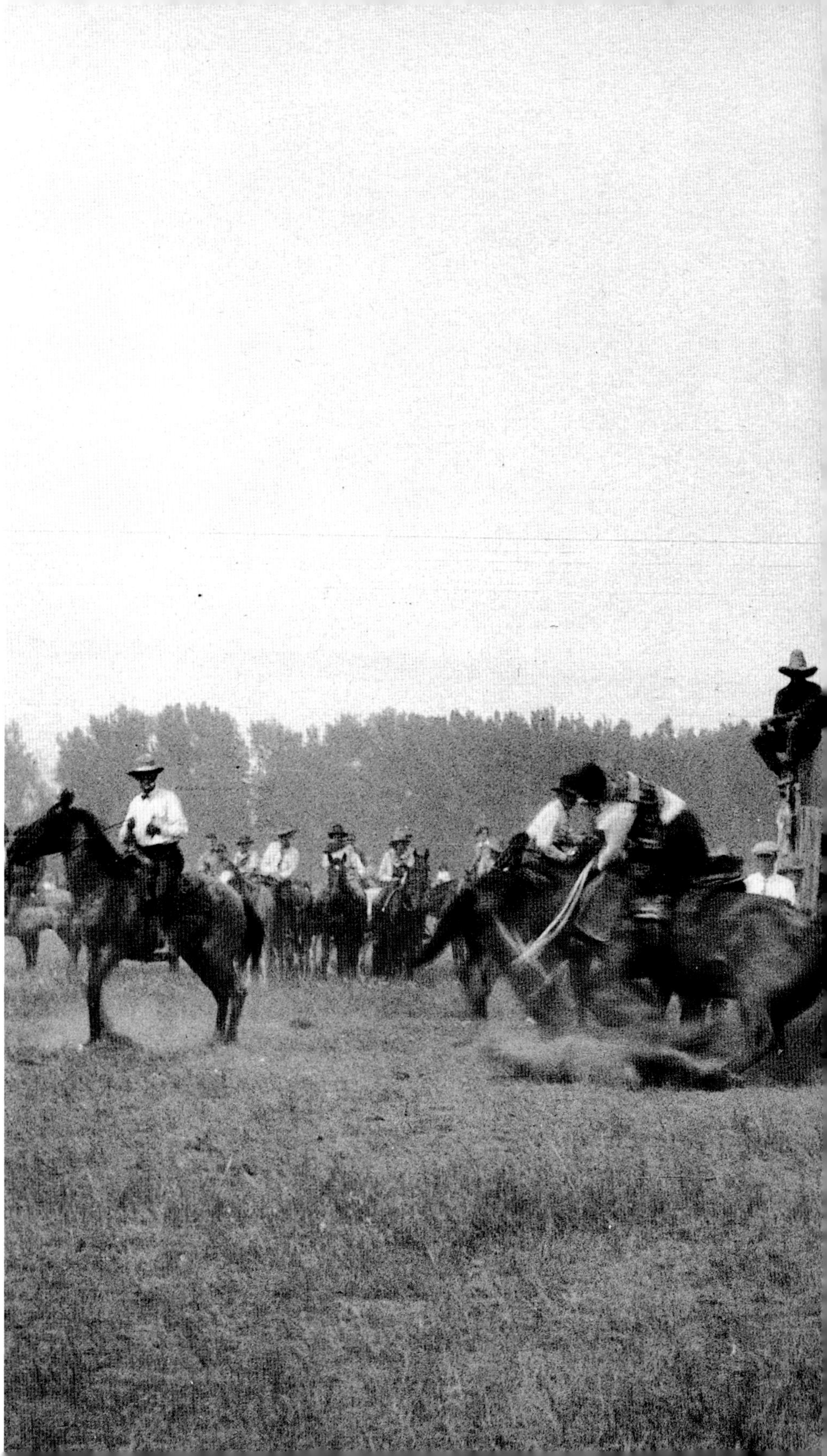

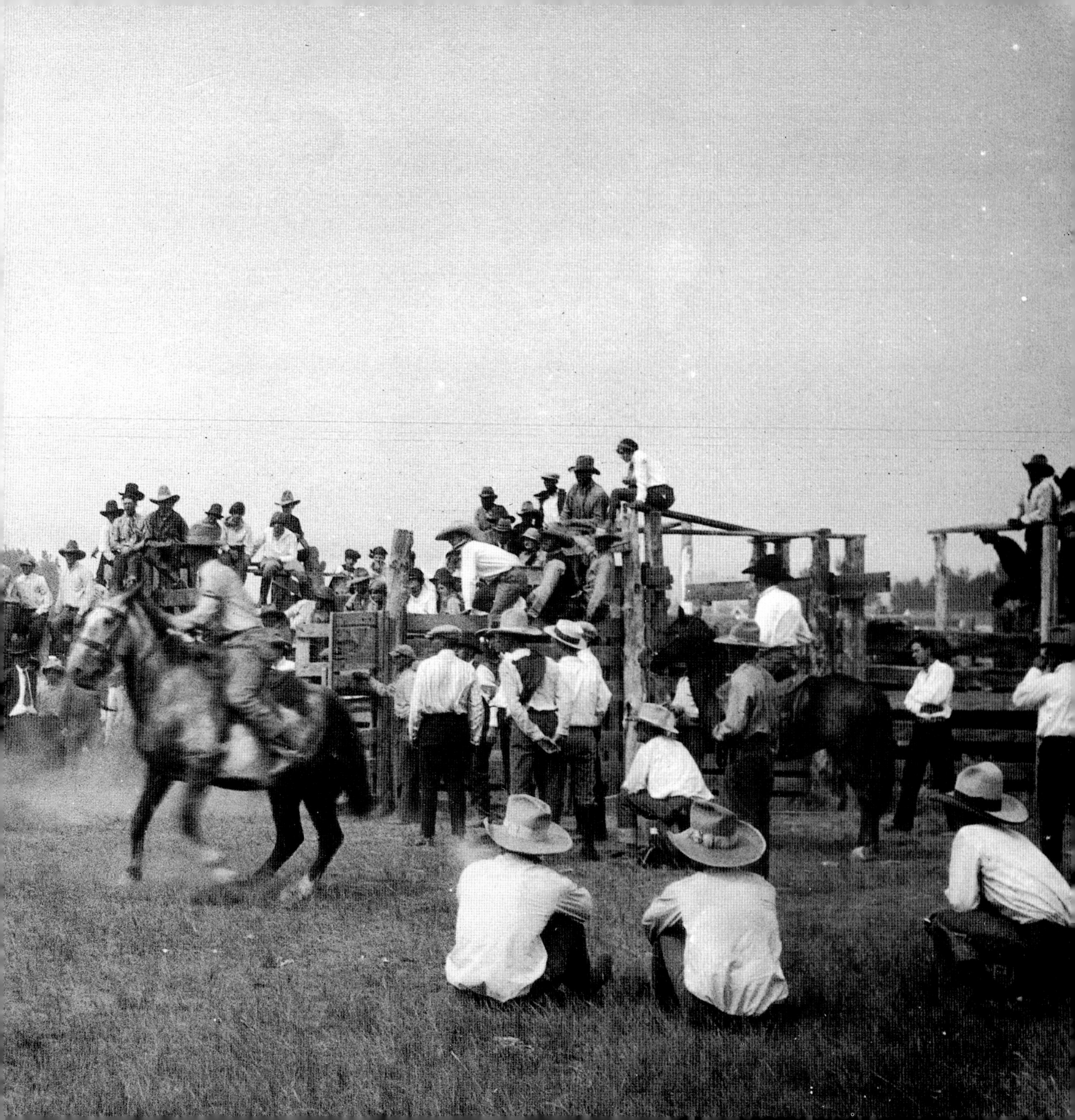

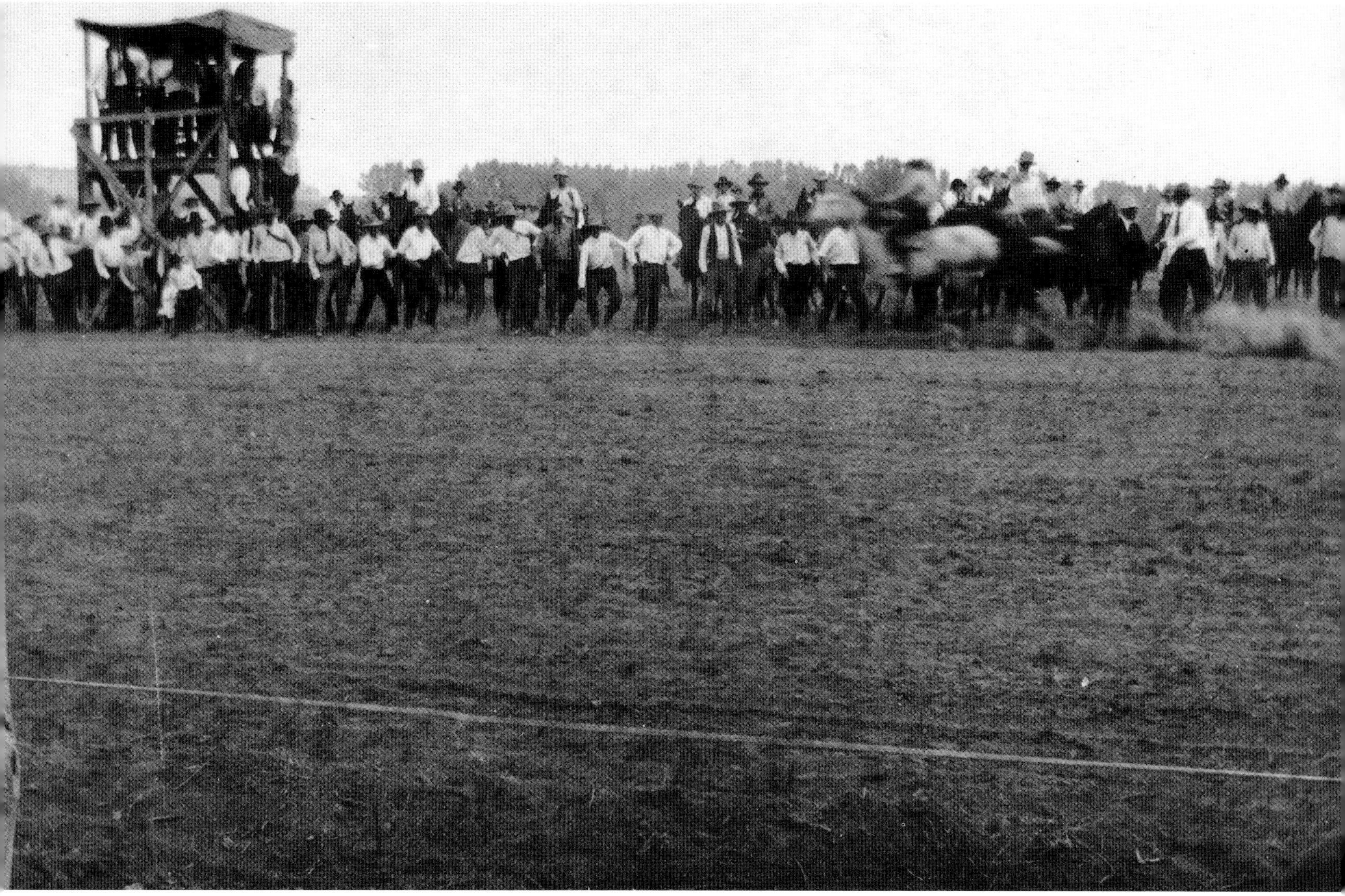

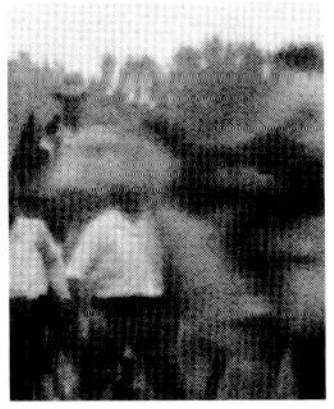

108. Coming down the Home Stretch

INFORMANT: JOHN WOODENLEGS

108a. This is a horse race at Ashland. That's the judges' stand and a whole bunch of people standing on foot. These people are really interested in that race! A whole bunch of them have white shirts and black ties on, and chaps and hats. I guess the Indian people were told to wear white shirts and ties by the government people or the missionaries. This might be a relay race—looks like one rider might have just jumped on. Cheyenne people sure liked races—foot races and horse races. They owned good horses.

108b. According to A History of the Cheyenne People *(Weist 1977), at the height of horse ownership the Cheyennes possessed some 15,000 head. On 450,000 acres that would have allowed some 30 acres each if they did not have to compete with cattle. This would seem incredible until we realize that horses left to themselves can double in number every few years, seriously taxing any grazing resource. The increase in Indian horses was vehemently protested by outside cattle owners, who coveted Indian grass. This led to the horse slaughter program of the 1920s, one of the worst blows to Cheyenne morale in the reservation period and indeed of all time.*

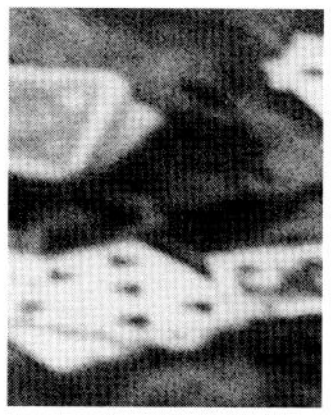

109. Playing "Got None"

INFORMANT: JOHN WOODENLEGS

109a. These are some Cheyenne women playing cards, something they never had before the white people came. They learned to gamble and everybody got to playing cards. There was one game they called "Got None." They are sitting in a circle—there's one old lady, a good looking lady sitting there watching the cards. Another has a cigarette in her mouth with a shawl covering her eyes. There's another one there nursing her baby, but she's playing at the same time! Everybody's watching real close. The men liked to play too. They never had cards before and they all got interested. Pretty soon they began to bet money. They played for hides and buckskins. Later on they got after them, but they got so used to playing cards that they hid. They would go in the woods or the bushes. If they got caught playing in a house, they had to go to court. Some of them had to serve time and go to jail. Sometimes they just were sitting in a circle—no cards, no nothing! Somebody said, "Policeman's coming!" When the police came, he saw no cards, no money, no nothing. My grandfolks played cards, and my dad and my uncle. Some of the people didn't play, they just tended to their business, tanning hides and doing their work, using their time in a good way.

109b. Although gambling in hand games or stick games was widespread in Plains communities, the use of playing cards was not known until white contact.

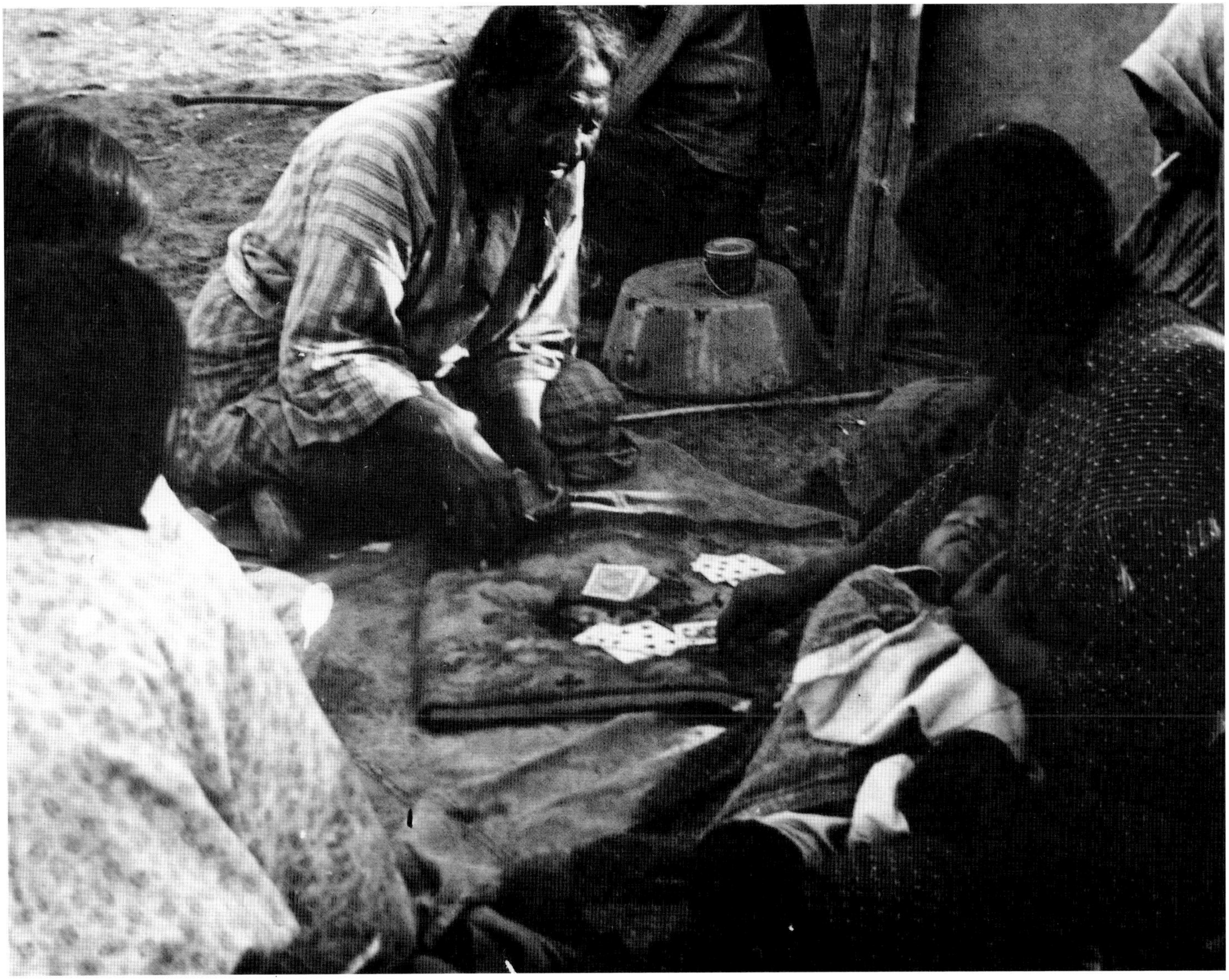

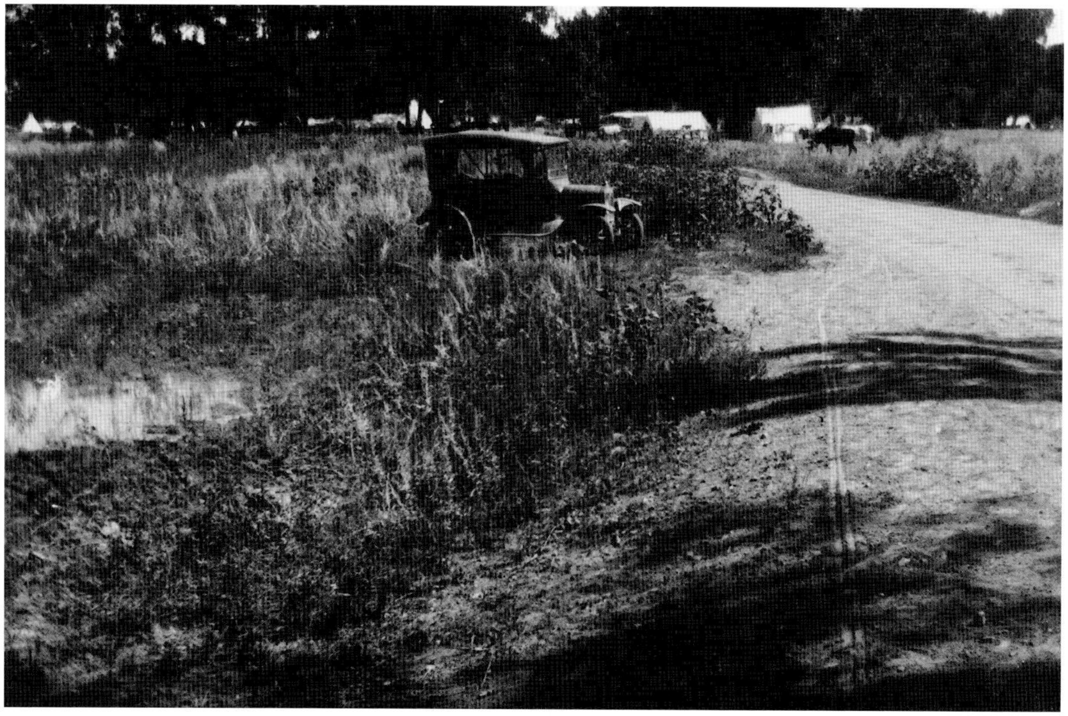

110. Camping at Crow Fair

INFORMANT: JOHN WOODENLEGS

110a. The Cheyennes are camping at the Crow Fair where they often took part. The cars are Model T Fords, and some have wagons and horses, tents and tepees. There are a lot of trees in the campground. A lot of the horses are pintos. They always celebrated together at Crow Agency. It was about 43 miles west of Lame Deer on the Crow Reservation.

110b. The Crows and Cheyennes have enjoyed a love-hate relationship for generations. Considerable intermarriage exists today, analogous to that between citizens of France and Germany. Original enmity and warfare over hunting territory existed through most of the nineteenth century. Crow scouts assisted U.S. military forces against the Sioux and Cheyennes in the final wars of the 1870s, which the latter have not forgotten.

The new Indian memorial at Custer Battlefield dedicated on June 25, 2003, honors not only the tribes who were defending their homelands against white invasion but also the Crow and Arikara scouts for the soldiers (to the displeasure of descendants of the defending tribes). A large proportion of Crow blood nonetheless flows in Cheyenne veins and vice versa, because of the many women and children taken captive in intertribal warfare who subsequently intermarried with members of the opposing tribe.

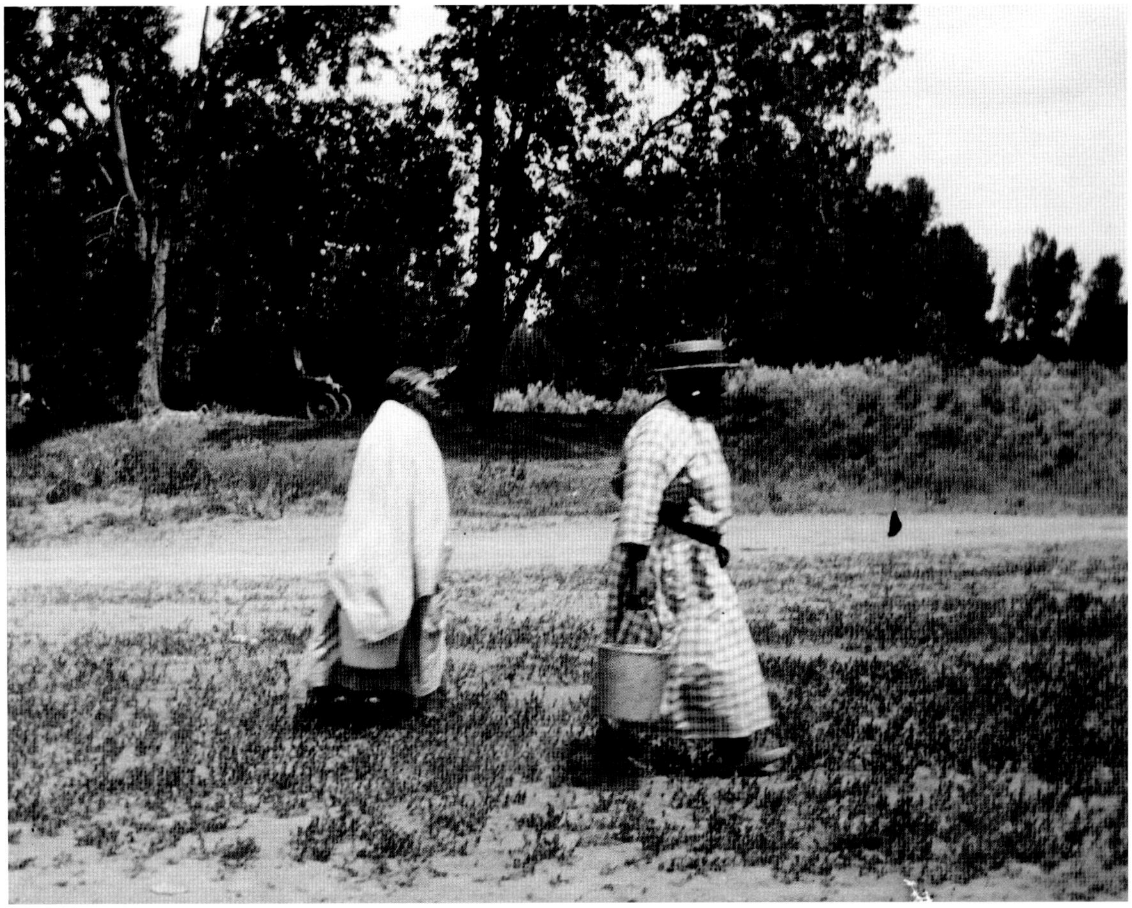

111. Carrying Water

INFORMANT: JOHN WOODENLEGS

111a. This is also at the Crow Fair. These Cheyenne women are carrying water. One is wearing a hard straw hat, the kind the men wore. Cheyennes and Crows always had a good celebration. These straw hats were flat on top. They were men's hats, but I never saw any men wear them, just older ladies. They'd wear them when they were picking berries when it's hot, to shade their eyes.

111b. Reservation millinery fashions soon responded to those of mainstream society. Hats were a novelty. The use of hats by white people is noted in the Plains sign language, which expresses the term "white man" by drawing a finger across the forehead to represent a hat brim. The big black "reservation hats" for men are no longer worn, having yielded to later cowboy styles ubiquitous in mainstream western communities.

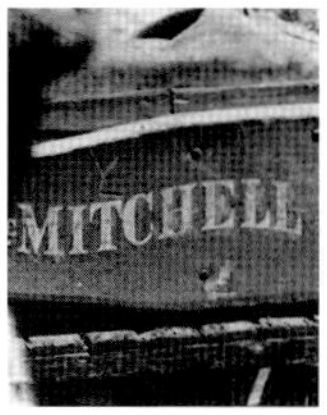

112. "Mitchell" Wagon

INFORMANT: JOHN WOODENLEGS

112a. These are the kind of wagons the Cheyennes used. On the end gate of one of these wagons is written "Mitchell." There's an old man standing there with his reservation hat. These four women are in the wagon, kind of getting on or getting off. Another man is holding his team. It must be some kind of celebration where the people are getting together. There's saddle horses, Model T cars, and the children ride horseback. One wagon has got some wood on it. They are moving in. The work horses they have seem to look fat. They're good horses.

112b. Travois or pole-drag use was discontinued at an early date. Long journeys were often made by families in wagons of this kind, especially in the days of government rations but also to attend fairs and celebrations as shown here.

A tale gathered in a recent Cheyenne tribal oral history project tells of two hungry girls in the back of such a wagon, returning home by starlight. One of them said, "I am so hungry I can even smell cabbages cooking." The other replied, "No, no. The horse just farted."

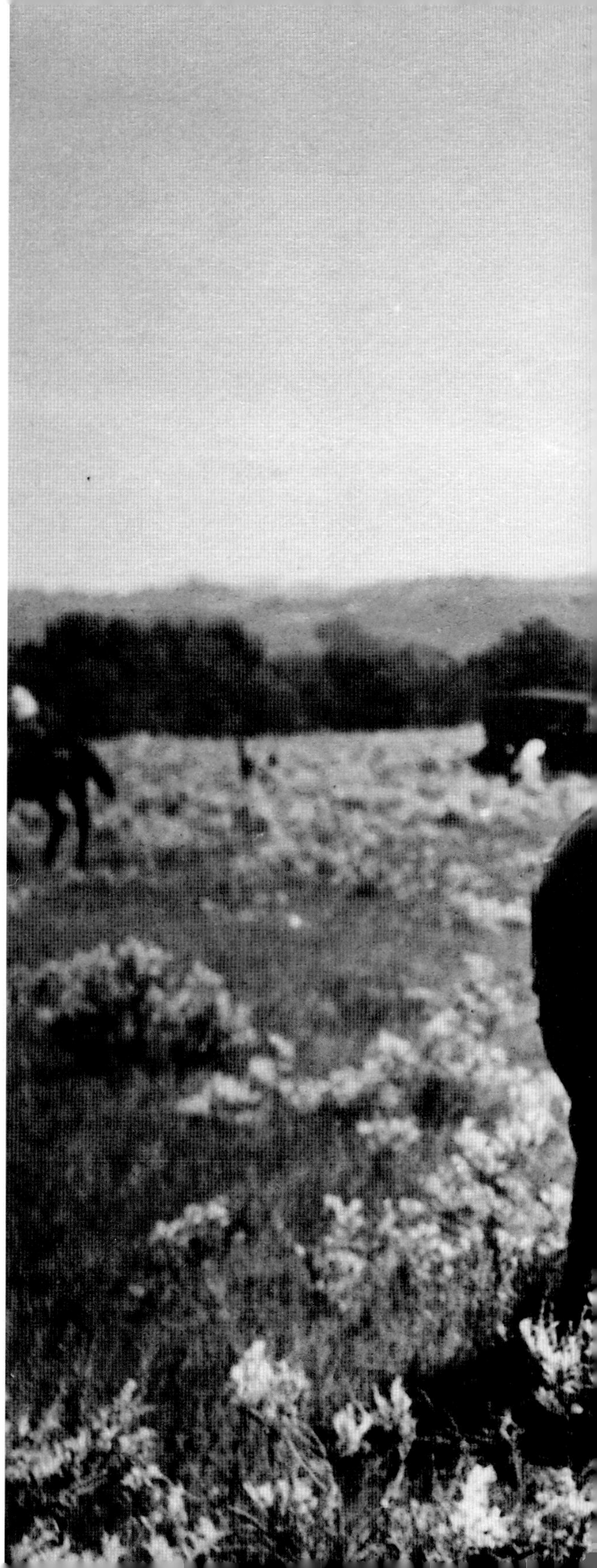

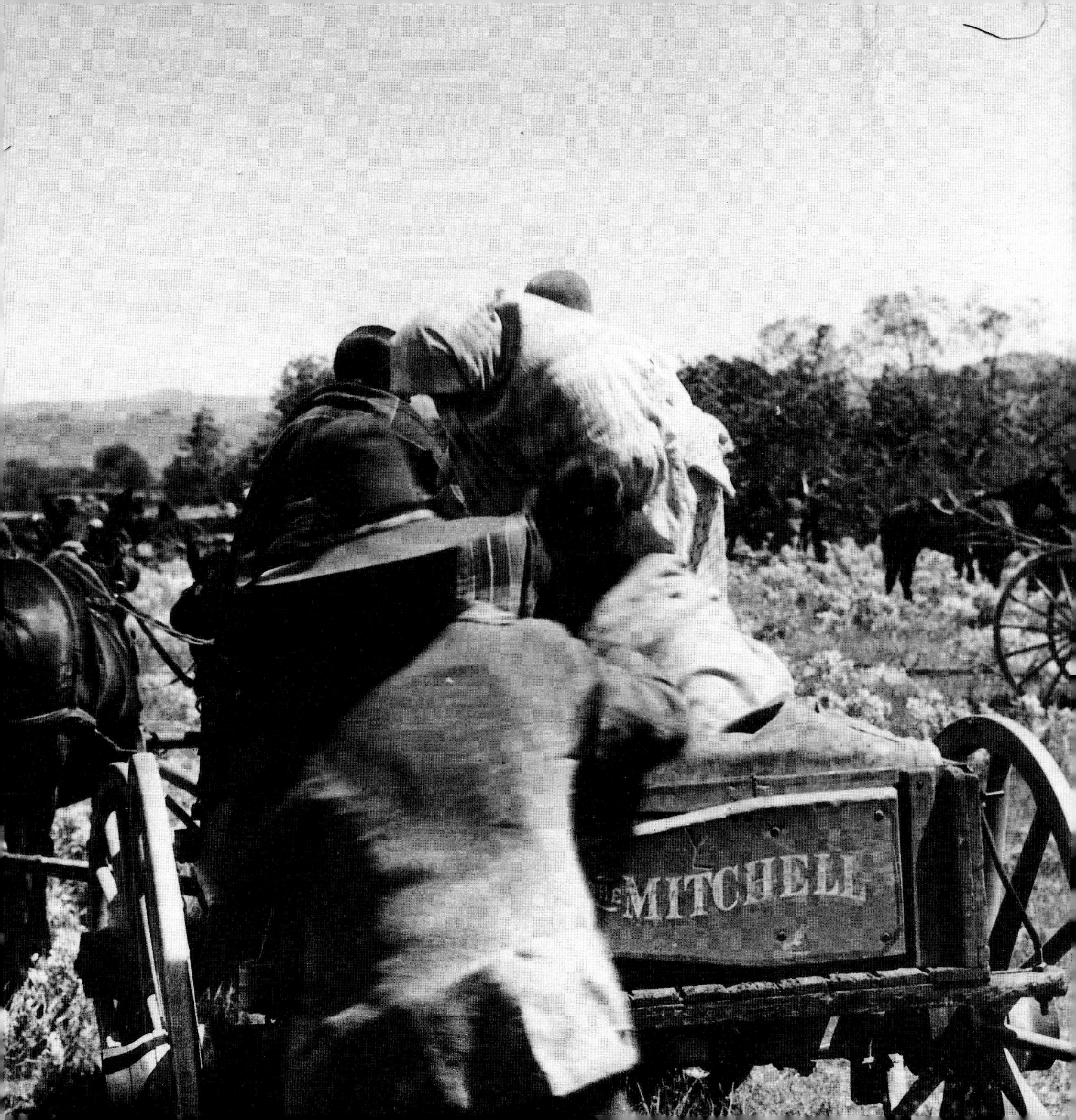
MITCHELL

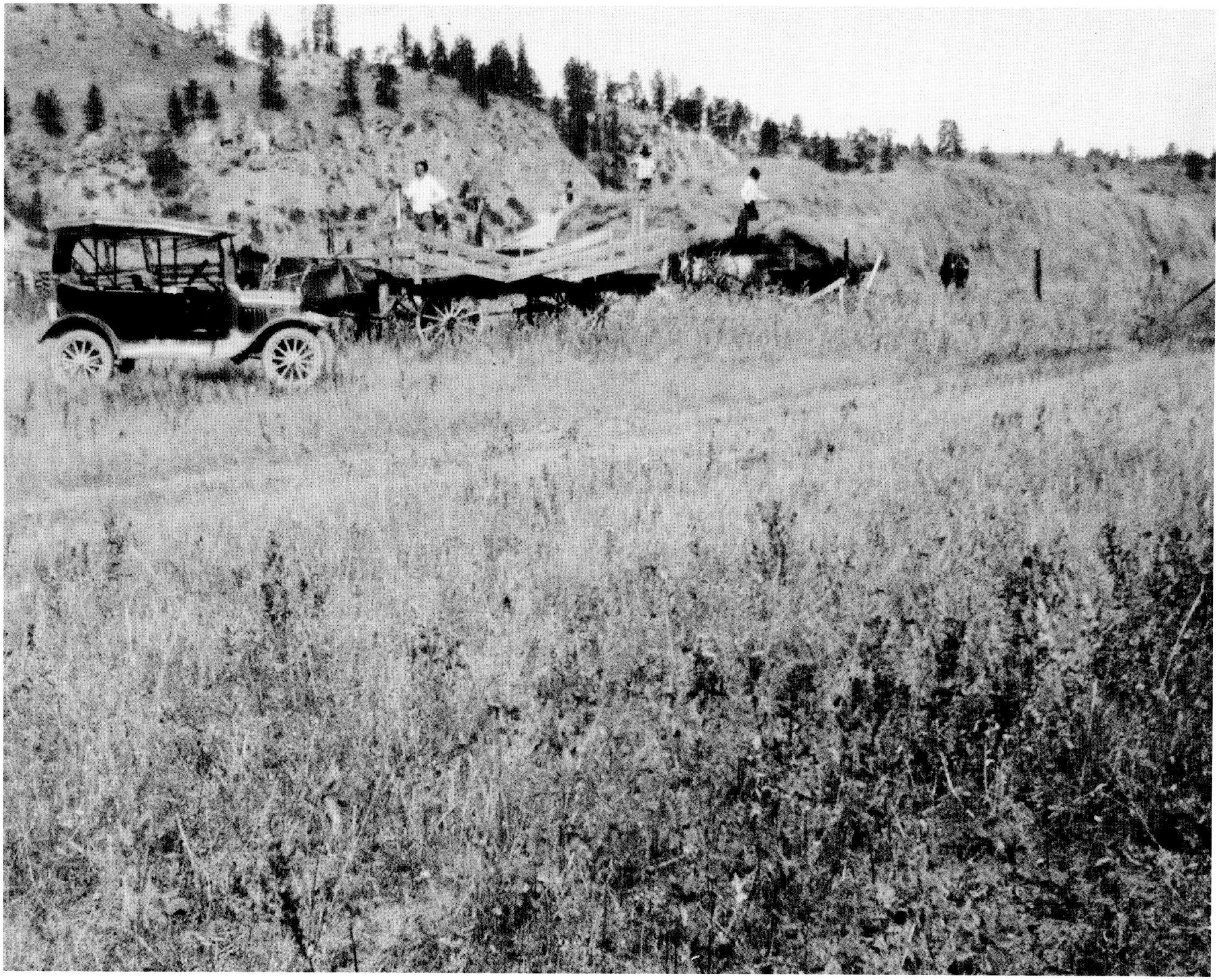

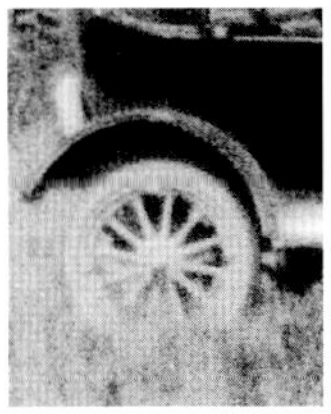

113. Unloading Hay for Winter

INFORMANT: JOHN WOODENLEGS

113a. These wagons are hauling hay and one fellow is already unloading his hay rack. These were feeding stations for the beef cattle. They issued out hay during the winter. They fed the cattle, and the Indians sold hay to the government. The hay had to be weighed. The people hauled it themselves. One fellow is stacking the hay. They made big long stacks of hay. Maybe the boss had this Model T Ford standing there.

113b. After the brutal winter of 1886–87, which put many cattle owners out of business, the winter feeding of hay cut in the summer became obligatory practice. Horses, which can paw through snow to exposed buried grass, are less susceptible to winter starvation than cattle; but often little grass remains on the ground from the previous summer.

The Model T shown prominently in some of these pictures was probably the one that Marquis used at the time.

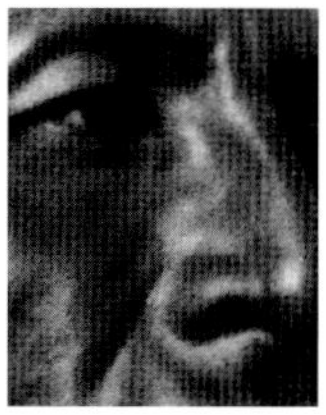

114. George Long Roach

INFORMANT: JOHN WOODENLEGS

114a. This is George Long Roach. He has his braids on and his earrings. It really looks good. He's alongside of a Model T Ford. He has a good shirt on; he's dressed up. He has his big hat with a braided hair hat band with a ring and kind of a star on it. He's married and has children and he was one of the religious ceremonial people. He only has one daughter living today; the rest of the children passed on. At one time he was interested in the Ghost Dance, but he got away from that. He was a good Native Church man.

114b. A ghost story was told by John Stands in Timber about the Long Roach pictured here (or possibly an older man by the same name). In early reservation times Long Roach went to visit his friend Looks Behind. Returning home after dark, he was overtaken near a burial ground by a small whirlwind that twisted along beside him. Seemingly it drove him out of his mind. He was found by relatives the next day lying on a grave with foam coming out of his mouth. He was almost stiff. "They took him on horseback a ways and then loaded him in a wagon. All he knew was the whirlwind hit him, and years later his mouth was still a little bit one sided" (Stands in Timber and Liberty 1997: 296).

Presumably the picture here—if it is the right Long Roach—was taken before this event.

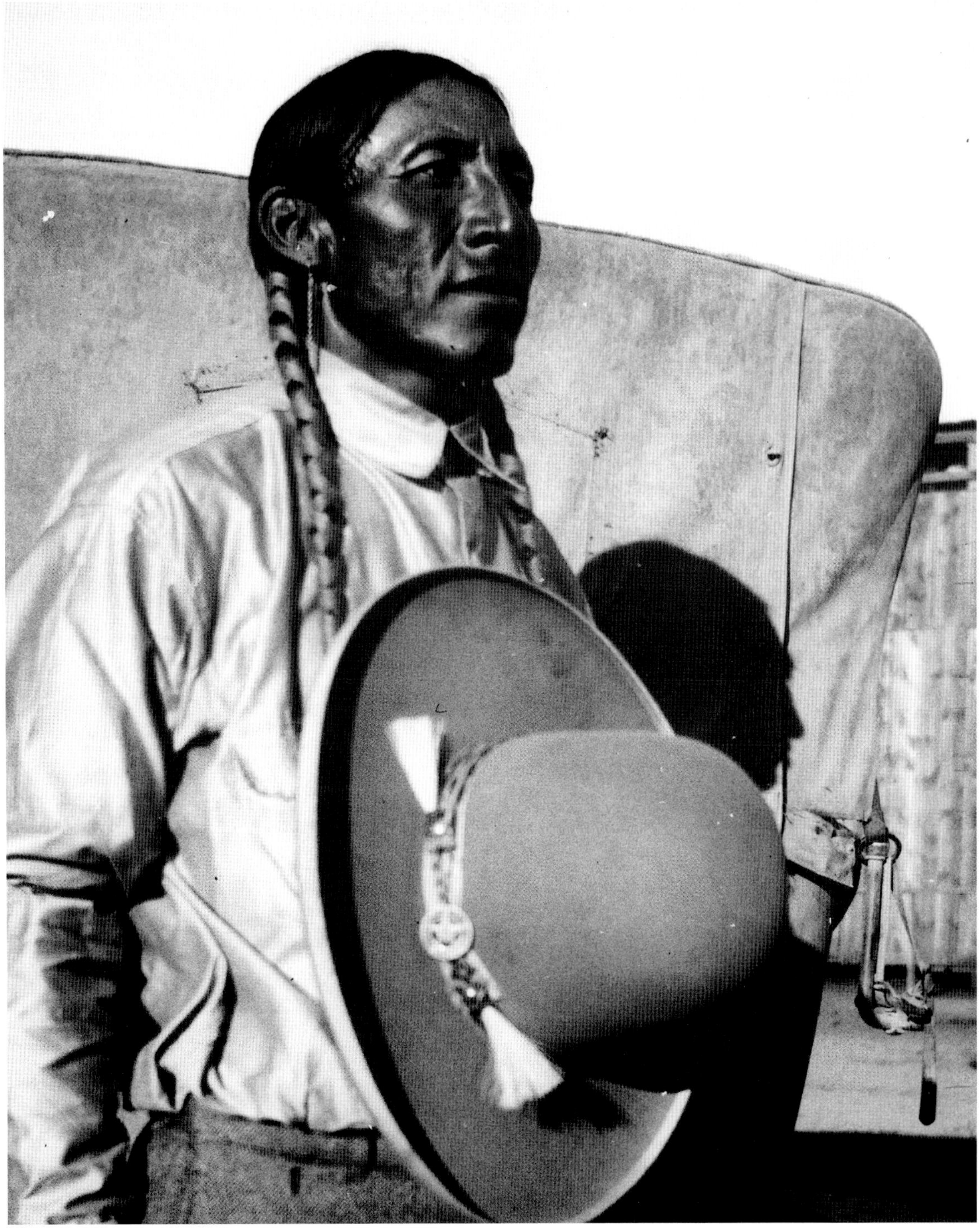

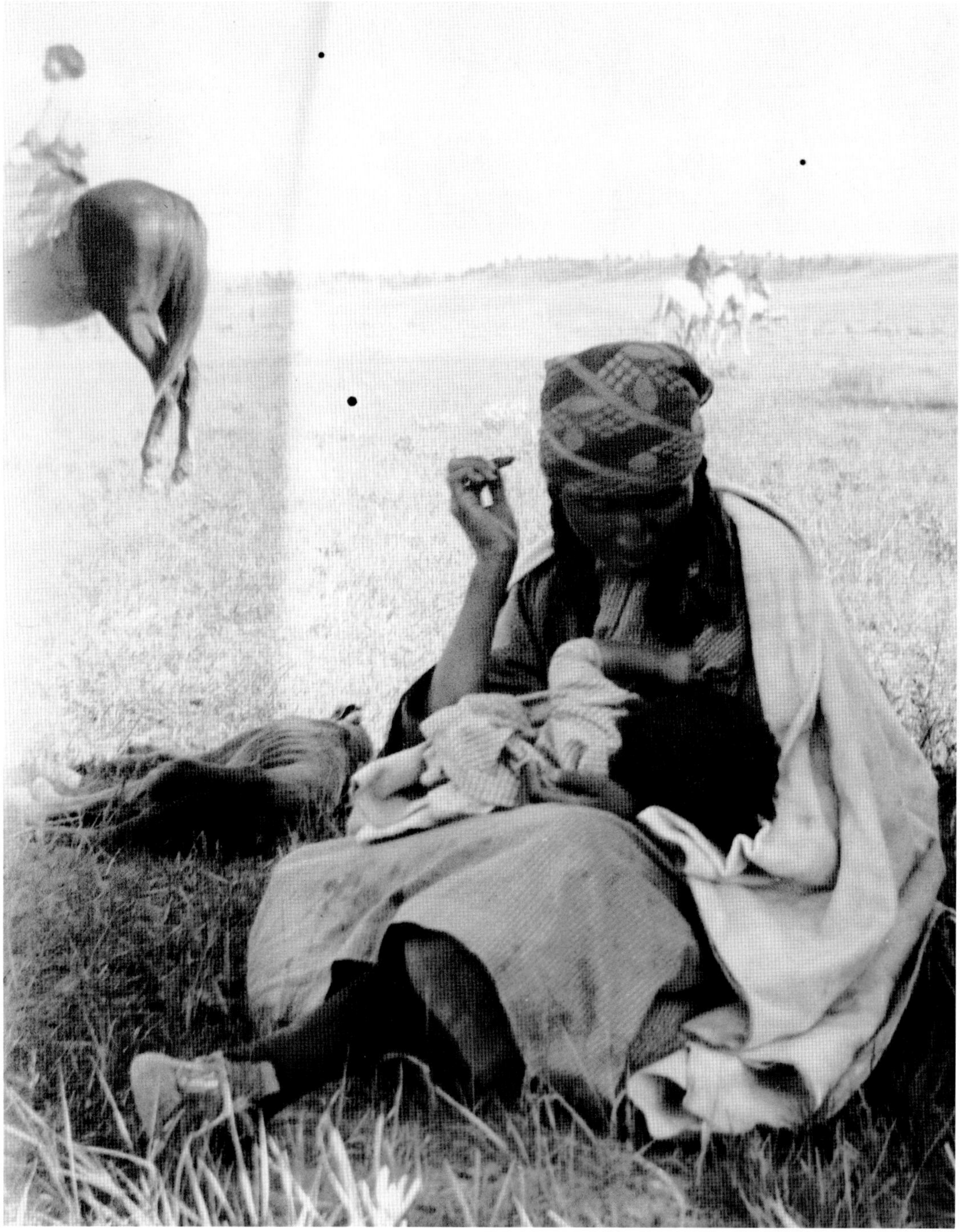

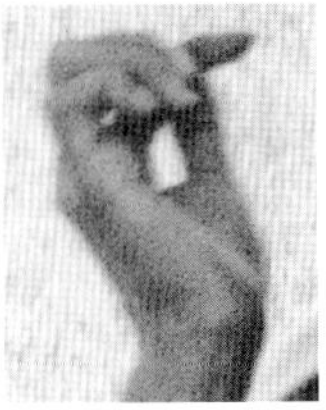

115. Time for Lunch

INFORMANT: JOHN WOODENLEGS

115a. This lady with a handkerchief around her head is nursing a baby. They are sitting on the ground. There's a dog laying close to her, and a girl on horseback close to her. Then there's two more children. One is riding a black horse and one a white one and one a pinto horse. I think this lady was married to Ben Big Head and they had three girls. You hardly ever see her, just once in a great while. She really stayed home and was a good housewife. Later on they split up and she married Pete Fire Crow. They were older then and they didn't have any children. Her name was Julia.

115b. The many relatives available to any Cheyenne child for babysitting were an advantage of traditional and early reservation life. Mothers' sisters were counted the same as mothers for most practical purposes, and mothers' sisters' children were the same as sisters and brothers. Fathers' brothers were equated with fathers in equally important ways.

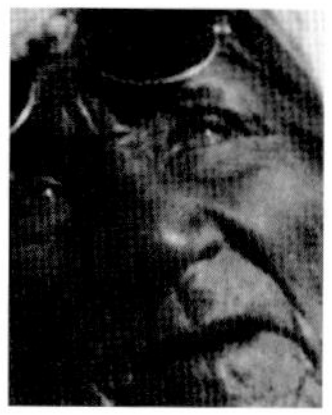

116. Buffalo Hump

INFORMANT: JOHN WOODENLEGS

116a. This is Buffalo Hump on horseback and he has a rag around his head. He's got glasses. He's riding a bald-faced roan horse. I know the man. This horse was a single-footer, kind of a pacer. This man lived on Rosebud Creek and a lot of times he'd come to Lame Deer. He's pointing with his left hand and he's holding on to the saddle horn. There's a white man with him. He's pointing up to the sky, maybe telling him about his eyesight as he is getting older. He was really active as a real old man. Now the white man is a doctor, I guess. He's probably telling him about how far he can still see. He was a good man, he talked about old times. He was Morning Star's son. He was called Buffalo Hump. He was kind of comical and he told stories. They tried to make him the next Chief after his father. He said, "No, you turn to the government and the Agency. My father did what he could for the tribe and coming back from Oklahoma. He's the one, so I don't want to be the next Chief. He's done a good job for us."

Buffalo Hump owned horses and he sure liked to ride this good roan horse. This picture was taken in 1922 when he was 77 years old. He was a Custer Battle veteran. The doctor is Dr. Ross, according to Dr. Marquis' notes.

116b. Dull Knife or Morning Star was one of the two famous chiefs who led the Northern Cheyennes back from imprisonment in Oklahoma in 1878–79. The other was Little Wolf. This episode was one of the most famous in American Indian history, because it led to the final settlement of the people in the northern country that they loved so much. Dull Knife was honored in the tribe as the greater of the two because Little Wolf subsequently killed a fellow tribesman, which disqualified him as a tribal leader.

The Cheyenne system of chiefs was extremely rigorous in matters of this kind. Its expectations were so high that later candidates like Buffalo Hump often chose not to burden themselves with chiefly responsibilities.

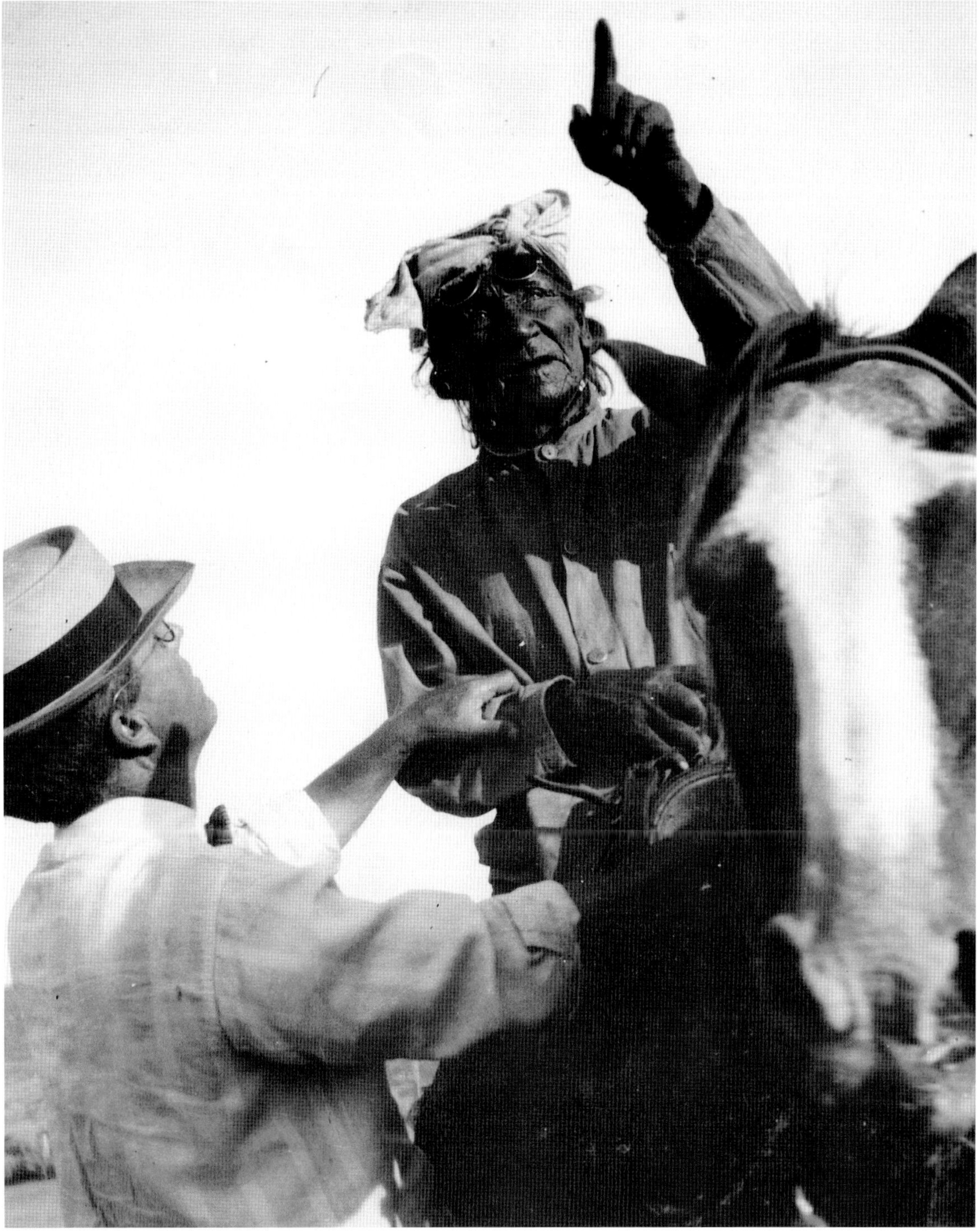

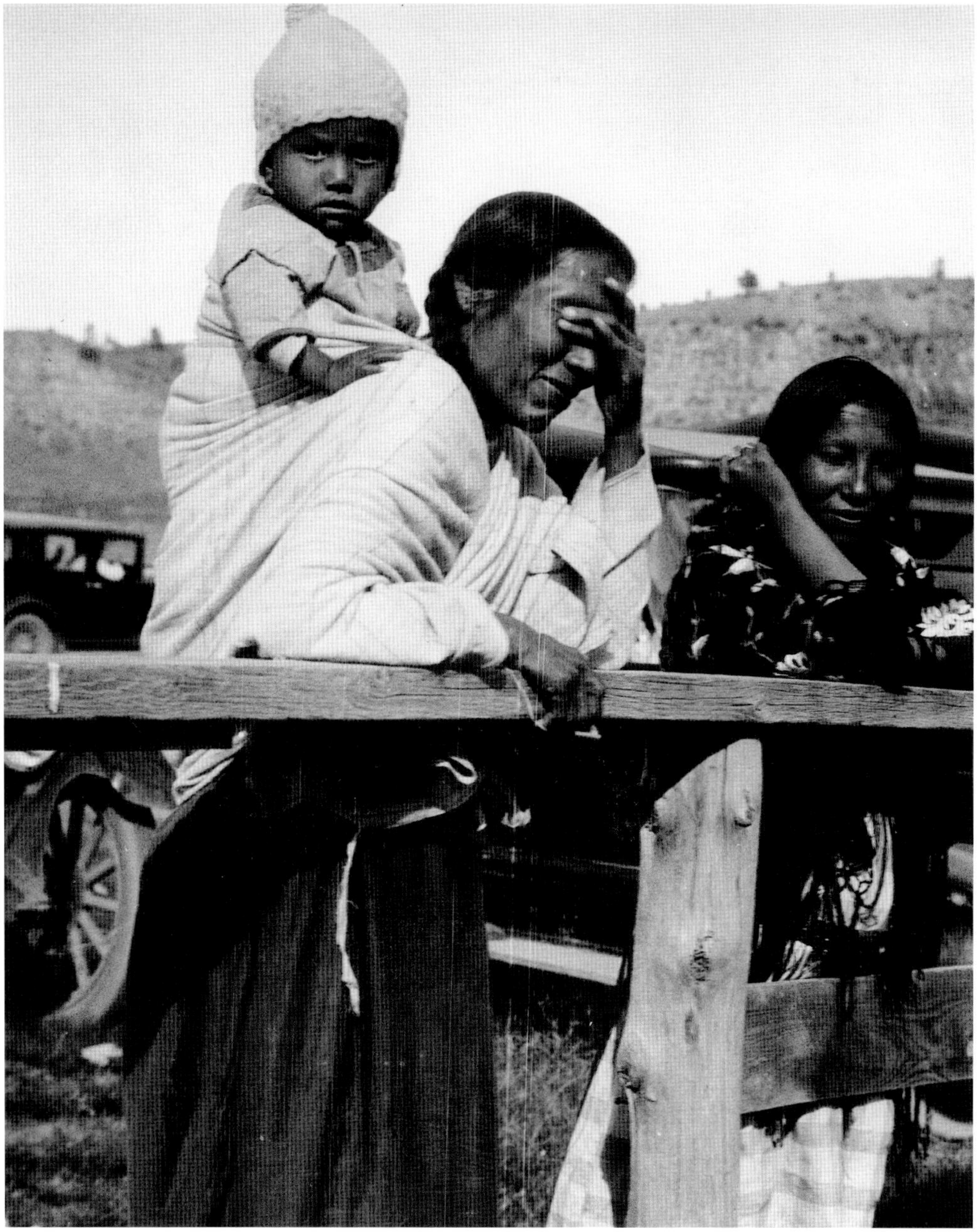

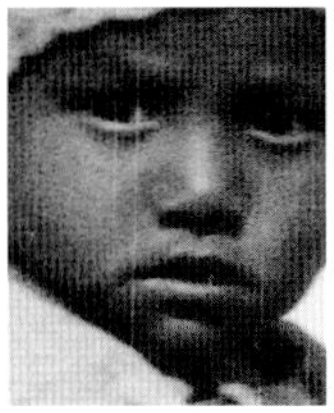

117. Mrs. Richard Wolf Chief and Children

INFORMANT: JOHN WOODENLEGS

117a. This is Mrs. Richard Wolf Chief with her baby, Anne, on her back and her daughter Alice in front of her. She has her hand over her eyes. This was near the fairground, I guess. There are Model T cars in the background. She has a blanket on and a dress and real Cheyenne braids. The girl is dressed in a light shawl. This lady was married to Richard Wolf Chief and I think they only raised that one girl. The rest of them died. Her husband didn't go to school, but he ran a Ford car like a mechanic. He always had his car running. They lived in Lame Deer. She's got her eyes covered with her hand, but she's smiling anyway, and the girl is smiling too. Maybe they were bashful, but the baby looked right straight at the photographer. She was safe on her mother's back. This is the way they carried their babies, on their back. Nowadays, some white ladies sometimes carry their babies on their back or in the front in a kind of pack-thing. They must be following an old Indian tradition!

This picture was taken in 1928.

117b. This comment on mainstreamers' use of backpack baby carriers is the kind relished by early Cheyenne observers of non-Indian reservation life.

118a. Maud Arapaho Chief and Lenora Arapaho Chief Two Birds in 1926 when Maud was 82 and her daughter perhaps 40 years. This is my great-grandmother, Maud, and my grandmother, Lenora. Lenora was the mother of my mother, Frances Two Birds Knows His Gun. Maud was a medicine woman and she and her husband did Indian doctoring. They owned many horses.

Now Peter Two Birds (Little Bear) had two wives who were sisters. One was Lenora, and the other was Laura, whose Indian name was "Skunk Woman." Lenora did fine beadwork and won many prizes at the fairs. They also won prizes on garden produce, especially watermelons. They raised cattle and fine horses. They lived around the Kirby area.

Lenora lived long enough to see my first two children. I don't know how old she was when she died. She was a hard-working woman, she could set up a tepee in a short time. She could butcher beef all by herself. When my brother Gordon passed away, she lost her zest for living and from then on, she went downhill. Sometimes when she cried she said, "I never thought my grandson would go on before me."

Here is a little history that was passed on from Maud: when Custer's men attacked, Arapaho Chief and his family were camped on the north side of the river. Lenora and Laura were very small then. When the soldiers came across the river, it was right by the Cheyenne camp. Before they made the charge to go across, they went along looking for a place to cross. Some got caught in a crossfire and one leader was shot.

Laura said, "Who are those people?" Maud said, "Those are the people who have come to kill us!" Laura was so frightened she fainted. When that man got shot, two riders came on either side and one to the front and grabbed the reins and they kept the man on his horse, turned around, and went back across. My grandmother thinks this man might have been Custer, and from my own reading of the battle, it seems this could be. If a lesser officer had been shot, it wouldn't have stopped the charge.

Lenora and Laura stayed in Oklahoma when the Cheyennes went there after the Custer Battle. They later went to Pine Ridge, S.D., and settled in the White River area. Later on they came to the Busby area after the reservation was set up in 1884.

Lenora's half-brother was taken by some white people and raised to go to school, possibly college. When he came to Pine Ridge, he tried to take Lenora and Laura with him to go to school. He and his father had trouble being reconciled to one another, and eventually the son committed suicide.

Lenora and her husband farmed and raised corn and livestock. They would make dry meat, Indian hominy and they would share food with older, needy people. I asked her once, "Why do you do all this?" She said, "These people have life and God is concerned about that life and if we do something to feed that life, God will bring us blessings. Some way if we give the last of whatever we have, God sees, God is concerned and He will help us."

Lenora went to the Mennonite Church in Busby and

before she died, she and my grandfather were baptized.

[According to the notes of Dr. Marquis, this picture was taken in 1926, when Maud was 82 years old.]

118b. This photograph and the photograph of Limpy and his wife (figure 22) are probably the most historically significant pictures in the collection. For years scholars have debated the closeness of Custer's approach to the Little Bighorn River when he attacked the big Indian village at the northern end of the camp on June 25, 1876. The Cheyennes are known to have occupied the northernmost campground, which was the farthest downstream. Many authorities say that the Custer column did not approach the ford to the village but remained at a final hillside position, where he and his soldiers died. According to this account, however, the soldier column approached the crossing closely enough to frighten a young girl who saw them from the other side.

If the soldiers were indeed kept out of the village at this point by four Cheyenne horsemen—as recounted in Crazy Horse *(Sandoz 1961)—an extraordinary action happened at this place. Had the soldiers penetrated the village, the battle's outcome might have been totally different. See also Grinnell,* The Fighting Cheyennes *(1956).*

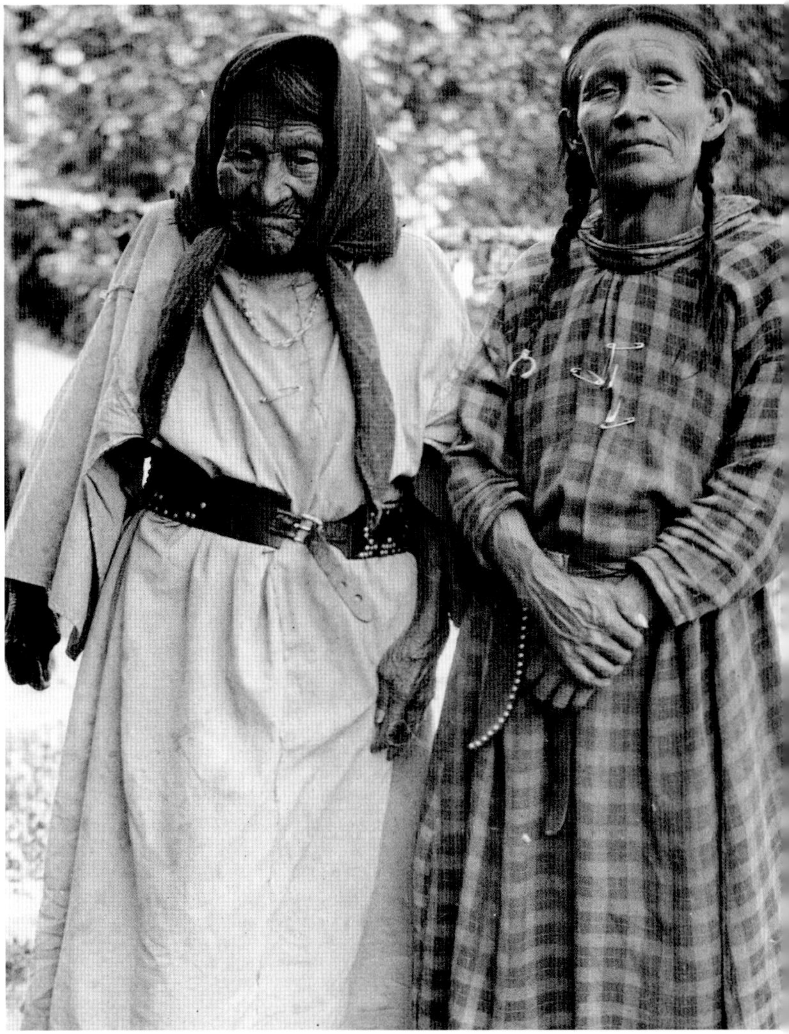

118. Maud Arapaho Chief and Lenora Arapaho Chief Two Birds

INFORMANT: SYLVESTER KNOWS HIS GUN

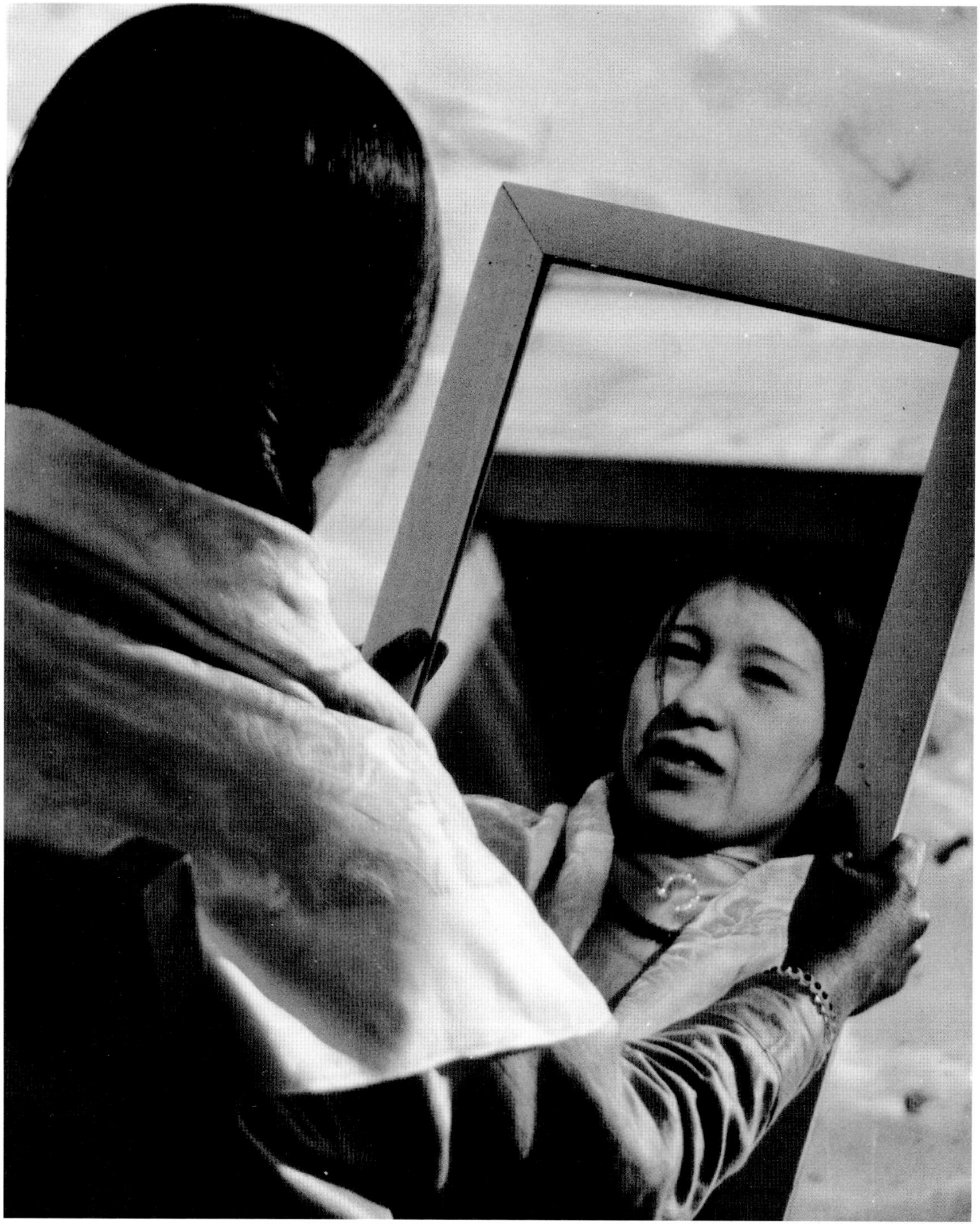

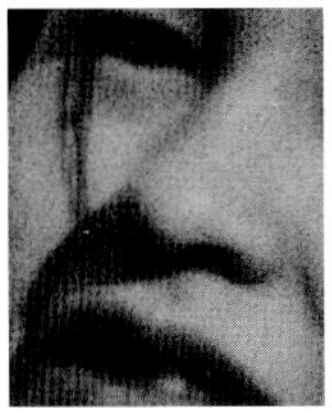

119. Frances Two Birds Knows His Gun

INFORMANT: SYLVESTER KNOWS HIS GUN

119a. This is a picture of my mother, taken in 1925. Her father was Peter Two Birds, but his original name was Peter Little Bear. When his nephew was born, he changed his name. Two Birds was his Indian name. Frances' Indian name was "Two Killer Woman." That name means a person counted two coups on the enemy.

Frances married Hector Knows His Gun, a Crow (with some Flathead and Kiowa). One of Hector's ancestors had been a Crow chief. Frances had nine children: Sylvester, Edith, Hector Jr., Gordon, Roger, Franklin, Genevieve, Diana, and Alvin. When they were first married, they lived near Lodge Grass. Later they lived near Kirby, where her relatives ranched. Frances' brother was Jacob Two Birds.

Frances taught her children the things they needed to withstand the battles of life. She was a Christian when she passed away in 1978. She was always willing to help people. She would not turn away anyone who was hungry, and she would pick up hitchhikers. She was a very strong in whatever she stood for. She was one of the few who could speak English and could speak up in her generation.

As a teenage girl, she saved Albert Longjaw from drowning when he fell into a creek that was in flood stage. That was in Busby. Frances was 73 when she died in 1978.

119b. This is another example of a multiplicity of Indian names. The personality of a strong woman with a mind of her own is also suggested.

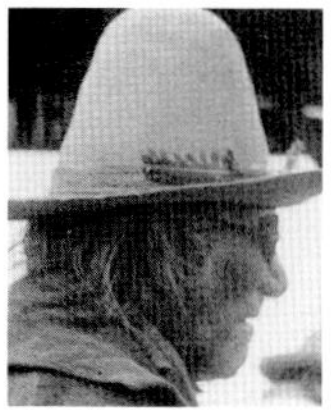

120. Iron Shirt at the Fair

INFORMANT: JOHN WOODENLEGS

120a. This is Iron Shirt on his horse at the Lame Deer Fair, September 3, 1927. According to Dr. Marquis' notes, he was 96 years old.

120b. Iron Shirt was one of about a hundred Cheyenne warriors in the Custer fight. Many of these survived until Marquis spent time as a reservation photographer four decades later. About twenty such battle veterans appear among the pictures presented in this volume.

Born in 1831, Iron Shirt would have been 45 on the date of the fight. At the age of 96, he still presents an impressive picture on horseback. Marquis took great care in recording such ages and dates and made few if any mistakes. He says that Indians knew their ages perfectly well at any given time.

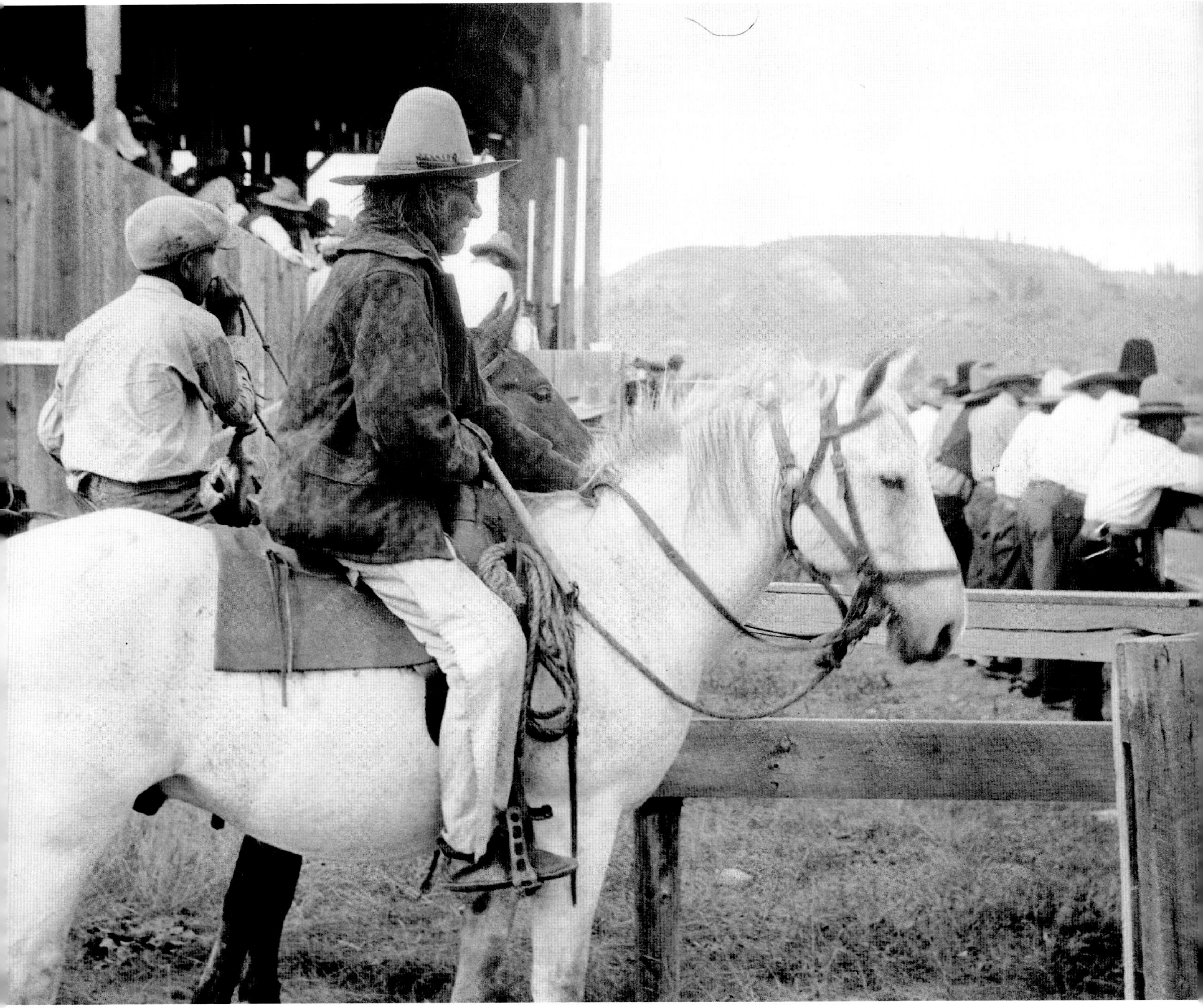

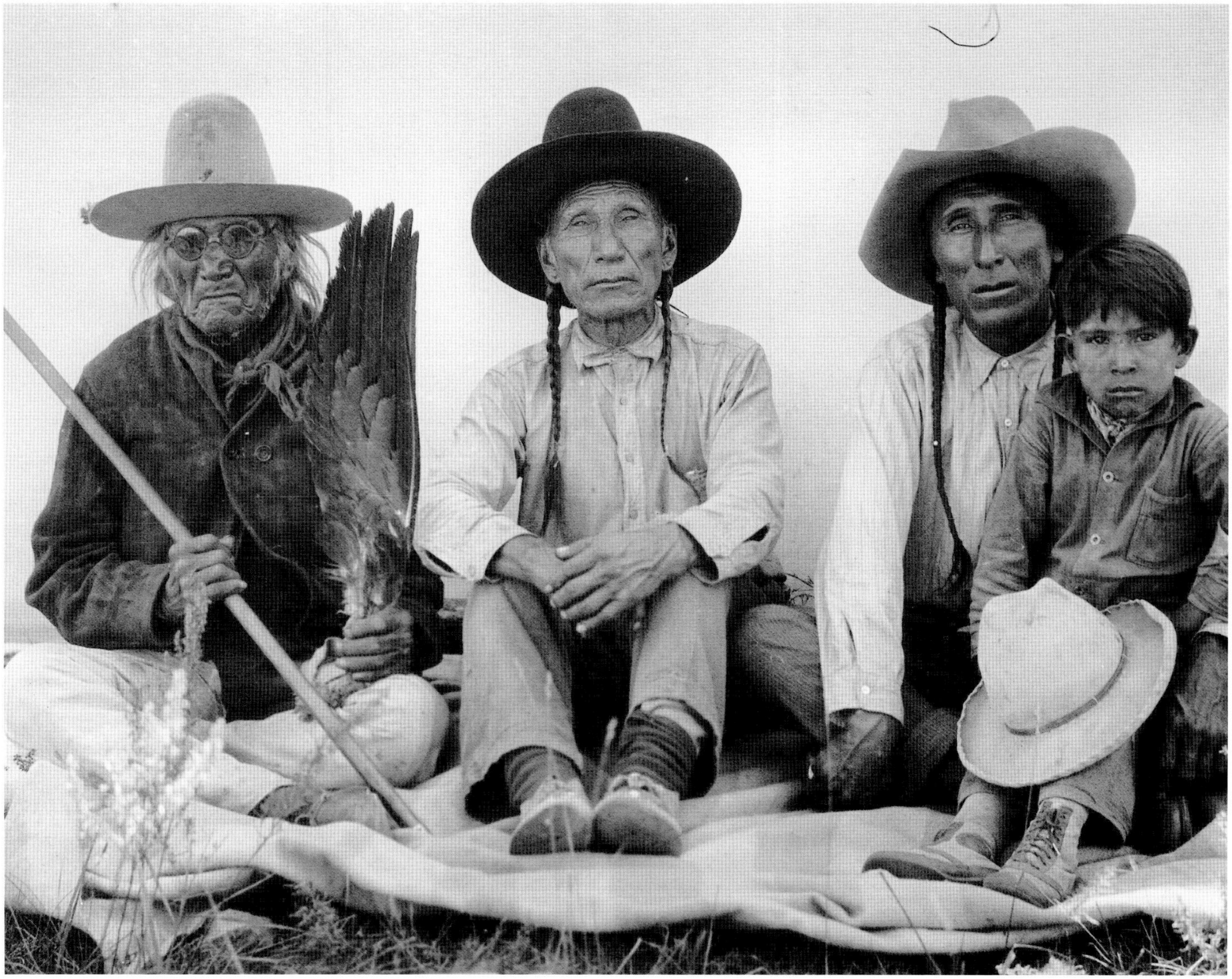

121. Iron Shirt and Family

INFORMANT: JOHN WOODENLEGS

121a. Here we have four generations: Iron Shirt, Philip Risingsun, Pete Risingsun, and Harry Risingsun, all sitting together. Iron Shirt has his cane and his eagle wing feather, his reservation hat, glasses on and a black handkerchief around his neck. Philip (his son) has his ten gallon hat and long braids. Harry (Pete's son) is just a young boy about six or seven. He's got his hat and his tennis shoes. They're all sitting on a blanket.

Now I have seen Iron Shirt. He raised some good horses. There's another picture of him riding a white horse to the fair where they were having races. I did have one of his horses that he raised, a good-looking little bay horse. This old man's brand was on the right hip—quarter circle Z. He raised these horses, they were Indian ponies. They were all good horses. Somehow I got this bay horse and I broke it to ride. It was that good color bay with black mane and tail and his hoofs were black. I have a picture of this horse. I used to relay race and I've got my relay saddle on this little bay horse. I liked the horse so much, he was such a cute horse. He carried me good, kind of a teenager horse. I dressed him up and we had a picture taken.

This Iron Shirt lived on Rosebud Creek west of the mouth of Lame Deer Creek. Philip Risingsun lived at Busby. He had horses and he had a good place on Rosebud Creek above Busby town or store. I have seen him and talked with him and his wife. He had these sons: Pete, Oliver, and John Risingsun, also Willie. I think he had one daughter that married James Big Back from Lame Deer, and another daughter was married to John Russell.

This was a big family—they were all good people. From this Iron Shirt there came to be lots of relatives. Pete Risingsun had a son who was in the Army in the Second World War, also a nephew. So he wanted to honor these soldiers and also to honor the flag. So they had a singing with the drums, and his wife used to help him, also some men and boys. They all had horses and cattle and worked at being cowboys. Oliver Risingsun was on the Tribal Council. They all took part in different ceremonial doings. Philip Risingsun had a four-room house, a fence around his place, good horses, cattle. They lived about five or six miles from the Busby school.

One brother of Iron Shirt was Alights on the Cloud who went to Washington in 1851 after the Horse Creek Treaty. He was killed by the Pawnees in 1852. Iron Shirt was named for his uncle, Iron Shirt, born in the late 1700s. The older Iron Shirt was owner of a famous coat of mail, probably procured from the Spanish. Alights on the Cloud was wearing this coat when a Pawnee left-hander killed him right through the eye.

The younger Iron Shirt was prominent in the fighting of the Custer Battle.

121b. These four patrilineally related members of the Iron Shirt family represent a distinguished group. Iron Shirt was also famous in early reservation days for resisting a rancher who tried to run cattle over his garden.

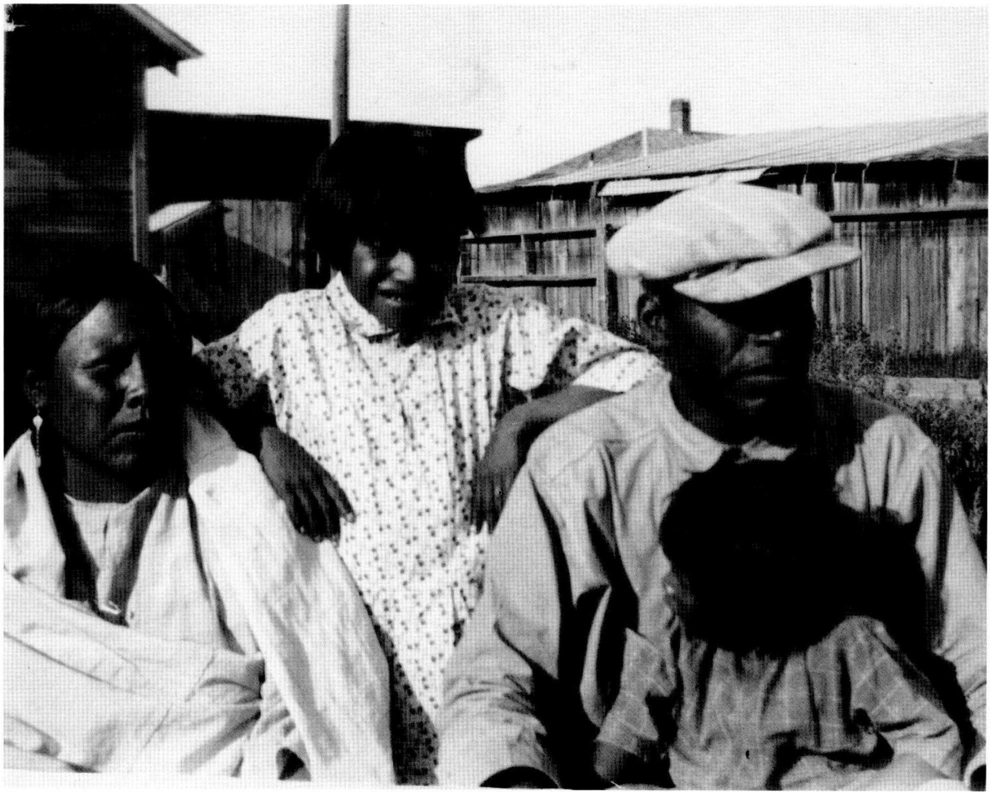

122. Albert Duster and Family

INFORMANT: JOHN WOODENLEGS

122a. This is Albert Monothy or Albert Duster and his wife, and their two girls. The girls seem to be about six and four. Marquis took the picture in 1928. Mr. Duster had some education; he must have gone away to school. He was a blacksmith and kind of a mechanic. His Indian name is "Wounded." His wife's relatives were Red Fox. The children died young. Duster was a hard worker, a Native Church man, talked good to people. He ran a taxi in Lame Deer, a Model T Ford. He had his own car. Duster was on the Tribal Council for a long time. He went to Washington, D.C., four times as a delegate.

122b. The occupation of taxi driver in Lame Deer was definitely not a common one.

Indian delegates to Washington sometimes picked up surprisingly detailed geographical knowledge. John Stands in Timber once as a joke mapped out for me the locations of six or seven men's rooms known to him in the Capitol building itself.

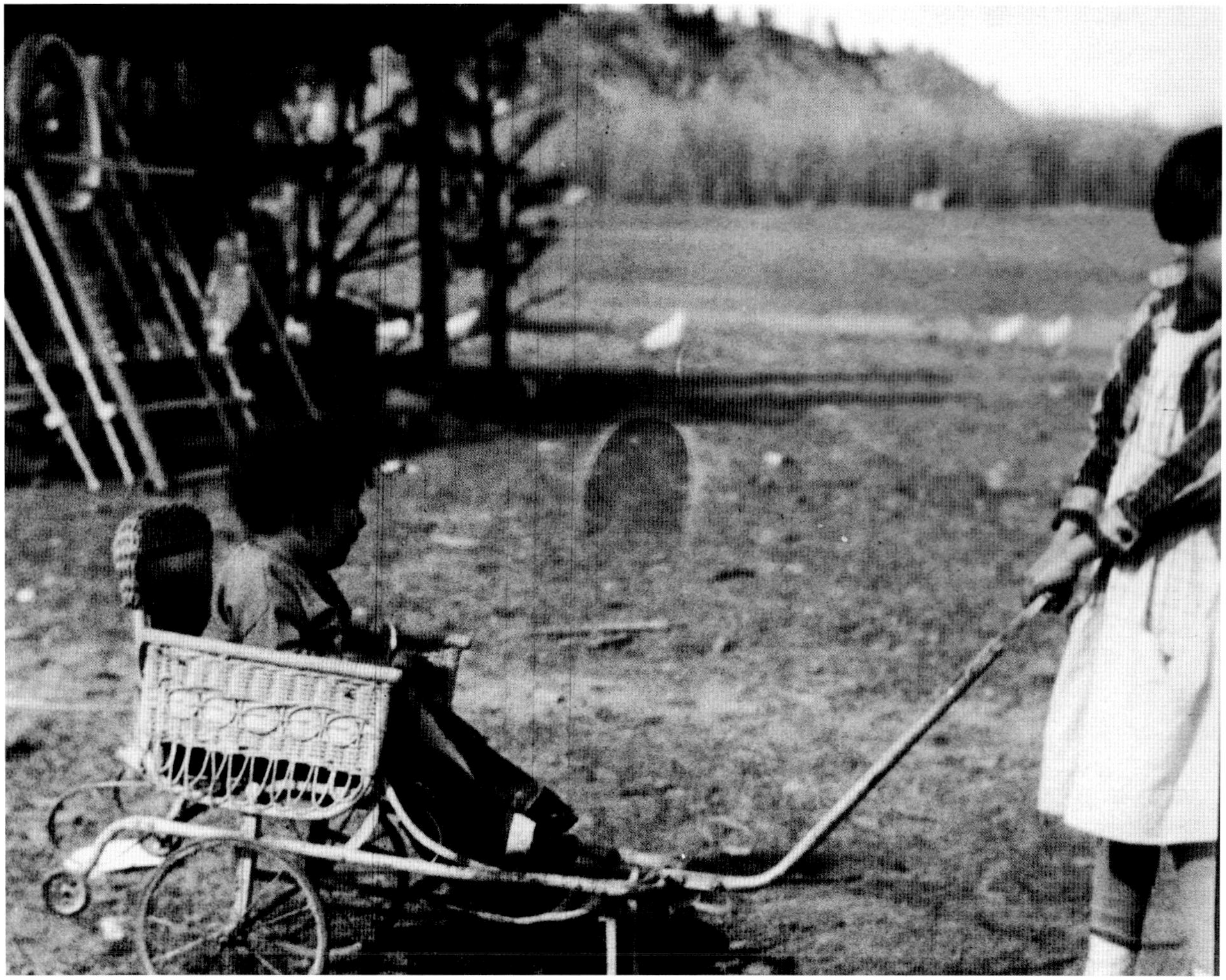

123. Getting a Ride

INFORMANT: JOHN WOODENLEGS

123a. This is a girl about seven or eight years old pulling a baby carriage or cart, and there's a baby in there and he's quite big. They took these carts and used them for any sized baby. There's some chickens and hills and cottonwood trees—might be along the river. I don't know who they are, I can't see the girl's face.

123b. This picture was probably taken to document the finest fashion in early reservation perambulators. Few Indian families would have been able to afford such a luxury.

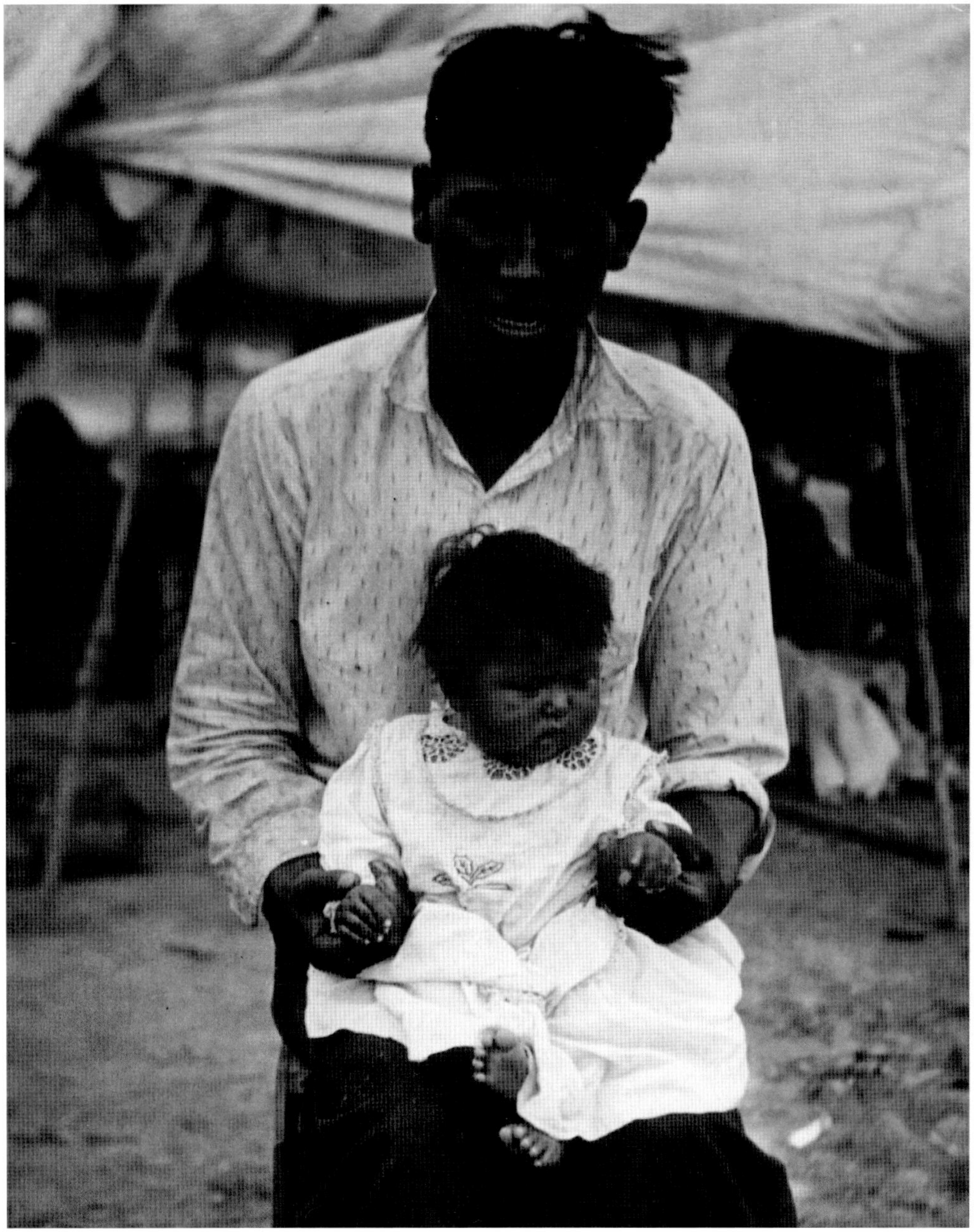

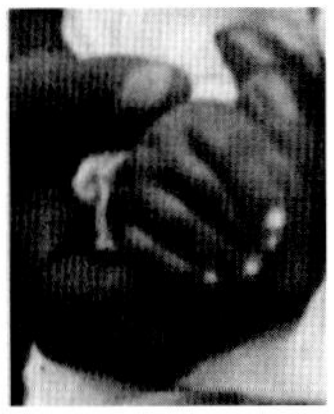

124. William Yellow Fox and Mary Yellow Fox

INFORMANT: JOHN WOODENLEGS

124a. This is William Yellow Fox as quite a young man. He's got a baby in his lap. He did live in Lame Deer and was raised by old ladies. He went to Ashland and married one of the Yellow Nose girls and they had two or three children. He only went to school a little bit. The children died except for one, I think. The child's name was Mary Yellow Fox. They have kind of a tent and a shade fixed just outside of it. The little girl's got no shoes on, her toes are sticking out. She has on a white dress, probably dressed up to have her picture taken. She's kind of chubby.

This picture was taken in 1930. When this baby grew up she married George Runs Above.

124b. Marquis took many photographs of young children.

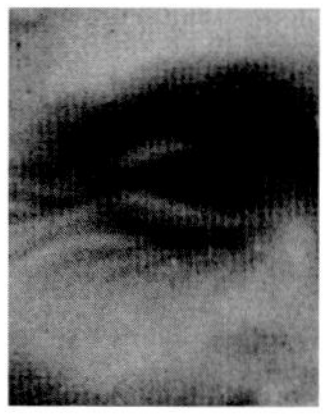

125. George American Horse

INFORMANT: JOHN WOODENLEGS

125a. This is George American Horse, with his braids really fixed the Cheyenne way. He has on a white shirt and dress pants. He's one of the elders that farmed, raised cattle and horses. He lived on Lame Deer Creek south of Lame Deer. I've seen that man plowing on foot, horses pulling one single plow. He worked hard. He didn't have an education, only his good Native ways. He abided by the rules and regulations. I think he went to the Catholic Church. He had two girls and a boy. He always wore his hair long. He worked on the Tribal Council. He was also one of the camp criers, tried to talk to young people of the good ways of the Cheyenne people. He had horses—he raised race horses. He had two horses that were mouse colored. They were good looking horses and they were strong. My father trained them and took them to races. My dad and American Horse were good friends. He lived in a good way and tried to raise his family in a good way.

125b. The information on this beautiful portrait of an early reservation farmer does not tell whether he was related to the older chief American Horse who took part in the Indian wars, including the Custer fight. George American Horse was a committee member during a reorganization of the traditional chiefs in May 1941. Another chiefs' meeting was held in July 1960 (Stands in Timber and Liberty 1997: chapter 3).

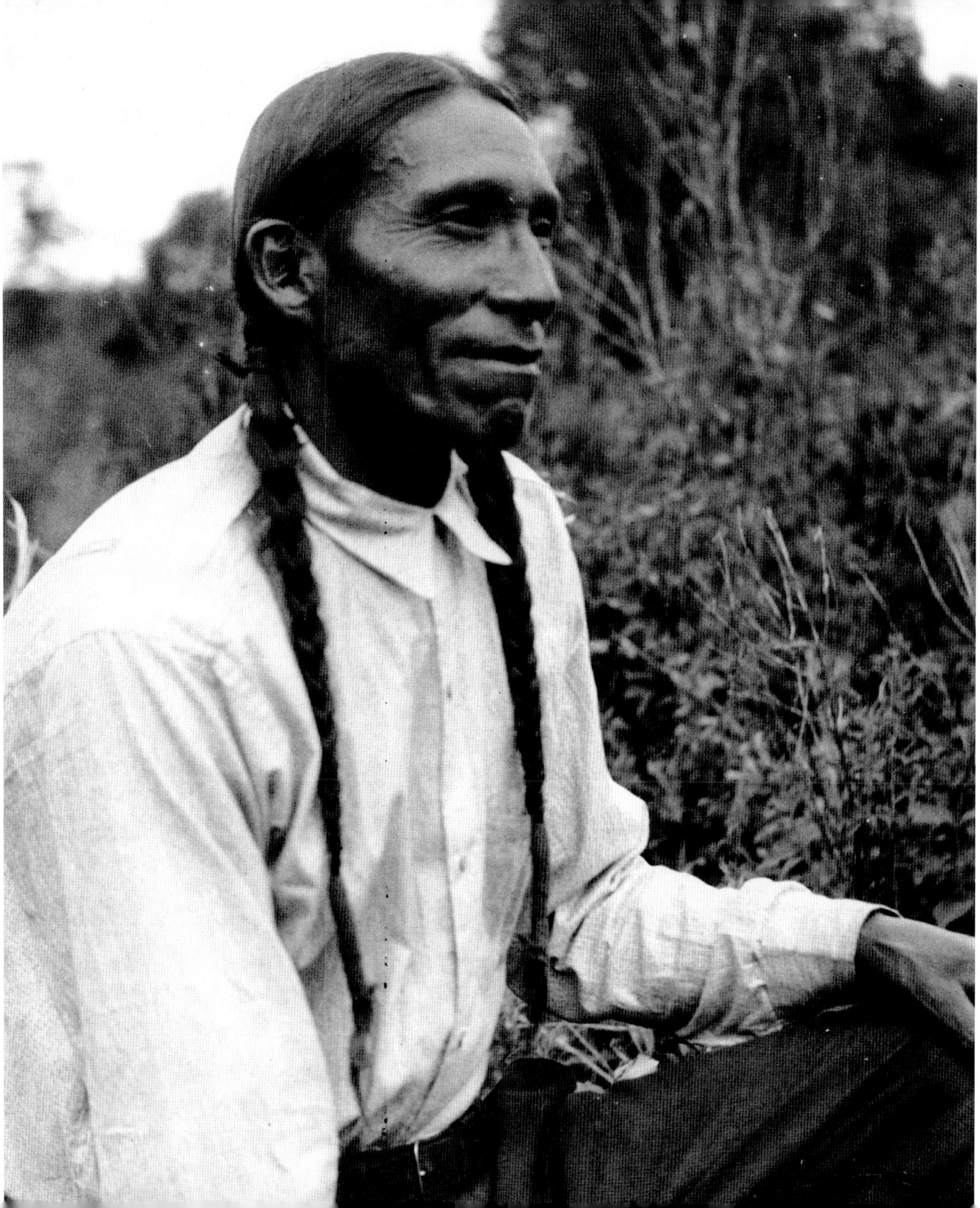

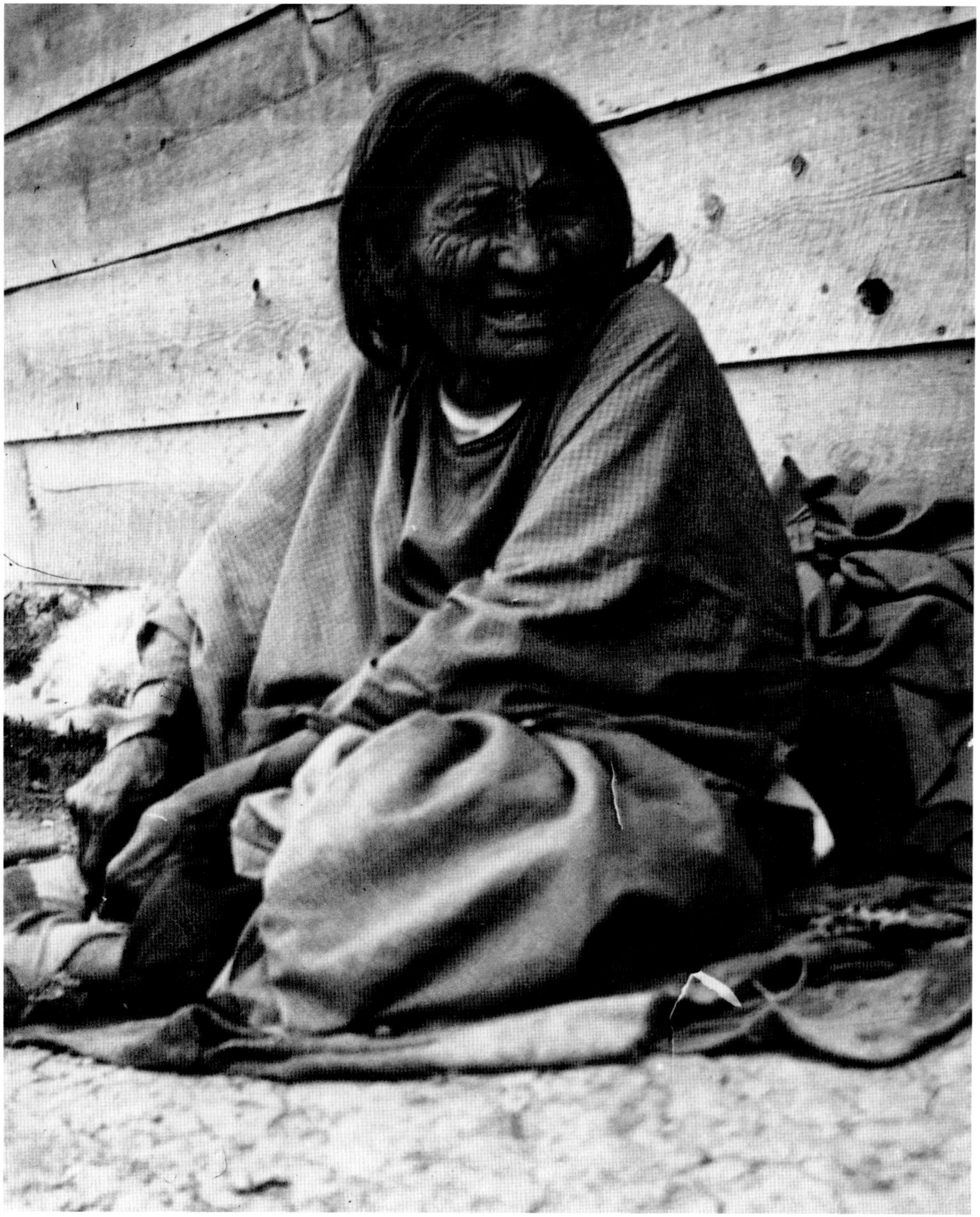

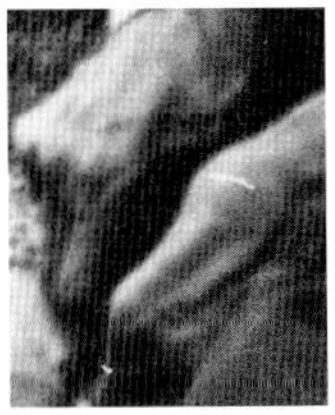

126. Howling Woman

INFORMANT: JOHN WOODENLEGS

126a. This is an older Indian woman. I don't know her English name, but her Indian name was Howling Woman. My aunt was married to Pius Shoulderblade, my uncle, and they lived over towards Ashland. This lady is his grandmother. His mother was living and his stepfather was living and his father and his stepmother were living, and he had a brother and a sister, half, but it seemed like he was the only child of the first marriage of his parents. And this is his grandmother. I have seen her when I was with him, talked to her. She still talked good and she was one of the real old Cheyenne women. She's tying up her moccasins, kind of fixing up to pose for this picture alongside of a building. This building looks like the house that Pius Shoulderblade's father and stepmother lived in, and they had taken care of her there. She must have lived to be quite old. She was really old when I knew her. See her face, it's just the way she looked when I saw her.

126b. Marquis made a strong effort to represent women among his subjects, although minimal information concerning their lives was likely to be available in comparison with the more obvious activities of men. Thus it has always been! Buffalo Calf Road Woman, Comes Together, and Sweet Woman are three whose achievements were specifically noted in Cheyenne Memories *(Stands in Timber and Liberty 1997). Marquis made particular mention of Susan Iron Teeth, portrayed in figures 41 to 43.*

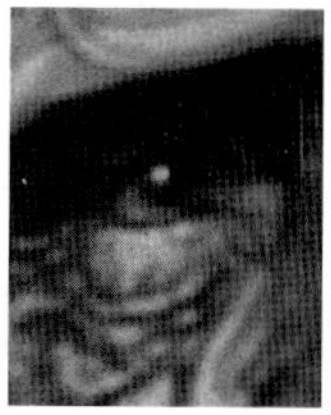

127. Cheyenne Lady

INFORMANT: JOHN WOODENLEGS

127a. This is a Cheyenne lady that I had seen when she was very old. She looks good in this picture. She has her handkerchief on her head, her shawl and her earrings, and her necklace and her dress. She has good braids for an old woman. She has bracelets. I never knew her English name, just her Indian name. She looks healthy for an older lady. One of her grandsons was John Kills on Top.

127b. Cheyenne women were noted throughout the plains for high standards of moral behavior. They kept track of the courtship behavior of young men by chaperoning their daughters and taunting any would-be suitor who had an inadequate war record, saying, "You are brave now but you were not so brave against the enemy."

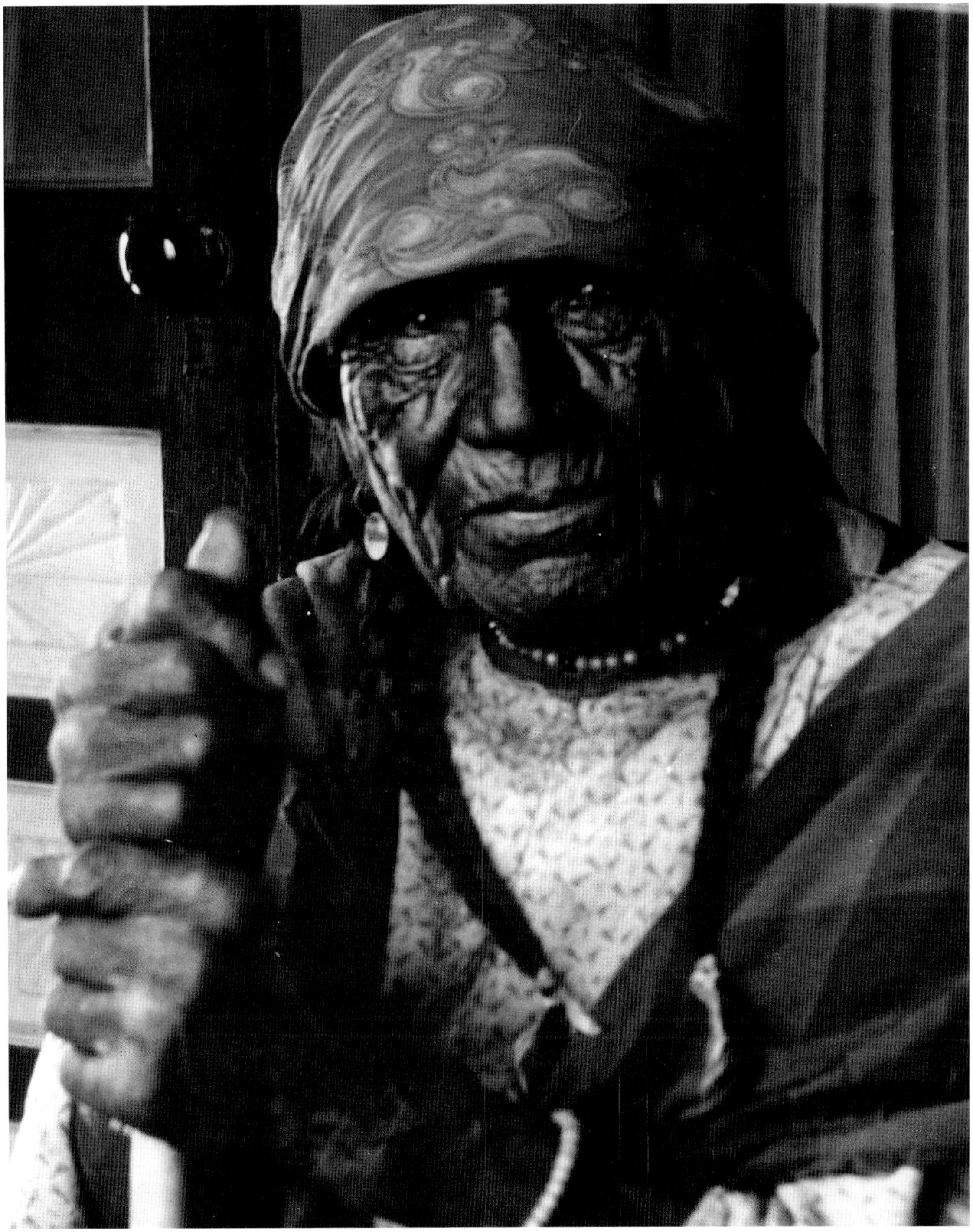

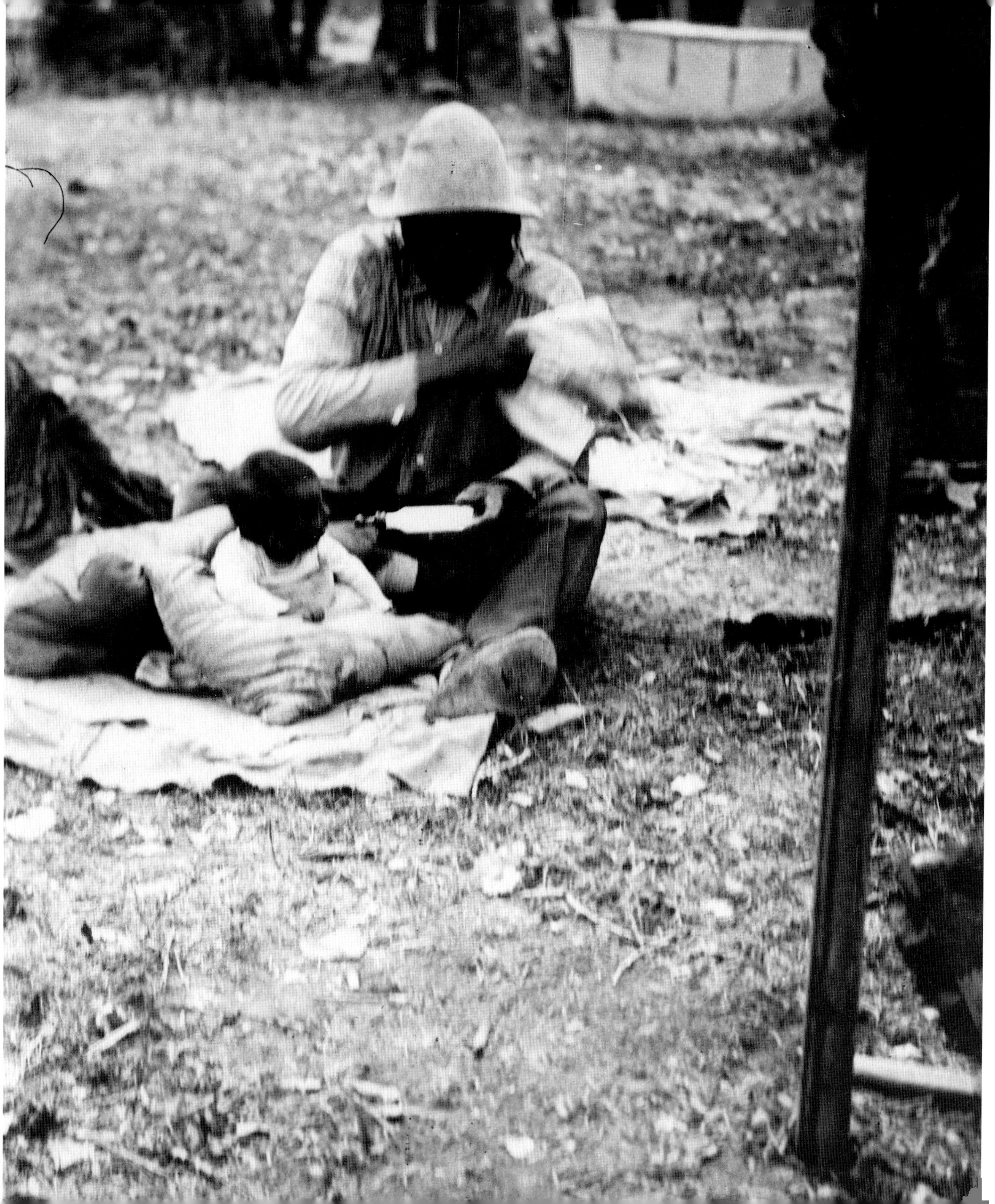

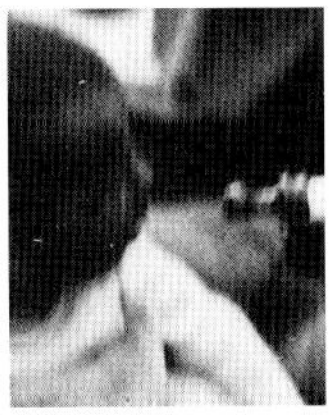

128. Baby Sitter

INFORMANT: JOHN WOODENLEGS

128a. This is an old man with a kind of little derby hat, shirt and shoes on. It's taken close to some trees, and there's some quilts on the ground. He is taking care of a little baby. This is an old man, named Big Crow, and he's trying to give the bottle to the baby and at the same time shooing flies away from it. He has a rag in one hand and the bottle in the other, and the baby is on its hands trying to get up to that bottle. I guess he's busy trying to shoo the flies away. That's a neat picture, kind of comical. Big Crow was such a good man, really a good dancer. At sixty or seventy years old, he was still really dancing. Such a kind man, talked good to everybody. So he's trying to help this baby with the bottle. In the back there's some white canvas or something. This picture was taken in 1927, according to Dr. Marquis' notes.

128b. The old man pictured babysitting here in 1927 was probably a fierce warrior and hunter in his day. For similar examples, see The Cheyennes of Montana *(Marquis 1978), especially Hollow Wood (see figure 86 in this volume). The notes that Woodenlegs refers to have been lost.*

Another Big Crow was killed in the last Cheyenne action with soldiers on the Tongue River in the fight with General Miles in January 1877.

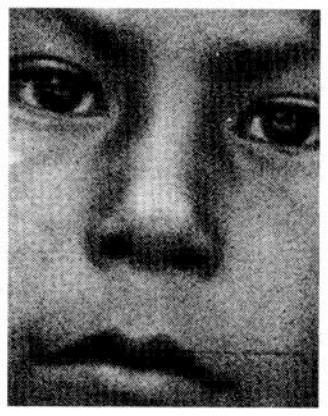

129. Spotted Black Bird and Family

INFORMANT: JOHN WOODENLEGS

129a. These folks lived in Birney. Their names are Clara Spotted Black Bird, Nellie, and Lee Spotted Black Bird. They were kind, good people, always worked hard.

129b. These were probably relatives of the Spotted Black Bird who was Keeper of the Sacred Medicine Hat at Birney. Birney, in its general isolation from other reservation communities, tended to be more traditional in language and religion and was termed by some of the missionaries "The Headquarters of Heathenism."

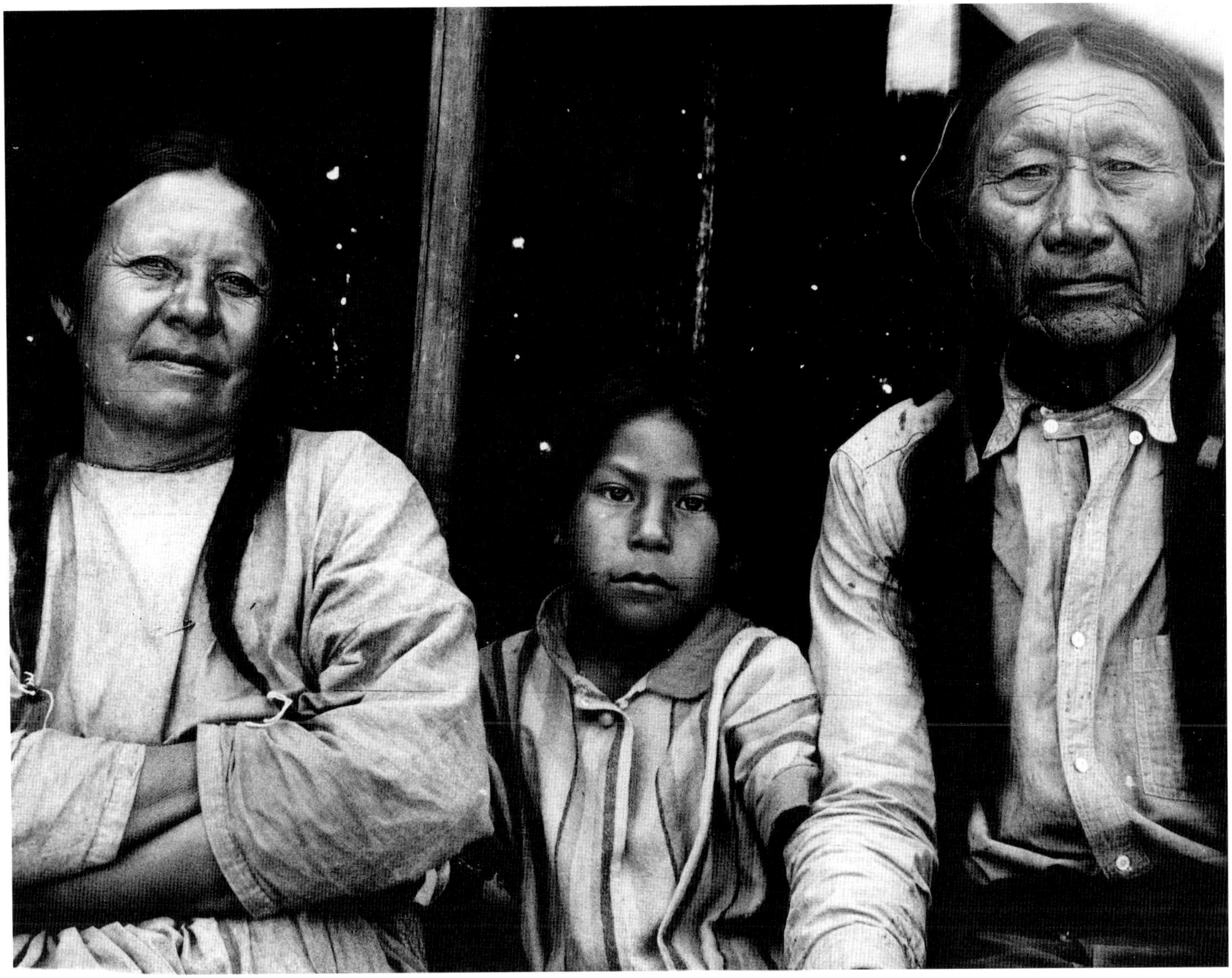

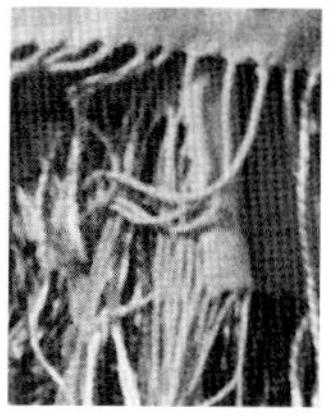

130. Sally Crazy Mule

INFORMANT: JOHN WOODENLEGS

130a. This is Sally Crazy Mule as a young girl. She looks sort of grown up—she has her hair braided good and has earrings, like a young lady, with her shawl and her dress bordered with lace. Later she married James Bites, Sr., and they had three girls and one boy. I know these people. Her father was Crazy Mule, a good man. He was small and he was really active—a good Native Church man. He raised cattle, horses. James Bites worked at the Busby school until he retired. He was a hard worker.

Sally was such a good lady and she was a good mother to her children. They all went to school some. Her children all got married and had children and now grandchildren.

130b. Crazy Mule was a well-known name in early reservation days. The first Birney school was built on the Crazy Mule allotment.

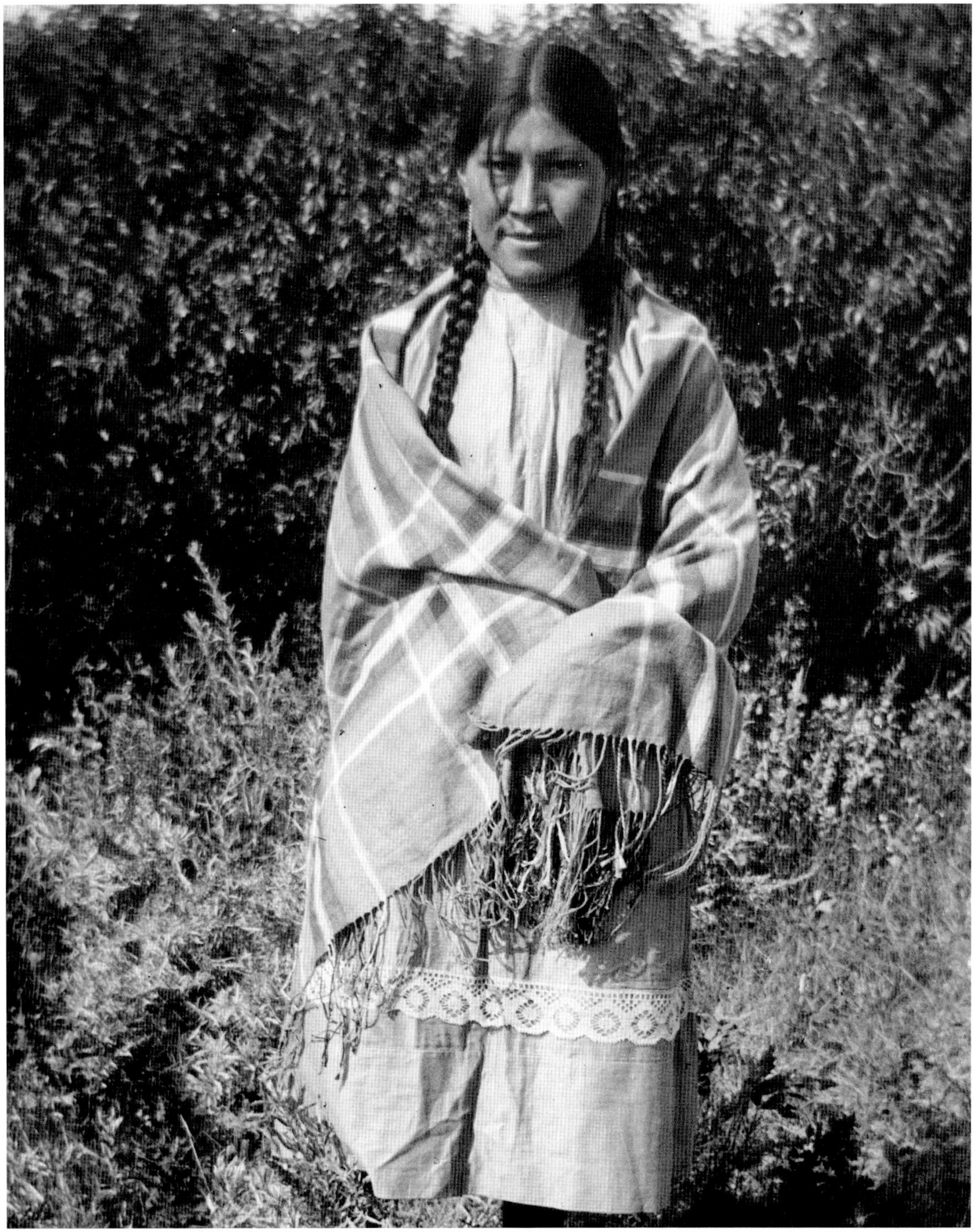

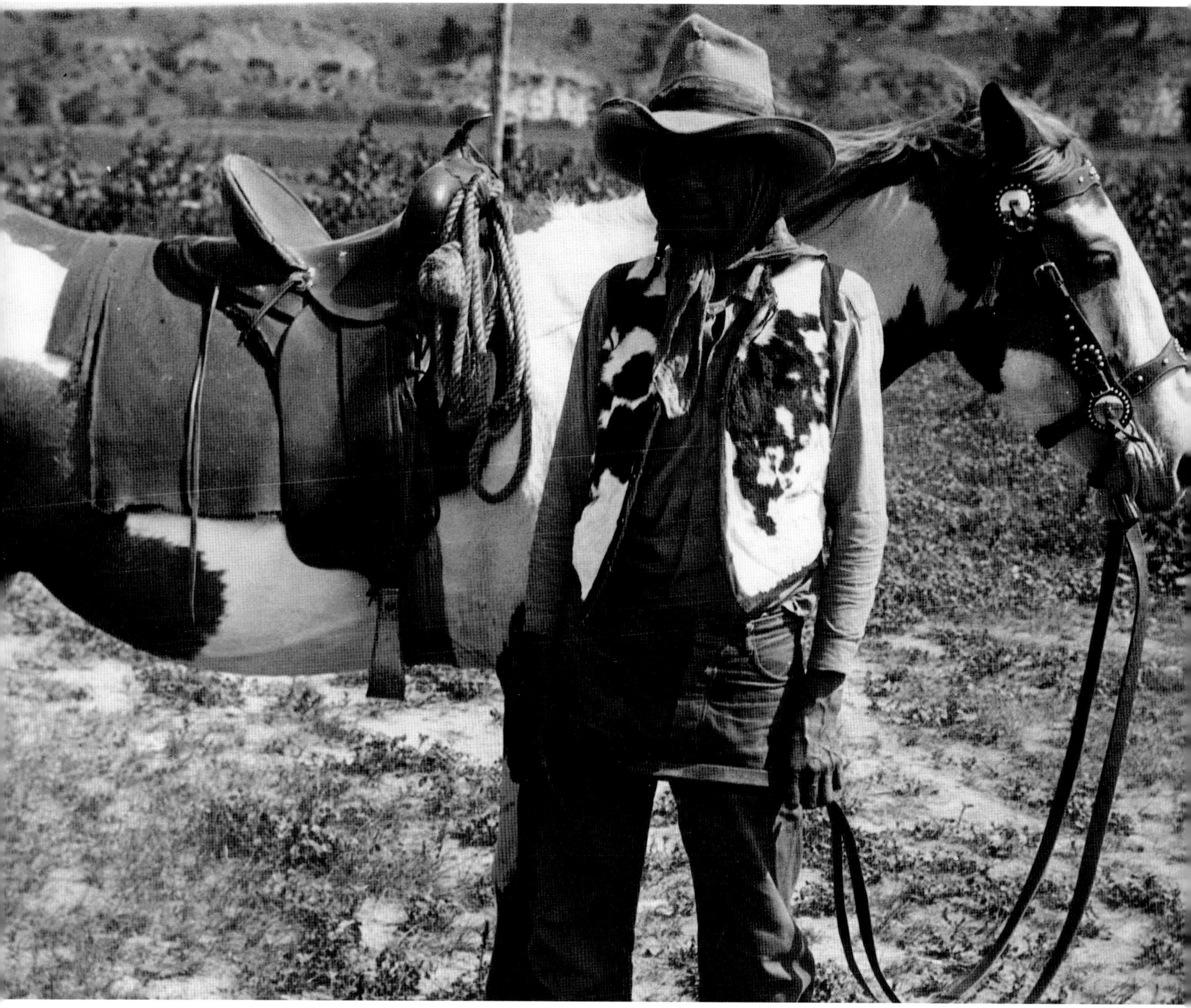

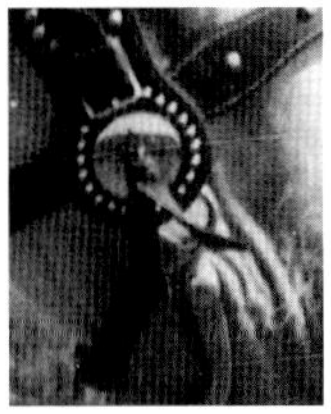

131. Lost Leg

INFORMANT: JOHN WOODENLEGS

131a. This is a man with a calfskin vest and overalls and a handkerchief around his head, almost closing his face and his glasses on and a big ten gallon hat, cowboy hat. He has a pinto horse, a sorrel pinto, saddle and rope. He and his horse both look like they are pintos. He was married. His name was Lost Leg. I know he had two children, one boy and one girl. I've talked to him and seen him, and he always had that handkerchief close to his eyes, maybe to shade them, I guess, and he still had glasses on. They raised horses and he lived between Birney and Lame Deer. There's a place between Birney and Lame Deer, half way up on top of the divide, down in a basin. It's called Lost Leg Basin, named after this man or his father. He was such a good, kind man. The family had lived there close to a spring in Lost Leg Basin. When I was just a young person, my father and some of my uncles went out to name some of these places where the springs, coulees, creeks were. Some are named after the people that lived there.

131b. A number of geographical locations on the reservation such as Lost Leg Basin were named after the first Indian allottees. Early maps of reservation grazing units clearly showed a number of these places.

Woodenlegs makes an amusing observation here concerning the "pinto" cowboy with his pinto horse.

132. Winter Camp at Ashland

INFORMANT: JOHN WOODENLEGS

132a. This is a picture of Tongue River at Ashland. Along the river there, the Cheyennes who lived along the river were kind of self-supporting. They had a lot of horses and a lot of cattle, and during the celebrations before Christmas, they collected money by having stick games at each other's places; whatever way they could collect money. They might have a dance and collect money there. Maybe a week or ten days before Christmas, they all move to this certain place there where they had built their own dance hall. They were called round houses and were built out of logs. They would have a Christmas committee: president, vice-president, secretary, and treasurer, and red-penny committee. They gathered their own money; they didn't ask anyone else. They all had cattle so some would donate cattle to eat during the Christmas celebrations. They would camp there even with the snow on the ground. They'd push the snow away and put up their tents, and they would have a Christmas celebration up to the New Year. This committee would have give-aways—really good give-aways; horses and tables and goods and blankets of all kinds, outfits and war bonnets. They all cooperated and worked together. A son or daughter might be president of the committee. Everyone was interested and cooperated together. I noticed as a young man when I danced there—came over from Lame Deer. My aunt's husband asked me to come over. He belonged over there. There were a lot of people danced—old people with bonnets and buckskin outfits. This picture has some horses and men and tents and the dance hall, with snow on the ground. They hauled hay to the horses. After the celebrations, they moved back to their own farms and places so that they could start to work again in the spring with their gardens and take care of their cattle and farms. Sometimes from the camp they would go back home to see that the water holes were open along the river so the cattle and horses could get water. So they all had a good time in the winter during Christmas celebrations. They called it "middle of the winter."

132b. Winter celebrations were a new pleasure for reservation Cheyennes. In the old days, because of limited horse pasturage and winter hunting, Plains tribes were only able to gather in big camps in the summer time and then only for a couple of weeks. Added reservation sociability was one of the assets gained when so much was lost in the transition from traditional life.

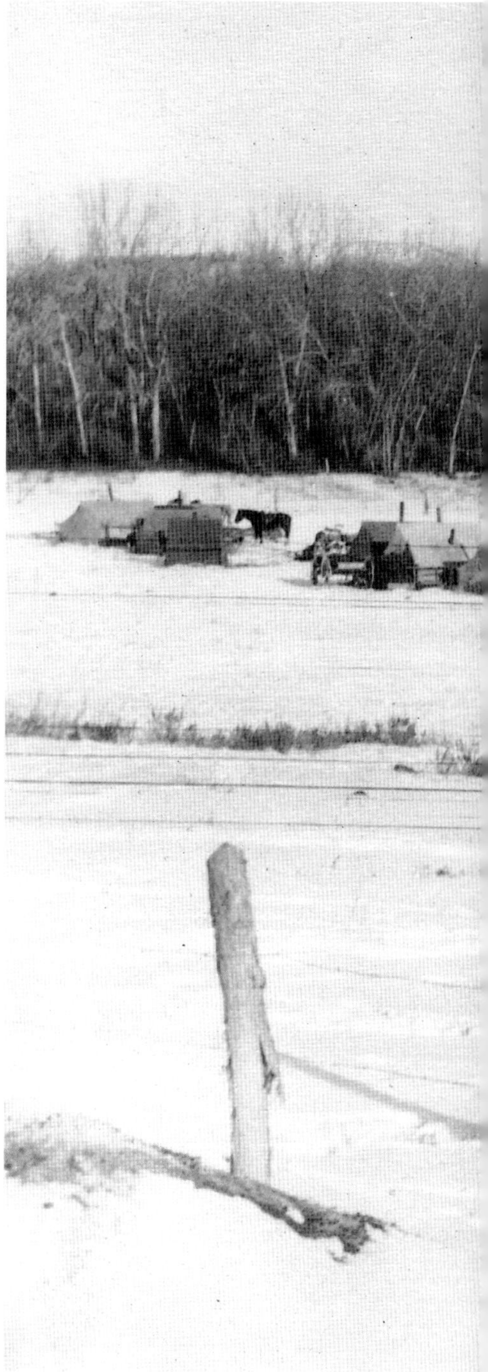

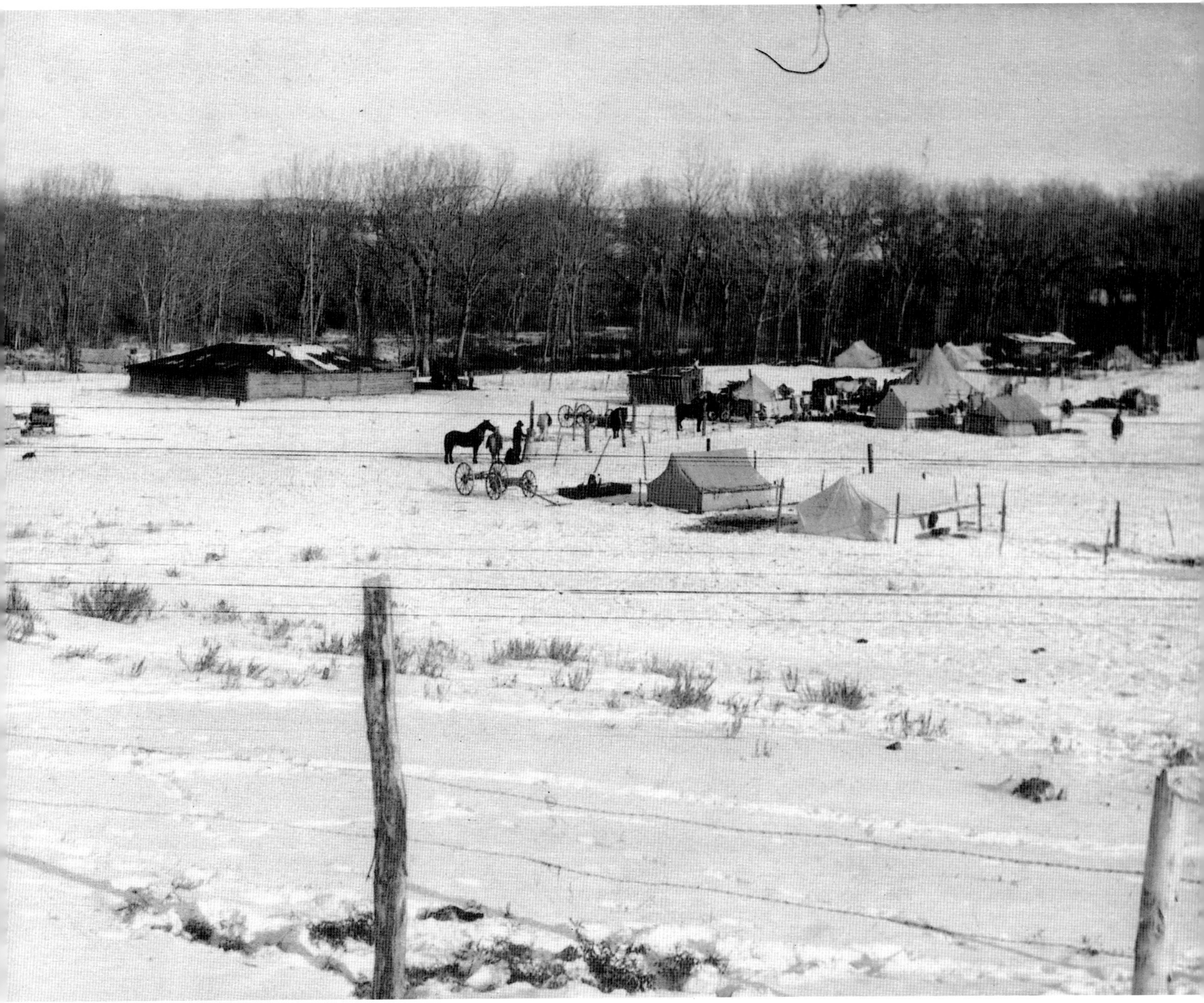

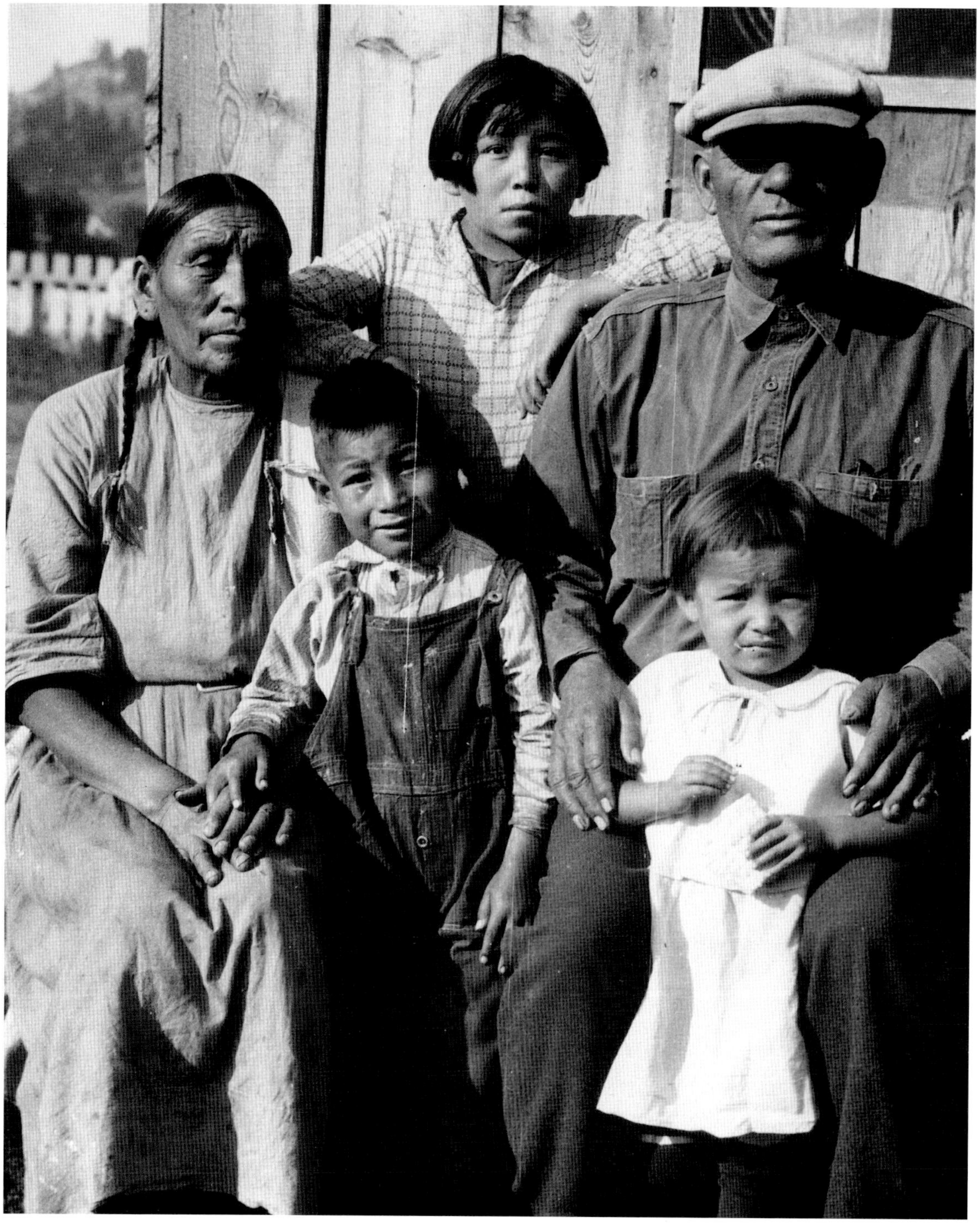

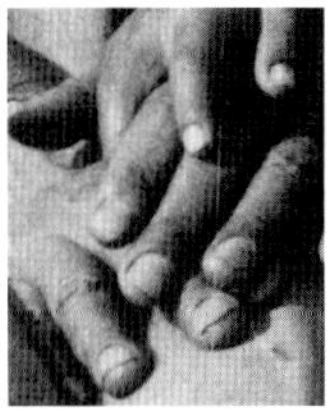

133. Willis Rowland and Family

Informant: John Woodenlegs

133a. This is Willis Rowland, his wife, and grandchildren.

William Rowland had married a Cheyenne woman. They had sons named Zachary, Willis, and James. Willis, as a young man of seventeen or eighteen, served as a scout at Ft. Keogh under General Miles and later under Lt. Ned Casey, as first sergeant. His father William served as interpreter. Both of them, in their lifetimes, did a lot of interpreting. Willis often interpreted for George Bird Grinnell, who wrote many books and articles about the Cheyennes. Willis' Indian name was High Forehead. Willis' wife, Bear Woman, was the daughter of Elk River, a Cheyenne noted in older times as an excellent catcher of wild horses.

The children pictured are their grandchildren. The girl standing in back is Grace. The boy is Frank. The small girl is Ardeth.

133b. William Rowland, called Long Knife by the Cheyennes, was an interpreter who married a Southern Cheyenne woman in Colorado and came north to become the first settler on the Northern Cheyenne reservation. Rowland's son Willis or High Forehead served with the Cheyenne scouts for the military and was famous among early Cheyenne ethnographers—much of what is known today was gathered through his services as an interpreter.

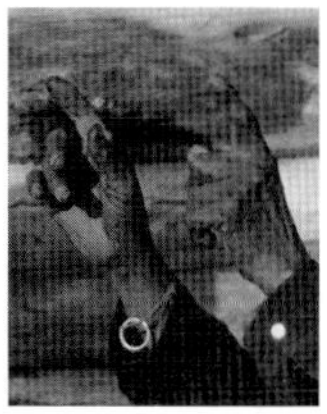

134. Willis Rowland and Stump Horn

INFORMANT: JOHN WOODENLEGS

134a. This is Willis Rowland visiting with Stump Horn. Stump Horn is making sign language. He was a scout at Ft. Keogh. He was a really good-natured man and liked to joke.

134b. In Cheyenne Memories *Stands in Timber mentions Stump Horn in a horse raid incident of August 1856 and also during the Cheyenne outbreak from Oklahoma in 1878 (Stands in Timber and Liberty 1997: 46, 165–66).*

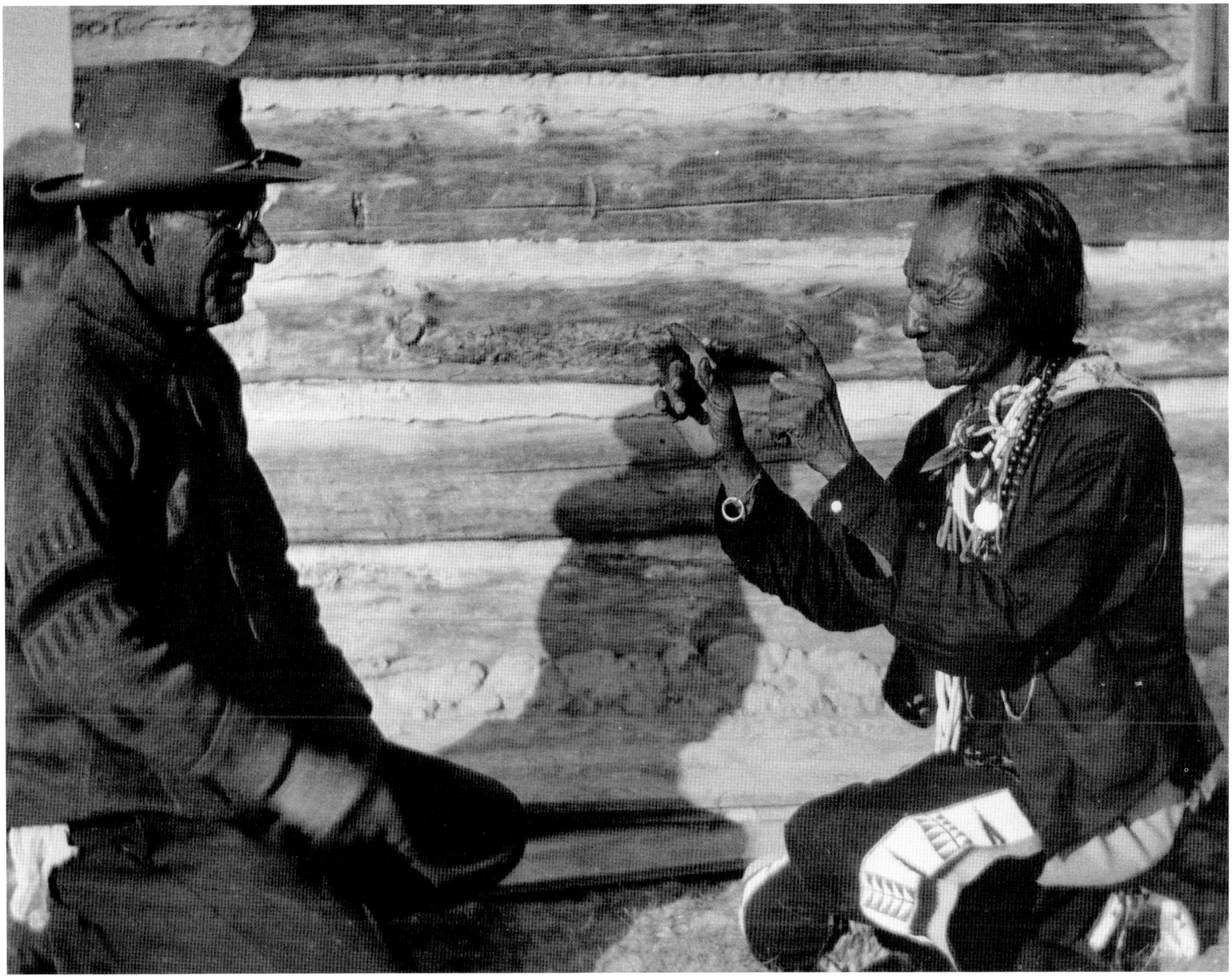

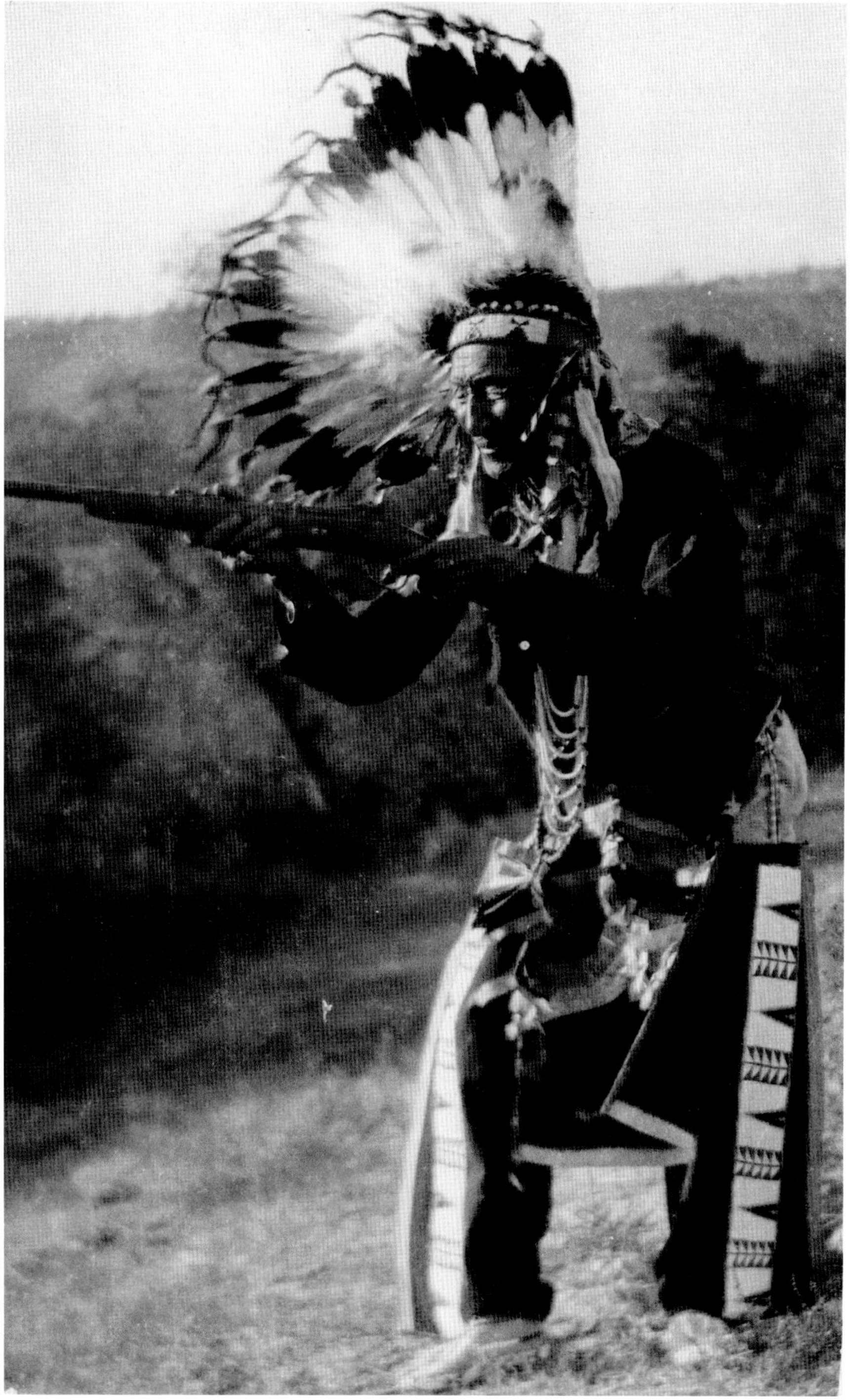

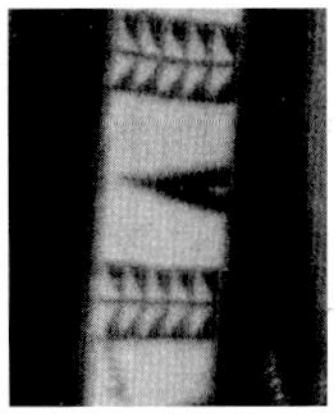

135. Stump Horn

INFORMANT: JOHN WOODENLEGS

135a. This is Stump Horn posing with a Custer gun. He has good beadwork on his outfit.

135b. Stump Horn is one of twenty or more Custer fight warriors photographed by Marquis after 1922. Marquis bought battle artifacts from a number of veterans and their families after 1927, using them as exhibits in his own small museum at Hardin, Montana. Many of these are now in the collections of the National Park Service at Little Bighorn Battlefield National Monument, Crow Agency, Montana.

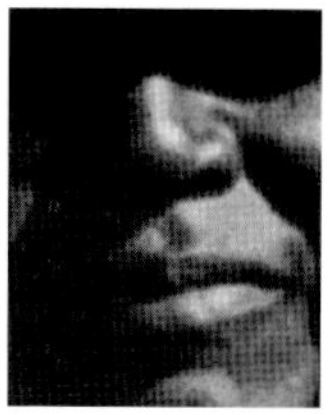

136. James Rock Roads

INFORMANT: JOHN WOODENLEGS

136a. This is James Rock Roads. He has a white handkerchief around his head, and braids and he's wearing a checkered shirt. Looks like he has something in his pocket. He used to always wear a blanket. He was the Keeper of the Sacred Hat, one of our sacred bundles. I knew him and his wife. He was a good man, he said prayers for everybody. He worked around his place. Rock Roads had a lot of relatives. After he passed on, his wife lived in Lame Deer. They were all kind people.

Rock Roads served as a scout in the Army under Lt. Ned Casey. He was with Casey when they went to the Sioux during the Ghost Dance trouble. Casey was shot and killed.

Rock Roads was a kind man, highly respected as a spiritual leader. This picture was taken in 1925. He died in 1927.

136b. Here and in the next picture Marquis has portrayed members of a leading Cheyenne family. Rock Roads was Keeper of the Sacred Medicine Hat, a holy tribal medicine object maintained in its own tepee by a tribally appointed priest. It continues to be of major importance today, although its major ceremonies are long forgotten.

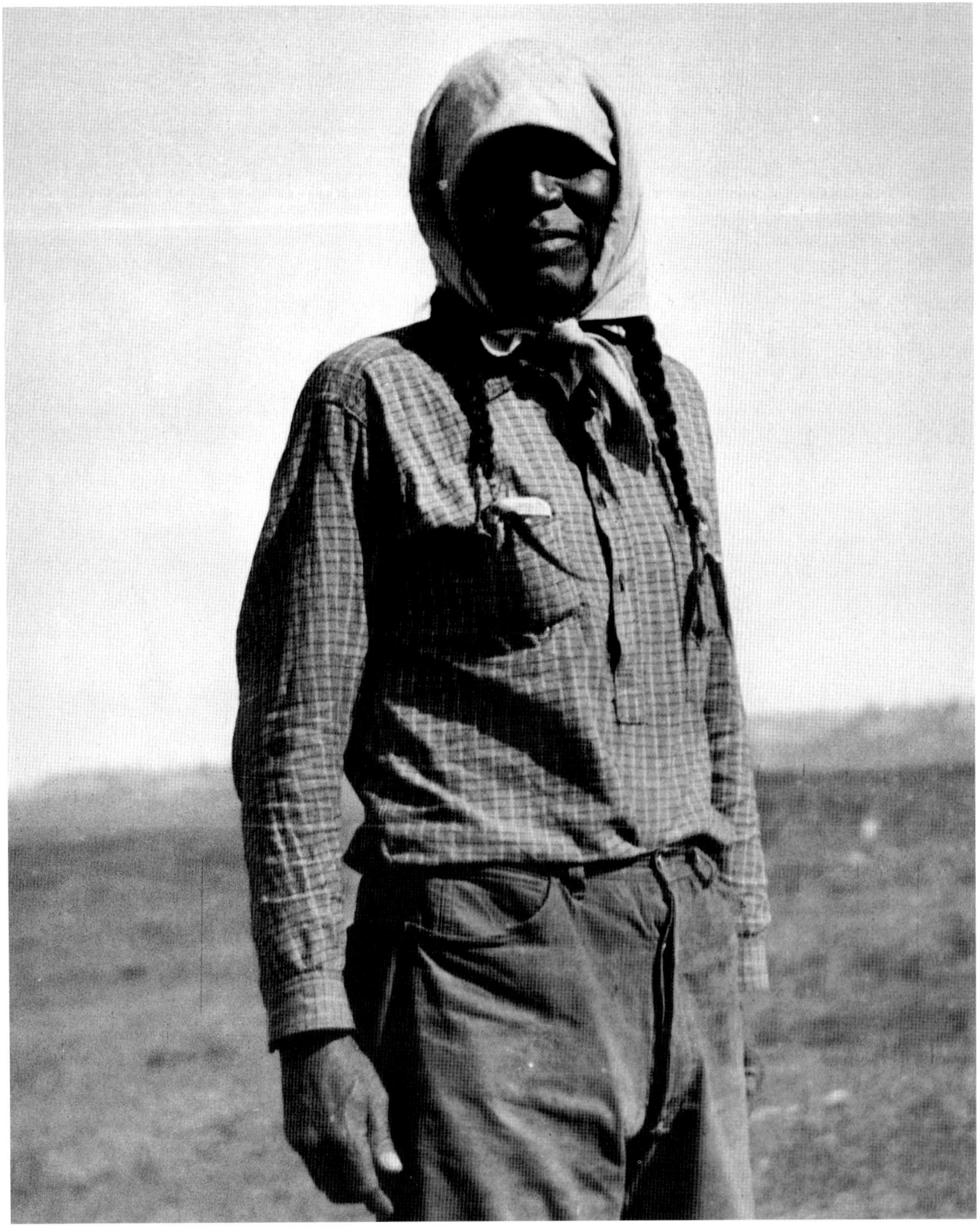

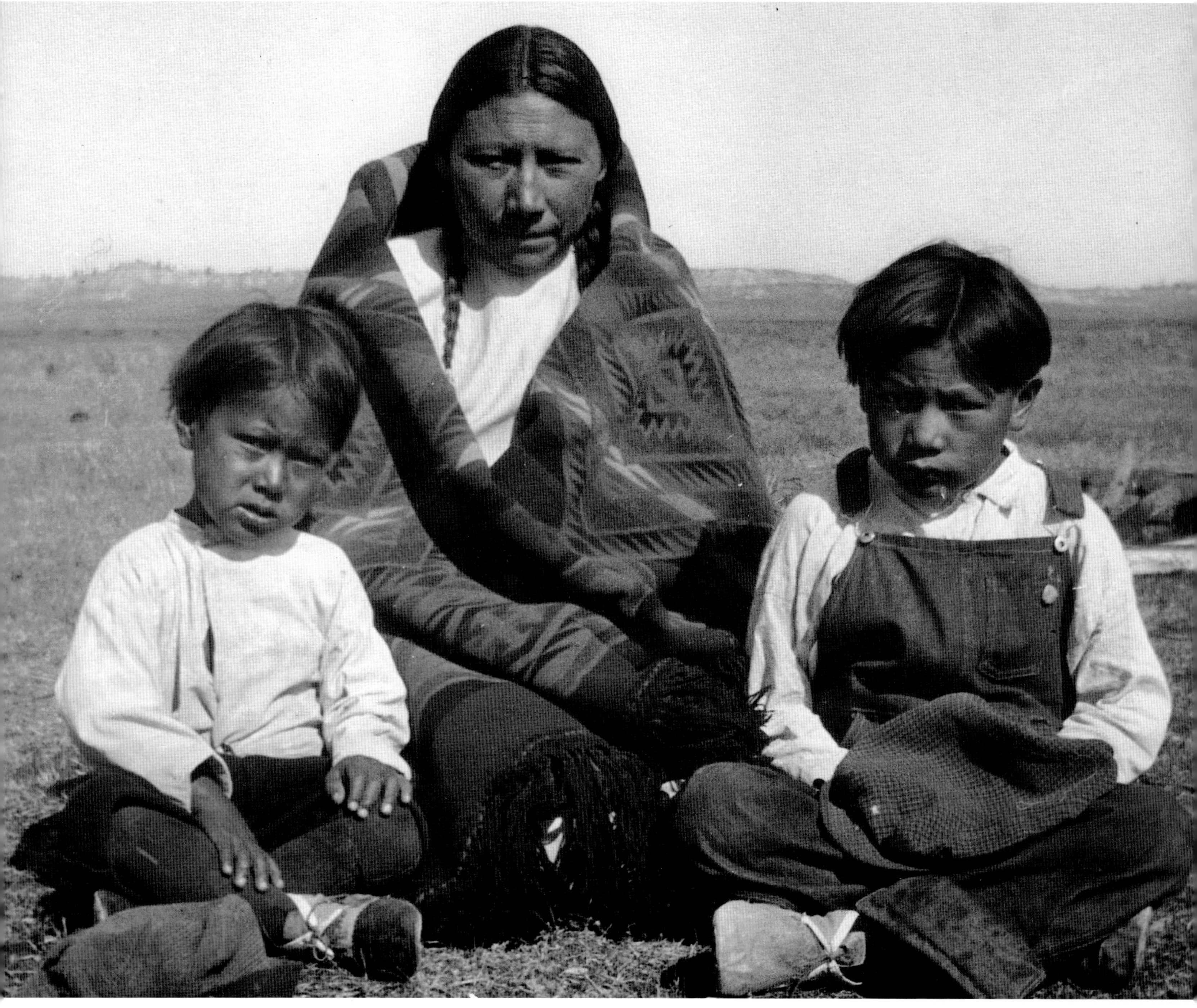

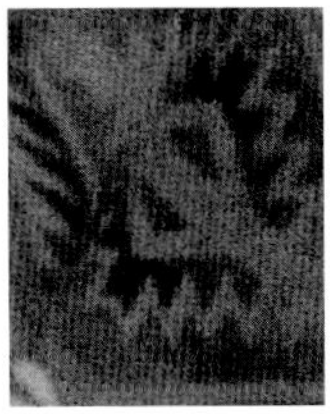

137. Nora Rock Roads and Boys

INFORMANT: JOHN WOODENLEGS

137a. This is Mack Rock Roads' wife, Nora, and his two boys, sitting alongside the mother. The boy on the left is Tom Rock Roads, Sr. The picture was taken in 1925. This is a very good picture. They have white shirts and bib overalls and a cap. Their hair is combed and they look real neat. They have moccasins on. The younger boy has two-tone moccasins on. They were leather with canvas tops sewed onto the sole. The mother has a very good Pendleton blanket. In those days those blankets were hard to get. They were a good family. They had their home on Rosebud Creek. They farmed, owned horses. Horses were the means of traveling back and forth.

Mack Rock Roads was a son of James Rock Roads.

137b. Grandsons of the Sacred Hat Keeper are seen with their mother. Their fine clothing indicates a special occasion or holiday.

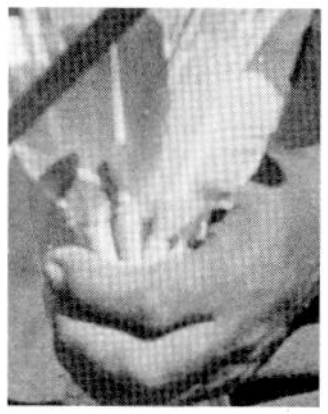

138. Fred Last Bull

INFORMANT: WILLIAM HOLLOW BREAST

138a. This is Fred Last Bull. He was a Sun Dancer. He pierced his flesh and on the third song, he tore loose. He was also a Native Church man. He is holding an eagle feather fan and a drumstick that was used in the peyote prayer service. This picture was taken at Crow Agency, September 1933.

138b. Piercing was not usually practiced in the Cheyenne Sun Dance or Medicine Lodge. It was a means of self-sacrifice in which skewers or pins put through the flesh of the breast were secured to the center pole of the Medicine Lodge and then torn loose by the dancer.

Fred Last Bull for a while cared for the Sacred Arrows in Montana, when there was trouble finding qualified Keepers among the Southern Cheyennes in Oklahoma. The Arrows are kept in a special lodge like the Sacred Hat. They were later returned to Oklahoma, where they remain under the care of a special Keeper. Last Bull also officiated during the 1959 opening of the Sacred Medicine Hat.

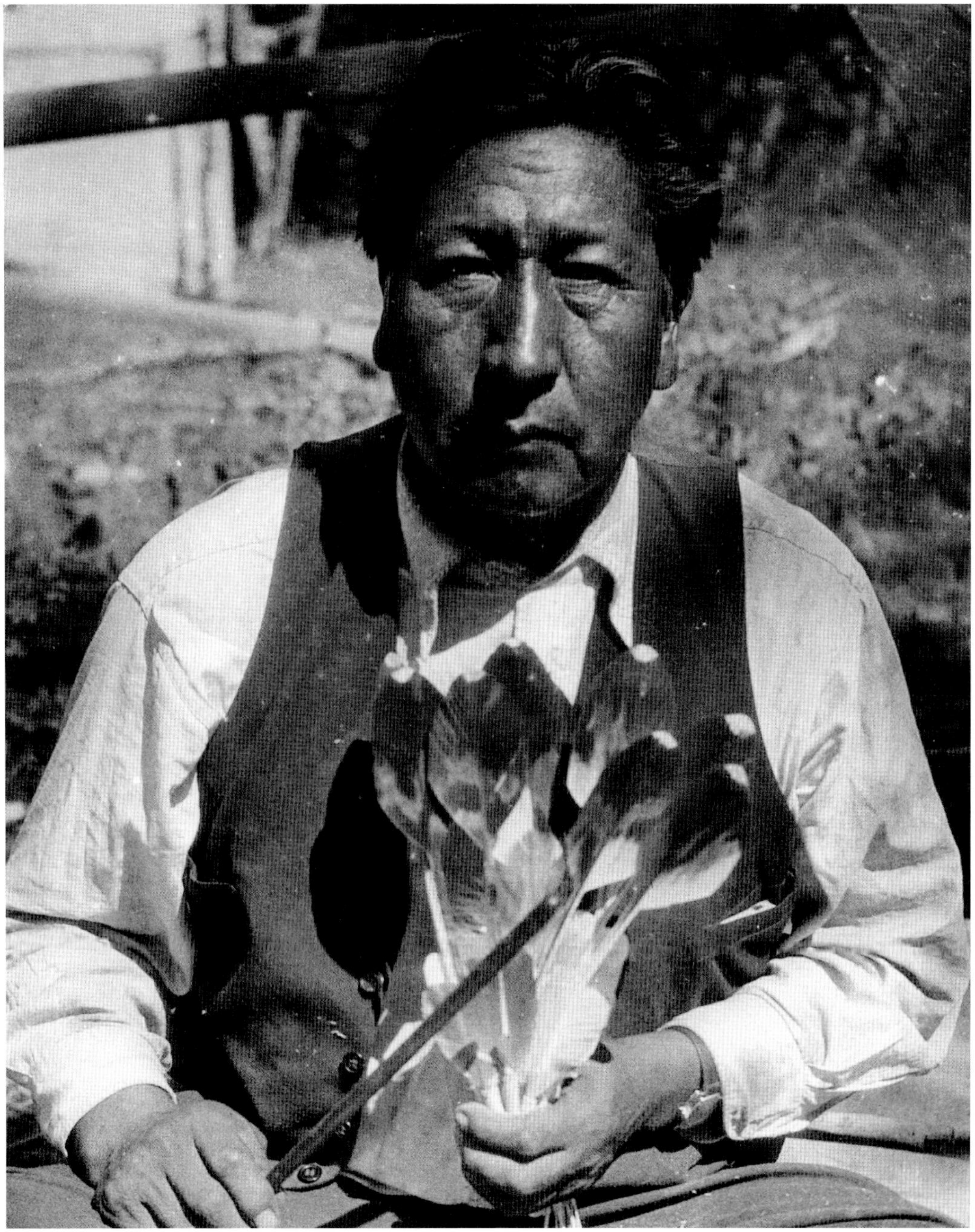

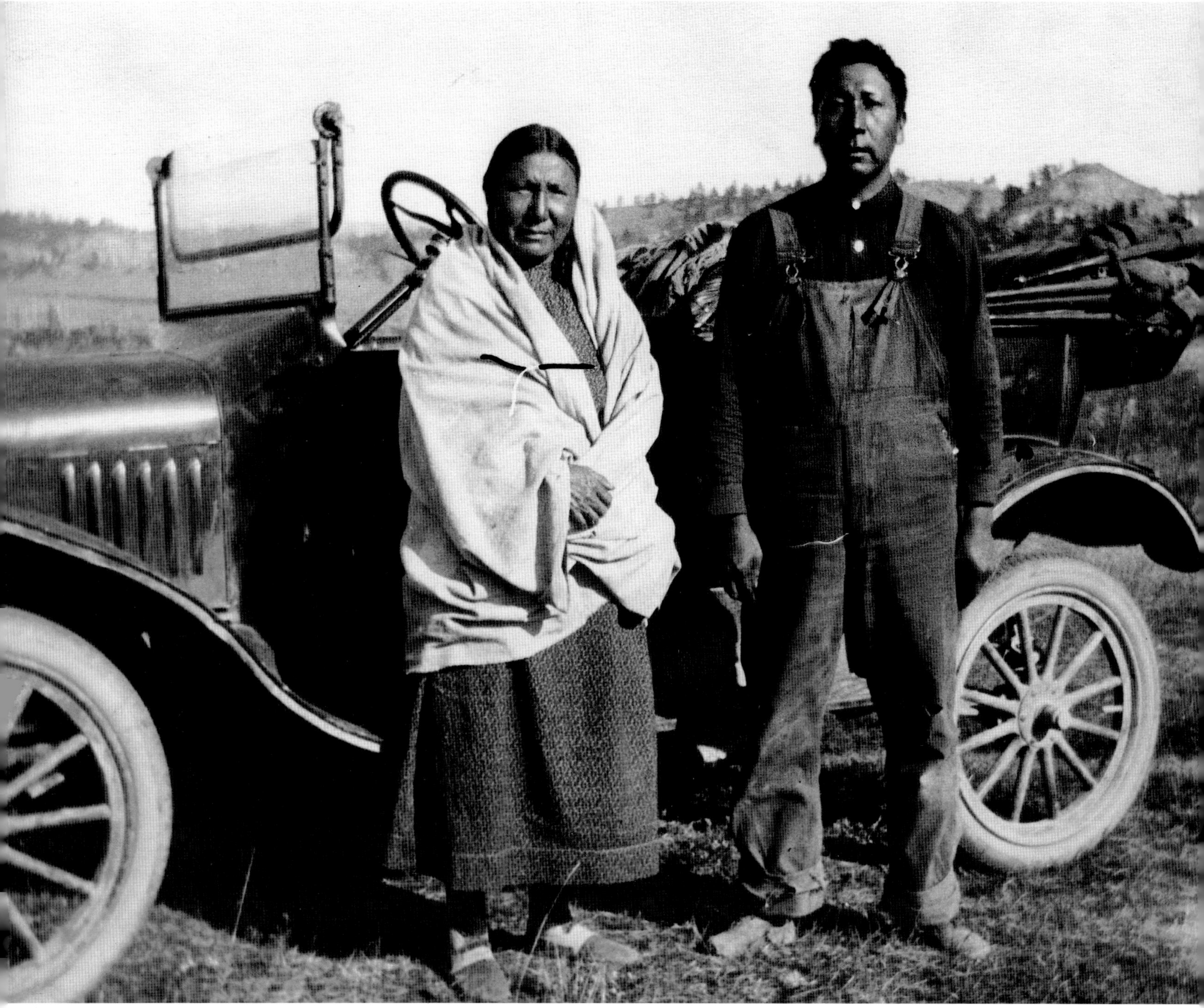

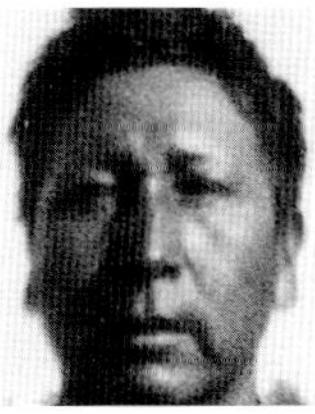

139. Fred and Mae Last Bull

INFORMANT: WILLIAM HOLLOW BREAST

139a. This is Fred Last Bull and his wife Mae. She was a Southern Cheyenne. They lived in the Busby area.

139b. John Stands in Timber gives an amusing account of Last Bull's performance as an extra in 1930 near Jackson Hole during the making of the Hollywood film The Oregon Trail. *He says that there were 300 Cheyennes, Crows, Arapahos, and Shoshones plus 200 whites hired for the attack scenes: "I never laughed so hard in my life" (Stands in Timber and Liberty 1997: 297–300).*

140a. **Woodenlegs:** This is Lucille Harris Fisher. This is a picture of her parents and brothers and sisters. I know they were hard-working people and they made it on their own. They lived on Muddy.

Lucille: What did they call that program where each person got two cows? That was how he got his start in the cattle business. I don't know how many of us there were at the time.

Woodenlegs: Yes, so that's your father, William Harris, and you mother, Margaret Twenty Stands, and she married Harris.

Lucille: My dad's brothers were Ed, Bryan, and Charles; his sisters were Alice Kinzel, Julia Burns, Lizzie Burns, and Emma. My mother's half-brother was James Twenty Stands Atwood. I can't think of her sister's name now. My dad got his start on Muddy when everybody got two cows each. There were eight of us at the time: Lizzie, Julia, George, Florence, Agnes, Mary, Raymond, and myself.

Woodenlegs: The government issued cattle, two head apiece, about 1909 and 1910. He must have took good care of them, because he had lots of cattle. What was his brand?

Lucille: X 3 was his brand.

Woodenlegs: He had a lot of horses too, he was really a hard-working man.

Lucille: He was a hard worker; he farmed and raised wheat and oats, had a garden all the time. He used to bring his wheat to the old flour mill, they used to have it over here. Mitchell used to have that flour mill.

Woodenlegs: He was good to everybody, an old cowpuncher and he cooked for the roundup.

Lucille: Yes. In our family, we all used to help and work hard. We helped put up hay and put up wheat, plant gardens, get ready for the winter. I went to Lame Deer school and also to St. Labre. Most of my brothers and sisters are still living. Florence passed away and a brother named Leo.

Woodenlegs: In this picture, left to right: William Harris, Margaret Twenty Stands Harris, Florence, Mary, Raymond, and George. The picture was taken in 1926, according to Dr. Marquis' notes. Lucille Fisher was interviewed in 1981.

140b. The Harrises were a noted family of mixed-blood reservation ranchers. Llevando Fisher (a son of Lucille Harris Fisher, who is interviewed here) served as chairman of the Northern Cheyenne tribal council in the 1980s. He was a fifth grader during my time at the Birney Day School in the late 1950s.

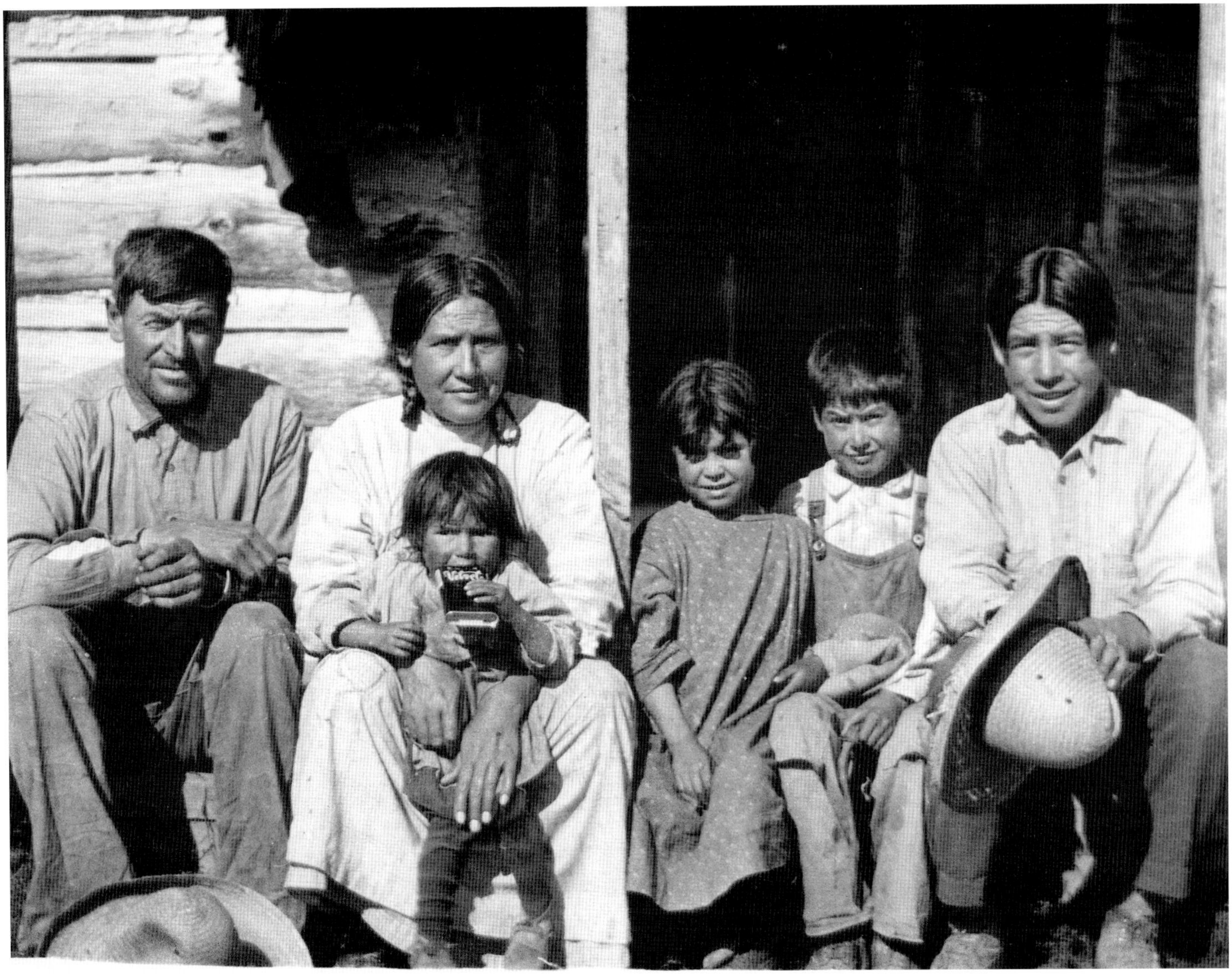

140. William Harris and Family

INFORMANTS: JOHN WOODENLEGS AND LUCILLE HARRIS FISHER

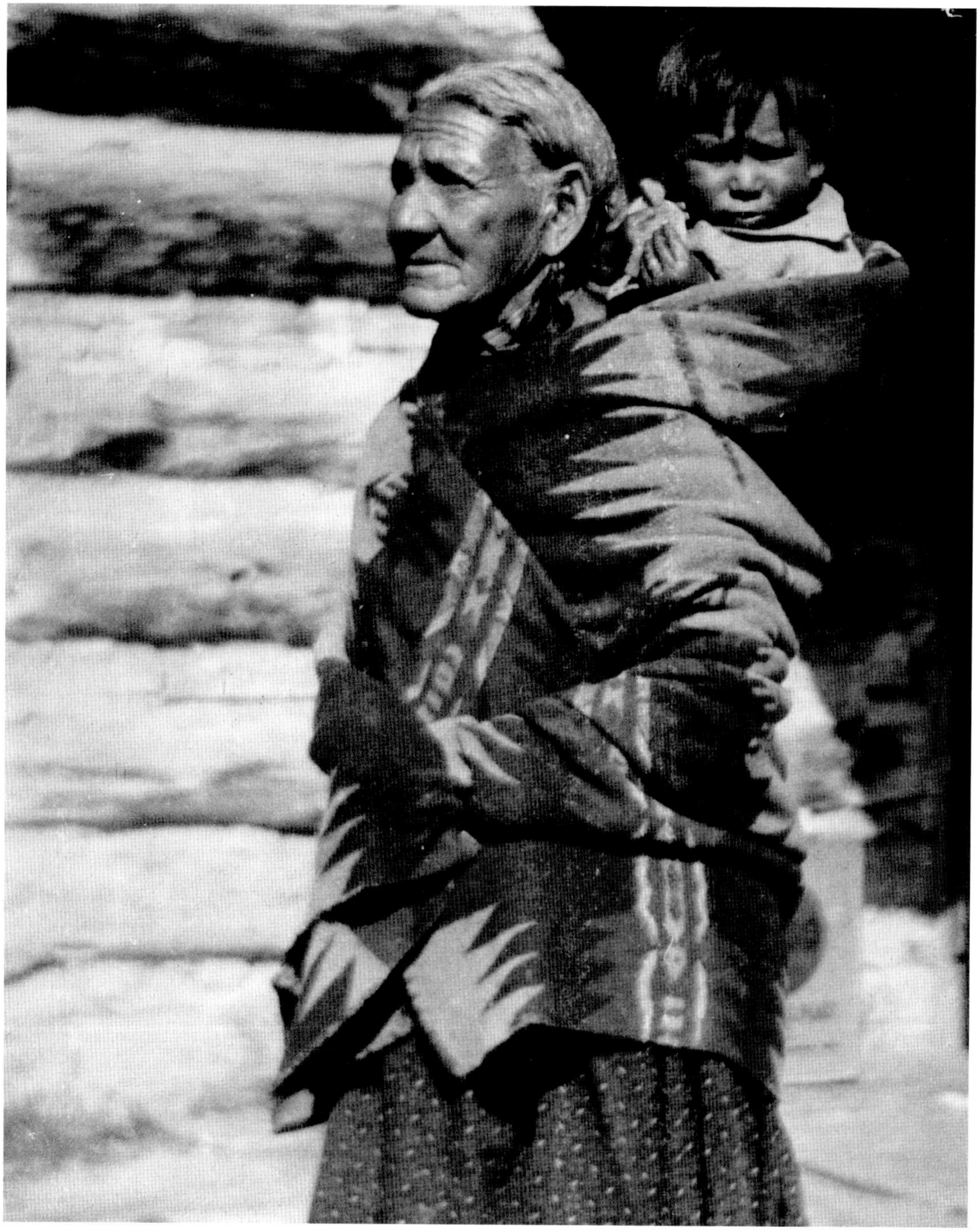

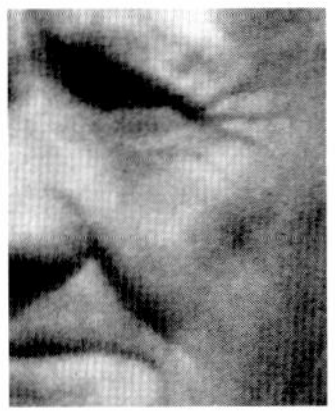

141. Sally Harris and Child

INFORMANTS: JOHN WOODENLEGS AND LUCILLE FISHER

141a. **Woodenlegs:** Now, your father's mother . . .

Lucille: Her name was Sally Harris.

Woodenlegs: She used to come up and play cards with my grandmother. They must have been related someway. This is her picture with a child on her back.

Lucille: I used to say that was George, but some of them say it is Carl.

Woodenlegs: This picture was taken in 1925 when Sally was 77, according to Dr. Marquis. Marquis notes: "A famous Cheyenne midwife, known as Granny Harris."

141b. This portrait once again indicates the interest and success of Marquis in photographing Cheyenne women.

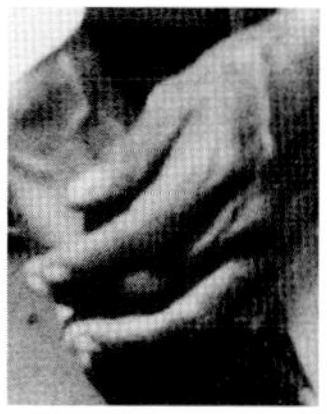

142. Charles Beaver Hart and Family

INFORMANT: JOHN WOODENLEGS

142a. This is Charles Beaver Hart, called "Hart" for short, and his wife, Louise. Her maiden name was Harris. The little girl is their child. Charles has long hair and braids. His father lived in the Kirby area above Busby. He had a home and place there. I know his brother David Beaver Hart. Charles used to come to Lame Deer and we worked with him—my father, and we hauled coal. He had a team of horses, and he had three daughters: Elizabeth, Eva, and Jessie. They are all living and married and have children. Charlie Hart was a good dancer and a hard worker—he always worked hard to make a living for his family. He farmed and ranched and hauled coal for the agency with his team and wagon. Worked hard shoveling coal, and later when he got older, he got arthritis. He could hardly get around. He was friends with my father and also Marion King. So they thought they would try to help him with peyote, this Native Church way. And it really did help him—that medicine, and he even went down to Texas. He got to be a really good member of the Native Church. He put up meetings and went down to Texas to get peyote and prayed down there where it grows.

Louise was a daughter of William and Sally Harris. She was a sister of Alice Kinzel. Louise lived to be 96 years old; passed on in 1978. She was a good person, did beautiful beadwork and made fine quilts.

At the time this picture was taken, Charles was age 42 and his wife was 37, according to Dr. Marquis' notes. Charles owned the new truck that is partially shown in the picture.

142b. An earlier Beaver Heart fought in the Battles of the Rosebud and the Little Big Horn. Charles was probably his son.

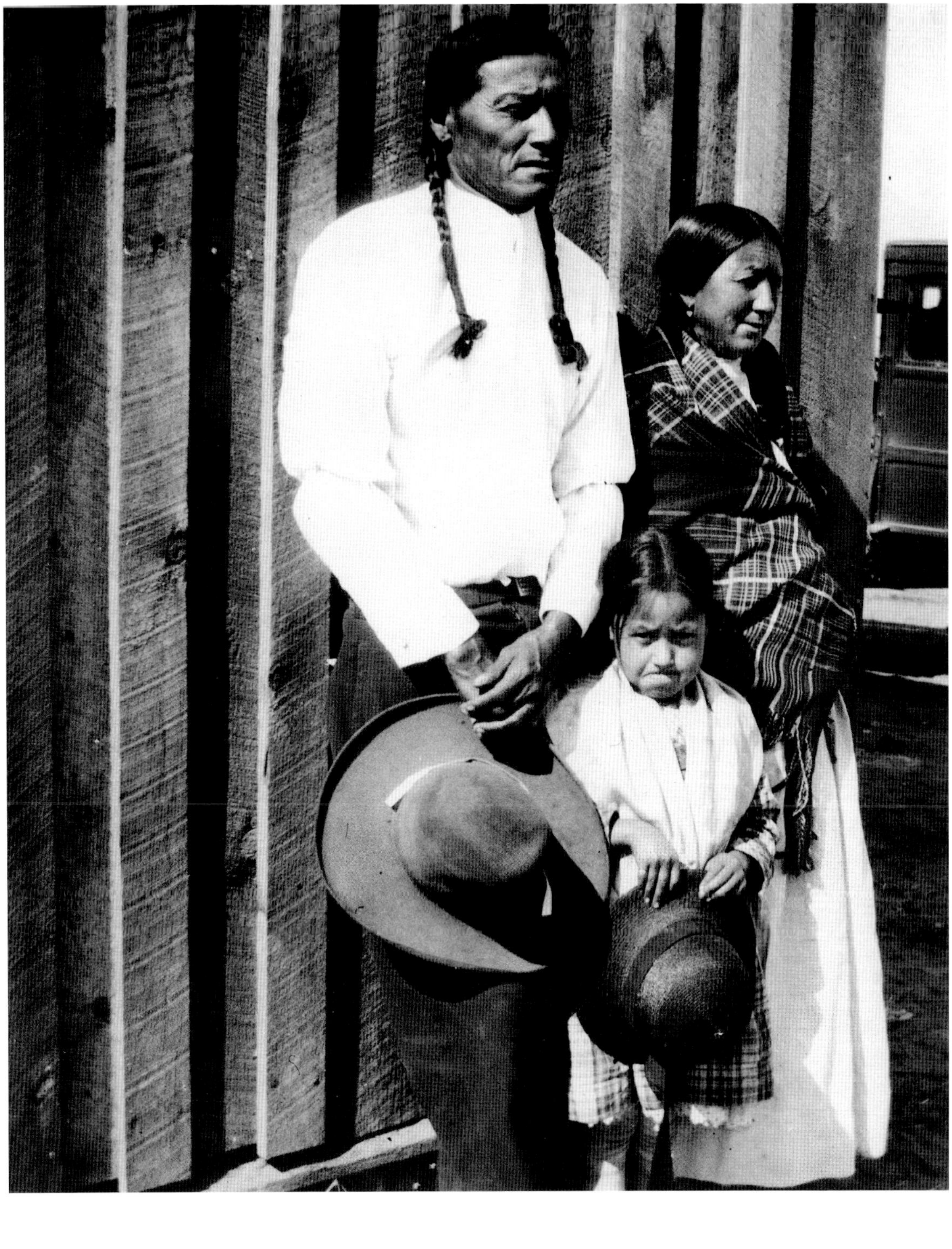

Afterword

The Northern Cheyennes were almost all located near the present community of Lame Deer, Montana, before the turn of the twentieth century. Now more than a century of reservation life has outstripped in duration the 100-odd years (ca. 1775–1875) of free-roaming equestrian life enjoyed by the Cheyennes after they obtained horses. The early reservation years portrayed by the photographs and interviews in this book represent an all but forgotten generation of Plains Indian life. The change from traditional to mainstream culture is seldom documented or written about.

The Marquis pictures portray these early reservation years, but change has continued. A rapidly growing population has expanded the original communities of Lame Deer, Busby, Ashland, Muddy, and Birney. Horses have been replaced by cars, and paved roads reach out in four directions. New housing projects have proliferated. Television is found in every home. The new Chief Dull Knife Memorial College adds a major force for ongoing education.

But strong elements of traditional life still continue, despite the three wrenching changes in economic lifestyle that the Cheyennes had already suffered by the 1920s. Buffalo hunting had been replaced by rations and subsistence gardening; these gave way to or were supplemented by cattle raising and then by dry farming before the drought years destroyed those too in the 1930s. Success in all of these was extremely limited.

Yet one of the surprises herein is that on the whole those years from 1922 to 1935 (the dates of the Marquis pictures) were not so bad in some ways.

Contrary to the common stereotypes of reservation life, the Northern Cheyennes have retained a great deal, including their sense of humor, as revealed in these pages. Living in settled villages derived from the old nomadic bands, they maintained the traditional kinship system and could visit distant relatives and gather for celebrations more often than in the past. They kept the original Fox, Elk, and Crazy Dog military societies. They retained their language, their arts and crafts (particularly beadwork), and their music, which linked them to expanding social networks with other tribes. The people kept most of their religious institutions—the Sun Dance, the Sacred Arrows, and the Sacred Hat—adding the Native American Church as well as the Catholic and Mennonite missions. Opportunities for social interaction throughout the year increased.

Most of the people today live in or near the

reservation communities in Montana. A great many attend the tribal powwows, which function as annual homecomings. In short, the Cheyennes have remained Cheyenne. These elders of the 1920s and their successors offer us a marvelous example of the resilience of the human spirit.

References

Abbott, E. C., and Helena Huntington Smith
1939 We Pointed Them North. New York: Rinehart.

Alderson, Nannie T., and Helena Huntington Smith
1942 A Bride Goes West. New York: Rinehart.

Cheyenne Elders
1960s–1981 Interviews by Reservation Research Team. About 100 pages of typewritten transcription copies. Currently in the possession of Margot Liberty, Sheridan, Wyoming. The location of the original tapes and transcriptions is unknown.

Frazier, Ian
2000 On the Rez. New York: Farrar, Straus and Giroux.

Frink, Maurice, and Casey E. Barthelmess
1958 Photographer on an Army Mule. Norman: University of Oklahoma Press.

Grinnell, George Bird
1956 (1915) The Fighting Cheyennes. Norman: University of Oklahoma Press.

Hagan, William T.
1966 Indian Police and Judges. New Haven: Yale University Press.

Highwalking, Belle, and Katherine M. Weist
1991 Belle Highwalking: The Narrative of a Northern Cheyenne Woman. Billings: Montana Council for Indian Edu-cation.

Hoebel, E. Adamson
1960 The Cheyennes: Indians of the Great Plains. New York: Holt, Rinehart and Winston.

La Barre, Weston
1975 The Peyote Cult. 4th ed. New York: Schocken Books.

Liberty, Margot
1965 Suppression and Survival of the Northern Cheyenne Sun Dance. *Minnesota Archeologist* 27:120–43.
1967 Narrative Account of the 1959 Sun Dance and Opening of the Sacred Medicine Hat. *Plains Anthropologist* 12:367–68.
1982 Hell Came with Horses: Plains Indian Women in the Equestrian Era. *Montana, the Magazine of Western History* 32(3):10–19.
1996 Oral and Written Indian Perspectives on the Indian Wars. Pp. 125–38 in Legacy:

New Perspectives on the Battle of the Little Bighorn. Charles E. Rankin, ed. Helena: Montana Historical Society.

Mader, Jerry
2002 The Road to Lame Deer. Lincoln: University of Nebraska Press.

Marquis, Thomas Bailey
1957 (1931) Wooden Leg: A Warrior Who Fought Custer. Lincoln: University of Nebraska Press.
1967 (1933–34) Custer on the Little Bighorn. Anna Rose Octavia Heil, ed. 5th printing. Lodi, Calif.: End-Kian Publishing Company. Republication in book form of pamphlet series originally published Scottsdale, Ariz.: Cactus Pony.
1933a She Watched Custer's Last Battle: Her Story, Interpreted in 1927 (1967 section VI).
1933b Sketch Story of the Custer Battle: A Clashing of Red and Blue (1967 section I).
1933c Which Indian Killed Custer? (1967 section III); and Custer Soldiers Not Buried (1967 section V).
1934a Rain-in-the-Face and Curly, the Crow (1967 sections IV and VIII).
1934b Sitting Bull and Gall the Warrior (1967 section VII).
1934c Two Days after the Custer Battle: A Clashing of Red and Blue as Viewed by a Gibbon Soldier (1967 section II).
1976 Keep the Last Bullet for Yourself: The True Story of Custer's Last Stand. Introduction by Joseph Medicine Crow. Algonac, Mich.: Reference Publications.
1978 The Cheyennes of Montana. Thomas B. Weist, ed. Algonac, Mich.: Reference Publications, Inc.

Petter, Rodolphe
1913–15 English-Cheyenne Dictionary. Kettle-Falls, Wash.: n.p.

Petter, Dr. Rodolphe, and Mrs. Bertha K. Petter
1936(?) Mission Memoirs: Reminiscences of Past Years in Mission Service among the Cheyenne (by R. Petter); and Two Life Sketches of Vxzeta and Vohokass (by B. Petter). No publication information, but possibly printed at Lame Deer, Montana, by the Mennonite Mission.

Pringle, Robert
1958 The Northern Cheyenne Indians in the Reservation Period. Honors thesis, College of Arts and Sciences, Harvard University.

Sandoz, Mari
1961 Crazy Horse: The Strange Man of the Oglalas. 2nd ed. Lincoln: University of Nebraska Press.

Schwartz, Warren E.
1989 The Last Contrary: The Story of Wesley Whiteman. (Sioux Falls?): Center for Western Studies.

Stands in Timber, John, and Margot Liberty
1997 (1967) Cheyenne Memories. 2nd ed. New Haven: Yale University Press.

Sturtevant, William C., ed.
1978 Handbook of North American Indians. Vol. 17: Languages. Washington D.C.: Smithsonian Institution.

Weist, Thomas B.
1977 A History of the Cheyenne People. Billings: Montana Council for Indian Education.
1978 Introduction and Biography of Thomas B. Marquis. Pp. 9–22, 23–49, and 101 in Thomas B. Marquis, Cheyennes of Montana. Thomas B. Weist, ed. Algonac, Mich.: Reference Publications, Inc.

Index

References to photographs are in italic type.

Y